The Syntax of Welsh

Welsh, like the other Celtic languages, is best-known amongst linguists for its verb-initial word order and use of initial consonantal mutations. However it has many more characteristics which are of interest to syntacticians. This book provides a concise, yet comprehensive and accessible overview of the major syntactic phenomena of Welsh. The authors cover a broad variety of topics, including finite and infinitival clauses, noun phrases, agreement and tense, word order, clause structure, dialect variation, and the historical background of the language. Contemporary colloquial Welsh serves as the main source of data and, where appropriate, is complemented by data from contemporary literary forms of the language. Data from Middle and Early Modern Welsh are also discussed. In each chapter, the authors first present a theory-neutral description of the data and then go on to examine theoretical analyses within Principles & Parameters theory and Head-driven Phrase Structure Grammar. The results shed new light not only on the syntax of Welsh but also on the merits of the respective theoretical frameworks. An engaging guide to everything that is interesting about Welsh syntax, this book will be welcomed by theoretical syntacticians, typologists, historical linguists and Celticists alike.

ROBERT D. BORSLEY is Professor in the Department of Language and Linguistics at the University of Essex. His previous books include *The Syntax of the Celtic Languages* (co-edited with Ian Roberts, 1996) and *Welsh Negation and Grammatical Theory* (co-authored with Bob Morris Jones, 2005).

MAGGIE TALLERMAN is Professor in the Linguistics Section at the University of Newcastle upon Tyne. Her previous books include *Understanding Syntax* (second edition 2005) and *Language Origins: Perspectives on Evolution* (2005).

DAVID WILLIS is Senior Lecturer in the Department of Linguistics at the University of Cambridge and Fellow of Selwyn College, Cambridge. He is the author of *Syntactic Change in Welsh* (1998).

CAMBRIDGE SYNTAX GUIDES
General editors:
P. Austin, B. Comrie, J. Bresnan, D. Lightfoot, I. Roberts, N. V. Smith

Responding to the increasing interest in comparative syntax, the goal of the
Cambridge Syntax Guides is to make available to all linguists major findings,
both descriptive and theoretical, which have emerged from the study of particular languages. The series is not committed to working in any particular
framework, but rather seeks to make language-specific research available to
theoreticians and practitioners of all persuasions.

Written by leading figures in the field, these guides will each include an
overview of the grammatical structures of the language concerned. For the
descriptivist, the books will provide an accessible introduction to the
methods and results of the theoretical literature; for the theoretician, they
will show how constructions that have achieved theoretical notoriety fit into
the structure of the language as a whole; for everyone, they will promote
cross-theoretical and cross-linguistic comparison with respect to a well-
defined body of data.

Other books available in this series
O. Fischer *et al*: *The Syntax of Early English*
K. Zagona: *The Syntax of Spanish*
K. Kiss: *The Syntax of Hungarian*
S. Mchombo: *The Syntax of Chichewa*
H. Thrainsson: *The Syntax of Icelandic*
P. Rowlett: *The Syntax of French*

The Syntax of Welsh

ROBERT D. BORSLEY
University of Essex

MAGGIE TALLERMAN
University of Newcastle upon Tyne

DAVID WILLIS
University of Cambridge

CAMBRIDGE UNIVERSITY PRESS

Cambridge, New York, Melbourne, Madrid, Cape Town,
Singapore, São Paulo, Delhi, Mexico City

Cambridge University Press
The Edinburgh Building, Cambridge CB2 8RU, UK

Published in the United States of America by
Cambridge University Press, New York

www.cambridge.org
Information on this title: www.cambridge.org/9781107407619

First published 2007
First paperback edition 2012

A catalogue record for this publication is available from the British Library

ISBN 978-0-521-83630-2 Hardback
ISBN 978-1-107-40761-9 Paperback

Er cof am Lewis Davies
1924–2006

Contents

Tables   xiii

Preface   xv

Abbreviations   xvii

1   Introduction   *1*

   1.1   The Celtic background   *1*

   1.2   The history and current position of Welsh   *2*

   1.3   Dialect variation and the literary language   *4*

   1.4   Some grammatical properties of Welsh   *7*

   1.4.1   Welsh as a head-initial language   *7*

   1.4.2   Clause structure   *9*

   1.4.3   Agreement   *17*

   1.4.4   Mutation   *19*

   1.4.5   Case and pronouns   *26*

   1.5   Research on Welsh syntax   *29*

   1.6   The structure of this book   *30*

2   Simple finite clauses   *32*

   2.1   Some basic properties   *32*

   2.1.1   Word order and agreement   *32*

   2.1.2   Pre-verbal particles   *34*

   2.1.3   Other Celtic languages   *37*

   2.2   Auxiliary-initial clauses   *38*

   2.2.1   Aspectual clauses   *39*

   2.2.2   *Gwneud*-clauses   *41*

   2.2.3   *Ddaru*-clauses   *42*

   2.2.4   Copular clauses   *43*

   2.2.5   Syntactic tests for auxiliaries?   *44*

   2.3   Transformational analyses of verb-initial clauses   *48*

   2.3.1   Preliminaries   *48*

   2.3.2   Possible analyses   *48*

   2.3.3   Further arguments for verb-fronting   *51*

   2.4   Constraint-based analyses of verb-initial clauses   *52*

2.4.1   Some analyses   *52*
2.4.2   More on the arguments for verb-fronting   *54*
2.5   Analyses of auxiliary-initial clauses   *56*
2.5.1   Aspectual and copular clauses   *56*
2.5.2   *Gwneud*-clauses and *ddaru*-clauses   *58*
2.6   Further issues   *60*
2.6.1   Null subjects   *60*
2.6.2   Expletive subjects   *61*
2.6.3   Further non-canonical subjects   *63*
2.6.4   The 'serial construction'   *64*
2.6.5   Verbless clauses   *66*
2.7   Conclusions   *67*

3   Non-finite verbs and infinitival clauses   *68*
3.1   Non-finite verbs: verbal and nominal properties   *68*
3.1.1   The non-finite verb form   *68*
3.1.2   Arguments against the 'verb-noun' categorization   *69*
3.1.3   Verb-noun phrases as DPs   *73*
3.2   Tensed complement clauses   *75*
3.3   *Bod*-clauses: finite clauses with the infinitive *bod*   *76*
3.3.1   The distribution of *bod*   *76*
3.3.2   Evidence that *bod* is finite   *78*
3.4   Infinitival *i*-clauses with overt subjects   *81*
3.4.1   Finite *i*-clauses   *82*
3.4.2   Non-finite *i*-clauses   *85*
3.5   Control predicates   *87*
3.6   The syntax of *i* in infinitival complements   *90*
3.6.1   An apparent paradox in the distribution of *i*   *90*
3.6.2   Evidence that functional *i* is not a preposition   *91*
3.6.3   Two distinct *i* elements in infinitival clauses:
         complementizer *i* versus inflectional *i*   *94*
3.6.4   Finiteness and clause structure   *97*
3.7   Raising predicates   *99*
3.7.1   A class of raising predicates   *99*
3.7.2   Complementizers in raising clauses   *102*

4   *Wh*-constructions   *104*
4.1   *Wh*-questions   *106*
4.1.1   The basic pattern   *106*
4.1.2   Antiagreement in subject *wh*-questions   *107*
4.1.3   Ungrammaticality of resumptive pronouns in subject
         and object position   *108*
4.1.4   Verb forms in *wh*-constructions   *109*
4.1.5   Object *wh*-questions in periphrastic clauses   *109*

4.1.6   Analysing subject and object *wh*-questions   *112*
4.1.7   Prepositional *wh*-questions   *114*
4.1.8   Possessor *wh*-questions   *116*
4.1.9   Adjunct *wh*-questions   *117*
4.1.10   Multiple *wh*-questions and superiority   *118*
4.2   Relative clauses   *118*
4.2.1   Subject and object relatives   *118*
4.2.2   Object of non-finite verbs   *120*
4.2.3   Object-of-preposition relatives   *120*
4.2.4   Possessor relatives   *121*
4.2.5   Adjunct relatives   *122*
4.3   Focus   *123*
4.3.1   Propositional adverbs   *124*
4.3.2   Agreement in focus constructions   *125*
4.3.3   Fronting of verbal phrases and minor constituent types   *126*
4.3.4   Embedded focus constructions   *128*
4.4.   Copular constructions   *129*
4.4.1   Fronting in identity copular constructions   *129*
4.4.2   Fronting in predicative copular constructions   *130*
4.4.3   Affinities with *wh*-constructions   *131*
4.5   Non-finite *wh*-constructions   *133*
4.6   Other *wh*-constructions: comparatives and correlatives   *136*
4.7   Particles in literary Welsh   *136*
4.8   Negative *wh*-constructions   *139*
4.9   Long-distance *wh*-constructions   *141*
4.9.1   *Wh*-constructions formed on embedded subject position   *141*
4.9.2   *Wh*-constructions formed on embedded object positions   *144*
4.9.3   *Wh*-constructions formed on other embedded positions   *145*
4.9.4   Resumptive embedded *wh*-constructions   *146*
4.9.5   Islands and subjacency   *146*
4.9.6   Successive cyclicity   *148*
4.10   Conclusion   *151*

5   **Noun phrases**   *152*
5.1   Introduction: major features of the Welsh noun phrase   *152*
5.2   Determiners and related elements   *154*
5.2.1   The definite article   *155*
5.2.2   Possessive clitics   *157*
5.2.3   Other determiners   *161*
5.2.4   Early postdeterminers   *162*
5.3   Numerals   *163*
5.3.1   Mutations with numerals   *163*
5.3.2   Agreement patterns with a numeral   *165*
5.3.3   The syntax of complex numerals   *166*
5.3.4   Noun phrases headed by numerals   *168*

5.3.5   Numeral + *o* 'of' + plural noun   *170*
5.3.6   Numeral-like quantifiers   *171*
5.3.7   Late postdeterminers   *174*
5.3.8   How much structure?   *174*
5.4   Adjectives and demonstratives   *175*
5.4.1   Mutations on adjectives   *177*
5.4.2   Number and gender agreement   *178*
5.4.3   Position of adjectives relative to the noun   *179*
5.4.4   Order of postnominal adjectives   *180*
5.4.5   Noun phrases headed by adjectives   *182*
5.4.6   The 'genitive of respect'   *183*
5.5   Possessor noun phrases and related constructions   *184*
5.5.1   The 'construct-state' effect   *184*
5.5.2   Possessor noun phrases versus attributive noun phrases   *185*
5.5.3   The mixed construction   *186*
5.6   Possible analyses of noun-phrase structure   *186*
5.6.1   Noun-raising approach   *186*
5.6.2   Non-movement approaches   *188*
5.6.3   Adjective mutation: phonology or morphosyntax?   *188*
5.6.4   Conclusions about possible analyses   *194*
5.7   Conclusion   *194*
        Appendix: Mutation triggers in the noun phrase   *195*

6   More on agreement   *198*
6.1   The basic data   *198*
6.2   Coordination and focus sentences   *205*
6.2.1   Coordination   *205*
6.2.2   Focus sentences   *206*
6.3   Generalizations   *208*
6.4   Implications   *211*
6.5   A Linearization-based HPSG approach   *215*
6.6   Reflexives   *220*
6.7   Conclusions   *222*

7   Syntax and mutation   *223*
7.1   Mutation environments: some basic data   *223*
7.2   Phrase-based approaches to syntactic SM   *226*
7.3   Early case-based approaches to syntactic SM   *231*
7.4   Roberts' case-linked approach   *235*
7.5   Problems with the case-linked account   *238*
7.5.1   Empirical issues   *238*
7.5.2   The question of head government   *243*
7.6   Recent work from a phrase-based perspective   *244*
7.7   Theoretical matters and structural considerations   *249*

7.7.1   Case and mutation   *249*
7.7.2   Structure and empty categories   *251*
7.8   Conclusion: common ground?   *253*

8   More on verbal syntax   *255*
8.1   The syntax of *bod*   *255*
8.1.1   Third-person forms   *256*
8.1.2   Omission of finite forms of *bod*   *260*
8.1.3   Analyses of *bod*   *261*
8.2   Negation   *263*
8.2.1   Negation in literary Welsh   *263*
8.2.2   Weak negative verbs and negative dependents   *265*
8.2.3   Negative quantifiers and pseudo-quantifiers   *268*
8.2.4   Strong negative verbs   *270*
8.2.5   The licensing of n-words   *271*
8.2.6   Analyses   *272*
8.2.7   Some other negative elements   *273*
8.3   Valency-changing processes   *275*
8.3.1   The passive   *275*
8.3.2   Other valency-changing processes   *278*
8.3.3   Impersonals   *282*
8.4   Conclusions   *284*

9   Historical syntax   *286*
9.1   Word order in main clauses   *287*
9.1.1   Verb-second structures   *287*
9.1.2   Expletive subjects and the emergence of the
        pre-verbal particle *fe*   *297*
9.1.3   Verb-initial order   *298*
9.2   Periphrastic verbal forms   *303*
9.2.1   Periphrastic aspectual constructions   *303*
9.2.2   The periphrastic passive   *304*
9.3   Agreement patterns and null arguments   *305*
9.3.1   General principles of agreement   *305*
9.3.2   Subject–verb agreement in V2-structures and
        the 'mixed' sentence   *306*
9.3.3   The decline of null arguments   *307*
9.4   Morphological case   *308*
9.5   Negation   *309*
9.5.1   The shift of negative-polarity indefinite pronouns to negative
        quantifiers   *310*
9.5.2   The Welsh Jespersen's Cycle   *311*
9.5.3   Definite direct objects in negative sentences   *312*
9.6   Mutations   *313*

9.6.1   Direct-object mutation in Welsh   *313*
9.6.2   Mutation of comparative adjectives in negative
        and interrogative clauses   *315*
9.7   Copular constructions and inversion structures   *316*
9.7.1   Delayed subjects and objects in Middle Welsh   *316*
9.7.2   Copular constructions   *317*
9.8   Pronouns   *319*
9.8.1   Loss of accusative clitics   *322*
9.8.2   Effects of phonological reduction of pronouns   *323*
9.9   Subordinate clauses   *326*
9.9.1   Embedded finite clauses   *326*
9.9.2   Embedded infinitival clauses   *327*
9.10   *Wh*-constructions   *334*
9.11   Noun phrases   *336*
9.12   Conclusion   *337*

10 Welsh as a VSO language   *338*
10.1   Traditional typology: universal ordering principles
        and VSO languages   *338*
10.1.1 Welsh and the Greenbergian universals   *339*
10.1.2 Some extensions and proposed explanations   *347*
10.2   Approaches to word-order typology in
        generative grammar   *350*
10.2.1 Proposals by Ouhalla (1991): are the Celtic languages
        typologically VSO?   *350*
10.2.2 Further proposals for correlates of verb-initial order   *358*
10.3   Conclusion: the derivation of verb-initial word order   *365*

References   *367*
Index   *382*

Tables

1.1   Some cognate items in the modern Celtic languages   *2*
1.2   Conventional period datings for Welsh   *3*
1.3   Paradigms of a regular colloquial Welsh verb   *9*
1.4   Paradigm for *am* 'about' in colloquial Welsh   *17*
1.5   Consonantal mutation in Welsh   *20*
2.1   Pre-verbal particles   *36*
3.1   Summary of properties of Welsh clause types   *98*
4.1   Summary of patterns of marking *wh*-constructions   *105*
4.2   Forms of *bod* 'be' in *wh*-constructions in colloquial Welsh   *110*
4.3   Choice of particle in *wh*-constructions in literary Welsh   *138*
5.1   Possessive proclitics   *157*
5.2   Possessive enclitics   *158*
5.3   Frequency of soft mutation of adjectives after *blynedd* 'year'   *166*
5.4   Restrictions on the syntactic environments in which quantifiers may occur   *172*
5.5   Forms of demonstratives in Welsh   *176*
6.1   Summary of Welsh agreement patterns   *198*
6.2   Agreement and grammatical function   *211*
9.1   Distribution of word-order patterns in affirmative main declarative clauses in Middle Welsh   *289*
9.2   Possible interpretation of agreement paradigms in modern colloquial Welsh   *308*
9.3   Traditional classification of personal pronouns in Middle Welsh   *320*
9.4   Paradigms of conjunctive and reduplicated pronouns in Middle Welsh   *322*
9.5   Reduction of pronominal forms in Early Modern Welsh   *325*
10.1   Literary Welsh present tense of *canu* 'sing'   *355*

Preface

Welsh has received a fraction of the attention from linguists that has been lavished on English and some other languages. However, it has been the object of generative research since the 1970s, and there is now a large and diverse body of generative research on Welsh syntax, assuming a number of different theoretical frameworks, and dealing with both synchronic and diachronic matters. In this book we outline what modern syntactic theory has said or can say about Welsh syntax and consider the kinds of issues which data from Welsh raise for syntactic theory. The book is not a reference grammar and we make no attempt to provide a completely comprehensive coverage of Welsh syntax. However, we consider a wide range of topics, and hope that we have dealt with most issues that syntacticians are likely to be interested in.

We draw extensively on the published literature, but we also go beyond it in various ways, offering both updated proposals and new analyses. Our work owes a great intellectual debt in particular to one of the pioneering works on Welsh syntax, Jones & Thomas (1977). Thirty years ago, that book tackled many of the important syntactic issues of the day from a generative standpoint. Since this is also one of our main aims, we feel that the current work has something in common with that earlier work; it may also in some sense stand as a replacement for it, since Jones & Thomas (1977) is now unfortunately out of print.

We hope that the book will be accessible in large part both to specialists in syntactic theory who are not familiar with Welsh (or any other Celtic language) and to specialists in Welsh who are not familiar with syntactic theory. Much of the book is concerned to provide a relatively theory-neutral description of Welsh syntax, but we also present more theoretically oriented treatments drawing on Principles and Parameters theory (P&P) and Head-driven Phrase Structure Grammar (HPSG). The three authors differ in their theoretical preferences, and we do not assume that any one framework has a monopoly of wisdom. We have tried to steer a neutral path when no particular theoretical issues are at stake. For instance, we typically refer to 'noun phrase' rather than NP or DP.

We have not attempted to produce a broadly uniform set of chapters. Different issues arise in different areas, and different areas have seen different amounts and different kinds of theoretical work. Every chapter has had extensive input from all three authors. However, with the exception of chapter 1 ('Introduction'), all the chapters had one primary author as follows: Borsley was primarily responsible for chapter 2 ('Simple finite clauses'), chapter 6 ('More on agreement') and chapter 8 ('More on verbal syntax'), Tallerman for chapter 3 ('Infinitival clauses'), chapter 7 ('Syntax and mutation') and chapter 10 ('Welsh as a VSO language'), and Willis for chapter 4 ('*Wh-*constructions'), chapter 5 ('Noun phrases') and chapter 9 ('Historical syntax').

Various people have helped the authors during the preparation of this work. We would like to extend our gratitude to Ian Roberts and Louisa Sadler for their careful reading of the draft manuscript and for their thought-provoking comments. Much of the material presented here was tested on Maggie Tallerman's Cross-Linguistic Syntax class at Durham in 2005; we are grateful for helpful comments from class members. We are also extremely grateful for the assistance we have received from the following data consultants: Emyr Davies, Lewis Davies, Bob Morris Jones and Heather Williams. Dr Lewis Davies spent most of his working life teaching and researching in Biological Sciences at the University of Durham; he was an eminent entomologist with a keen interest in all the natural sciences, amongst which he was happy to include linguistics. Sadly, Lewis died while this book was in its final stages of preparation. His loss, both as a long-standing friend and as an ardent supporter of everything concerning Welsh language and society, will be greatly felt. This book is dedicated in his memory in recognition of his contribution to the natural sciences and his unstinting help as a data consultant over the course of many years.

Abbreviations

List of glosses

ABS	absolute verb form (in Celtic examples); absolutive case (in examples from other languages)
ACC	accusative
AFF	(on a pronoun) affixed form; (alone) affirmative particle
AGR	agreement
COMP	complementizer
COND	conditional
CONJ	conjunctive pronoun
COP	copula
CORREL	correlative particle
DAT	dative case
DEM	demonstrative
DEP	dependent form
DUAL	dual number
EQ	equative adjective
FOCUS	focus marker
F	feminine
FS	feminine singular
FUT	future
GEN	genitive
GENERAL	adjective form unmarked for gender or number
GENN	genitive–noun
IMPER	imperative
IMPERS	impersonal form of verb
IMPF	imperfect
IND	independent pronoun
INF	infinitive (verb-noun)
INT	interrogative particle
MS	masculine singular

NS	neuter singular
NEG	negative
NGEN	noun–genitive
NOM	nominative case
NUM	numerative form
P	plural
PART	participle
PAST	past tense
PASTPART	past participle
PERF	perfect marker or verb
PLUPERF	pluperfect
PRED	predicate marker
PRES	present
PRET	preterite
pro	null argument
PROG	progressive marker
PRT	verbal particle
Q	question tag particle
QUOT	quotative particle
REDUP	reduplicated pronoun
REL	relative (*wh*) form of verb
S	singular
STRONG	strong (independent) form of pronoun
SUBJ	subjunctive
SUPERL	superlative adjective
t	trace (of movement)
3	third person [object]
3s etc.	third-person singular

Other abbreviations

AP	Adjective Phrase
Asp	Aspect
AspP	Aspect Phrase
Aux	auxiliary
BDT	Branching Direction Theory
C	complementizer
CP	Complementizer Phrase
DOM	direct object mutation (except in chapter 6)

DP	Determiner Phrase
ECM	Exceptional Case Marking
EIC	Early Immediate Constituents
EMW	Early Modern Welsh
FocP	Focus Phrase
ForceP	Force Phrase
HPSG	Head-driven Phrase Structure Grammar
I	Inflection
IP	Inflectional Phrase
LFG	Lexical Functional Grammar
MB	Middle Breton
ModW	Modern Welsh
MW	Middle Welsh
NP	Noun Phrase
NomP	Nominalizer Phrase
OW	Old Welsh
P&P	Principles and Parameters
PerfP	Perfect Phrase
PP	Prepositional Phrase
ProgP	Progressive Phrase
QP	Quantifier Phrase
SM	soft mutation
Spec	Specifier
TP	Tense Phrase
V1	verb-initial
V2	verb-second
VoiceP	Voice Phrase
vP	light verb Phrase
VP	Verb Phrase
XP	any phrase
XPTH	XP trigger hypothesis

1

Introduction

1.1 The Celtic background

Welsh is a member, along with Breton and Cornish, of the Brythonic subgroup of the Celtic branch of Indo-European. It is currently spoken by something over half a million speakers, mostly in Wales, but also by the Welsh community in the Chubut province of Argentina and by scattered pockets of speakers elsewhere, particularly in the major English cities.

The modern Celtic languages are descendants of the Common Celtic language once spoken in central Europe. By the first millennium BC, and probably for several millennia before, various Continental Celtic languages were spoken over large parts of western and central Europe. Gaulish in particular is well attested in a large corpus of inscriptions from the third century BC onwards, but there is also material in Hispano-Celtic, spoken in central eastern Spain, from the fifth century BC, and in Lepontic and Cisalpine Gaulish, spoken in northern Italy. Celtic migrations to the British Isles gave rise to the modern Insular Celtic languages. Of these, closely related Irish, Scots Gaelic and Manx form the Goidelic branch, and, somewhat less closely related Welsh, Cornish and Breton form the Brythonic branch. The Brythonic languages derive from the language spoken by the Britons across all of present-day England and Wales and much of southern Scotland before and during the Roman occupation. With the Anglo-Saxon migrations of the sixth and seventh centuries, speakers of the Brythonic (British) language were pushed west and north, and some migrated to Brittany, leading to the split of Brythonic into the separate languages that we see today.

The genetic relationship between the modern Celtic languages is exemplified in Table 1.1, which gives a selection of items that are cognate in all six of them. The reflexes of the word for 'four' demonstrate the /kʷ/ > /p/ sound change which is found in the Brythonic languages but not in the Goidelic languages and which forms the basis of the division of Celtic languages into P-Celtic and Q-Celtic.

Table 1.1. *Some cognate items in the modern Celtic languages.*

	Welsh	Breton	Cornish	Irish	Scots Gaelic	Manx
'dog'	*ci*	*ki*	*ky*	*madra* (OIr. *cú*)[a]	*cù*	*coo*
'four'	*pedwar*	*pevar*	*padzhar*	*ceathair*	*ceithir*	*kiare*
'house'	*tŷ*	*ti*	*chy*	*teach*	*tigh*	*chaagh*
'hunt (v.)'	*hela*	*hemolc'h*[b]	*helfia*	*seilg*	*sealg*	*shelg*
'summer'	*haf*	*hañv*	*haf*	*samhradh*	*samhradh*	*sourey*
'swallow (v.)'	*llyncu*	*lonkañ*	–	*slog*	*sluig*	*slug*
'wet (adj.)'	*gwlyb*	*gleb*	*gleb*	*fliuch*	*fliuch*	*fliugh*

Note: [a] OIr - Old Irish;   [b] *hem-* is a reflexive prefix; only the root *-olc'h* is cognate with the other items listed.

1.2   The history and current position of Welsh

Welsh is conventionally divided into the periods given in Table 1.2.[1] The term 'Early' (also 'primitive') is used to describe the languages after the period of the phonological changes (principally loss of final syllables) that are taken to indicate the splitting up of the Brythonic parent language into the Neo-Brythonic languages (see Jackson 1953, Sims-Williams 1990, 1991), but before the earliest written records.

Old Welsh is the language of the earliest written records in Welsh, principally a number of short prose texts, including some charters, legal documents and an astronomical text, some fragments of poetry and numerous glosses on Latin works. There is also a larger body of poetry whose date of composition is usually located within the Old Welsh period but which is attested largely in later manuscripts.

There is a far richer body of material in Middle Welsh, which survives in a large number of texts, including both native and translated tales and romances, legal codes, chronicles, saints' lives and other religious texts, medical and scientific works, and an extensive corpus of fixed-metre poetry. With the exception of some Anglo-Norman and Flemish settlements along the south coast and in some of the towns which grew up around English-built castles after the conquest of Wales in 1282, Welsh at this time was the language of the overwhelming majority in all parts of Wales.

---

[1] The exact temporal extent of each of the periods varies from author to author, as witnessed by the slightly different periodizations given by D. S. Evans (1964: xvi–xxi), Heinecke (1999: 132–4), Jackson (1953: 5–6), Lewis (1931: 96–108), Morris-Jones (1913: 6–8) and Russell (1995: 1).

Table 1.2. *Conventional period datings for Welsh.*

Period	Date
Early Welsh	550–800
Old Welsh	800–1150
Middle Welsh	1150–1500
Modern Welsh	1500–present day
[Early Modern Welsh	1500–1700]

Translations of parts of the Bible, particularly the New Testament, appeared from the mid sixteenth century, culminating in the publication of a full Bible translation in 1588, which, along with a revised version in 1620, greatly facilitated standardization of the written literary language. Although the official status of the language declined with the exclusive use of English for official purposes after the Act of Union with England in 1536, the Reformation and the invention of printing substantially increased the production of Welsh literature. Printing in Welsh began with the publication in 1546 of a short collection of instructional material commonly known as *Yny lhyvyr hwnn* 'In this book', and a steady stream of printed books and almanacs appeared in Welsh throughout the late sixteenth and seventeenth centuries. This literature was particularly of a religious nature, but included also grammars such as those by William Salesbury (1969[1550]), Gruffydd Robert (1939[1567]) and Siôn Dafydd Rhys (1592).

Increased literacy and the religious revivals of the eighteenth and early nineteenth century strengthened the literary use of the language and maintained its status. These factors also promoted the emergence of a lively journalistic tradition in the language in the nineteenth century. However, by the mid nineteenth century it was clear that large-scale unassimilated immigration of English and Irish workers to industrial south Wales was beginning to lead to language shift to English in many areas. Official policy which viewed the language as a cause of Welsh 'backwardness' aimed at the eradication of the language from the mid nineteenth century onwards, and education through the medium of Welsh ceased. The proportion of Welsh speakers in the population declined steadily from perhaps 80% in 1800 (R. O. Jones 1993: 543–4) to 49.9% (930,000 people) according to the census of 1901, and to a low of 18.9% (504,000 people) in the 1981 census.

Conversely, from the mid twentieth century onwards, campaigns by Welsh speakers have led to an improved official status for the language and a rapid growth in Welsh-medium education throughout Wales since the 1960s. Improved status came with the Welsh Language Act of 1967, which guaranteed the right to use Welsh in court and allowed its use in public administration. A further Welsh Language Act of 1993 required public bodies to treat Welsh and English equally, establishing the Welsh Language Board (*Bwrdd yr Iaith Gymraeg*) to promote the use of Welsh and oversee the delivery of equal treatment. More significant has been the growth of Welsh-medium education: as of 2005/06, 20.1% of Welsh primary school pupils received all or most of their education through the medium of Welsh (Welsh Assembly Government Statistical Directorate 2007: 67).

The current number of speakers of Welsh is a much measured statistic. According to the 2001 UK Census, Welsh is spoken by 20.8% of the population of Wales (582,000 people), with a further 2.8% (79,000) able to understand the language but not speak it. A Welsh Language Use Survey conducted by the Welsh Language Board in 2004 estimated the number of speakers at 611,000 (21.7%). The Welsh Local Labour Force Survey, an annual survey which consistently returns higher numbers of Welsh speakers, put the number at 747,000 (26.7%) in 2005. The majority of Welsh speakers, around 60%, are in south Wales, but the areas with the highest proportion of Welsh speakers are mostly in the northwest. In north Wales, Welsh is spoken by a majority of the population in Gwynedd and on the Isle of Anglesey; in the south, it is spoken by a majority in Ceredigion and by around half the population in Carmarthenshire.

Attitudes towards Welsh have transformed in the last fifty years, such that the goal of language maintenance is now viewed in an overwhelmingly positive light within Wales, and policies aimed towards language maintenance, particularly via the education system, have been far more successful in Wales than in the other Celtic nations. Although the language is still in decline in its southern heartlands, and still threatened by outmigration and decreasing fluency of its speakers, the overall picture for the future is much more promising than it was thirty years ago. Non-Welsh-speaking parents whose grandparents or greatgrandparents spoke Welsh often have Welsh-speaking children, and the children of migrants, particularly in the northwest, are now often Welsh-speaking. The use of Welsh in public life is increasing, and there are good reasons to be optimistic about the long-term future of the language.

1.3   Dialect variation and the literary language

From the seventeenth to the mid twentieth century, the standard literary language based on the Bible translations of 1588 and 1620 remained fairly constant and evolved only gradually. Some minor points of orthographic detail (use of accents, doubling of consonant characters, spelling of consonant clusters beginning with /s/) were gradually standardized. However, the morphology of the literary language hardly changed at all, and, although the verb-initial word order of spoken Welsh eventually ousted the subject-initial order frequently found in the Bible translation and in earlier Welsh, other innovative patterns from speech failed to make their way into the literary language. As the gulf between the literary language and the various spoken dialects widened, the literary language increasingly had to be learned as a distinct variety, taught and maintained through its use in religion. The situation emerged that prevails today, where most speakers do not have active control of the elevated style of highly literary Welsh, and none speak this variety as their native language. By the early twentieth century, and well before, it was fair to speak of two distinct varieties, 'literary Welsh' and 'colloquial Welsh', the latter subject to a good deal of dialectal variation ('the dialects'). These terms will be used extensively in this book to refer to (some-what idealized) versions of these distinct varieties.

While in the mid twentieth century it was possible to speak of a diglossic situation between two well-defined varieties (albeit with regional variation within 'colloquial Welsh'), the sociolinguistic changes of the twentieth and twenty-first centuries have had profound effects on the relationship between the literary language and colloquial Welsh. The diglossic situation reflected in the earlier strict dichotomy between literary Welsh and the dialects has become blurred.

On the one hand, written Welsh has admitted forms previously confined mostly to speech, for instance, *dydy e* 'he isn't' and *rydyn ni* 'we are' for more literary *nid yw* and *yr ydym*. Some literary forms felt to be far removed from speech, for instance *efe* 'he (stressed, reduplicated form)' or pluperfect verbal morphology, have become very limited in their use and are now markers of elevated or deliberately archaic style. Furthermore, written Welsh has begun to admit limited regional variation. Some northern forms, for instance, *o* '(unstressed) he' or the affirmative particle *mi*, are now regularly found in stylistically neutral written contexts such as journalism. The same goes to a lesser extent for some marked southern forms, such as the embedded focus marker *taw*, or lexical items such as *mas* 'out'.

A second complication comes from the rise of Welsh-medium education and the reintroduction of the language into districts, mostly in the northeast and southeast of Wales, where use of the language had largely died out. This partial discontinuity in language transmission means that the new varieties in these areas have much more in common with the language of neighbour-ing areas where the language did not die out than with the former local dialects (see M. C. Jones 1998). Welsh-medium education has also tended to level out dialect differences. Increasingly, with some local exceptions, two fairly uniform spoken standards are emerging in north and south Wales respectively.

Since not all variants differ in the same way stylistically, the result is the emergence of a complex stylistic continuum. Two examples are given in (1) and (2). In each case, a highly elevated literary Welsh version, unacceptable in speech, is given, along with one or two possible neutral versions, acceptable in journalism or in careful educated speech, followed by spoken forms for the two major dialect areas, north and south. The four or five forms given do not exhaust the possibilities, since further systematic mixing of forms is possible giving rise to different levels of formality.

(1)   Ni   ddywedodd   ddim   wrthyf.   ELEVATED WRITTEN STYLE
        Ddywedodd e(f) ddim byd wrtha   i.   NEUTRAL STYLE
        Wedodd   e   ddim byd wrtha   i.   COLLOQUIAL SOUTHERN
        NEG say.PAST.3S   he nothing to.1s   me

        Ddaru o ddim   deud   dim byd wrtha i.   COLLOQUIAL NORTHERN
        PAST   he NEG   say.INF nothing to.1s me
        'He didn't say anything to me.'

(2)   Nid ydyw   wedi dy weled heddiw.   ELEVATED WRITTEN
        NEG be.PRES.3S   PERF 2S see.INF today

        Dyw   e(f) ddim wedi dy weld   di   heddiw.   NEUT. SOUTHERN
        Dydy   o   ddim wedi dy weld   di   heddiw.   NEUT. NORTHERN
        Smo   fe   'di   gweld   ti   heddi.   COLL. SOUTHERN
        Tydy   o   ddim 'di   gweld   chdi heddiw.   COLL. NORTHERN
        NEG.be.3s he   NEG PERF 2s see.INF you today
        'He hasn't seen you today.'

In view of these register differences in Welsh, decisions have had to be made in this book about which forms of Welsh to describe and to use in examples. The focus of this book is not on literary Welsh, partly because the most extreme forms of literary Welsh are now little used, and partly because literary Welsh is not and never has been the native language of any group of speakers. We have nevertheless made reference to literary Welsh where the literary variant seems to be of particular interest, or where it has received particular attention in the existing linguistic literature. In the main, however, we have attempted to focus on neutral syntactic patterns, and to use phonological and morphological forms which are relatively neutral stylistically. Regionally marked forms that have widespread currency and are found in neutral written styles have been used freely. Where regionally marked syntactic patterns are in use over a wide area and differ structurally from the main syntactic pattern, they have been discussed separately. We also point out colloquial variants and patterns which are considered substandard, but which are very widespread in speech. However, this book does not attempt to cover the full range of syntactic variation found in the dialects. Inevitably this means that the examples do not all come from the same region or the same stylistic level, and this should be understood when interpreting them.

Although we have tried to point out major regional or stylistic syntactic differences in the text, there are a large number of phonological and morphological differences that are not the focus of attention in this book, but which inevitably appear in examples. Here, we have tried as far as possible to avoid forms restricted to one region or style, and have consequently used some literary spellings in examples from colloquial Welsh. Thus, for 'I saw', we have used *gwelais*, with the literary spelling of the past tense ending *-ais*, avoiding the choice between various regional forms such as northern *gwelish* or southern *gweles*. Similarly for 'he / she did', we have used *gwnaeth* rather than northern colloquial *naeth* or southern colloquial *nâth*. These are also the forms used in neutral written Welsh. Such spellings should be understood, in examples from colloquial Welsh, as a cover encompassing various possible regional or stylistic forms.

1.4   Some grammatical properties of Welsh

1.4.1   Welsh as a head-initial language

Like all the Celtic languages, Welsh is strongly head-initial, in the sense that heads precede their complements across all phrase types. This is shown for the major categories of verb (V), noun (N), adjective (A) and preposition (P) in (3) to (6) respectively:

(3)   a. Mae   Elin wedi **prynu**   [ceffyl du].
          be.PRES.3S Elin PERF buy.INF horse black
          'Elin has bought a black horse.'
        b. Dw   i 'n   **gwybod** [bydd   Elin yn   mynd].
          be.PRES.1S I PROG know.INF be.FUT.3S Elin PROG go.INF
          'I know Elin will be going.'

(4)   a. **pryder** [am   y   dyfodol]
          worry about the future
          'worry about the future'
        b. y   **profiad**   [o wneud rhywbeth diddorol]
          the experience of do.INF something interesting
          'the experience of doing something interesting'

(5)   a. Roedd   hi   'n   **benderfynol** [o ddeall].
         be.IMPF.3S she PRED determined of understand.INF
         'She was determined to understand.'
       b. Mae   'n   **amlwg** [mai   gadael oedd   o].
         be.PRES.3S PRED obvious COMP.FOCUS leave.INF be.IMPF.3S he
         'It's obvious that he was leaving.'

(6)   a. **gan** [fy mrawd]
         with 1s brother
         'with my brother'
       b. **cyn** [i ti   fynd]
         before to you go.INF
         'before you go'

Typically, adjuncts also follow the head that they modify, though verbal adjuncts have a notable amount of positional freedom within the clause. Attributive adjectives follow the head noun in the unmarked case; relative clauses always do so. Chapter 10 discusses the typology of word order in these and other instances in more detail. Possessor noun phrases also follow the head noun; word order within the noun phrase is examined in detail in chapter 5.

Functional heads also precede their phrasal complements, as shown in (7) for the predicate marker *yn*, in (8) for the perfective aspect marker *wedi*, and in (9) for the conditional complementizer *os*:

(7)   Mae   'r wefan **yn**   [llawn o gyngor da].
       be.PRES.3S the website PRED full   of advice good
       'The website is full of good advice.'

(8)   Roedd   Aled **wedi** [golchi 'r llestri].
       be.IMPF.3S Aled PERF wash.INF the dishes
       'Aled had washed the dishes.'

(9)   **Os** [yw   'r rheolwr yn   ddoeth . . .]
       if be.PRES.3S the manager PRED wise
       'If the manager is wise . . .'

Within the noun phrase, determiners and postdeterminers of all kinds (see chapter 5) precede the head noun, as do numerals, as shown in (10), (11) and (12):

(10)   y   tri   llyfr newydd
       the three book new
       'the three new books'

(11)   pob yn   ail   fis
       every PRED second month
       'every other month'

(12)   yr   holl broblemau
       the all   problems
       'all the problems'

If the noun phrase is analysed as a Determiner Phrase (DP), the determiner head can be seen as taking a following NP complement; see chapter 5 for discussion of the structure.

1.4.2   Clause structure

1.4.2.1   Finite clauses

Welsh has synthetic verbal morphology. Lexical verbs in the active voice display inflections from one of three paradigms, characterized in this book as future, past and conditional. We have chosen to use terminology which reflects the general semantics of the verb forms in the colloquial rather than in the literary language, and have therefore adopted terms which generally correspond to the semantics of these forms in speech. In some earlier literature (e.g. Williams 1980: 80–1), the terms 'present', 'past/preterite' and 'imperfect' are used, but since our focus is a broad range of Welsh data, it seems to us inappropriate to use terminology which presupposes that the literary language is the norm.[2] Typical colloquial Welsh paradigms for the regular verb *cerdded* 'walk' are given in Table 1.3. The verb *bod* 'be' is exceptional, and has additional paradigms (see section 3.3.1).

Some morphological differences exist between the colloquial forms given in Table 1.3 and the equivalent literary forms, such as first person plural past literary *cerddasom* vs. colloquial *cerddon ni* 'we walked', but these are fairly minor. However, there are also three major differences between literary and

Table 1.3. *Paradigms of a regular colloquial Welsh verb.*

	future	past	conditional
first-person singular	*cerdda(f)*	*cerddais*	*cerddwn*
second-person singular	*cerddi*	*cerddaist*	*cerddet*
third-person singular	*cerddiff*	*cerddodd*	*cerddai*
first-person plural	*cerddwn*	*cerddon*	*cerdden*
second-person plural	*cerddwch*	*cerddoch*	*cerddech*
third-person plural	*cerddan*	*cerddon*	*cerdden*
impersonal	*(cerddir)*	*cerddwyd*	*(cerddid)*

---

[2] For a fuller survey of the various terms used to refer to the Welsh verbal paradigms, see Heinecke (1999: 283–6).

colloquial Welsh in this area. Literary Welsh has two additional paradigms: a pluperfect paradigm, which functions also as a conditional perfect: *cerddaswn* 'I would have walked, I had walked'; and a present subjunctive paradigm: *cerddwyf* 'that I walk'. Both are highly formal.[3]

Secondly, the semantics of the forms differs between the varieties. The *cerdda(f)* paradigm of most verbs functions only as a modal future in colloquial Welsh, conveying a future action accompanied by willingness of the subject or high probability of the action being fulfilled. In literary Welsh this paradigm functions also as a true present tense.[4] In the third-person singular, neutral registers of Welsh distinguish the present and the future: *cerdda* 'he, she walks' (narrative present) vs. *cerddiff* or *cerddith* 'he, she will walk' (modal future), whereas colloquial Welsh has only the latter form. The *cerddwn* paradigm functions as a conditional in colloquial Welsh, but also as an imperfect in literary Welsh.

Finally, whereas literary Welsh freely allows null arguments with heads that bear agreement (null subjects of finite verbs, null objects of prepositions etc.), use of such null elements is highly restricted in colloquial Welsh.

Both colloquial and literary Welsh also inflect verbs for the imperative mood and have a single non-finite (verb-noun) form. Welsh has no inflected present or past participles. Some verbs have a deverbal adjective in -*edig*, for instance *printiedig* 'printed', but this suffix is clearly derivational rather than inflectional, being lexically restricted to a minority of verbs and often having an idiosyncratic meaning.

In all neutral finite clauses in Welsh, the finite verb or auxiliary is in clause-initial position in unmarked word order. This applies both to main (root) clauses and to embedded clauses:

(13)   Prynodd   Elin dorth o fara.
        buy.PAST.3s Elin loaf of bread
        'Elin bought a loaf of bread.'

(14)   Mae   o 'n   dweud [(y) bydd   Elin yn prynu torth o fara].
        be.PRES.3s he PROG say.INF PRT be.FUT.3s Elin PROG buy.INF loaf of bread
        'He says that Elin will buy a loaf of bread.'

(15)   y   ddynes [(a) brynodd   dorth o fara]
        the woman PRT buy.PAST.3s loaf of bread
        'the woman who bought a loaf of bread'

---

[3] A distinct imperfect subjunctive, used after the complementizer *pe* 'irrealis if', survives marginally in literary Welsh for a few verbs, for instance, *elwn* '(if) I were to go'.

[4] A few verbs in colloquial Welsh use the future paradigm to convey a present tense meaning, e.g. *gwela i* (see.FUT.1s I) 'I see', *gwn i* (know.FUT.1s I) 'I know'.

Any adverbial elements typically occur in clause-final position, or, with slightly more emphasis, in clause-initial position. We can say, then, that the unmarked word order in Welsh is VSOX, as in (16):

(16)   Prynodd   Elin dorth o fara   yn y   farchnad ddydd Llun.
        buy.PAST.3s Elin loaf   of bread in the market   Monday
        'Elin bought a loaf of bread at the market on Monday.'

The finite element may be preceded by one of a small set of pre-verbal particles, the use of which depends largely on register. For instance, in (14), the presence of the particle *y* in the embedded clause is a marker of formal Welsh, and is absent in speech. On the other hand, it is common in the spoken language to find one of the affirmative markers *mi* or *fe* (the choice is largely dialectally determined), which occur in root clauses:

(17)   **Mi/Fe** brynodd   Elin dorth o fara.
        PRT   buy.PAST.3s Elin loaf   of bread
        'Elin bought a loaf of bread.'

Note that these particles both trigger soft mutation; see section 1.4.4. In what follows, we normally show a verb in initial position with no pre-verbal particle.

The past tense occurs in examples (13), (15), (16) and (17) above. The future tense is shown in (18):

(18)   Ceith   hi siom   fawr wythnos nesa'.
        get.FUT.3s she disappointment big week   next
        'She'll be very disappointed next week.'

The conditional paradigm is illustrated in (19):

(19)   Hoffet   ti   banad o de?
        like.COND.2s you   cupful of tea
        'Would you like a cup of tea?'

The conditional paradigm also has other uses, most notably in literary Welsh, to refer to habitual events in the past (see Jones & Thomas 1977: 84, 89–93):

(20)   Âi   Elin allan bron   bob   nos.
        go.COND.3s Elin out   nearly every night
        'Elin used to go/would go out nearly every night.'

In speech, the most frequent kinds of finite clauses are not the VSO clauses illustrated in examples such as (16) to (20), but rather, clauses with a finite auxiliary in initial position, as shown in both the main and the embedded clause in (14). These are sometimes known as AuxSVO clauses: they have an initial auxiliary followed by the subject, and the lexical verb occurs in its non-finite form later in the clause. In (21) to (23) we show three different clause types of this kind:

(21)   Mae   Elin **wedi/ yn**   prynu   torth o fara.
        be.PRES.3S Elin PERF PROG buy.INF loaf of bread
        'Elin has bought/is buying a loaf of bread.'

(22)   Gwnaeth Elin brynu   torth o fara.
        do.PAST.3S Elin buy.INF loaf of bread
        'Elin bought a loaf of bread.'

(23)   Ddaru Elin brynu   torth o fara.
        PAST   Elin buy.INF loaf of bread
        'Elin bought a loaf of bread.'

In (21), we have an example of an overtly aspectual clause, with an aspect marker in pre-verbal position. Welsh has a small set of grammaticalized aspect markers, most of which are descended from – and homophonous with – prepositions. The two most common are shown in (21), *wedi* (PERFECT) and *yn* (PROGRESSIVE). However, the standard progressive gloss does not give an accurate indication of how and when *yn* is used. Clauses containing it have a broader distribution than the English progressive aspect (*is buying*), and can, for instance, contain stative verbs or express habitual aspect.[5] Note that only one auxiliary occurs in aspectual clauses, namely *bod* 'be'; unlike various other European languages, Welsh has no 'have' auxiliary, though one does occur in closely related Breton.

There are no aspectual particles in (22) or (23). These examples again have a finite initial auxiliary, with the non-finite lexical verb in post-subject position. The auxiliary in (22), *gwneud* 'do', is widely used in all dialects, and is especially frequent in northern dialects. Unlike its English counterpart, *gwneud* confers no special emphasis. *Ddaru* in (23) is etymologically a verb (meaning 'happen') but is simply a past tense marker in the modern language, having only the one form. The auxiliary-initial examples in (22) and (23) have the same meaning as the VSO sentences in (13) and (16), and all these examples are largely interchangeable, though (23) is restricted to northern dialects. However, it is clear that the periphrastic verb forms – i.e., forms with an initial auxiliary and a non-finite main verb – are spreading at the expense of synthetic verbs in the modern language. This spread is particularly advanced in northern dialects, somewhat unusually, since these dialects are generally more conservative.

---

[5] Consider, for instance, example (i), which shows that there is no prohibition on stative verbs appearing with the progressive aspect:

(i)   Dw   i 'n   gwybod yr ateb.
       be.PRES.1S I PROG know.INF the answer
       'I know the answer.'

More detail on the structure of finite clauses, including copular clauses, can be found in chapter 2.

So far, we have considered active verbs. Welsh, like English, has no specifically passive verbal morphology, but it does have both a passive construction and impersonal morphology. In the passive, the notional object is promoted to subject position, and the passive is expressed via an auxiliary *cael* 'get', plus the non-finite form of the lexical verb, which takes an agreement proclitic agreeing with the new subject, as shown in (24):

(24)   Mae   'r lladron wedi cael   eu dal   gan yr heddlu.
        be.PRES.3S the thieves PERF get.INF 3P catch.INF by   the police
        'The thieves have been caught by the police.'

The impersonal, shown in (25), is generally restricted to literary Welsh:

(25)   Daliwyd   y   lladron gan yr heddlu.
        catch.PAST.IMPERS the thieves by   the police
        'The thieves were caught by the police.'

More detail on the impersonal, the passive, and other valency-changing processes is given in chapter 8.

One additional factor concerning finite clauses is worth mentioning at this stage. It is often the case that verb-initial languages have alternative unmarked word orders: for instance, a VSO language may alternate that word order with VOS, or SVO (see chapter 10 for more on this). In Welsh, however, the unmarked word order always has a finite verb or auxiliary in initial position, as illustrated in this section, and there are no neutral alternative possibilities. Any constituent can be fronted for focus (see section 4.3), but focus clauses are always pragmatically marked to some extent.

1.4.2.2 Non-finite clauses

A particularly interesting characteristic of Welsh concerns the syntax of clauses which are formally non-finite. One reason for interest is that some of these clauses are in fact demonstrably *finite*, despite having no visible tensed element. Two examples are shown in the bracketed embedded clauses in (26) and (27):

(26)   Mae   'n   ymddangos [bod llawer o dai   yn y pentre 'n   hen].
        be.PRES.3S PROG appear.INF be.INF many of houses in the village PRED old
        'It appears that many houses in the village are old.'

(27)   Dywedodd Ifan [iddyn nhw gymryd tystiolaeth ledled   Cymru].
        say.PAST.3S Ifan to.3P them take.INF evidence   throughout Wales
        'Ifan said that they had gathered evidence throughout Wales.'

In (26), the embedded clause is a *bod*-clause (see section 3.3), and in (27) we have one type of *i*-clause (section 3.4). In both cases, there is an overt subject in the complement clause, but no formally finite verb or auxiliary; yet the bracketed clause in (26) is interpreted as present tense, and that in (27) as relative past tense.

On the other hand, the subordinate clause in (28) appears to be syntactically parallel to that in (27), but is not interpreted as finite at all; rather, it is a genuinely infinitival clause, here with relative future time reference.

(28)   Disgwyliodd   Elen [iddyn nhw beidio ag   aros   dros nos].
        expect.PAST.3s Elen to.3P   them NEG   with stay.INF over night
        'Elen expected them not to stay overnight.'

Alongside embedded clauses with overt subjects, there are also contexts with no overt subject, as shown in (29) and (30):

(29)   Rydyn   ni 'n   bwriadu   [cynnal   ymgynghoriad cyhoeddus].
        be.PRES.1P we PROG intend.INF hold.INF consultation   public
        'We intend to hold a public consultation.'

(30)   Rydyn   ni 'n   tueddu [i gymryd ein cymdogion yn   ganiataol].
        be.PRES.1P we PROG tend.INF to take.INF 1P neighbours PRED granted
        'We tend to take our neighbours for granted.'

These are also genuinely non-finite contexts. Note that the subordinate clause in (30) is introduced by a functional element *i*, as are the bracketed clauses in (27) and (28). One question then concerns the status and function of these *i* elements, and whether or not they instantiate the same morpheme in each case. Chapter 3 investigates the syntax of non-finite clauses in detail.

1.4.2.3   Syntactic alignment

Welsh, like the vast majority of European languages, has subject/ object alignment. This is indicated syntactically via word order (in the unmarked order, subjects always precede objects) and morphologically via head-marking (in Welsh, subject – verb agreement) on the verb or auxiliary.

Consider first verbal morphology. The finite verb or auxiliary inflects to agree with the person and number of a pronominal subject (see section 1.4.3), as shown in (31) and (32), but does not agree with the object.

(31)   Gwelodd   hi 'r   ddraig.
        see.PAST.3s she the dragon
        'She saw the dragon.'

(32)   Gwelon   nhw gath yn yr   ardd.
        see.PAST.3P they cat in the garden
        'They saw a cat in the garden.'

Non-finite verbs, however, display object agreement proclitics; see section 1.4.5.

Transitive verbs bear the same inflections as intransitive verbs, and there are no distinctions between unergative and unaccusative clauses in terms of verbal agreement, as shown by the absence of any difference between (33) with the unergative verb *rhedeg* 'run' and (34) with the unaccusative verb *diflannu* 'disappear':

(33)   Rhedon   nhw i ffwrdd.
            run.PAST.3P they away
            'They ran away.'

(34)   Diflannon   nhw.
            disappear.PAST.3P they
            'They disappeared.'

The verbal dependents in a clause are morphologically unmarked, and there is no morphological case in Welsh, either on nouns or pronouns; see section 1.4.5 below. Compare then (31) and (35), which show that both the noun phrase *y ddraig* 'the dragon' and the pronoun *hi* 'she' can appear in both subject and object position.[6]

(35)   Gwelodd   y   ddraig hi.
            see.PAST.3S the dragon her
            'The dragon saw her.'

The same forms also occur as the objects of prepositions:

(36)   a. â   'r   ddraig
             with the dragon
             'with the dragon'
       b. â   hi
             with her
             'with her'

There is, however, a long-running debate concerning the form of direct objects in examples like (32). Here, the object bears soft mutation ($<$ *cath*) (see section 1.4.4) and it is sometimes proposed that in this context mutation marks accusative case. In literary Welsh, the availability of null subjects may very occasionally lead to ambiguity which is sometimes resolved by this mutation. So, for instance, (37) is interpreted with *pawb* 'everyone' as subject, because it does not undergo mutation. Conversely, in (38), *pawb* undergoes soft mutation to *bawb*, and is interpreted as the direct object.

---

[6] The slight difference in form between *y ddraig* and *'r ddraig* is due to phonological rather than syntactic factors. The form of the definite article is *'r* in post-vocalic contexts, *y/yr* elsewhere; see Hannahs & Tallerman (2006) for full details.

(37)   Deallai   pawb.
        understand.COND.3s everyone
        'Everyone would understand.'

(38)   Deallai   bawb.
        understand.COND.3s everyone
        'He/she would understand everyone.'

Although this mutation gives the impression of being accusative case morphology, there are good reasons for believing that it is not; chapter 7 discusses this issue in detail.

As expected with a subject/object alignment, the subjects of both intransitive and transitive clauses are differentiated syntactically from direct objects. Consider the examples in (39) to (41):

(39)   Deffrodd   Mair a   mynd allan.
        wake.PAST.3s Mair and go.INF out
        'Mair woke up and went out.'

(40)   Gwelodd   Mair y ddraig a   rhedeg i ffwrdd.
        see.PAST.3s Mair the dragon and run.INF away
        'Mair saw the dragon and ran away.'
        (≠ 'Mair saw the dragon and the dragon ran away.')

(41)   *Gwelodd Mair a   Rhiannon y ddraig a   'u bwyta nhw.
        see.PAST.3s Mair and Rhiannon the dragon and 3P eat.INF them
        ('Mair and Rhiannon saw the dragon and it ate them.')

This construction (termed the serial construction by Rouveret 1994) has the following properties: the first conjunct is tensed, the second infinitival; the subject of the second conjunct is obligatorily empty, and must be co-referential with the subject of the first conjunct. Examples (39) and (40) show that the construction has a subject pivot, since the subject of both intransitive and transitive clauses can be the antecedent for the covert subject in the second conjunct. In (41), on the other hand, we see that the object in the first conjunct, *y ddraig* 'the dragon', cannot be the antecedent for the unexpressed noun phrase in the second conjunct.[7] Clearly, the subject grammatical relation is the salient one here.

---

[7] Note that (i) is grammatical on the reading shown, where, in the second conjunct, the subject is null, referring back to *Mair*, and *hi* 'her' is the object, referring back to the dragon (which is feminine).

(i)   Gwelodd   Mair y ddraig a   'i   bwyta hi.
       see.PAST.3s Mair the dragon and 3FS eat.INF her
       'Mair saw the dragon and she ate it.'
       (≠'Mair saw the dragon and it ate her.')

1.4.3   Agreement

Agreement in Welsh operates only between a head and a personal pronoun, never between a head and a lexical noun phrase. So, in (42), the third person plural verb *cerddon* appears with the pronominal subject *nhw* 'they', but, in (43), the lexical third person plural subject, *Aled a Sara* 'Aled and Sara', requires the default form of the verb, namely the third person singular.

(42)   Cerddon   nhw adre.
        walk.PAST.3P they home
        'They walked home.'

(43)   Cerddodd   / *Cerddon   Aled a   Sara adre.
        walk.PAST.3S / walk.PAST.3P Aled and Sara home
        'Aled and Sara walked home.'

This pattern is replicated with all types of agreement in Welsh. For instance, as in all Celtic languages, most prepositions in Welsh inflect for the person and number of their object. A few prepositions, such as *â* 'with', are invariant. As with subject – verb agreement, the inflected form is used if the object is pronominal, but not if it is lexical. The paradigm for *am* 'about' is given in Table 1.4. Notice that, in Table 1.4, we have *amdanyn nhw* 'about them', with an inflected preposition, but the preposition fails to inflect in (44), where the object is lexical.

(44)   am   / *amdanyn y   myfyrwyr
        about / about.3P   the students
        'about the students'

This pattern of agreement is similar to that found in other Celtic languages, but also subtly different. In all the other Celtic languages, as in Welsh, agreement marking reflects a relationship between a head and a pronominal element, never a lexical noun phrase.[8] Thus, in Breton, the verb in (45) must appear in the default third-person singular form even though the subject is a

Table 1.4. *Paradigm for* am *'about' in colloquial Welsh.*

	singular	plural
first person	*amdana(f) i*	*amdanon ni*
second person	*amdanat ti*	*amdanoch chi*
third person	*amdano fe / fo*	*amdanyn nhw*

---

[8] There are some systematic exceptions to this statement, such as negative clauses in Breton, but the basic pattern nevertheless remains clear.

plural noun phrase, whereas, with a pronominal subject in (46), the verb shows the usual third-person plural inflection.

(45)   Bremañ e   lenn   / *lennont   ar vugale al levrioù.
        now   PRT read.PRES.3S / read.PRES.3P the children the books.
        'Now the children are reading the books.'

(46)   Bremañ e   lennont   al levrioù.
        now   PRT read.PRES.3P the books.
        'Now they are reading the books.'

This is the same principle that Welsh manifests in (42) and (43).

However, in Celtic languages other than Welsh, it is usually impossible for a pronoun to be overtly expressed if there is agreement. This is seen most clearly in Irish. In (47), where the verb *chuirfinn* 'would put' is inflected for first person singular, an overt pronoun *mé* is impossible. Contrast this with (48). Here the verb appears in a default third-person singular form (as can be seen from a comparison with (49)), and an overt pronoun is possible, in fact required.

(47)   Chuirfinn   (*mé) isteach ar an phost sin.
        put.COND.1S (I)   in   on the job   that
        'I would apply for that job.'   (Irish, McCloskey & Hale 1984)

(48)   Chuirfeadh sibh isteach ar an phost sin.
        put.COND.3S you in   on the job   that
        'You would apply for that job.'   (Irish, McCloskey & Hale 1984)

(49)   Chuirfeadh Eoghan isteach ar an phost sin.
        put.COND.3S Owen   in   on the job   that
        'Owen would apply for that job.'   (Irish, McCloskey & Hale 1984)

This phenomenon has been referred to as the Complementarity Principle (Stump 1984: 292, see also Anderson 1982, Borsley & Stephens 1989, Doron 1988 and Stump 1989):

(50)   The Complementarity Principle
        Within a clause, overt argument noun phrases never appear with concording personal affixes.

Overt pronouns are sometimes possible with agreement in Breton, but are usually avoided. In Welsh, however, the Complementarity Principle does not hold, and an overt pronoun is quite normal, as illustrated in (51) (see also Rouveret 1991).

(51)   Hoffwn   i ymgeisio am y   swydd honno.
        like.COND.1S I apply.INF for the job   that
        'I would like to apply for that job.'

Although these two phenomena (lack of agreement with a lexical noun phrase and impossibility of a subject pronoun alongside agreement) have often been linked, Welsh, which manifests the former but not the latter, demonstrates that they are distinct. We understand the Complementarity Principle to refer strictly to the second phenomenon, as expressed in (50), and we will therefore not use it with reference to Welsh.

1.4.4   Mutation

After verb-initial word order, probably the best-known aspect of all the Celtic languages, including Welsh, is the feature known as initial conso-nantal mutation. The term 'mutation' refers to a set of alternations in the initial segments of words or morphemes. Note that the distribution of the various mutated forms is generally determined by lexical and morphosyntac-tic factors, and never by phonological factors. Although any Welsh grammar will provide a list of triggering contexts (see, for instance, King 2003, Thorne 1993), not all the mutations are consistently observed in speech in all dialects.

There are three basic series of initial mutations in Welsh, traditionally known as soft mutation (*treiglad meddal*), nasal mutation (*treiglad trwynol*) and aspirate mutation (*treiglad llaes*).[9] The canonical form of a word or morpheme with no mutation is its citation form, and is also the form used generally in dictionary entries. These basic forms with no mutation are known as the radical forms: the radical initial consonants are shown in the first column in Table 1.5. In each column, Welsh orthographic representations are given on the left, and the phonetic values on the right.

As can be seen from Table 1.5, a total of nine consonants formally partici-pate in the mutation system, though only soft mutation affects all nine. Although the phonetic processes involved are not entirely straightforward, some generalizations can be made. Soft mutation is a general process of leni-tion, so voiceless stops and liquids become voiced, and voiced stops become fricatives. Note, however, that [g] deletes in the modern language, rather than becoming a fricative. Nasal mutation affects only the stop consonants; these become homorganic nasals, retaining both voicing and place of articulation.

---

[9] Although it is sometimes regarded as a mutation, hard mutation (*treiglad caled*), the fortition process seen in *teg* 'fair', *tecaf* 'fairest' is, in our view, a morphophonologi-cal alternation of the ordinary kind, and therefore should not be included with the discussion of initial consonant mutation. Also often included in lists of the conso-nantal mutations is the process known as aspiration, whereby *h-* [h] is added to vowel-initial words in certain contexts, for instance, following the proclitics *ei* (3FS) and *ein* (1P): *ei harian* (< *arian*) 'her money'; *ein hoes* (< *oes*) 'our lifetime'.

Table 1.5. *Consonantal mutation in Welsh.*

Radical	Soft	Nasal	Aspirate
p [p]	b [b]	mh [m̥ʰ]	ph [f]
t [t]	d [d]	nh [n̥ʰ]	th [θ]
c [k]	g [g]	ngh [ŋ̊ʰ]	ch [x]
b [b]	f [v]	m [m]	
d [d]	dd [ð]	n [n]	
g [g]	– zero	ng [ŋ]	
m [m]	f [v]		
ll [ɬ]	l [l]		
rh [r̥ʰ]	r [r]		

Only the three voiceless stops undergo aspirate mutation, becoming homorganic voiceless fricatives.

As a result of mutation, a single morpheme may appear in as many as four distinct forms, depending on the context. For instance:

(52)   radical: *tad* 'father'
        soft mutation: *dy dad* (2s father) 'your father'
        nasal mutation: *fy nhad* (1s father) 'my father'
        aspirate mutation: *ei thad* (3FS father) 'her father'

Note that mutation is always on the initial segment of the constituent which is the target for mutation (and not, for instance, necessarily on the head word). If the first word happens not to have a mutable initial consonant, then the target will bear no sign of mutation at all.

Obviously, a comprehensive account of mutation would include, amongst other factors, both a morphophonological analysis (see, for instance, Lieber 1983) and a full list of the environments in which the mutations occur. Here, we give a brief overview of the main contexts for mutation. In what follows, we refer to the item causing the mutation (where there is such an item) as the trigger, and the item undergoing the mutation as the target.

As noted above, the triggering contexts are mainly either lexical or morphosyntactic (and sometimes both), and in the general case, the mutation is triggered by an immediately preceding lexical item. Typical lexical triggers include various agreement clitics (as in (52)), prepositions (53a), numerals (53b), determiners (53c), conjunctions (53d), pre-verbal particles (53e) and a number of other small functional elements, such as the predicate marker *yn* (53f) and the comparative marker *mor* (53g). Where the mutation is relevant to the discussion, we adopt the practice of underlining the mutated item and showing its radical form in parentheses. Where the mutation is not germane to the discussion, we will not indicate it in the examples or glosses.

(53) a. gan <u>flodau</u>   (*blodau*)
         with flowers
         'with flowers'
      b. dau <u>fachgen</u>   (*bachgen*)
         two boy
         'two boys'
      c. pa   <u>ddiwrnod</u>   (*diwrnod*)
         which day
         'which day'
      d. te neu <u>goffi</u>   (*coffi*)
         tea or   coffee
         'tea or coffee'
      e. Mi <u>brynais</u>   i docyn.   (*prynais*)
         PRT buy.PAST.1s I ticket
         'I bought a ticket.'
      f. yn   <u>ofalus</u>   (*gofalus*)
         PRED careful
         'careful(ly)'
      g. mor <u>fawr</u>   (*mawr*)
         so   big
         'so big'

The vast majority of lexical triggers cause soft mutation, as is the case with all the examples in (53). Examples of triggers for the other two series of mutation are shown in (54): in (a), *yn* 'in' triggers nasal mutation on *de*; in (b), *a* 'and' triggers aspirate mutation on *coffi*; and in (c), *â* 'with' triggers aspirate mutation on *poeni*.

(54) a. yn <u>ne</u>   Cymru   (*de*)
         in south Wales
         'in south Wales'
      b. te a   <u>choffi</u>   (*coffi*)
         tea and coffee
         'tea and coffee'
      c. Paid   â   <u>phoeni</u>.   (*poeni*)
         NEG.IMPER.2s with worry.INF
         'Don't worry.'

Note that not all prepositions, numerals, clitics, determiners and other functional elements are mutation triggers: knowing the word class of an item does not predict anything about its status as a mutation trigger. Furthermore, homophonous elements may trigger different mutations. For instance, the morpheme *yn* 'in' triggers nasal mutation, as shown in (54a), but the progressive aspect marker *yn* is followed by the radical initial consonant. And while the third-person masculine singular proclitic *ei* triggers soft mutation, as in *ei dad* 'his father', the homophonous third-person feminine singular proclitic *ei* triggers aspirate mutation, as in (52); unsurprisingly, this is one of the more robust environments for aspirate mutation in the modern spoken language.

Although the examples of mutation shown so far are all triggered across word boundaries, a number of prefixes also trigger various mutations (mainly soft). For instance, *di-* 'without' and *cyd-* 'co-, con-' both trigger soft mutation: *diddefnydd* 'useless' (< *defnydd* 'use' n.); *cydfynd* 'agree' (< *mynd* 'go.INF'); the negative prefix *an-* triggers nasal mutation: *anghofio* 'forget' (< *cofio* 'remember'); and the prefix *dy-* is in some cases a trigger for aspirate mutation: *dychanu* 'satirize' (< *canu* 'sing').

Morphosyntactic factors come into play when the target (or less often, the trigger) is restricted in some way. Welsh, like the other Celtic languages and like the Romance languages, has a grammatical gender system in which the two options are masculine and feminine. Nouns generally display no inherent marking for gender, but distinct mutations are associated with feminine singular nouns. For instance, in (55), the feminine singular noun *cath* 'cat' bears soft mutation following the definite article in (a), but the feminine plural noun *cathod* 'cats' in (b) and the masculine noun *ci* / *cŵn* 'dog(s)' in (c) do not.[10]

(55)   a. y <u>gath</u>   (*cath*)
             the cat
             'the cat'
      b. y cathod
             the cats
             'the cats'
      c. y ci / y cŵn
             the dog / the dogs
             'the dog' / 'the dogs'

Similarly, in (56), the adjective bears soft mutation following a feminine singular noun in (a), but not following a feminine plural noun in (b), or a masculine noun in (c):

---

[10] Unlike in many European languages, the definite article in Welsh does not vary according to the gender of the following noun (see section 5.2.1). Nor do adjectives generally have masculine and feminine allomorphs (but see section 5.4.2). Gender is therefore less visible in Welsh than in many other languages.

(56)   a. y   gath <u>fawr</u>   (*mawr*)
    the cat big
    'the big cat'
  b. y   cathod mawr
    the cats big
    'the big cats'
  c. y   ci   mawr / y   cŵn mawr
    the dog big / the dogs big
    'the big dog' / 'the big dogs'

However, there are also certain purely structural conditions for mutation. For instance, any adjective in pre-nominal position triggers soft mutation on the following item (mostly, a noun), irrespective of the head noun's gender or number:

(57)   a. hen <u>gathod</u>   (*cathod*)
    old cats
    'old cats'
  b. hen <u>gŵn</u>   (*cŵn*)
    old dogs
    'old dogs'

Mutation in the noun phrase is discussed in more detail in chapter 5 (especially section 5.4.1).

There are also contexts in which no mutation trigger can be identified. For example, adverbials tend to undergo soft mutation, as in (58), though not all speakers observe this environment consistently.

(58)   <u>Ddwy</u> flynedd yn ôl, aethon   ni i 'r   Alban.   (*dwy*)
   two   year   ago   go.PAST.1P we to the Scotland
   'Two years ago, we went to Scotland.'

In a somewhat different category come contexts in which there is formally a lexical trigger, and where the mutation remains even though the trigger itself is often absent in the colloquial language. One context of this type involves the proclitics which precede nouns and non-finite verbs (see sections 4.1.5, 4.2.2 and 5.2.2); (59) illustrates:

(59)   Mae   Elin wedi (ei) <u>weld</u> o.   (*gweld*)
   be.PRES.3S Elin PERF 3MS see.INF him
   'Elin has seen him.'

The 3MS proclitic *ei* triggers soft mutation, but in a context like that in (59) it is rarely overt in the spoken language; nonetheless, the mutation typically remains. However, there is room for debate about when mutation is triggered by some covert element and when it is just the realization of some features on the target. In some instances, the mutation which would be triggered by an overt element is not the one which occurs when that element is missing. For example, in the literary language, the negative pre-verbal particle *ni* triggers aspirate mutation of /p t k/ and soft mutation of the remaining consonants.[11] In the colloquial language the particle is generally omitted, and only a handful of verbs systematically retain aspirate mutation in this context (see sections 8.2.1 and 8.2.2); instead, soft mutation is generalized to the majority of finite verbs.

In general, the lexical environments for mutation are not of huge theoretical interest. Some structural contexts, however, have been the topic of great debate over a long period, particularly in the generative literature on Welsh. One particularly contentious environment, which we term syntactic soft mutation, is illustrated in (60) and (61):

(60)   Cafodd   hi [ddau fachgen].   (*dau*)
        have.PAST.3S she two   boy
        'She had two boys.'

(61)   Mae   gynnon ni [ormod   o broblemau].   (*gormod*)
        be.PRES.3S with.1P us too.many of problems
        'We have too many problems.'

In (60), the direct object of a finite verb bears the mutation, and in (61), a noun phrase following a PP bears the mutation. The syntax of this environment for soft mutation is discussed in detail in chapter 7, where we propose that the mutation is triggered by a preceding and c-commanding phrase. A different structural context is illustrated in chapter 4 (especially section 4.9.6.2), where we discuss the mutations occurring in relative clauses in the colloquial language.

Finally, note that some words appear to have an initial mutable consonant, but nonetheless do not mutate. These fall into various categories. Consider first proper nouns. Names of people do not undergo mutation: 'to Dafydd' is *i Dafydd*, not **i Ddafydd*. Names of places do mutate, but unassimilated foreign words, including foreign place names, do not undergo mutation. For instance, the preposition *i* 'to' is a trigger for soft mutation, so 'to Bangor' is *i Fangor* and 'to Paris' is *i Baris* (< *Paris*), since *Paris* is a phonologically assimilated form. But 'to Durham' is *i Durham* and not **i Ddurham*, since this place name has no assimilated form.

---

[11] This is known as the mixed mutation, and is one of two special types of mutation. The other is the restricted soft mutation, which occurs in a small number of contexts, for instance after the triggers *yn* (PREDICATIVE) and *mor* 'so'. This mutation affects only seven of the nine mutable consonants, and excludes *ll-* and *rh*-initial words: *yn llawn* (PRED full) 'full'; *mor rhesymol* (so reasonable) 'so/as reasonable'.

Secondly, there are numerous lexically idiosyncratic restrictions imposed by the mutation target, resulting in items which fail to undergo one or more types of mutation. These are often small functional elements, such as the second person singular proclitic *dy* in (62) and *mor* 'so', in (63).

(62)　　Gwelais　i dy/*ddy　　dad.
　　　　see.PAST.1s I 2s/ (+SM) father
　　　　'I saw your father.'

(63)　　Mae　　　fy swyddfa newydd mor/*for　　fawr!
　　　　be.PRES.3s 1s office　　new　　so/ (+SM) big
　　　　'My new office is so big!'

Also in this category come a handful of loanwords from English with initial /g/, such as *gêm* 'game', *g(i)ât* 'gate' and *braf* (< English or French *brave*) 'nice'.

Thirdly, some words appear to have a fossilized mutation as their citation form in the modern language, so fail to undergo further mutation. For instance, a number of prepositions fall into this category, such as *gan* 'with, from, by', *dan* 'under' and *dros* 'over, for', all of which normally appear in these forms, i.e. with soft mutation. Some adverbials are also in this category, for instance *ddoe* 'yesterday' and *gartre(f)* 'at home'; again, these items are fixed in their soft mutated form for all speakers.

It is also worth noting that, although we have presented the three series of mutations as if their status in the modern language were equal, this is not in fact the case. First, by far the majority of mutation triggers are triggers for soft mutation, and there are substantially fewer lexical triggers for both aspirate and nasal mutation. Secondly, it is mainly the environments for soft mutation which tend to be robust in the modern language: contexts for the other two series are less stable, and again are subject to much dialectal and idiolectal variation. Some lexical triggers have simply ceased to trigger the mutation with which they are historically associated; for instance, *efo*, *gyda* and *â* (all meaning 'with') are triggers for aspirate mutation in formal Welsh, but this is rarely observed in the modern spoken language.

Furthermore, certain environments which are formally (and historically) contexts for nasal and aspirate mutation tend to be supplanted by soft mutation in the modern spoken language (or sometimes exhibit no mutation). For instance, *yn* 'in' is formally a trigger for nasal mutation, which is fairly stable in the spoken language, e.g. *yng Nghaerdydd* (< *Caerdydd*) 'in Cardiff'; but, in some dialects, *yn* triggers soft mutation instead: *yn Gaerdydd*.[12] A second

---

[12] The preposition *yn* itself has a set of allomorphs (*yn, ym, yng*) which are conditioned by the phonological environment.

example, mentioned above, is the spread of soft mutation onto negative finite verbs, where formally, the negative particle *ni* would trigger aspirate mutation on voiceless stops.

Another reason for the prevalence of soft mutation is the stability of the syntactic context for this mutation, illustrated in (60) and (61). In the modern colloquial language syntactic soft mutation is extremely robust and shows no signs of dying out.

1.4.5   Case and pronouns

As already noted, Welsh nouns have no case morphology. Grammatical functions are indicated using fairly rigid word order. Subject and object are distinguished by appearing rigidly in that order:

(64)   Lladdodd   Myrddin y   ddraig.
        kill.PAST.3s Merlin   the dragon.
        'Merlin killed the dragon.'

In the absence of a genitive case, possession in noun phrases is indicated by juxtaposition of possessed noun and possessor noun phrase in that order:

(65)   cŵn y   cymdogion
        dogs the neighbours
        'the neighbours' dogs'

Case on personal pronouns is a more complex issue. Sometimes, differences in the form of pronouns give the impression of reflecting case distinctions. Thus, the distinction between *i* and *fi* in (66) and (67) might lead to the conclusion that *i* is a nominative form and *fi* is an accusative form.

(66)   Gwelais   i 'r   ddraig.
        see.PAST.1s I the dragon
        'I saw the dragon.'

(67)   Gwelodd   y   ddraig **fi**.
        see.PAST.3s the dragon me
        'The dragon saw me.'

This conclusion, however, would be misguided. Although Welsh has a complex system of pronouns, which varies extensively in detail between different dialects and between the literary and the colloquial language, the basic distinctions hinge on phonological strength, and not on case (see sections 5.2 and 9.8).

Personal pronouns have both clitic and non-clitic forms. The pronoun *i* in (66) above is a clitic, whereas *fi* in (67) is not. Both proclitic and enclitic forms exist. The second-person singular pronoun, for instance, has four possible simple forms: free form *ti*, post-head enclitic ('affixed') *di* (*ti* after /t/), and pre-head clitics, proclitic *dy* and enclitic *'th*. The weak, post-head enclitic forms are used in conjunction with an agreement morpheme or with another clitic. A distinction between accusative clitics (used as the object of a finite verb) and genitive proclitics (used as the object of a non-finite verb) is made in literary Welsh, but not in colloquial Welsh (see section 9.8).

In (68), we see enclitic subjects after an agreeing verb, and, in (69), the enclitic object of a nonfinite verb, used in conjunction with a proclitic (*dy*) attached to the same verb.

(68)   Gweli   **di**   / Gwelaist **ti**   'r   cyfan.
        see.FUT.2S you   see.PAST.2S you the whole
        'You'll see everything.' / 'You saw everything.'

(69)   Mae   Steffan yn   dy garu   (**di**).
        be.PRES.3S Steffan PROG 2S love.INF you
        'Steffan loves you.'

Although post-head enclitic pronouns may bear contrastive stress and may be coordinated with another noun phrase, they form a phonological unit with the preceding verb, from which they may not be separated, and may not form an utterance on their own.

The free, non-clitic forms are used when there is no corresponding agreement suffix or agreement proclitic. They may occupy a focus position, as in (70), or may be used alone, as in (71).[13]

(70)   **Ti** yw   'r   gorau.
        you be.PRES.3S the best
        'You are the best.'

(71)   Pwy sy   eisiau chwarae? **Ti**?
        who be.PRES.REL want   play.INF you
        'Who wants to play? You?'

---

[13] *Eisiau* 'want' in example (71) is one of a number of items in Welsh that express psychological predicates that have a mixture of nominal and verbal syntactic properties. Although they appear in construction with auxiliary verbs, as here with progressive auxiliary *bod*, they may not co-occur with aspect markers. If aspect other than progressive needs to be expressed, then another auxiliary must be inserted:

(i)   Mae   Aled wastad wedi bod   eisiau chwarae 'r ffidil.
        be.PRES.3S Aled always PERF be.INF want   play.INF the violin
        'Aled has always wanted to play the violin.'

Other items that behave similarly are *rhaid* 'must, necessity', *ofn* 'be afraid, fear' and *angen* 'need, requirement'. For further details, see section 2.6.3.

They also appear in syntactic environments where there is no agreement, as with the direct object of a finite verb in (72), or, in colloquial Welsh, the direct object of a non-finite verb, as in (73).

(72)   Clywais   i **ti**   'n   gadael   y   tŷ.
         hear.PAST.1S I you PROG leave.INF the house
         'I heard you leaving the house.'

(73)   Mae   Rhiannon yn   hoffi   **ti**.
         be.PRES.3S Rhiannon PROG like.INF you
         'Rhiannon likes you.'

In very literary Welsh, the free forms are sometimes replaced by longer 'reduplicated' forms, which exist only as independent, non-clitic elements:

(74)   **Myfi**   / **Tydi**   yw   'r gorau.
         I.REDUP / you.REDUP be.PRES.3S the best
         'I am/You are the best.'

Welsh pronouns also convey pragmatic meaning concerning information structure. Use of 'conjunctive' forms of pronouns, for instance, often indicates a change of topic, with the pronoun being the new topic, or else indicates comparison with some other (often implied) entity. Conjunctive pronouns are available in both clitic and non-clitic forms, illustrated in (75) and (76) respectively.

(75)   Yn 1970, cefais   innau fy newis   i   ddarllen y   neges.
         in   1970 get.PAST.1S I.CONJ 1S choose.INF to read.INF the message
         'In 1970, I (in my turn) was chosen to read the message.'

(76)   Roedd   fy nhad yn   chwarae dros Gymru fel finnau.
         be.IMPF.3S 1s father PROG play.INF for   Wales like me.CONJ
         'My father played for Wales like me.'

Proclitics appear before non-finite verbs, as in (77), and on nouns, as in (78).[14]

(77)   Mae   Rhiannon yn   **dy** hoffi   (di).
         be.PRES.3S Rhiannon PROG 2s like.INF you
         'Rhiannon likes you.'

(78)   Mae   Dafydd wedi cymryd **dy** fodur (di).
         be.PRES.3S Dafydd PERF take.INF 2s car   you
         'Dafydd has taken your car.'

Here, (77) represents a more formal or neutral register than colloquial (73) above. Proclitics like *dy* may never be stressed. If contrastive stress is required, it must be borne by the post-head enclitic (*di*).

---

[14] Note that with an agreement proclitic in (77) the object pronoun appears in the enclitic form *di*, whereas, in the absence of an agreement proclitic in (73), the pronoun appears in the independent non-clitic form *ti*.

There is frequently doubling of a pre-head proclitic (*dy*) and a post-head enclitic (*di*) as in (77) and (78), although the proclitic alone is sufficient to ensure grammaticality. The existence of doubling raises the question of which of the two elements is the 'real' object of the verb or possessor of the noun. Traditional Welsh grammar takes the view that the proclitic is the 'real' pronoun, and the enclitic has a supporting role. Generative literature has generally taken the reverse perspective, namely that the enclitic is the 'real' pronoun and the proclitic is an agreement morpheme. This book adopts the latter view. One piece of evidence in favour is that it is the enclitic that occupies the position that would have been occupied by a lexical noun phrase. For instance, *di* in (77) occupies the same position as *Dafydd* in (79); and *di* in (78) occupies the same position as *Rhiannon* in (80). Fuller discussion of this issue and further reasons for favouring the second view will be given in sections 3.1.2 and 5.2.2.

(79)   Mae   Rhiannon yn   hoffi   Dafydd.
        be.PRES.3s Rhiannon PROG like.INF Dafydd
        'Rhiannon likes Dafydd.'

(80)   Mae   Dafydd wedi cymryd modur Rhiannon.
        be.PRES.3s Dafydd PERF take.INF car   Rhiannon
        'Dafydd has taken Rhiannon's car.'

Our glossing practices will reflect this view. Hence, we gloss the proclitics as agreement markers (1s, 2s etc.) and the enclitics as pronouns (*me*, *you* etc.).

Under certain circumstances which vary between registers, the proclitics may instead appear as enclitics (for instance as second person '*th*) on the previous word. The conditions on this are quite complex and are to a large extent phonological and hence not of central concern here (for further details, see section 5.2.2).

1.5   Research on Welsh syntax

Welsh syntax has had a fraction of the attention that has been lavished on the major Germanic and Romance languages. Early work on Welsh linguistics in the late nineteenth and early twentieth centuries focused mainly on phonetics, phonology and morphology and dealt with syntax only indirectly. This is the case with the major historical and comparative grammars of the time, such as those by John Morris-Jones, *A Welsh grammar, historical and comparative* (1913), and Holger Pedersen, *Vergleichende Grammatik der keltischen Sprachen* (1909–13, later revised in English as Lewis & Pedersen 1937). From the 1930s onwards, however, work focusing specifically on syntax began to appear. Particularly noteworthy are works by John Morris-Jones, *Welsh syntax* (published posthumously in 1931), Melville Richards, *Cystrawen y frawddeg Gymraeg* ('Syntax of the Welsh sentence', 1938), T. J. Morgan, *Y treigladau a'u cystrawen* ('The mutations and their syntax', 1952), and the work of Henry Lewis and Emrys Evans. The rich tradition of Welsh dialectology, although again often primarily focused on phonological and morphological variation, also indirectly contains much work of syntactic interest. Particularly noteworthy is this regard is O. H. Fynes-Clinton's *The Welsh vocabulary of the Bangor district* (1913), as well as *A glossary of the Demetian dialect of north Pembrokeshire* by Meredith Morris (1910) and Alf Sommerfelt's *Studies in Cyfeiliog Welsh* (1925).

Much of the work of the first half of the twentieth century had a strong historical bias, either explicitly or implicitly. Although work of a historical nature continued in the second half of the twentieth century, it was joined now by research of a purely synchronic nature conducted against a background of European structuralism. The earliest major work of this kind is perhaps *Ieithyddiaeth* ('Linguistics') by T. Arwyn Watkins (1961). A number of extensive descriptive grammars have also appeared, particularly in the last fifteen years, most notably those by Stephen J. Williams (1959, 1980), David Thorne (1993), Peter Wynn Thomas (1996), and, for colloquial Welsh, Gareth King (1993, revised 2003).

Generative work dates from the mid 1970s, and there is now a sizeable and diverse body of work within this tradition too. The generative tradition has addressed new questions, but has also brought a different approach to some familiar questions. Major book-length treatments of aspects of Welsh syntax within a generative framework include Awbery (1976), Jones & Thomas (1977), Sadler (1988), Rouveret (1994), Willis (1998), Borsley & Jones (2005) and Roberts (2005).

1.6   The structure of this book

In the following chapters (chapters 2 to 8), we consider the major issues in synchronic Welsh syntax, before turning to historical and typological issues in the final two chapters.

An important issue in generative literature on Welsh has been the correct analysis of verb-initial word order. Most work, following Harlow (1981) and Sproat (1985), has argued for an analysis in which verb-initial order is the result of a verb-fronting process, although other work, including the earliest research on Welsh syntax within generative grammar, Awbery (1976), has assumed a basic VSO structure, a position developed within the Head-driven Phrase Structure Grammar (HPSG) analyses of Borsley (1989a, 1995). We begin by discussing the main patterns of word order in chapter 2, considering both analyses that treat verb-initial word order as derived by verb-fronting, and such works as Tallerman (1990) and Borsley (2006), which have advanced objections to this approach and treated verb-initial order as underlying.

Non-finite clauses have received less attention than finite clauses, but there is important discussion in Borsley (1986), Rouveret (1994) and Tallerman (1998). We discuss such clauses in chapter 3.

What are often known as A′-binding constructions, for instance, relative clauses and *wh*-questions, have also received considerable attention. Important works here are Harlow (1981), Rouveret (1994, 2002), and Willis (2000). This is the focus of chapter 4.

Noun phrases have figured quite prominently in the most recent literature, being discussed in Rouveret (1994), Sadler (2000), Mittendorf & Sadler (2005) and Willis (2006a), and are considered in chapter 5. Chapter 6 deals with the peculiarly Celtic patterns of agreement between heads and pronominal elements only.

Another major topic is direct object mutation. One approach, developed in Zwicky (1984) and Roberts (1997, 2005), takes this mutation to be a realization of case. However, various objections to this approach have been advanced in Borsley (1997) and Tallerman (2006). An alternative approach, developed in Harlow (1989), Borsley & Tallerman (1996), Borsley (1999) and Tallerman (2006), argues that this mutation is triggered by an immediately preceding phrase of some kind. We discuss this matter in chapter 7.

Negation has been discussed at length in Borsley & Jones (2005), and, along with other aspects of verbal syntax, such as the syntax of 'be' and grammatical function-changing processes (passive, impersonal), this is the focus of chapter 8.

Most generative work on Welsh syntax has adopted a synchronic perspective. However, Willis (1998) provides a major diachronic study of clausal word order, and such historical questions are discussed in chapter 9.

Finally, chapter 10 looks at the broader context, examining the features of Welsh against the background of work in language typology, examining in particular the question of whether there is such a thing as a 'VSO-type' of language, and whether Welsh would fit into such a type.

2

Simple finite clauses

In this chapter, we look at simple finite clauses, largely ignoring *wh*-interrogatives, relative clauses and focus sentences, which we consider in chapter 4. As noted in chapter 1, Welsh, like the other Celtic languages, is a VSO language with a verb or an auxiliary in pre-subject position in all finite clauses. In the latter case, a non-finite form of the lexical verb follows the subject. We outline the main features of verb-initial and auxiliary-initial clauses and discuss how they should be analysed. In transformational work it has generally been assumed that verb-initial clauses are the result of movement, and this has often been assumed for some auxiliary-initial clauses as well.[1] There has been considerable debate about the precise location of both the verb/auxiliary and the following subject. It is possible to have an analogue of verb/auxiliary-movement in a non-transformational framework. However, the main non-transformational analysis has assumed a flat structure, in which subject and object are both sisters of the verb. There is a major unresolved issue here. Do Welsh finite clauses contain a VP like finite clauses in many other languages? Or not?

We begin in section 2.1 by looking at some basic properties of simple finite clauses. Then, in section 2.2, a number of types of auxiliary-initial clauses are discussed. In sections 2.3 and 2.4 we consider first transformational and then non-transformational analyses of finite clauses. Then, in section 2.5, we discuss analyses of auxiliary-initial clauses. Finally, in section 2.6, we consider a number of additional issues that arise here.

2.1 Some basic properties

2.1.1 *Word order and agreement*

As noted in section 1.4.2.1, finite main clauses in Welsh have a verb or auxiliary in pre-subject position:

---

[1] We use the term 'transformational' to refer to the transformational grammar of the 1970s and to its successors: Principles and Parameters theory and Minimalism.

(1)   Gwelodd   Rhiannon ddraig.
        see.PAST.3S Rhiannon dragon
        'Rhiannon saw a dragon.'

(2)   Mae   Rhiannon wedi gweld   draig.
        be.PRES.3S Rhiannon PERF see.INF dragon
        'Rhiannon has seen a dragon.'

This is also true of finite subordinate clauses, including relative clauses. (The bracketed particles in these examples are discussed in section 2.1.2.)

(3)   Dw   i 'n   credu [(yr) hoffai   Gwyn fynd   adre].
        be.PRES.1S I PROG believe PRT like.COND.3S Gywn go.INF home
        'I believe Gwyn would like to go home.'

(4)   Dw   i 'n   gwybod [(y) bydd   Sioned yn   canu].
        be.PRES.1S I PROG know.INF PRT be FUT.3S Sioned PROG sing.INF
        'I know Sioned will be singing.'

(5)   y dyn [(a) welais   i]
        the man PRT see.PAST.1S I
        'the man that I saw'

(6)   y llyfr [(y) mae   Gwyn yn ei   ddarllen]
        the book PRT be.PRES.3S Gwyn PROG 3MS read.INF
        'the book that Gwyn is reading'

Non-finite subordinate clauses are different, as discussed in chapter 3.

As also noted in section 1.4.2.1, there is no possibility of subject-initial order in an unmarked sentence. The subject of a finite clause may precede the verb if it is focused, but so may any constituent. Both (7) and (8) are possible.

(7)   Rhiannon (a) welodd   ddraig.
        Rhiannon PRT see.PAST.3S dragon
        'It was Rhiannon that saw a dragon.'

(8)   Draig   (a) welodd   Rhiannon.
        dragon PRT see.PAST.3S Rhiannon
        'It was a dragon that Rhiannon saw.'

See chapter 4 for further discussion of such sentences.

As noted in sections 1.4.2.1 and 1.4.3, most Welsh verbs have three paradigms: future, past and conditional. *Bod* 'be' has two further paradigms: present and imperfect.[2] Finite verbs agree with the following subject if it is pronominal. (9) is the literary past tense paradigm of *gweld* 'see', and (10)

---

[2] In the case of *bod* we call the past tense preterite. See section 3.3.1 for further discussion.

is a past tense paradigm from the New Quay dialect (see Thomas & Thomas 1989: 67):

(9)   a. gwelais   (i)
          see.PAST.1S I
       b. gwelaist   (ti)
          see.PAST.2S you.S
       c. gwelodd   (ef/hi)
          see.PAST.3S he she

       d. gwelasom   (ni)
          see.PAST.1P we
       e. gwelasoch (chwi)
          see.PAST.2P you.P
       f. gwelasant (hwy)
          see.PAST.3P they

(10)   a. gweles   i
          see.PAST.1S I
       b. gwelest   ti
          see.PAST.2S you.S
       c. gwelodd   e/ hi
          see.PAST.3S he she

       d. gwelon   ni
          see.PAST.1P we
       e. gweloch   chi
          see.PAST.2P you.P
       f. gwelon   nhw
          see.PAST.3P they

On the face of it, the literary paradigm has six different forms whereas the colloquial paradigm has just five. However, the colloquial forms do not normally appear without the following pronoun, and it is possible that both the first- and the second-person singular form should be analysed as *gweles* and the plural forms as *gwelo*. If so, there are just three forms here. With a non-pronominal subject, either singular or plural, the verb is in the third-person singular form, which can be seen as the default form. The following illustrate:

(11)   Gwelodd   y   bachgen/bechgyn ddraig.
        see.PAST.3S the boy boys   dragon
        'The boy/boys saw a dragon.'

(12)   *Gwelon   y   bechgyn ddraig.
        see.PAST.3P the boys   dragon
        ('The boys saw a dragon.')

We will see in later chapters that not just verbs, but also a number of other heads show agreement with pronouns but not with non-pronominal noun phrases.

In the literary language the subject of a finite clause is commonly omitted. Hence, literary Welsh is a null-subject language. In colloquial Welsh the subject is rarely omitted. Hence, colloquial Welsh is not a typical null-subject language. See section 2.5 for further discussion.

2.1.2   Pre-verbal particles

As noted in section 1.4.2.1, finite clauses show a number of pre-verbal particles, which have often been analysed as complementizers, e.g. in Sadler

(1988) and Rouveret (1994), although this analysis has sometimes been questioned, notably in Borsley & Jones (2005).

In the literary language, present and imperfect forms of *bod* 'be' are preceded in affirmative declarative sentences by a particle *y* (*yr* before a vowel):

(13)   a. Y   mae   Gwyn yn yr ardd.
             AFF be.PRES.3S Gwyn in the garden
             'Gwyn is in the garden.'
    b. Yr oedd   Gwyn yn yr ardd.
             AFF be.IMPF.3S Gwyn in the garden
             'Gwyn was in the garden.'

This particle does not occur in the colloquial language although a remnant of *yr* in the form of an initial *r-* sometimes occurs in affirmative colloquial forms. Thus, colloquial counterparts of the examples in (13) would have *mae* with no preceding particle and *roedd*, respectively.

Colloquial Welsh has two other affirmative declarative particles, *mi* and *fe*. It is traditionally said that *mi* is used in northern dialects, and *fe* in southern ones. However, the situation is more complex than this; for discussion, see C. Thomas (1974). *Fe* occurs with any finite verb except present or imperfect forms of *bod*, while *mi* occurs with any finite verb except third-person present tense forms of *bod*. Here are some examples:

(14)   a. Mi/*Fe (r)oedd   Gwyn yn yr ardd.
             AFF   be.IMPF.3S Gwyn in the garden
             'Gwyn was in the garden.'
    b. Mi/Fe fydd   Gwyn yn yr ardd.
             AFF   be.FUT.3S Gwyn in the garden
             'Gwyn will be in the garden.'
    c. Mi/Fe welodd   Rhiannon ddraig.
             AFF   see.PAST.3S Rhiannon dragon
             'Rhiannon saw a dragon.'

Both *mi* and *fe* trigger the morphophonological alternation known as soft mutation. Hence the verb in (14b) is *fydd* with initial [v] and not the basic form *bydd*. Similarly, the verb in (14c) is *welodd* and not the basic *gwelodd*. In current colloquial Welsh there is a tendency for these particles to be dropped but for the mutation to remain (see Ball 1987–8). Thus, (1) could have *welodd*. In this situation it is widely assumed that the mutation is triggered by a phonologically empty version of the particle.

Affirmative declarative subordinate clauses such as (3) are introduced by *y* (*yr* before a vowel) in literary Welsh, but this is commonly omitted in the colloquial language.

Interrogative clauses, both main and subordinate, are introduced by *a* in literary Welsh. This does not normally occur in colloquial Welsh. However, the mutation which it triggers in the literary language also occurs in the colloquial language. Thus, (15a) is literary Welsh, and (15b) is its colloquial Welsh equivalent.

(15)   a. A fydd   Gwyn yn yr ardd?
           INT be.IMPF.3S Gwyn in the garden
           'Will Gwyn be in the garden?'
       b. Fydd   Gwyn yn yr ardd?
           be.FUT.3S Gwyn in the garden
           'Will Gwyn be in the garden?'

Given that the affirmative declarative particles *mi* and *fe* are not always used, a declarative and the corresponding interrogative are sometimes distinguished only by intonation.

In literary Welsh, negative declarative main clauses are introduced by *ni* (*nid* before a vowel), and negative declarative subordinate clauses are introduced by *na* (*nad* before a vowel). The former, *ni*, does not occur in colloquial Welsh, but the latter, *na*, is used. We discuss this matter more fully in section 8.2. A further negative particle is *oni* (*onid* before a vowel), which is used in negative interrogatives in literary Welsh.

There are two further particles that should be noted: *a* and *y* (*yr* before a vowel) which are used in *wh*-constructions, e.g. *wh*-interrogatives, relatives and focus sentences. The particle here is mainly a feature of the literary language. See sections 4.1 and 4.7 for further discussion. Table 2.1 summarizes the preceding paragraphs to show the pre-verbal particles we have in Welsh.

As noted above, the particles have often been analysed as complementizers, and such an analysis is quite plausible. The meanings they encode are often encoded by complementizers in other languages. Moreover, if they are not analysed as complementizers, there will be no complementizer in typical

Table 2.1. *Pre-verbal particles*

Main affirmative declarative	*fe, mi, y(r)*
Embedded affirmative declarative	*y(r)*
Interrogative	*a*
Main negative declarative	*ni(d)*
Embedded negative declarative	*na(d)*
Negative interrogative	*oni(d)*
Relative clauses, *Wh*-interrogatives	*a, y(r)*

subordinate clauses even in literary Welsh, which some might see as an odd state of affairs. However, they are intimately associated with the following verb in a way that contrasts at least with English complementizers. We have noted that *mi* may not co-occur with third-person present tense forms of *bod*, while *fe* may not co-occur with present or imperfect forms of *bod*. Also relevant is the fact, noted in Borsley & Jones (2005: chapter 3), that *na(d)* unlike English 'that' must appear in each conjunct of a coordinate structure: Thus, (16a) is ungrammatical and only (16b) is possible.

(16) a. *Mae   Gwyn yn   dweud na   ddaw   o i Lundain
         be.PRES.3S Gwyn PROG say.INF NEG come.FUT.3S he to London
         a   welith   o Megan.
         and see.FUT.3S he Megan

      b. Mae   Gwyn yn   dweud na   ddaw   o i Lundain
         be.PRES.3S Gwyn PROG say   NEG come.FUT.3S he to London
         ac   na welith   o Megan.
         and NEG see.FUT.3S he Megan
         'Gwyn says that he won't come to London and see Megan.'

Facts like these lead Harlow (1983) and Borsley & Jones (2005) to propose that the particles form a constituent with the following verb. Harlow still labels them complementizers, but this position is abandoned by Borsley & Jones.[3] It is probably fair to say that the correct analysis is still an open matter. However, we will assume in later discussion that these elements are complementizers.

2.1.3   Other Celtic languages

Welsh finite clauses are quite like finite clauses in Irish and Scots Gaelic but less like finite clauses in Breton, although Breton is more closely related to Welsh. Both Irish and Scots Gaelic have a verb or an auxiliary in pre-subject position in finite clauses, both main and subordinate. The following Irish example illustrates:

(17) Shíl   mé [go   mbeadh sé ann].
      think.PAST I   PRT be.COND he there
      'I thought he would be there.'   (Borsley & Roberts 1996b: 21)

Breton is rather different. Subordinate clauses normally have an initial finite verb, but finite verbs do not generally appear in initial position in main clauses. This is a reflection of the fact that Breton is a type of verb-second language. Simple affirmative main clauses commonly have a non-finite verb in initial position separated from any complements. Consider, for example (18):

---

[3] A position rather like Harlow's is assumed in Willis (2004).

(18)   Lenn   a   ra   Anna al levr.
        read.INF PRT do.PRES.3S Anna the book
        'Anna reads the book.'   (Borsley, Rivero & Stephens 1996: 54)

Modern Welsh does not have examples like this although, as noted in section
9.1.1, they occur in Middle Welsh. Breton also has clauses in which an auxiliary is immediately followed by a non-finite verb, followed by the subject and
any complements. The negative sentence in (19a) and the subordinate clause
in (19b) illustrate.

(19)   a. N' en deus   ket lennet   Tom al levr.
           NEG 3MS have.PRES NEG read.PASTPART Tom the book
           'Tom has not read the book.'   (Borsley, Rivero & Stephens 1996: 55)
        b. Lavaret   he deus   Anna [en deus   lennet
           say.PASTPART 3FS have.PRES Anna 3MS have.PRES read.PASTPART
           Tom al   levr].
           Tom the book
           'Anna said Tom read the book.'
                                               (Borsley, Rivero & Stephens 1996: 59)

Modern Welsh does not have anything like this. As we will see in the next
section, in sentences with an auxiliary, the lexical verb always follows the
subject.

2.2   Auxiliary-initial clauses

As noted in section 1.4.2.1, Welsh has a number of types of auxiliary-
initial clause. We apply the term auxiliary to certain verbal elements which
appear with a verbal complement of some kind and allow the expression of a
meaning which would be expressed by a single verb in some languages. We will
consider later whether there are any clear syntactic tests for auxiliaries. These
clauses are sometimes referred to as AuxSVO clauses. However, this label is
potentially misleading since the subject is sometimes followed not by the verb
but by an aspect marker and the first verbal element may be a non-finite
auxiliary, hence not a V if V means non-auxiliary verb. The combination of
auxiliary and non-finite verb is sometimes called a periphrastic verb while the
verb in a simple VSO clause is sometimes called a synthetic verb. We will make
some use of these terms in later chapters. Three types of auxiliary-initial
clause will be considered here, which we will refer to as aspectual clauses,
gwneud-clauses, and *ddaru*-clauses. We also consider what we call copular
clauses.

2.2.1   *Aspectual clauses*

Aspectual clauses involve a form of *bod* 'be' and a non-finite verb phrase preceded by an aspectual particle, most commonly either *yn* (progressive) or *wedi* (perfect). We have examples in (2)–(4), (6) and (16). Here are some further examples:

(20)   Mae   Rhiannon yn   cysgu   rwan.
        be.PRES.3s Rhiannon PROG sleep.INF now
        'Rhiannon is sleeping now.'

(21)   Mae   Rhiannon wedi mynd   adre.
        be.PRES.3s Rhiannon PERF go.INF home
        'Rhiannon has gone home.'

Progressive clauses may include stative verbs such as *gwybod* 'know' (which is seen in (4)) or *deall* 'understand'. This means that Welsh has an aspectual clause where English would have a simple clause with no auxiliary, and that the term 'progressive' should not be taken literally. The aspectual particle *yn* seen in (20) is homophonous with the preposition *yn* in (22).

(22)   Mae   Rhiannon yn yr   ardd.
        be.PRES.3s Rhiannon in the garden
        'Rhiannon is in the garden.'

However, the particle triggers no mutation, while the preposition triggers nasal mutation. Thus, *tŷ* 'house' appears as *nhŷ* in the following:

(23)   Mae   Rhiannon yn nhŷ   Megan.
        be.PRES.3s Rhiannon in house Megan
        'Rhiannon is in Megan's house.'

The aspectual particle *wedi* seen in (21) is also homophonous with the preposition in (24).

(24)   wedi 'r   rhyfel
        after the war
        'after the war'

There are a number of other aspectual particles which are homophonous with prepositions. In the following, we have what look like the prepositions *ar* 'on', *heb* 'without' and *am* 'about' (hence the glosses):

(25)   a. Mae   Rhiannon **ar** adael.
           be.PRES.3s Rhiannon on leave.INF
           'Rhiannon is about to leave.'
        b. Mae   Rhiannon **heb**   adael.
           be.PRES.3s Rhiannon without leave.INF
           'Rhiannon has not left.'

c. Mae   Rhiannon **am** adael.
be.PRES.3S Rhiannon for leave.INF
'Rhiannon wants to leave.'

Unlike *yn*, these elements also trigger the same mutation (soft mutation) as the homophonous prepositions. There is also one aspectual particle which looks like an adjective. In the following, we have what looks like the adjective *newydd* 'new':

(26)   Mae   Rhiannon **newydd** adael.
be.PRES.3S Rhiannon new   leave.INF
'Rhiannon has just left.'

Heb is a special case because it is a negative element as discussed in section 8.2. *Am* is also a special case because it can have a clausal complement:

(27)   Mae   o **am** i ti fynd.
be.PRES.3S he for to you go.INF
'He wants you to go.'

It is sometimes possible to have two aspectual particles. For example, *wedi* can co-occur with *yn* but must come first.

(28)   a. Mae   Rhiannon **wedi** bod **yn** cysgu.
be.PRES.3S Rhiannon PERF be.INF PROG sleep.INF
'Rhiannon has been sleeping.'
b. *Mae   Rhiannon **yn** bod **wedi** cysgu.
be.PRES.3S Rhiannon PROG be.INF PERF sleep.INF
(*Rhiannon is having slept.)

Heb and *newydd* can also co-occur with *yn* and must also come first. As the translations in (28) make clear, English has a similar restriction. Such facts are a central concern of Cinque (1999).

As one might expect, there is evidence, for example from fronting, that the material following the subject in an aspectual clause is a constituent. However, *yn* does not appear in a fronted constituent. Thus, corresponding to (20), we have (29a) and not (29b). Corresponding to (21), we have (30).

(29)   a. [Cysgu   rwan] mae   Rhiannon.
sleep.INF now be.PRES.3S Rhiannon
'Rhiannon is sleeping now.'
b. *[Yn   cysgu   rwan] mae   Rhiannon.
PRED sleep.INF now be.PRES.3S Rhiannon
('Rhiannon is sleeping.')

(30)   [Wedi mynd adre] mae   Rhiannon.
PERF go.INF home be.PRES.3S Rhiannon
'Rhiannon has gone home.'

Sproat (1985: 1.2.3) draws attention to examples like these and proposes that the material following the subject in an aspectual clause is a VP. He sees it as quite important that Welsh has superficial VPs. However, it seems likely that the aspectual particles are heads of the constituents that they introduce since they influence their distribution. This would mean that these constituents are AspPs or that an *yn*-phrase is a ProgP and a *wedi*-phrase a PerfP. It could be, however, that the complement of *yn* and *wedi* is a VP. In other words, it could be that we have the structure in (31) or those in (32).

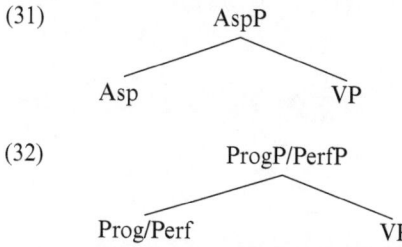

(31)   AspP
        Asp   VP

(32)   ProgP/PerfP
        Prog/Perf   VP

It could also be that the initial constituent in (29a) is a VP although an alternative would be to assume that it is an AspP or ProgP with a phonologically empty head.

2.2.2   Gwneud-*clauses*

We turn now to *gwneud*-clauses, which involve the auxiliary *gwneud* 'do'. Unlike its English counterpart, this occurs where there is no particular emphasis. Thus (33b) is as likely to occur as (33a) in the colloquial language.

(33)   a. Agorodd   Emrys y   drws.
           open.PAST.3s Emrys the door
           'Emrys opened the door.'
        b. Gwnaeth   Emrys agor   y   drws.
           do.PAST.3s Emrys open.INF the door
           'Emrys opened the door.'

As with periphrastic clauses, there is evidence from fronting that the material following the subject is a constituent:

(34)   [Agor   y   drws] wnaeth   Emrys.
        open.INF the door do.PAST.3s Emrys
        'Emrys opened the door.'

As Rouveret (1994: 81) notes, the non-finite form *gwneud* does not appear with an in-situ verbal complement. Thus, it is not possible in examples like the following:

(35)   Mae   Gwyn yn   ceisio (*gwneud) canu   'r   anthem.
        be.PRES.3S Gwyn PROG try.INF do.INF   sing.INF the anthem
        'Gwyn is trying to sing the anthem.'

However, *gwneud* is possible with a fronted complement, as (36) illustrates:

(36)   Canu   'r anthem y   mae   Gwyn yn   ceisio ei **wneud**.
        sing.INF the anthem PRT be.PRES.3S Gwyn PROG try.INF 3MS do.INF
        'Singing the anthem is what Gwyn is trying to do.'

This suggests that *gwneud* is a verb, as assumed by Jones & Thomas (1977: 112, fn. 3) and Rouveret (1994: 81), and not just the realization of some functional category. The appearance of the clitic also supports this conclusion since as noted in chapter 1, and as discussed in section 3.1.2 and section 5.2.2, clitics appear with non-finite verbs and nouns.

2.2.3   Ddaru-*clauses*

We can now consider *ddaru*-clauses, which are confined to northern dialects. These contain the form *ddaru*, which is historically a verb meaning 'happen, finish', but is now just a marker of past tense. The following illustrates:

(37)   Ddaru Megan fynd   adre.
        PAST   Megan go.INF home
        'Megan went home.'

Unlike other auxiliaries *ddaru* does not standardly agree with the following subject, and is invariant for most speakers, although for some speakers it has an inflectional paradigm. In more literary Welsh, *ddaru* (or *ddarfu*) is followed by what looks like the preposition *i* 'to', as in (38).

(38)   Ddarfu   i Megan fynd   adref.
        happen.PAST.3S to Megan go.INF home
        'Megan went home.'

Whatever may be the correct analysis for examples like this, it is fairly clear that examples like (37) contain a subject and a complement. Like other subjects and complements, they can be separated by the negative adverb *ddim* in a negative sentence.

(39)   Ddaru Megan ddim mynd   adre.
        PAST   Megan NEG go.INF home
        'Megan didn't go home.'

Again there is evidence from fronting that the material following the subject is a constituent:

(40)   [Mynd adre] ddaru Megan.
        go.INF home PAST Megan
        'Megan went home.'

2.2.4   Copular clauses

We now consider what we call copular clauses, clauses where *bod* has a non-verbal complement. We have already seen that it can take a PP complement in (22) and (23). It can also take what can be called a predicative phrase, a phrase containing the predicative particle *yn* and an AP or noun phrase. Unlike the homophonous aspectual particle, predicative *yn* triggers soft mutation. Thus, the following examples have *ddiog* and *feddyg* rather than *diog* and *meddyg*:

(41)   a. Mae   Gwyn [yn   ddiog].
           be.PRES.3S Gwyn PRED lazy
           'Gwyn is lazy.'
        b. Mae   Gwyn [yn   feddyg].
           be.PRES.3S Gwyn PRED doctor
           'Gwyn is a doctor.'

There is evidence that the same *bod* appears in examples with a non-verbal complement as in aspectual clauses. Like English *be*, *bod* can combine with a coordinate structure with various verbal and non-verbal conjuncts. The following illustrate:

(42)   a. Mae   Gwyn yn   ddiog ac yn   cysgu.
           be.PRES.3S Gwyn PRED lazy   and PROG sleep.INF
           'Gwyn is lazy and sleeping.'
        b. Mae   Gwyn yn   ieithydd ac yn   astudio Cymraeg.
           be.PRES.3S Gwyn PRED linguist and PROG study.INF Welsh
           'Gwyn is a linguist and studying Welsh.'
        c. Mae   Gwyn dan y   bwrdd ac yn   cysgu.
           be.PRES.3S Gwyn under the table and PROG sleep.INF
           'Gwyn is under the table and sleeping.'

It seems, then, there is a single *bod* taking a number of types of complement. Aspectual phrases, PPs and predicative phrases also appear in what traditional Welsh grammars refer to as 'absolute clauses' (Anwyl 1899: 121–2) or *ymadroddion annibynnol* 'independent phrases' (Richards 1938: 26–8, Williams 1959: 230). These are typically introduced by a coordinating conjunction, especially *a* 'and', and contain a subject and the kind of phrase that appears with *bod*. Consider, for example, the following:

(43)   a. Roedd   Mair yn   canu,   a   finnau 'n   gwrando
            be.IMPF.3S Mair PROG sing.INF and me.CONJ PROG listen.INF
            'Mair was singing and I was listening.'

        b. Mae   Nia wedi diflannu,   a   finnau wedi aros
            be.PRES.3S Nia PERF disappear.INF and me.CONJ PERF wait.INF
            oriau amdani.
            hours for.3FS
            'Nia has disappeared and I've been waiting for her for hours.'

        c. Dydy   o ddim yn   deall,   ac   yntau yng
            NEG.be.PRES.3S he NEG   PROG understand.INF and him   in
            Nghymru.
            Wales
            'He doesn't understand, and he's in Wales.'

        d. Dydy   o ddim yn   deall,   ac   yntau
            NEG.be.PRES.3S he NEG   PROG understand.INF and him
            'n   glyfar iawn.
            PRED clever very
            'He doesn't understand, and he's very clever.'

        e. Dydy   o ddim yn   deall,   ac   yntau 'n
            NEG.be.PRES.3S he NEG PROG understand.INF and him   PRED
            athro.
            teacher
            'He doesn't understand, and he's a teacher.'

Thus, it seems that these constituents form a natural class.

2.2.5   *Syntactic tests for auxiliaries?*

English has a number of syntactic tests for auxiliaries. In particular, only auxiliaries can precede the subject in an interrogative and only auxiliaries can be negated by a following *not*. Clearly we should ask whether there are comparable tests for auxiliaries in Welsh. Neither interrogatives nor negation are relevant here. Interrogatives have the same word order as declaratives, and negation does not distinguish between auxiliaries and lexical verbs. With both, negation is normally realized by the adverb *ddim* in post-subject position.[4] The following illustrate:

(44)   a. Dw   i ddim yn   mynd i Aberystwyth.
            be.PRES.1S I NEG PROG go.INF to Aberystwyth
            'I am not going to Aberystwyth.'

---

[4] There are certain complications here. See section 8.2.

b. Es   i ddim i Aberystwyth.
go.PAST.1s I NEG to Aberystwyth
'I didn't go to Aberystwyth.'

There are two properties that distinguish *bod* and *gwneud* from most other verbs: they appear in tag questions and in responsives, that is, *yes-no* words and their equivalents. The former are illustrated, using northern forms in (45) and (46).

(45)   a. Oedd   Sioned yn   gweithio, ynd oedd?
be.IMPF.3s Sioned PROG work.INF Q   be.IMPF.3s
'Sioned was working, wasn't she?'
b. Doedd   Sioned ddim yn   gweithio, nac oedd?
NEG.be.IMPF.3s Sioned NEG PROG work.INF NEG be.IMPF.3s
'Sioned wasn't working, was she?'

(46)   a. Gwnei   di   agor   y   drws, yn gwnei?
do.FUT.2s you.s open.INF the door Q do.FUT.2s
'You will open the door, won't you?'
b. Wnei   di   agor   mo 'r drws, na   wnei?
do.FUT.2s you.s open.INF NEG the door NEG do.FUT.2s
'You won't open the door, will you?'

The positive tags contain the particle *yn(d)*. This derives historically from the negative interrogative particle *oni(d)*, mentioned in section 2.1.2, but has no negative content, hence the gloss 'Q'. Negative tags contain the negative particle *na(c)*. Note that this is different from the negative particle *na(d)*, mentioned in the last section.[5]

Responsives are quite complex.[6] Past tense *yes-no* questions are answered with *do* 'yes' and *naddo* 'no', as in (47).

(47)   A: Welaist   ti   ddraig?
see.PAST.2s you.s dragon
'Did you see a dragon?'
B: Do / Naddo.
yes / no
'Yes / No.'

Questions with an initial focused phrase are answered with *ie* 'yes' and *nage* 'no', as in (48)

(48)   A: Draig   welaist   ti?
dragon see.PAST.2s you.s
'Was it a dragon that you saw?'

---

[5] For detailed discussion of tag questions including dialect variation, see Rottet and Sprouse (2006).
[6] For detailed discussion of responses, see Jones (1999).

B: Ie /   Nage.
   yes /   no
   'Yes / No.'

With other tenses, there is no equivalent of 'yes' and 'no'.[7] Instead a short answer echoes the form of the question, repeating the auxiliary, preceded by *na(c)* in the case of a negative. Normally there is no overt subject. The following illustrate:

(49)   A: Oedd   Sioned yn   gweithio?
             be.IMPF.3s Sioned PROG work.INF
             'Was Sioned working?'
         B: Oedd /   Nac oedd.
             be.IMPF.3s / NEG be.IMPF.3s
             'Yes / No.'

(50)   A: Gwnei   di   agor   y   drws?
             do.FUT.2s you.s open. INF the door
             'Will you open the door?'
         B: Gwnaf /   Na   wnaf.
             do.FUT.1s / NEG do.FUT.1s
             'Yes / No.'

Most verbs that would not be regarded as auxiliaries cannot appear in either tags or responsives and must be replaced by *gwneud* 'do'. However, a small number of verbs with irregular morphology can appear in both. These include *mynd* 'go' and *dod* 'come':

(51)   a. Eith   hi heno,   ynd eith?
             go.FUT.3s she tonight Q   go.FUT.3s
             'She will go tonight, won't she?'
         b. Eith   hi ddim heno,   nac eith?
             go.FUT.3s she NEG tonight NEG go.FUT.3s
             'She won't go tonight, will she?'

(52)   a. Ddaw   hi fory,   yn daw?
             come.FUT.3s she tomorrow Q   come.FUT.3s
             'She will come tomorrow, won't she?'

---

[7] Questions with aspectual *wedi* can be answered with the appropriate form of *bod* or with with *do/naddo*:

(i)   A: Wyt   ti   wedi gweld y   ffilm?
             be.PRES.2s you.S PERF see   the film
             'Have you seen the film?'
         B: Ydw/   Nac ydw /   Do / Naddo.
             be.PRES.1s NEG be.PRES.1s / yes / no
             'Yes / No.'

    b. Ddaw   hi ddim fory,   na ddaw?
      come.FUT.3s she NEG   tomorrow NEG come.FUT.3s
      'She won't come tomorrow, will she?'

(53)   A: Eith   hi heno?
         go.FUT.3s she tonight
         'Will she go tonight?'
      B: Eith /   Nac eith.
         go.FUT.3s / NEG go.FUT.3s
         'Yes / No'

(54)   A: Ddaw   hi fory?
         come.FUT.3s she tomorrow
         'Will she come tomorrow?'
      B: Ddaw /   Na ddaw.
         come.FUT.3s / NEG come.FUT.3s
         'Yes / No'

Moreover, the third auxiliary we have highlighted, *ddaru*, does not appear in tags or responsives. Instead we have the forms *do* and *naddo*, which are used with all past tense forms. (In tags the former is commonly preceded by *yn*.)

(55)   a. Ddaru Megan fynd   adre, (yn) do?
        PAST   Megan go.INF home Q   yes
        'Megan has gone home, hasn't she?'
      b. Ddaru Megan ddim mynd adre, naddo?
        PAST   Megan NEG   go.INF home no
        'Megan hasn't gone home, has she?'

(56)   A: Ddaru Megan fynd   adre?
        PAST   Megan go.INF home
        'Has Megan gone home?'
      B: Do / Naddo.
        yes / no
        'Yes / No.'

The fact that *ddaru* does not appear in responsives is expected if it is a past tense form, but the fact that it does not appear in tags suggests that they do not provide a test for auxiliaries.

Thus, neither tags nor responsives are restricted to auxiliaries, and neither occurs with all the auxiliaries that we have discussed. Hence, neither provides a syntactic test for auxiliaries.

It may be that further research will provide some tests for auxiliaries, but it could be that Welsh does not have a clear-cut class of auxiliaries in the way that English does. It may be, then, that 'auxiliary' is just a convenient label here with no theoretical significance.

2.3   Transformational analyses of verb-initial clauses

2.3.1   *Preliminaries*

Almost all work on Welsh within transformational grammar has assumed that the verb-initial order of finite clauses is derived through a verb-movement process, and this position has been developed by a number of linguists within Principles and Parameters theory (P&P). Various arguments have been advanced for such an analysis. One, which can be traced back to Jones & Thomas (1977), is that it allows all forms of a verb to originate in the same kind of structure. Non-finite verbs are immediately followed by their complements, and are preceded by their subject if they have one. We have seen this in auxiliary-initial clauses and absolute clauses. We also see it in the main type of non-finite clause, which we highlighted in section 1.4.2.2 and which we discuss in detail in section 3.4. The bracketed material in the following illustrates:

(57)   Mae   Siôn yn   disgwyl   [i Emrys ddarllen llyfr].
        be.PRES.3S Siôn PROG expect.INF to Emrys read.INF book
        'Siôn expects Emrys to read a book.'

A movement analysis allows finite verbs to originate in the same position as their non-finite counterparts. We will note some other arguments for a verb-movement analysis after we have looked at exactly what form such an analysis should take.

2.3.2   *Possible analyses*

In transformational analyses of Germanic and Romance languages, it is standardly assumed that a pre-subject verb occupies the C position. One might, therefore, propose the same analysis for pre-subject verbs in Welsh. This would give the structure in (58) for the example in (1).

(58)

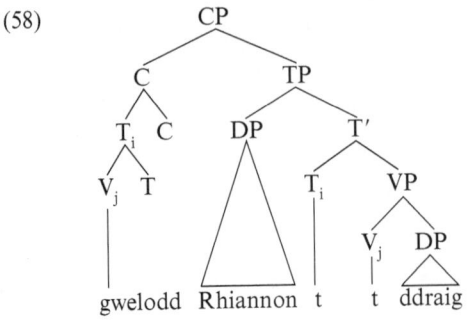

However, the Germanic languages only have pre-subject verbs in main clauses. Thus, as the following show, Standard English has a pre-subject auxiliary in main clause interrogatives but not in subordinate clause interrogatives.

(59)   a. What is Lee doing?
         b. I wonder [what Lee is doing].

Similarly, in German, the finite verb appears in second position and before the subject if some other constituent is in first position, but it appears in clause final position in subordinate clauses.

(60)   a. Er **hat** ihn gestern   gesehen.
            he has him yesterday seen
            'He saw him yesterday.'
         b. Gestern   **hat** er ihn gesehen.
            yesterday has he him seen
            'Yesterday he saw him.'
         c. dass er ihn gestern   gesehen **hat**.
            that he him yesterday seen   has
            'that he saw him yesterday'

It is widely assumed that such contrasts reflect the impossibility of movement to a C-position that is filled by an overt complementizer. This seems problematic because the auxiliary is in post-subject position in (59b) and the verb is clause-final in German subordinate *wh*-interrogatives even though there is no overt complementizer in either case. However, if there is some universal principle that precludes movement to C in a subordinate clause, the fact that Welsh has pre-subject verbs in subordinate as well as in main clauses means that pre-subject verbs cannot generally be in C. Hence alternative analyses must be considered.

One alternative arises from the widely accepted idea that subjects originate within VP. If this is right, it is possible that subjects remain in VP in some languages. If the verb moves out of VP to T, the result will be verb-subject order. These ideas give the structure in (61), proposed in Rouveret (1990).

(61)

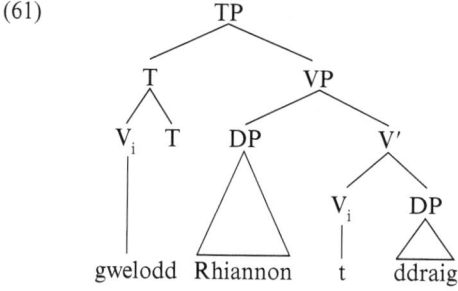

However, problems arise for this approach from the widely accepted idea that certain adverbs mark the left edge of VP. Combining this idea with the analysis in (58) one would expect to find adverbs between the verb and the subject. Some adverbs may appear between a verb and an indefinite subject, as (62) shows.

(62)   Mae   **wastad** lefrith yn y   ffrij.
        be.PRES.3s always milk   in the fridge
        'There is always milk in the fridge.'

However, as Roberts (2005: 10) notes, adverbs never appear between the verb and a definite subject. We do not find examples like the following:

(63)   *Gwelith **yfory**   Emrys ddraig.
        see.FUT.3s tomorrow Emrys dragon
        'Emrys will see a dragon tomorrow.'

Moreover, as Roberts also notes, a definite subject can be followed by an adverb. Examples like the following illustrate:

(64)   Mae   'r bws **eisoes** wedi gadael.
        be.PRES.3s the bus already PERF leave.INF
        'The bus has already left.'

Within a transformational approach the facts suggest that while indefinite subjects may be inside VP, and thus preceded by certain adverbs, definite subjects are outside, and thus followed by these adverbs. This is possible if there are two functional heads between C and VP. The verb can be in the higher one and definite subjects in the specifier position of the lower one. If we call these heads F1 and F2, this will give the following structure:

(65)

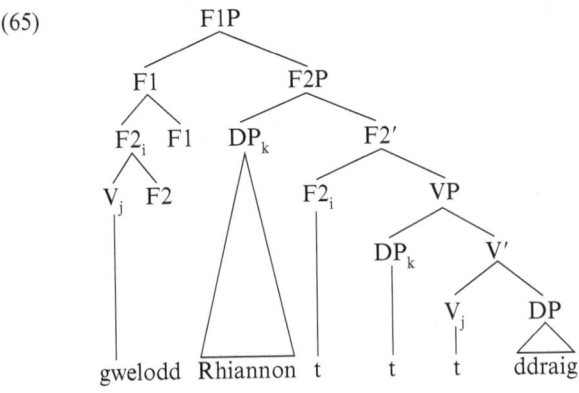

Rouveret (1994) proposes essentially this structure with F1 as AgrS and F2 as T. (See also Tallerman (1998) and Willis (2000).) Roberts (2005) proposes a somewhat more complex structure with separate Pers(on) and Num(ber) heads instead of Rouveret's Agr head.

2.3.3   *Further arguments for verb-fronting*

We can now consider some further arguments that have been advanced for a verb-movement analysis. One involves *gwneud*-clauses like (33b). Harlow (1981: 223) and Sproat (1985: 202) propose that such clauses have the same structure as simple VSO clauses but with *gwneud*-insertion instead of verb-movement. Essentially, the idea is that they reveal the underlying structure of simple finite clauses.

Another argument for a verb-movement analysis involves reflexives. Welsh reflexives closely resemble their English counterparts, and like English reflexives they require a local antecedent. The subject of a finite clause can be the antecedent of a reflexive in object position, but the object of a finite clause cannot be the antecedent of a reflexive in subject position.

(66)   a. Gwelodd   Gwyn ei   hun.
             see.PAST.3S Gwyn 3MS self
             'Gwyn saw himself.'
          b. *Gwelodd ei   hun Gwyn.
             see.PAST.3S 3MS self Gwyn
             ('Himself saw Gwyn.')

This is just like the situation in *gwneud* clauses.

(67)   a. Gwaeth   Gwyn weld   ei   hun.
             do.PAST.3S Gwyn see.INF 3MS self
             'Gwyn saw himself.'
          b. *Gwaeth   ei   hun weld   Gwyn.
             do.PAST.3S 3MS self see.INF Gwyn
             ('Himself saw Gwyn.')

In these clauses the object is inside a constituent which does not contain the subject. Hence the subject c-commands the object but the object does not c-command the subject. Given the standard assumption in transformational work that a reflexive must be c-commanded by its antecedent, the contrast in (67) is predicted. So is the contrast in (66) given the assumption that the object is inside a VP. Hence, if anaphora does involve c-command, there is some important evidence here for verb-movement.

Further arguments for verb-fronting might be advanced on the basis of ellipsis and coordination.[8] In the case of ellipsis, we can consider the following examples from Jones (1999):

---

[8] Arguments of this kind are advanced for a verb-movement analysis of Irish verb-initial clauses in McCloskey (1991).

(68)   a. Mi newidith   Siôn ei   feddwl
        PRT change.FUT.3S Sion 3MS mind.INF
        'Siôn will change his mind.'
        b. Neith   o ddim (newid   ei   feddwl).
        do.FUT.3S he NEG   change.INF 3MS mind.INF
        'He won't (change his mind).'

Here, the second sentence is a *gwneud* clause, and as the bracketing indicates, the complement may be omitted. If it is omitted, the antecedent for the ellipsis is apparently the finite verb and the object in the first sentence. If one assumes that an antecedent for ellipsis must be a constituent, this suggests that verb and object must be a constituent at some level. In the case of coordination, we can consider the following:

(69)   Rhoddodd   yr un dyn **lyfr i Mair** a   **darlun i Megan**.
        give.PAST.3S the one man book to Mair and picture to Megan
        'The same man gave a book to Mair and a picture to Megan.'

This contains two conjuncts (in bold) consisting of two complements of a finite verb. If one assumes that a conjunct must be a constituent, this suggests that the complements of a finite verb must be a constituent. On any verb-fronting analysis the complements of a finite verb will be a VP whose verb has been extracted. It looks, then, as if there is some evidence here for such analyses.

A final point that should be noted here is that the obvious alternative to a verb-fronting analysis, a flat structure in which verb, subject and complement(s) are daughters of S, is not available within transformational approaches which assume that no phrase may have more than two daughters. Within such approaches, unless verb and subject form a constituent, subject and complement(s) must form a constituent, as they do on a verb-movement analysis.

2.4   Constraint-based analyses of verb-initial clauses

2.4.1   *Some analyses*

We turn now to non-transformational, constraint-based analyses. It is not possible to assume a verb-fronting analysis in such frameworks. However, similar analyses are available in these frameworks, and an analysis of this kind has been proposed in Lexical Functional Grammar (LFG).

It is possible within LFG for a verb to appear outside the associated VP, and Bresnan (2001: 127–31) proposes that this is the situation in Welsh finite clauses. Within her approach, (1) would have the following structure, which is rather like that in (61):

(70)

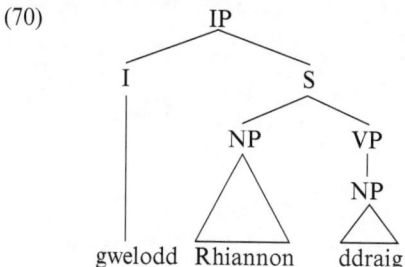

It is also possible to have an analogue of verb-fronting within HPSG. See, for example, Borsley (1989b). However, as far as we are aware, no one has proposed such an analysis for Welsh.

Within constraint-based frameworks there is no a-priori objection to a flat structure. Borsley (1989a, 1995) has proposed analyses within Head-driven Phrase Structure Grammar (HPSG) which involve such a structure. Within HPSG, heads have a feature SUBJ, which generally indicates what subject a head requires, and a feature COMPS, which generally indicates what complements a head requires. Assuming these features, the obvious HPSG analysis for (1) is the following, where the clause is headed by the verb – hence the label V – and the integers show that *Rhiannon* is a subject and *ddraig* a complement:[9]

(71)

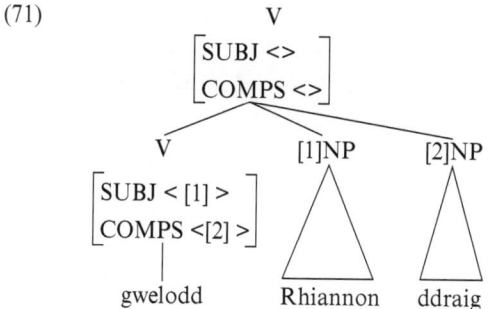

However, Welsh has certain subject-initial clauses, notably the absolute clauses in (43). This being so, if finite verbs take a subject, a stipulation is necessary to prevent the generation of subject-initial finite clauses. Borsley argues instead for an analysis in which subjects of finite verbs are the realization not of the single member of the SUBJ list, but of an extra member of the COMPS

---

[9] For textbook discussion of HPSG, see Sag, Wasow & Bender (2003).

list, in other words an analysis in which subjects are extra complements. On this approach, (1) has the following analysis, where the integers show that *Rhiannon* and *ddraig* are both complements:

(72)

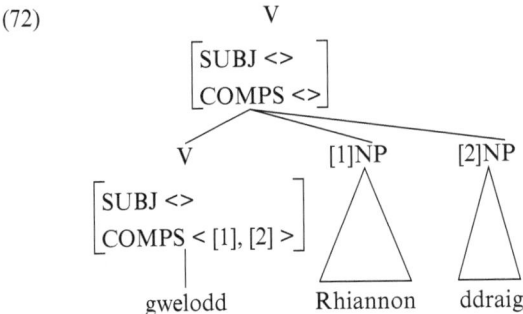

This approach automatically accounts for the impossibility (except in focus sentences) of subject-initial finite clauses. It also plays a role in the approach to mutation developed in Borsley (1999), which is discussed in section 7.6.[10]

2.4.2   *More on the arguments for verb-fronting*

What about the various arguments for a verb-fronting analysis? Borsley (2006) argues that these are a lot less persuasive than has generally been assumed.

Consider first the argument that such an analysis allows all forms of a verb to originate in the same kind of structure. One point to note is that it is not really true that all forms of a verb originate in the same kind of structure in much transformational work. As discussed in section 2.5.2, Rouveret (1994) assumes that non-finite verbs but not finite verbs are embedded in a DP. Similarly, Roberts (2005: chapter 3) assumes that non-finite verbs are embedded in a VoiceP. Finite and non-finite verbs originate in the same kind of structure in Tallerman (1998), but all that Rouveret (1994) and Roberts (2005) can say is that all forms of a verb originate in similar environments. Is this an advantage? It is generally assumed that it is within transformational work, which as Culicover & Jackendoff (2005) document, has been dominated by

---

[10] Borsley (1989a, 1995) suggests that this analysis is also supported by the fact that finite verbs agree with their subjects in much the same way as non-finite verbs agree with their objects. However, if agreement refers not to grammatical functions but to linear order, as suggested in chapter 6, this is irrelevant. Essentially the same analysis is proposed for English auxiliary-initial clauses in Sag, Wasow & Bender (2003). Borsley (1995) argues that the analysis in (71) is preferable for verb-initial clauses in Syrian Arabic.

certain notions of uniformity. However, these notions are rejected in other frameworks, and it is not clear that rejecting them leads to any problems. Thus, Borsley & Jones (2005: 9.2.1) show that it is a simple matter within HPSG to associate finite and non-finite verbs with different structures. On the other hand, as Culicover & Jackendoff show, uniformity considerations lead to very complex syntactic structures. Thus, it is only if one accepts some controversial transformational assumptions that there is an argument here.

Turning to the suggestion that *gwneud*-clauses reveal the underlying structure of simple VSO clauses, this is undermined by the evidence that *gwneud* is a verb and not just some functional element. It follows, if one assumes verb-fronting, that it must be fronted like other verbs and hence that *gwneud*-clauses are more complex than simple VSO clauses. Evidence that they are indeed more complex comes from negation. While simple VSO clauses can be negated by a negative pronoun in object position, this is not possible with a *gwneud*-clause.

(73)   a. Welodd   Siôn neb.
          see.PAST.3s Siôn no one
          'Siôn did not see anyone.'
    b. *Wnaeth   Siôn weld   neb.
          do.PAST.3s Siôn see.INF no one
          ('Siôn did not see anyone.')

This suggests that the object is more deeply embedded in a *gwneud*-clause than in a simple VSO clause. Thus the idea that *gwneud*-clauses reveal the underlying structure of simple VSO clauses seems untenable.

What about the argument from anaphora? As Borsley (2006) points out, there is only an argument here if conditions on anaphora refer to constituent structure. However, it is generally accepted in constraint-based work that they refer to other kinds of structure. In HPSG, they refer to the argument structure of lexical heads, and in LFG they refer to functional structure. Hence, outside transformational approaches there is no argument from anaphora.

Consider next ellipsis. Here, Borsley (2006) points out that examples like (74), traditionally referred to as bare argument ellipsis, cast doubt on the assumption that it is a good test for constituency.

(74)   Gwelodd   Gwyn Emrys, ond dim Sioned.
        see.PAST.3s Gwyn Emrys but NEG Sioned
        'Gwyn saw Emrys, but not Sioned.'

Like its English translation, this is ambiguous. It can mean that Gwyn did not see Sioned or that Sioned did not see Emrys. On the second interpretation, the antecedent for ellipsis is the verb and the object, which is a constituent on a verb-fronting analysis. However, on the first interpretation, the antecedent for ellipsis is the subject and the verb, which obviously do not form a constituent. Thus, the antecedent for ellipsis is not necessarily a constituent. It may be that someone can show that the antecedent for ellipsis in (68) must be a constituent, but until this has been shown there is no argument from ellipsis.

Finally, consider coordination. As noted in Borsley (2006), examples like the following cast doubt on the idea that it always involves a constituent:

(75)   Mae   Gwyn wedi rhoi   **llyfr i Mair** a   **darlun i Megan**.
        be.PRES.3S Gwyn PERF give.INF book to Mair and picture to Megan
        'Gwyn has given a book to Mair and a picture to Megan.'

Here, the conjuncts (in bold) consist of a pair of complements of a non-finite verb. It has generally been assumed in P&P since Larson (1988) that such sequences are constituents, but this assumption is rejected in many other frameworks. See, for example, Sag *et al.* (1985), Maxwell & Manning (1996), Beavers & Sag (2004). If examples like this involve coordination of non-constituents, then the assumption that a conjunct must be a constituent is untenable. Again, then, there is no argument outside some controversial transformational assumptions.

It seems, then, that the case for a verb-fronting analysis of Welsh is not as strong as has often been assumed. Hence, the alternative analysis in (72) cannot be lightly dismissed.

2.5   Analyses of auxiliary-initial clauses

We now consider the analysis of the various kinds of auxiliary-initial clauses that we discussed in section 2.2.

2.5.1   *Aspectual and copular clauses*

Aspectual clauses have been discussed by Ouhalla (1991: 72–9) and Hendrick (1991, 1994, 1996). The obvious suggestion within P&P is that the aspectual markers are functional heads – Prog, Perf, etc. If one assumes that finite verbs and auxiliaries are in Agr and subjects in Spec TP, one might suggest that (20), repeated here as (76), has the structure in (77), and this is essentially what Ouhalla (1991: 72–9) proposes. (See also Willis 1998: 19–29 and Tallerman 1998.)

(76)   Mae   Rhiannon yn   cysgu   rwan.
        be.PRES.3S Rhiannon PROG sleep.INF now
        'Rhiannon is sleeping now.'

(77)   [$_{\text{AgrP}}$ Mae$_i$ [$_{\text{TP}}$ Rhiannon t$_i$ [$_{\text{ProgP}}$ yn [$_{\text{VP}}$ cysgu rwan]]]]]

We have seen, however, that *bod* has a non-finite form, which suggests that it is a verb and not some functional element. Evidence for this also comes from the fact that we appear to have the same element in copular clauses, where no other verb is present. This suggests that it is a verb that moves to T (and then Agr), a position widely assumed for English *be*. Accepting this position, Hendrick (1996) proposes an analysis in which *bod* is a verb taking a phrase headed by an aspectual functional head as its complement.[11] This gives the following structure for (76):

(78)   [$_{\text{AgrP}}$ Mae$_i$ [$_{\text{TP}}$ Rhiannon t$_i$ [$_{\text{VP}}$ t$_i$ [$_{\text{ProgP}}$ yn [$_{\text{VP}}$ cysgu rwan]]]]]]

Given such structures for aspectual clauses, copular clauses could have very similar structures differing only in the kind of complement that *bod* has. If aspectual clauses and copular clauses have similar structures, the existence of 'mixed' coordination examples like those in (42) is not surprising.

A central issue for any analysis of aspectual clauses is the order of aspect markers. As the examples in (28), repeated here as (79), show, we have *wedi* followed by *yn* but not the reverse.

(79)   a. Mae   Rhiannon wedi bod   yn   cysgu.
             be.PRES.3S Rhiannon PERF be.INF PROG sleep.INF
             'Rhiannon has been sleeping.'
          b. *Mae   Rhiannon yn   bod   wedi cysgu.
             be.PRES.3S Rhiannon PROG be.INF PERF sleep.INF.

Within Hendrick's (1996) approach, these examples will have the structures in (80).

(80)   a. [$_{\text{AgrP}}$ Mae$_i$ [$_{\text{TP}}$ Rhiannon t$_i$ [$_{\text{VP}}$ t$_i$ [$_{\text{PerfP}}$ wedi [$_{\text{VP}}$ bod [$_{\text{ProgP}}$ yn [$_{\text{VP}}$ cysgu]]]]]]]]
          b. [$_{\text{AgrP}}$ Mae$_i$ [$_{\text{TP}}$ Rhiannon t$_i$ [$_{\text{VP}}$ t$_i$ [$_{\text{ProgP}}$ yn [$_{\text{VP}}$ bod [$_{\text{PerfP}}$ wedi [$_{\text{VP}}$ cysgu]]]]]]]]

It looks as if we have the following restriction here:

(81)   If Prog has a complement headed by *bod*, *bod* may not have PerfP as its complement.

---

[11] In earlier work Hendrick (1991, 1994) proposes that *bod* originates in the specifier position of the aspectual functional heads. Applied to (20), this gives the following structure:

(i)   [$_{\text{AgrP}}$ Mae$_i$ [$_{\text{TP}}$ Rhiannon t$_i$ [$_{\text{ProgP}}$ t$_i$ yn [$_{\text{VP}}$ cysgu]]]]

This analysis assumes that *bod* in aspectual clauses is a different element from *bod* elsewhere, something which the examples in (42) suggest is dubious. Notice also that it involves movement from a specifier to a head position. A specifier normally moves to a specifier position. Hence, this is not a normal kind of movement.

It is normal for a head to impose restrictions on the head of its complement, but it is not normal for a head to impose restrictions on the complement of the head of its complement, which is what we seem to have here. One might suppose that *yn* simply doesn't allow a complement headed by *bod*. However, examples like the following, where *bod* has a predicative complement, show that this is not the case:

(82)   Mae   Gwyn yn   bod   yn   ddiog.
        be.PRES.3s Gwyn PROG be.INF PRED lazy
        'Gwyn is being lazy.'

Thus, there seems to be a problem here. One solution would be to assume that *bod* and other non-finite verbs have some aspectual feature when they head the complement of an aspect marker. This would mean that *bod* is marked as progressive when it heads the complement of *yn*. One could, then, stipulate that progressive *bod* may not have a PerfP complement.

2.5.2   Gwneud-*clauses and* ddaru-*clauses*

We turn now to *gwneud*-clauses. We saw in the last section that the idea that such clauses have the same structure as simple VSO clauses but with *gwneud*-insertion instead of verb-movement is quite dubious. It seems that *gwneud* is a verb, albeit one with some special properties. Thus, within a transformational approach (33b), repeated here as (83), should have something like the structure in (84):

(83)   Gwnaeth Emrys agor   y   drws.
        do.PAST.3s Emrys open.INF the door
        'Emrys opened the door.'

(84) $[_{AgrP}$ Gwnaeth$_i$ $[_{TP}$ Emrys t$_i$ $[_{VP}$ t$_i$ $[_{?P}$ agor y drws]]]]

We label the complement here '?P' to indicate that there is room for debate about its nature. Rouveret (1994: 76) proposes that it is a DP containing a VP, as follows:

(85) $[_{AgrP}$ Gwnaeth$_i$ $[_{TP}$ Emrys t$_i$ $[_{VP}$ t$_i$ $[_{DP}$ $[_{VP}$ agor y drws]]]]]

The main motivation for this view is that it allows one to analyse the clitics in both (86) and (87) as determiners:[12]

(86)   Gwnaeth Emrys ei   gweld.
        do.PAST.3s Emrys 3FS see.INF
        'Emrys saw her.'

---

[12] The appearance of clitics with non-finite verbs and nouns is discussed in sections 3.1.2 and 5.2.2.

(87)   Gwelodd Emrys ei   char.
        see.PAST.3s Emrys 3FS car
        'Emrys saw her car.'

However, extraction argues against this approach. An object can be extracted from a verbal complement of *gwneud* but a possessor cannot be readily extracted from a DP, as the following illustrate:

(88)   Pwy wnaeth   Emrys ei   weld?
        who do.PAST.3s Emrys 3MS see.INF
        'What did Emrys see?'

(89)   ??Pwy welodd   Emrys ei   gar?
        who see.PAST.3s Emrys 3MS car
        'Whose car did Emrys see?'

Instead of (89), we have (90), where the whole DP has been fronted:

(90)   [Car pwy] welodd   Emrys?
        car who see.PAST.3s Emrys
        'Whose car did Emrys see?'

We do not have similar examples where a verbal complement of *gwneud* is fronted.

(91)   *[Gweld beth] wnaeth   Emrys?
        see.INF what do.PAST.3s Emrys
        'What did Emrys see?'

If the complement of *gwneud* is not a DP containing a VP, the obvious suggestion is that it is just a VP.

What then of *ddaru*-clauses? We have noted that *ddaru* is invariant and is essentially a marker of past tense. Within a transformational framework, it would be natural to assume that it originates in T. In a framework like HPSG which doesn't have elements like T, it would be analysed as an irregular verb. Again it seems natural to assume that it has a VP complement.

Both *ddaru*-clauses and *gwneud*-clauses are rather like raising clauses such as (92) (see section 3.7).

(92)   Dechreuodd Emrys agor   y   drws.
        begin.PAST.3s Emrys open.INF the door
        'Emrys began to open the door.'

In all three clause types an expletive subject is possible:

(93)   a. Neith   hi fwrw   glaw.
           do.FUT.3s she strike.INF rain
           'It will rain.'

b. Ddaru hi   fwrw   glaw.
   PAST   she   strike.INF rain
   'It rained.'

c. Dechreuodd   hi   fwrw   glaw.
   begin.PAST.3S she   strike.INF rain
   'It began to rain.'

In constraint-based approaches, it is assumed that ordinary raising sentences also have a VP complement. However, in transformational approaches they are generally assumed to have a clausal complement of some kind. Thus, there is an issue as to how similar *ddaru*-clauses and *gwneud*-clauses are to raising verbs.

2.6   Further issues

There are a number of further issues that are of interest here, mainly involving subjects.

2.6.1   Null subjects

As we noted in section 2.1, the subject of a finite clause is optional in literary Welsh. Thus, we have superficially subjectless examples such as the following:

(94)   Gwelais   y   ci.
        see.PAST.1S the dog
        'I saw the dog.'

Within various versions of transformational grammar, the unexpressed subjects of such examples would be analysed as the empty category *pro*. An interesting argument for such an analysis comes from mutation. An important fact about objects of finite verbs, which we consider in some detail in chapter 7, is that they bear soft mutation. Thus, the object in (95) is the mutated form *geffyl* and not the basic form *ceffyl*.

(95)   Gwelais   i geffyl.
        see.PAST.1S I horse
        'I saw a horse.'

As discussed in chapter 7, a number of researchers have argued that this mutation is one of a number of instances of mutation triggered by an immediately preceding phrase. Here, the crucial phrase is the subject. Notice now that we have the same mutation in a sentence with an unexpressed subject:

(96)   Gwelais   geffyl.
        see.PAST.1S horse
        'I saw a horse.'

If the mutation in such examples is triggered by an immediately preceding phrase, then they must contain a phonologically empty subject.

2.6.2   Expletive subjects

Like many languages, Welsh has an expletive pronoun in subject position under various circumstances. The main expletive is the third-person singular feminine form *hi*. This appears with metereological predicates, as (97) illustrates:

(97)   Mae   hi 'n   bwrw   glaw.
        be.PRES.3S she PROG strike.INF rain
        'It is raining.'

It also appears in examples involving what one might think of as an extraposed clausal subject.

(98)   a. Mae   hi 'n   ymddangos [bod   Mair yn   gadael].
           be.PRES.3S she PROG appear.INF   be.INF Mair PROG leave.INF
           'It appears that Mair is leaving.'
        b. Mae   hi 'n   amlwg   [bod   Mair wedi dod   yn ôl].
           be.PRES.3S she PROG obvious be.INF Mair PERF come.INF back
           'It is obvious that Mair has come back.'
        c. Synnodd   bawb   [y   byddai   angen mwy o arian].
           surprise.PAST.3S everyone PRT be.COND.3S need more of money
           'It surprised everyone that more money was needed.'

There is no overt expletive in (98c). However, the fact that the object is the mutated form *bawb* and not the basic form *pawb* suggests that it must contain an empty expletive.

One might suppose that these examples would have paraphrases with a clausal subject. However, Welsh does not generally allow finite clausal subjects. Thus, the following are ungrammatical.

(99)   a. *Mae   [bod   Mair yn   gadael] yn   ymddangos.
           be.PRES.3S be.INF Mair PROG leave.INF PROG appear.INF
           ('It appears that Mair is leaving.')
        b. *Mae   [bod   Mair wedi dod   yn ôl] yn   amlwg.
           be.PRES.3S be.INF Mair PERF come.INF back PROG obvious
           ('That Mair has come back is obvious.')

    c. *Synnodd   [y byddai   angen mwy o arian] bawb.
       surprise.PAST.3S PRT be.COND.3S need   more of money everyone
       ('That more money was needed surprised everyone.')

One might think that the situation is rather like English, in which examples like the following are ungrammatical:

(100)   *Is [that Kim is clever] obvious?

However, clausal subjects are also ungrammatical in sentence-initial position. Thus whereas (101) is grammatical, the examples in (102) are no better than those in (99):

(101)   [That Kim is clever] is obvious.

(102)   a. *[Bod Mair yn   gadael]   mae   'n   ymddangos.
            be.INF Mair PROG leave.INF be.PRES.3S PROG appear.INF
            ('It appears that Mair is leaving.')
       b. *[Bod Mair wedi dod   yn ôl] mae   'n   amlwg.
            be.INF Mair PERF come.INF back be.PRES.3S PROG obvious
            ('That Mair has come back is obvious.')
       c. *[Y byddai   angen mwy o arian] synnodd   bawb.
            PRT be.COND.3S need   more of money surprise.PAST.3S everyone
            ('That more money was needed surprised everyone.')

Unlike finite clauses, subjectless non-finite clauses of the kind that are assumed in much work to have a PRO subject can appear in subject position, as the following show:

(103)   a. Mae   [mynd yno] yn   syniad da.
          be.PRES.3S go.INF there PROG idea   good
          'Going there is a good idea.'
       b. Mae   [darllen llyfrau] yn   dda i   ti.
          be.PRES.3S read.INF books PRED good for you.S
          'Reading books is good for you.'

A rather different type of example which may involve an expletive subject is illustrated by the following:

(104)   Mae   'n   well gan Mair goffi.
       be.PRES.3S PRED better with Mair coffee
       'Mair prefers coffee.'

Here, however, many speakers do not allow an overt expletive, and there is no evidence from mutation that an empty subject is present. Hence, it is not clear whether this is the right analysis.

Welsh has a second expletive element *yna* 'there'. Like the superficially similar English *there*, this is associated with an indefinite noun phrase. Thus, we have both (105a) and (105b).

(105)   a. Mae   dafad   yn yr ardd.
         be.PRES.3S sheep.S in the garden
         'A sheep is in the garden.'
         b. Mae   yna   ddafad yn yr ardd.
         be.PRES.3S there sheep.S in the garden
         'There is a sheep in the garden.'

However, *yna* is much more restricted than *there*. It appears only between a
finite verb and an indefinite noun phrase. *There* can appear in a non-finite
clause, such as that in (106).

(106)   I arranged [for there to be a sheep in the garden].

Welsh has non-finite clauses which resemble the English clause here, as discussed in section 3.4. However, they do not allow *yna*.

(107)   *Disgwyliodd Gwyn [i yna   fod   dafad yn yr ardd].
         expect.PAST.3S Gwyn to there be.INF sheep.S in the garden
         ('I expected there to be a sheep in the garden.')

Yna is also impossible in a finite clause where it is not immediately followed
by the associated noun phrase. Thus, (108) is ungrammatical, unlike its
English translation.

(108)   *Dylai   yna   fod   dafad yn yr ardd.
         ought.COND.3S there be.INF sheep.S in the garden
         ('There ought to be a sheep in the garden.')

2.6.3   Further non-canonical subjects

An expletive subject could be regarded as a non-canonical subject.
Welsh has a number of other types of non-canonical subject. Consider first
the following; see also section 10.2.2.4:

(109)   a. Mae   car newydd gan Megan.
         be.PRES.3S car new   with Megan
         'Megan has a new car.'
         b. Mae   gan Megan gar newydd.
         be.PRES.3S with Megan car new
         'Megan has a new car.'

In (109a) it is fairly clear that *car newydd* is the subject, and it seems reasonable to assume that the same is true of *gar newydd* in (109b). If this is
right, it is a subject which is non-canonical in being separated from the associated verb.

Another type of non-canonical subject is seen in the following, where both
angen and *eisiau* are verbs:

(110)   a. Mae   angen dwy bunt   arnaf i.
         be.PRES.3S need   two pound on.1S me
         'I need two pounds'
         b. Mae   arnaf i eisiau mynd adref.
         be.PRES.3S on.1S I want go.INF home
         'I want to go home.'

It seems reasonable to assume that *angen dwy bunt* is the subject of (110a) and
that the subject of (110b) is *eisiau fynd adref*.[13] One might think of these subjects as semantically non-canonical. In both cases, the object of the preposition *ar* (with which *ar* agrees) corresponds to the subject of the English
translation. In both cases, there is an alternative colloquial construction which
looks more like English. The following illustrate:

(111)   a. Dw   i angen dwy bunt.
         be.PRES.1S I need   two pound
         'I need two pounds.'
         b. Dw   i eisiau mynd adref.
         be.PRES.1S I want go.INF home
         'I want to go home.'

Welsh has a variety of examples like those in (110), all involving predicates of
the general 'psych' type; see also section 10.2.2.4. The following provide a
further illustration:

(112)   a. Mae   ofn arni   hi.
         be.PRES.3S fear on.3FS her
         'She is afraid.'
         b. Mae   syched arna' i.
         be.PRES.3S thirst on.1S me
         'I am thirsty.'
         c. Mae'r   ddannodd arno   fo.
         is   the toothache on.3MS him
         'He has toothache.'

2.6.4   The 'serial construction'

We look now at what Rouveret (1994: 302) calls the 'serial construction'. This is illustrated by the following:

(113)   Daeth   Megan i mewn ac eistedd i lawr.
         come.PAST.3S Megan to in   and sit.INF to down
         'Megan came in and sat down.'

---

[13] In both cases the prepositional phrase *arnaf i* can either precede or follow the other
constituent, but the preferred orders are as indicated.

Here, we have a coordinate structure which appears to involve a finite clause conjoined with a non-finite VP. As an alternative to (113) one might have (114), in which both conjuncts are finite clauses.

(114)   Daeth   Megan i   mewn ac   eisteddodd hi i lawr.
         come.PAST.3s Megan to in   and sat.PAST.3s she to down
         'Megan came in and sat down.'

Examples like this pose no special problems, but examples like (113) provide a challenge for theories of syntax. Within P&P, it is standardly assumed that meaning reflects structure quite closely. The second conjunct is understood as having the same subject and the same tense as the first conjunct. Hence, there is no real possibility of assuming that we really have a finite clause conjoined with a VP, as in (115).

(115)   [s [s Daeth Megan i mewn] ac [vp eistedd i lawr]].

Rouveret (1994) develops a P&P analysis of examples like (113) in which they involve conjoined TPs with extraction of the verb from the first, as in the following:

(116)   [Daeth_i [TP [TP Megan t_i i mewn] [ac [TP eistedd i lawr]]]].

This is somewhat unusual in involving extraction from one conjunct. However, Rouveret argues that this is independently motivated by examples like the following:

(117)   Gwelais   i a   Megan ddafad.
         see.PAST.1s I and Megan sheep.s
         'Megan and I saw a sheep.'

Here, the subject is a coordinate structure and the verb agrees with the first conjunct. Rouveret proposes that agreement is in fact the incorporation of a Num(ber) head. If one accepts this view of agreement, then such examples involve extraction from the first conjunct. We return to examples like these in section 6.2.1.

In other frameworks, which allow a more complex relation between meaning and structure, the second conjunct could be a VP. An analysis of this kind is developed within LFG in Sadler (2006). In LFG, constituents have a functional-structure which incorporates information about grammatical functions like subject and object and about properties like tense. Sadler shows that this makes it quite easy to ensure that the second conjunct has the appropriate interpretation.

Whatever the correct analysis of examples like (113), it is clear that somewhat similar examples occur in other languages. For example, Sadler cites the following Breton example from Ternes (1992: 396):

(118)   Per a   savas   ha mont d'ar prenestr.
        Per PRT stand.PAST.3S and go.INF to the window
        'Peter rose and went to the window.'

Here the first clause has an initial subject, reflecting the fact mentioned at the end of section 2.1, that Breton is a verb-second language. Otherwise, however, this is very similar to (113). Sadler also suggests that similar examples occur in the Australian language Wambaya. Thus, examples like (113) are not particularly unusual.

2.6.5   Verbless clauses

Finally, we consider certain main clauses which are either verbless or have a non-canonical verb. The following is a typical example:

(119)   Rhaid   i mi adael.
        necessity to me leave.INF
        'I must leave.'

Here the noun *rhaid* 'necessity' is followed by what looks like a non-finite clause, and there is no finite verb. This example has a present tense interpretation. If some other tense is intended an appropriate form of *bod* is used, as the following illustrate:

(120)   a. Bydd   rhaid   i mi adael.
           be.FUT.3S necessity to me leave.INF
           'I will have to leave.'
        b. Roedd   rhaid   i mi adael.
           be.IMPF.3S necessity to me leave.INF
           'I had to leave.'

One might suppose that examples like (119) involve a phonologically empty form of *bod*. Examples like (121) with a tag containing a form of *bod* provide support for this idea.

(121)   Rhaid   i mi adael, ynd oes?
        necessity to me leave.INF Q   be.PRES.3S
        'I must leave, mustn't I?'

However, many speakers allow a tag containing *rhaid*.

(122)   Rhaid   i mi adael, yn rhaid?
        necessity to me leave.INF Q necessity
        'I must leave, mustn't I?'

It looks, then, as if some speakers either allow a verbless analysis for examples like (119) or reanalyse *rhaid* as a verb.

2.7   Conclusions

This chapter has looked at the properties of simple finite clauses and considered the analytic issues that they raise. It has considered both transformational and constraint-based analyses, highlighting the unresolved question of whether finite clauses contain a VP like finite clauses in many other languages. It has also discussed the various types of auxiliary-initial clauses which play an important role in Welsh. Finally, it has looked at a number of other issues, especially null subjects, expletive subjects and certain non-canonical subjects.

3

Non-finite verbs and infinitival clauses

3.1   Non-finite verbs: verbal and nominal properties

3.1.1   The non-finite verb form

Welsh verbs have only one non-finite form, which we will generally refer to as a non-finite verb or an infinitive; the form is glossed throughout as 'INF(INITIVE)'. In Welsh traditional grammar, the non-finite form is known as a 'verb-noun' (*berfenw*), reflecting the traditional view that the form has the properties of both a verb and a noun, and is therefore neither fully in one category nor the other. In this section, we will show that this is a misleading characterization.

The non-finite form consists either of the bare verb stem, or of the stem plus one of a number of suffixes. Examples of the former include *darllen*, 'read', *disgwyl*, 'expect', *eistedd*, 'sit', *ennill*, 'win' and *ateb*, 'reply'. Infinitives formed by the addition of a suffix are often derived from nouns or adjectives. The most common suffixes by far are *-u*, *-i* and *-o/-io*, as in *credu* (*cred-u*), 'believe', *meddwi* (*meddw-i*) 'to get drunk', *bwydo* (*bwyd-o*) 'feed' and *herio* (*her-io*) 'challenge'. Established loan words from English commonly take the *-io* suffix too, such as *peint-io* 'paint', and this suffix is also heavily used to form Welsh verbs in nonce borrowings. A number of other infinitival suffixes occur in addition, but with a much more limited distribution: for instance, *-ed*, e.g. *clywed*, 'hear', *cerdded*, 'walk'; *-ian*, e.g. *sgrechian*, 'screech'; and *-a*, used in some infinitives formed from nouns, e.g. *gwledda* 'feast' (< *gwledd* 'feast' (n.)).

Although closely related Breton has a past participle, Welsh has no participial forms at all, and the infinitival form is used in all syntactic contexts requiring a non-finite verb. Examples (1) and (2) illustrate two contexts which in English require (present and past) participial verb forms. Note that while English also uses two different auxiliaries, the distinction in Welsh is obtained simply through the use of different aspect markers (see section 2.2.1):

(1)   Mae   Aled yn   canu   cân.
       be.PRES.3s Aled PROG sing.INF song
       'Aled is singing a song.'

(2)   Mae   Aled wedi canu   cân.
       be.PRES.3s Aled PERF sing.INF song
       'Aled has sung a song.'

There are a small number of expressions of the form P + non-finite verb, shown in (3), which are used in contexts such as (4) where a participial might otherwise be found in various languages:

(3)   a. ar agor   b. ar gau
          on open.INF   on close.INF
          'open'   'closed'

(4)   Mae   'r siop ar gau.
       be.PRES.3s the shop on close.INF
       'The shop is closed.'

There is also a derivational suffix -(i)edig which forms adjectives from the verb-noun, and these occur in contexts in which English would typically use a participial form:

(5)   y   safon   **ddisgwyliedig**
       the level   expected
       'the standard expected'

(6)   Mae   chwedl ddiddorol yn   **gysylltiedig** â   'r   pentref hwn.
       be.PRES.3s tale   interesting PRED connected with the village DEM.MS
       'There's an interesting tale connected with this village.'

There is clear evidence that -(i)edig derivatives are adjectives, however: they occur in adjectival contexts, for instance following predicative *yn*, as in (6), and following *mor* 'as, so':

(7)   gwlad   mor **ddatblygedig** â   Chymru
       country as developed   as Wales
       'a country as developed as Wales'

Moreover, these forms take the *an-* 'un-' adjectival prefix, as in *annisgwyliedig* 'unexpected', *anghysylltiedig* 'unconnected'.

3.1.2   Arguments against the 'verb-noun' categorization

As noted above, Welsh traditional grammar regards the 'verb-noun' as a single category with both nominal and verbal properties. Work in the generative tradition has taken a different view, regarding these forms as non-finite verbs where they correspond to non-finite verbs in English, and elsewhere analysing the 'verb-noun' simply as a noun. Detailed arguments for this view are developed by Borsley (1993). Conversely, P. Willis (1988) and Fife (1990) regard the 'verb-noun' as a noun in all its manifestations. In this section we outline some objections both against this latter view and against the traditional 'verb-noun' characterization.

In some contexts, the 'verb-noun' is clearly a true noun. A form such as *canu*, 'sing(ing)' takes the definite article, and can also be modified by an attributive adjective, as shown in (8):

(8)   Clywodd   Emyr **y   canu   hyfryd**.
       hear.PAST.3S Emyr the singing(n.) pleasant
       'Emyr heard the pleasant singing.'

Data like these indicate that we have a nominal element, *canu*, which has the same wordform as the corresponding verbal element *canu* in (1) and (2) – parallel, then, to an English form like *singing*, which can be a verb (*She was singing in the bath*) or a noun (*John's singing was awful*).

Both properties illustrated in (8) contrast with the behaviour of non-finite verbs. These cannot take the definite article, as (9) shows. Nor are they modified by an adjective, but instead must be modified by an adverb, which is formed from predicative *yn* + adjective, as in (10):[1]

(9)   Dylai   Emyr (***yr**) anfon   y   llythyr.
       ought.COND.3S Emyr the   send.INF the letter
       'Emyr ought to send the letter.'

(10)   Dylai   Rhiannon ganu   ***(yn)** hyfryd.
       ought.COND.3S Rhiannon sing.INF PRED pleasant
       'Rhiannon ought to sing pleasantly.'   (Borsley 1993: 46)

These two aspects of behaviour are predictable if the 'verb-noun' is in fact a non-finite verb in (9) and (10).

What, then, is the motivation behind the traditional 'verb-noun' classification? The most obvious point is that both non-finite verbs and ordinary nouns take the same set of agreement proclitics (see section 5.2.2), examples of which are shown in bold in (11) and (12). Not only are the proclitics themselves identical, they also trigger exactly the same set of consonantal mutations on the following head (verb or noun); the mutation effects are shown following each example. When they co-occur with a non-finite head verb, the proclitics represent agreement with the object of the verb; when they co-occur with a head

---

[1] We find *ganu* rather than *canu* in (10) because the non-finite verb is in an environment for soft mutation; see chapter 7.

noun, the proclitics represent agreement with a possessor. As elsewhere in the Welsh agreement system, a head only displays overt agreement with a pronominal argument, and never with a non-pronominal argument; see section 6.1 for full details. The pronominal argument itself follows the head verb or noun, but since the pronominal can also be null (i.e. *pro*), it is shown here in parentheses after each relevant head in (11) and (12) (data from Borsley 1993: 37–8):

(11) a. Ceisiodd   Emrys **ei** weld (o).   (gweld > weld)
         try.PAST.3S Emrys 3MS see.INF him
         'Emrys tried to see him.'
      b. Dechreuodd Gwyn **fy** nharo (i).   (taro > nharo)
         begin.PAST.3S Gwyn 1S hit.INF me
         'Gwyn began to hit me.'

(12) a. Gwelodd   Emrys **ei** wraig (o).   (gwraig > wraig)
         see.PAST.3S Emrys 3MS wife   him
         'Emrys saw his wife.'
      b. Prynodd   Gwyn **fy** nhŷ   (i).   (tŷ > nhŷ)
         buy.PAST.3S Gwyn 1S house me
         'Gwyn bought my house.'

Thus, nouns and non-finite verbs display the same agreement morphology, in the form of the proclitics. However, this is insufficient reason to categorize them as members of the same word class: see section 5.2.2 for further discussion. As Borsley (1993: 40–1) points out, finite verbs and prepositions also share a very similar agreement morphology (see section 6.1), but this is not considered grounds for categorizing these elements as members of a single syntactic category.

Moreover, the anaphoric possibilities are crucially not the same in (11) and (12). In (11a), whether the pronominal object is overt or covert, it must be disjoint in reference to the subject, *Emrys*: in other words, it can never mean 'Emrys tried to see himself.' This indicates that the subject and the object are in the same binding domain: a pronominal object cannot be bound within this domain. Conversely, in (12a), if the pronominal is covert (*pro*), then the object may be co-referential with the subject, giving the reading 'Emrys saw his (own) wife.' This indicates that the subject, *Emrys*, is in a different binding domain from the possessor, so allowing the possessor to be free in its own domain yet still bound by the subject. An overt pronominal argument in (12a) will, for some speakers, force the interpretation of disjoint reference with the subject (i.e. Emrys saw someone else's wife):[2]

---

[2] Various sociolinguistic factors influence the availability of the interpretations, however, and in particular the age of the speaker, with older speakers restricting the co-referential reading to the case where the argument is *pro*, and having obviation effects with an overt pronoun. See section 5.2.2.

(13)   Gwelodd   Emrys$_j$ ei   wraig *pro$_j$ / o$_i$*
        see.PAST.3S Emrys 3MS wife   him
        'Emrys$_j$ saw his (own)$_j$/his$_i$ wife.'

There are a number of other clear indications that non-finite verbs are distinct from nouns. In terms of their complementation and distribution, the two syntactic categories display a number of crucial differences. First, a transitive non-finite verb takes a noun phrase complement, as shown in (14), whilst a noun takes an (optional) PP complement, as shown in (15):

(14)   Dylai   Gwyn **ddisgrifio**   'r   llun.
        ought.COND.3S Gwyn describe.INF the picture
        'Gwyn ought to describe the picture.'

(15)   Ceir   **disgrifiad**   o 'r rhes o dai.
        get.PRES.IMPERS description of the row of houses
        'We are given a description of the row of houses.'

Second, consider focalization: phrases headed by nouns display quite distinct behaviour to those headed by non-finite verbs. In both (16) and (17), the focalized XP is itself the complement of a 'verb-noun'. The basic sentences are shown in the two (a) examples, and the focalizations in the two (b) examples (data from Borsley 1993):

(16)   a. Mae   Gwen yn   darllen [llyfr Emrys].
           be.PRES.3S Gwen PROG read.INF book Emrys
           'Gwen is reading Emrys's book.'
        b. [Llyfr Emrys] mae   Gwen yn   **ei   ddarllen.**
           book Emrys be.PRES.3S Gwen PROG 3MS read.INF
           'It's Emrys's book that Gwen is reading.'

(17)   a. Mae   Gwen yn   ceisio [canu   'r   anthem].
           be.PRES.3S Gwen PROG try.INF sing.INF the anthem
           'Gwen is trying to sing the anthem.'
        b. [Canu   'r   anthem] mae   Gwen yn   ceisio /*ei   **geisio.**
           sing.INF the anthem be.PRES.3S Gwen PROG try.INF 3MS try.INF
           'Gwen is trying to *sing the anthem.'*

In (16b) we have a fronted nominal expression (head noun + possessor), and in (17b), a fronted verbal expression (head non-finite verb + object). A resumptive element in the form of an agreement proclitic *ei*, 3MS, occurs on *ddarllen*, 'read', in (16b); the proclitic agrees with the fronted nominal phrase, which has a masculine singular head noun, *llyfr*, 'book'. But in (17b), neither the proclitic nor its associated soft mutation (*ceisio > geisio*) can occur.

Third, consider the difference between the *wh*-questions in (18) and (19); see also section 2.5.2. *Pwy*, 'who', is understood as the object of the non-finite head verb *gweld*, 'see', in (18), and as the possessor of the head noun *gwraig*, 'wife' in (19) (data from Borsley 1993):

(18)   Pwy geisiaist   ti   ei   weld?
         who try.PAST.2S you 3MS see.INF
         'Who did you try to see?'

(19)   ??Pwy welaist   ti   ei   wraig?
         who see.PAST.2S you 3MS wife
         'Whose wife did you see?'

Both constructions have a resumptive element in the form of an agreement proclitic (*ei* 3MS) on the head verb or noun. As noted in section 2.5.2, the difference is that constructions like (19) are marginal, whilst those in (18) are fully grammatical. Rather than (19), speakers generally prefer (20), with pied-piping of the whole possessive construction and no resumptive element:

(20)   **Gwraig pwy** welaist   ti?
         wife   who see.PAST.2S you
         'Whose wife did you see?'

But if a similar construction is used with the non-finite verb *gweld*, the result is highly degraded:

(21)   ?***Gweld pwy** geisiaist   ti?
         see.INF who try.PAST.2S you
         ('Who did you try to see?')

In sum, we have seen that the syntactic behaviour of nouns is very different from that of non-finite verbs. A number of other arguments are outlined in Borsley (1993). It seems clear that the element traditionally referred to as a 'verb-noun' is not a hybrid category at all, nor a pure noun, but simply a noun in certain clearly defined positions, and a non-finite verb in other, equally clearly defined contexts. There is no overlap in syntactic behaviour, and no uncertainty or fuzziness regarding the syntactic category of any given 'verb-noun'.

3.1.3   Verb-noun phrases as DPs

In the previous section we examined the problems posed by the view that 'verb-nouns' are nominal categories in all their manifestations. A distinct, though clearly allied, view is proposed by Rouveret (1994: Chapter 4). Under this proposal, 'verb-noun' phrases are in fact determiner phrases, DP, with the following structure:

(22)   [$_{DP}$ .... D [$_{NomP}$ .... [$_{Nom}$ affix] [$_{VP}$ .... V ....]]]   (Rouveret 1994: 263)

According to the structure in (22), the phrase has a non-finite verb heading a VP, but also contains a nominalizing affix, responsible for making the verb a nominalized form (NomP), which in turn is the complement to a determiner. The nominalizing affixes are the suffixes on the verb which we discussed in section 3.1.1. This proposal for Welsh has a clear parallel to Abney's (1987) structure for English POSS-*ing* constructions, for instance in [$_{DP}$ John [$_D$'s] [$_{VP}$ skilfully building a boat]]. However, whilst Abney's analysis of English (and indeed, various other languages) appears to us genuinely insightful, Rouveret's proposed structure for Welsh verb-noun phrases does not seem similarly appropriate.

Rouveret does acknowledge that nominal and verbal usages of the 'verb-noun' phrase are differentiated, but nonetheless regards all instances of the phrase, including verbal ones, as instances of DP; see also the discussion of his analysis of *gwneud* 'do' in section 2.5.2. Part of the motivation for this analysis (Rouveret 1994: 266) is the fact that both non-finite verbs and nouns take the same set of agreement proclitics, as seen in section 3.1.2. Rouveret (1994: 252) also cites as evidence for the DP analysis the fact that the objects of non-finite verbs do not undergo soft mutation (section 7.3 below), just as the argument in a possessive construction does not undergo soft mutation:

(23)   a. gweld   pererin/*bererin
           see.INF pilgrim/pilgrim(+SM)
           'to see a pilgrim'
        b. troed   pererin/*bererin
           foot   pilgrim/pilgrim(+SM)
           'a pilgrim's foot'

Conversely, the object of a finite verb does undergo soft mutation (see chapter 7):

(24)   Gwelais   bererin.   (*pererin*)
        see.PAST.1S pilgrim
        'I saw a pilgrim.'

In fact, following Welsh grammatical tradition, Rouveret proposes that the objects of non-finite verbs have (abstract) genitive case, whereas the objects of finite verbs have (abstract) accusative case.[3] The proposal to treat non-finite verb phrases as nominal categories is thus intended to account both for

---

[3] There is no morphologically distinct genitive case on lexical noun phrases; as noted in section 1.4.5, Welsh displays no case morphology. Rouveret's analysis parallels the situation in Irish and Scots Gaelic, where the objects of verb-nouns are visibly genitive under certain conditions.

the mutation patterns and the appearance of a parallel set of agreement proclitics on nouns and non-finite verbs: the proclitics are analysed as members of the Determiner category. However, in chapter 7 we argue that the contrast in mutation seen in (23a) and (24) has nothing whatever to do with case-marking.

Furthermore, Rouveret's proposal that 'verb-noun' phrases are DPs is equally problematic in light of the data examined in section 3.1.2, which very clearly showed non-finite verbs to be verbs in verbal contexts. The anaphoric possibilities illustrated in (11) to (13), the contrasting focalization possibilities in (16) and (17), and the contrasting possibilities for *wh*-extraction seen in (18) to (21) all show that a non-finite verb phrase is *not* syntactically parallel to a possessor noun phrase. Given such problems, we find no support for Rouveret's proposal that 'verb-noun' phrases are DPs.

3.2   Tensed complement clauses

Tensed complement clauses in Welsh are largely parallel in structure to main clauses: they either contain a simple finite verb and have VSO word order, as in (25), or alternatively are auxiliary-initial with a non-finite lexical verb lower down in the clause, as in (26). As usual, the finite element (in bold) is clause-initial, though in literary Welsh this may be preceded by the pre-verbal particle *y*, which is not normally found in speech:

(25)   Mae   Aled yn   credu   [(y) **darllenith**   Elen y   llyfr].
        be.PRES.3s Aled PROG believe.INF PRT read.FUT.3s Elen the book
        'Aled believes that Elen will read the book.'

(26)   Meddyliodd Aled [(y) **byddai**   Elen yn   darllen y   llyfr].
        think.PAST.3s Aled PRT be.COND.3s Elen PROG read.INF the book
        'Aled thought that Elen would be reading the book.'

The matrix verbs in these examples illustrate members of the large class of epistemic and declarative predicates, which includes *credu*, 'believe', *meddwl*, 'think', *gwybod*, 'know (a fact)', *deall*, 'understand' and *dweud*, 'say', amongst many others. Such predicates always take finite complement clauses, but as we will see, these complement clauses do not always contain a tensed verb: 'finite' in Welsh crucially does not always equate with 'tensed'. Tensed embedded clauses contain verbs inflected either for the future, as illustrated in (25), or the conditional/habitual, as in (26). Beyond this, however, various restrictions apply. These involve the substitution of what we might call a pseudo-non-finite clause for an ordinary tensed complement clause, as we show in sections 3.3 and 3.4.1.

In the following sections, we turn to the behaviour of the infinitival verb form. This form occurs in various types of complement clauses with overt subjects, as we discuss in sections 3.3 and 3.4. In these sections we outline the syntax of three distinct infinitival clause types: *bod*-clauses (section 3.3) and two varieties of *i*-clause (sections 3.4.1 and 3.4.2). All of these clause types have the *form* of a non-finite clause – that is, they contain no morphologically tensed element at all. However, one of the interesting features of Welsh syntax is that it is possible for a clause which contains only the infinitival form of the verb – and no morphologically finite elements – nonetheless to be a syntactically finite clause. We will see that *bod*-clauses and one type of *i*-clause have the syntax of a finite clause, while a completely distinct type of *i*-clause has the syntax of a non-finite clause.

Verbal infinitives also occur in complements with no overt subjects: the infinitival complements to control and raising predicates. These are discussed respectively in sections 3.5 and 3.7. The remaining section, 3.6, considers the status of *i* in infinitival clauses and examines the nature of finiteness in Welsh.

3.3   *Bod*-clauses: finite clauses with the infinitive *bod*

3.3.1   *The distribution of* bod

One restriction on clausal complements to the epistemic and declarative class of predicates (section 3.2) concerns the availability of tensed forms of *bod*, 'be', in the embedded clause. *Bod* exhibits more tense contrasts than lexical verbs in Welsh; specifically, it distinguishes a future tense (*bydd* 'be.FUT.3s') from a present tense (*mae* 'be.PRES.3s'), and an imperfect tense (*(r)oedd* 'be.IMPF.3s') from a preterite (*buodd/bu* 'be.PRET.3s'). However, not all of these forms are available in embedded contexts.

First, in affirmative and declarative contexts, embedded clauses cannot contain the present tense of *bod*, as (27) shows. Instead, the present tense form is replaced by the infinitival form *bod* itself, as shown in (28):

(27)   *Mae   Aled   yn   credu   [**mae**   Elen yn   darllen   y   llyfr].
         be.PRES.3s Aled PROG believe.INF be.PRES.3s Elen PROG read.INF the book
         ('Aled believes that Elen is reading the book.')

(28)   Mae   Aled   yn   credu   [**bod**   Elen yn   darllen   y   llyfr].
        be.PRES.3s Aled PROG believe.INF be.INF Elen PROG read.INF the book
        'Aled believes that Elen is/was reading the book.'

Secondly, it is also common for speakers to disallow imperfect tensed forms
of *bod* in these contexts too, though various idiolects do permit this; see Jones
& Thomas (1977: 216):

(29)   %Mae   Aled   yn   credu   [**roedd**   Elen yn   darllen   y   llyfr].
        be.PRES.3s Aled PROG believe.INF be.IMPF.3s Elen PROG read.INF the book
        'Aled believes that Elen was reading the book.'

For speakers who do not allow the imperfect here, the alternative would again
be (28), which is grammatical for all speakers, including those who accept (29).
The infinitival form, *bod*, then, translates either present and imperfect tense in
these contexts, and is a neutralization of these two tenses. We will use the term
'*bod*-clause' to refer to embedded clauses such as that in (28), with the infinitive
form *bod* in pre-subject position rather than a morphologically tensed form.
Schematically, *bod*-clauses are as shown in (30):

(30)   [*bod* Subject [Aspect-marker Verb(non-finite) Object/other complements
        Adjuncts]]

Apart from occurring as complements to verbs, *bod*-clauses may also be
complements to adjectives, such as *balch* 'glad', *siŵr* 'sure', and *sicr* 'certain',
as in (31), or to nouns, such as *si* 'rumour' and *syniad* 'idea', as in (32):

(31)   Dw   i 'n   sicr   [**bod**   Elen yn   darllen   y   llyfr].
        be.PRES.1s I PRED certain be.INF Elen PROG read.INF the book
        'I'm certain Elen is reading the book.'

(32)   Byddwn   yn   gwrthod   yn   llwyr   y
        be.FUT.1P PROG refuse.INF PROG complete the
        syniad [**bod**   methiant systematig].
        idea   be.INF failure   systematic
        'We reject completely the idea that there was a systematic failure.'

Bod-clauses are also frequently adverbial, following a preposition such as
cyn 'before', or *er* 'although':

(33)   Es   i allan [cyn   **bod**   y   plant   wedi codi].
        go.PAST.1s I out   before be.INF the children PERF rise.INF
        'I went out before the children had got up.'

In all types of embedded clause, *bod* formally takes a proclitic agreement
marker agreeing with a pronominal subject. As elsewhere in the agreement
system (see section 6.1), there is no agreement with a full noun phrase subject.

Although the proclitics themselves are typically absent in the colloquial language, the various mutations that they trigger still remain, except in the most colloquial usage. Thus, *fy* (1s) triggers nasal mutation (*bod* > *mod*), and *ei* (3MS) triggers soft mutation (*bod* > *fod*):

(34)   a. Dywedodd y   ferch [(fy) mod   i 'n   hwyr].
             say.PAST.3s the girl   1s be.INF I PRED late
             'The girl said that I was late.'
          b. Dywedodd y   ferch [(ei) fod   o 'n   hwyr].
             say.PAST.3s the girl   3MS be.INF he PRED late
             'The girl said that he was late.'

In very colloquial Welsh, both the agreement proclitic and the mutation on *bod* can be absent, and an independent (strong) subject pronoun is used, rather than the (weak) dependent forms such as *i* 'I' and *o* 'he' in (34); (35) is a more colloquial variant of (34a):

(35)   Wedodd   y   ferch [bo' fi   'n   hwyr].
          say.PAST.3s the girl   be.INF I.STRONG PRED late
          'The girl said that I was late.'

Where proclitics on *bod* do occur – in the somewhat more formal context in (34) – it is the same set of proclitics which occur as object agreement markers on non-finite verbs, as illustrated in (11), and as possessive agreement markers on nouns, as illustrated in (12); see also section 6.1. In Modern Welsh, *bod* is the only infinitival verb form to take the proclitics as *subject* agreement markers. As we will see in section 3.6.4, the explanation for this is that *bod* is the only morphologically non-finite verb to appear in the pre-subject position, where heads inflect to agree with a pronominal subject.

3.3.2   *Evidence that* bod *is finite*

Despite its being morphologically non-finite in form, there is much evidence that infinitival *bod* in complement clauses such as (28) and (31) to (35) is actually syntactically *finite* (Harlow 1992, Tallerman 1998). Note first that infinitival *bod* in these examples occurs in the same clause-initial position as any finite verb; in other words, it occurs in pre-subject position. This contrasts with other infinitival verb forms in embedded clauses, which only occur in post-subject position; see section 3.4. Second, *bod* complement clauses complete the set of 'normal' finite clausal complements, with the same distribution as the tensed clausal complements seen in (25) and (26); as Harlow (1992: 103) notes, 'they fill a gap in an otherwise plainly finite clausal paradigm'. Third, as we saw in (34), *bod*-clauses are like ordinary tensed clauses in that they exhibit subject agreement with pronominal subjects. In terms of position, distribution and agreement patterns, then, *bod* is finite in these cases.

Fourth, *bod*-clauses can coordinate with complement clauses containing ordinary tensed forms of *bod* (or indeed, other tensed verbs):[4]

(36)   Dywedodd Aled [**fod**   Mair wedi mynd   yn   barod] a
        say.PAST.3S Aled be.INF Mair PERF go.INF PRED ready   and
        [**byddai**   Gwen yn   mynd yn   fuan].
        be.COND.3S Gwen PROG go.INF PRED soon
        'Aled said that Mair had gone already and that Gwen would be going
        soon.'

Fifth, *bod*-clauses such as (37a) have the negation properties of ordinary tensed clauses such as (37b), in that they negate using adverbial *ddim* (see section 8.2), rather than using *peidio (â)*, the element which negates non-finite verbs:

(37)   a. Mae   Aled yn   dweud [bod   Mair **ddim** yn   barod].
           be.PRES.3S Aled PROG say.INF be.INF Mair NEG PRED ready
           'Aled says that Mair isn't ready.'
        b. Mae   Aled yn   dweud [fyddai   Mair **ddim** yn   barod].
           be.PRES.3S Aled PROG say.INF be.COND.3S Mair NEG PRED ready
           'Aled says that Mair wouldn't be ready.'

In fact, an alternative to (37a) replaces *bod* itself with a tensed form in the embedded clause, as in (38), adding more weight to the argument that a *bod*-clause is finite. This is closer to the more formal Welsh *nad yw Mair . . .*, (NEG is Mair):

(38)   Mae   Aled yn   dweud [**dydy**   Mair ddim yn   barod].
        be.PRES.3S Aled PROG say.INF NEG.be.PRES.3S Mair NEG PRED ready
        'Aled says that Mair isn't ready.'

Thus, we find the following sociolinguistic continuum of stylistic variation, from the most literary form with the negative complementizer *nad* and the tensed form *yw* 'is', to the most colloquial form with no complementizer, *bod* rather than a tensed form, and the negative adverb *ddim*:

(39)   Mae Aled yn dweud [**nad yw**   Mair   yn barod].   LITERARY WELSH
        Mae Aled yn dweud [**dyw/dydy** Mair **ddim** yn barod].
        Mae Aled yn deud [**bod**   Mair **ddim** yn barod].
                                                    COLLOQUIAL WELSH

---

[4] *Bod* mutates to *fod* following the subject of the matrix clause; see chapter 7 for more
  details of syntactic soft mutation.

Sixth, subjects of *bod*-clauses have the anaphoric properties of nominals in ordinary tensed clauses (Harlow 1992: 105):

(40)   a. Dywedodd Aled$_i$ [(ei) fod o$_{i/j}$ wedi gadael].
        say.PAST.3S Aled   3MS be.INF he   PERF leave.INF
        'Aled$_i$ said that he$_{i/j}$ had left.'

        b. *Dywedodd Aled [(ei) fod **ei hun** wedi gadael].
        say.PAST.3S Aled   3MS be.INF 3MS REFL PERF leave.INF
        (*'Aled said that himself had left.')

A pronominal such as *o* 'he' in the embedded clause in (40a) can be bound by a nominal element in the matrix clause, or can be free. The anaphor *ei hun* 'himself' in (40b) cannot be bound by a nominal element in the matrix clause, and has no antecedent in its own clause, so the sentence is ungrammatical. The *bod*-clause is therefore the binding domain for the subject nominals.

Seventh, since they are finite, *bod*-clauses cannot be sentential subjects: only non-finite clauses can form sentential subjects in Welsh. Thus, (41) illustrates a grammatical clausal subject with a non-finite verb:

(41)   Mae   [**dod**   yn   rhiant]   yn   anodd.
        be.PRES.3S come.INF PRED parent   PRED difficult
        'Becoming a parent is difficult.'

Finite *bod*-clauses have an overt lexical or pronominal subject (including *pro*). Conversely, non-finite *bod* constituents never have an overt subject: in other words, within a Principles & Parameters approach, these would be infinitival clauses containing the null subject PRO. Example (42) illustrates such a constituent with non-finite *bod* as a clausal subject:

(42)   Mae   [**bod**   yn   hoff o win] yn   arwydd o chwaeth.
        be.PRES.3S be.INF PRED fond of wine PRED sign of taste
        'To be fond of wine is a sign of taste.' (B. M. Jones 1993: 30)

In contrast, finite clauses, including ordinary tensed clauses and finite *bod*-clauses, are ungrammatical in this position (data from Tallerman 1998: 96):[5]

(43)   *Mae   [**bydd**   Aled/*pro* yn   dod]   yn   bosib.
        be.PRES.3S be.FUT.3S Aled   PROG come.INF PRED possible
        ('That Aled/(s)he will be coming is possible.')

---

[5] The grammatical alternative involves extraposition of the clause:

(i)   Mae   'n   amlwg   [**bod**   Aled yn   athro].
       be.PRES.3S PRED obvious be.INF Aled PRED teacher
       'It's obvious that Aled is a teacher.'

(44)   *Mae   [**bod**   Aled yn   athro]   yn   amlwg.
        be.PRES.3s be.INF Aled PRED teacher PRED obvious
        ('That Aled is a teacher is obvious.')

The fact that the *bod*-clause in (44) cannot occur here indicates that it is indeed finite.

Eighth, as seen in section 2.6.2, expletive *yna* 'there' only appears in finite clauses, so the fact that it can occur in *bod*-clauses provides more evidence that these are finite:

(45)   Mae   Gwyn yn   meddwl [bod   **yna** ddafad yn yr ardd].
        be.PRES.3s Gwyn PROG think.INF be.INF there sheep.s in the garden
        'Gwyn thinks that there is a sheep in the garden.'

We conclude, then, that clauses containing infinitival *bod* with an overt subject or *pro* are indeed finite, despite the lack of a tensed element in the clause. *Bod*-clauses thus form our first example of pseudo-non-finite clauses.

3.4   Infinitival *i*-clauses with overt subjects

In sections 3.4.1 and 3.4.2 we examine two more dependent clause types with overt (or null pronominal) subjects. Examples (46) and (47) illustrate:

(46)   Meddyliodd   Aled [i Mair fynd   adre'].
        think.PAST.3s Aled   to Mair go.INF home
        'Aled thought that Mair had gone home.'

(47)   Dymunai   Aled [i Mair fynd   adre'].
        wish.COND.3s Aled   to Mair go.INF home
        'Aled would want Mair to go home.'

Superficially, both are very similar, in that both are introduced by an element *i*, homophonous with the preposition *i* 'to'. This is followed by the subject and then the lexical verb, which appears in its non-finite form, and finally, any complements to the verb. Schematically, infinitival *i*-clauses are as shown in (48):

(48)   [i Subject [Verb(non-finite) Object/other complements Adjuncts]]

While the verb and its complements and adjuncts form a constituent, the subject forms a separate constituent from the *i* element; see section 3.6.2. Note that unlike *bod*-clauses, in which the subject follows infinitival *bod* – see (30) – the subject of an *i*-clause *precedes* the infinitival verb form. Nonetheless, *bod*-clauses and *i*-clauses are actually very similar, since in both clause types, the pre-subject element inflects to agree with a pronominal subject, while the lexical verb lower down in the clause is non-finite. This is also true of finite AuxSVO clauses such as (1) and (2). We return to this point in section 3.6.4.

The clause structure sketched in (48) in fact relates to two syntactically distinct clause types. The type of *i*-clause in (46) is finite, as section 3.4.1 shows, while that in (47) is clearly non-finite, as we see in section 3.4.2.

3.4.1   Finite i-*clauses*

Section 3.3 showed that there are restrictions on complement clauses which contain a form of *bod*, 'be'. Morphologically tensed forms of *bod* are generally only permissible in embedded clauses if they come from the future, preterite (*bu* etc.) or conditional paradigm. In this section we outline a further restriction in embedded clauses.

This second restriction also occurs in the complements to verbs such as *meddwl*, 'think', *dweud*, 'say' and *gwbod* (literary form *gwybod*), 'know', i.e. the epistemic and declarative predicates. We saw in (25) and (26) that such predicates take ordinary complement clauses containing a synthetic verb if this verb is in the future tense, or in the conditional. However, the dependent clause cannot freely contain the *past* tense of a lexical verb. As the '%' sign in these examples indicates, some speakers do permit this, but in a number of spoken varieties, as well as in literary Welsh, the past tense is ungrammatical:

(49)   %Meddyliodd Aled [aeth   Mair adre'].
        think.PAST.3S Aled go.PAST.3S Mair home
        'Aled thought that Mair had gone home.'   (Tallerman 1998: 72)

(50)   %Dw   i 'n gwbod [**gwelodd**   Siôn y gêm].
        be.PRES.1S I PROG know.INF see.PAST.3S Siôn the game
        'I know that Siôn saw the game.'   (B. M. Jones 1993: 44)

What replaces a dependent clause containing a finite verb is an infinitival clause introduced by a functional element *i* (literally 'to, for'), which is followed by the subject and the verbal infinitive (and any dependents to the verb). The alternative to the past tense in the embedded clause in (49) would be (51), which is grammatical in all spoken and literary varieties:

(51)   Meddyliodd Aled [i Mair **fynd**   adre'].
        think.PAST.3S Aled to Mair go.INF home
        'Aled thought that Mair had gone home.'

An *i*-clause complement to epistemic and declarative predicates is always interpreted as tensed. Strictly speaking, its tense is anterior to that in the main clause, since the time frame of the *i*-clause is established with reference to the tense of the matrix verb, as the translations of (51) versus (53) illustrate.

The *i*-clause also regularly occurs as a complement to various nouns and adjectives:

(52)   Roedd   y   ffaith [i   Mair adael]   yn   ofnadwy.
        be.IMPF.3s the fact   to Mair leave.INF PRED awful
        'The fact that Mair had left was awful.'

(53)   Mae   Aled yn   sicr   [i   Mair fynd].
        be.PRES.3s Aled PRED certain to Mair go.INF
        'Aled is certain that Mair has gone.'

As in the case of the *bod*-clauses in section 3.3, there is clear evidence that *i*-clauses of the type illustrated in (51) to (53) are syntactically finite, despite the lack of a tensed element. The arguments here are based on Sadler (1988), Harlow (1992) and Tallerman (1998).

First, the distribution is again significant: *i*-clauses complete the set of ordinary tensed clausal complements, and they have the same interpretation as an ordinary independent tensed clause.

Second, these finite *i*-clauses coordinate freely with ordinary tensed clauses:

(54)   Meddyliodd Aled [i   Alys fynd   adre'] a   [byddai   Mair yn
        think.PAST.3s Aled to Alys go.INF home and be.COND.3s Mair PROG
        mynd hefyd].
        go.INF too
        'Aled thought that Alys had gone home and that Mair would be going too.'

Here, the second conjunct contains a synthetic form of *bod* with a conditional inflection, and the first conjunct is an *i*-clause interpreted as finite. As Harlow (1992: 104) points out, such examples contrast notably with the coordination of an infinitival clause and a finite clause in English, which is at best degraded:

(55)   ??John believes [Bill to be intelligent] and [that he will be successful].

Third, anaphora in these *i*-clauses is parallel to that found in more typical finite clauses containing a synthetic verb. A pronominal subject can be bound by a nominal element in the matrix clause, or can be free, whilst a subject anaphor cannot be bound by a nominal element in the matrix clause (data from Tallerman 1998: 90):[6]

---

[6] (56) and (57) show that the element *i* inflects to agree with a pronominal subject. We return to this property in due course. The form *'i hun* in (57) is a contraction of the reflexive form *ei hun* (here, third person masculine singular).

(56)   Dywedodd Aled$_i$ [iddo   fo$_{i/j}$ fynd].
         say.PAST.3S Aled   to.3MS he go.INF
         'Aled said that he'd gone.'

(57)   *Dywedodd Aled [iddo   '-i   hun   fynd].
         say.PAST.3S Aled   to.3MS 3MS REFL go.INF
         (*'Aled said that himself had gone.')

This indicates that the lower clause constitutes the binding domain for the subject of that clause, just as in ordinary tensed clauses.

Fourth, negation facts again demonstrate that these *i*-clauses are finite. Non-finite clauses are negated using the negative element *peidio (â)* (see section 8.2.4), as shown in the embedded infinitival clause in (58):

(58)   Mae   hi eisiau [**peidio** â   mynd].
         be.PRES.3S she want(n.) NEG with go.INF
         'She wants not to go.'

But the *i*-clauses which are complements to matrix epistemic and declarative predicates cannot be negated using *peidio*, as (59) shows:[7]

(59)   *Dywedodd Aled [i Elen **beidio** â   darllen y llyfr].
         say.PAST.3S Aled to Elen NEG with read.INF the book
         ('Aled said that Elen did not read the book.')   (Tallerman 1998: 91)

The grammatical alternative in fact provides the fifth piece of evidence that this type of *i*-clause is finite: *i* + infinitive is replaced by an ordinary VSO clause with a tensed finite verb, as in (60); see section 8.2.3 for a discussion of the negative element *mo*:

(60)   Dywedodd Aled [**ddarllenodd**   Elen mo 'r llyfr].
         say.PAST.3S Aled NEG.read.PAST.3S Elen NEG the book
         'Aled said that Elen did not read the book.'

It seems relatively uncontroversial, then, that here we have a second type of pseudo-non-finite clause: the *i*-clause infinitival complements illustrated in this section are actually syntactically finite. Despite containing no tensed verbal elements, they are also semantically finite. *I*-clauses of this type – along with *bod*-clauses – occur as complements to a specific set of matrix predicates, namely the epistemic and declarative set, which in all other contexts select an ordinary finite complement clause containing a tensed verb.

However, an additional complication which we have already noted is that a second type of *i*-clause exists which is syntactically *non-finite*. Our discussion turns next to these, showing that other classes of matrix predicates

---

[7] *Peidio* mutates to *beidio* following the subject of the matrix clause; see chapter 7 for more details of syntactic soft mutation.

also subcategorize *i*-clausal complements containing overt subjects, but that these behave very differently from the finite *i*-clauses seen in the present section.

3.4.2   Non-finite i-*clauses*

We saw in section 3.4.1 that for many speakers, the synthetic past tense clausal complements to epistemic and declarative predicates are replaced by an infinitival *i*-clause, which is interpreted as finite. The infinitival clauses in the current section have contrasting properties to those in the previous section; see also Sadler (1988: section 1.5), Tallerman (1998). First, these clauses form the complements to a distinct set of matrix predicates. These are predicates of expectation and volition, such as *dymuno*, 'wish/want'; *mynnu*, 'wish, insist'; *hiraethu am*, 'long for'; *disgwyl*, 'expect'; *hoffi, licio/leicio*, 'like'; and *ofni*, 'fear'; see Jones & Thomas (1977: 239).

The second difference between this type of *i*-clause and those in section 3.4.1 concerns the interpretation of the complement clause. Here, there is no anterior tense interpretation, as (61) and (62) make clear. Instead, the *i*-clause is interpreted in a very similar way to the English translation – as an infinitival clause with future time reference, often with a modal interpretation (data from Tallerman 1998: 73):[8]

(61)   Dymunai   Aled [i   Mair fynd   adre'].
        wish.COND.3s Aled   to Mair go.INF home
        'Aled would want Mair to go home.'
        i.e. *not* 'Aled would wish that Mair had gone home.'

(62)   Disgwyliodd   Aled [i   Elen ddarllen y   llyfr].
        expect.PAST.3s Aled   to Elen read.INF the book
        'Aled expected Elen to read the book.'
        i.e. *not* 'Aled expected that Elen had read the book.'

Note, moreover, that the *i*-clausal complements to the expectation-and-volition class of predicates do *not* complete a normal finite set of complement clauses –

---

[8] Note that the matrix predicates discussed in section 3.4 are typically members of the class of ECM (exceptional case marking) predicates in English, which contains verbs such as *believe, think, expect, want* and so on; the translation of (62) illustrates. In Welsh, the ECM construction appears only in what are sometimes considered to be small clauses, as in (i), which are discussed briefly in section 8.3.1:

(i)   Maen   nhw 'n   galw   Gwyn yn   ffŵl.
      be.PRES.3P they PROG call.INF Gwyn PRED fool
      'They call Gwyn a fool.'

in contrast to the situation outlined in section 3.4.1. This is further indication that these *i*-clauses are non-finite.

Non-finite *i*-clauses also occur as the complements to various nouns and adjectives:

(63)   Byddai   'n   drueni [i ti   werthu 'r   car].
         be.COND.3S PRED pity   to you sell.INF the car
         'It would be a pity for you to sell the car.'

(64)   Mae   Aled yn   awyddus [i Rhys fynd].
         be.PRES.3S Aled PRED keen   to Rhys go.INF
         'Aled is keen for Rhys to go.'

Although *bod*-clauses (section 3.3) also occur as complements to the predicates in this section, they do not generally occur as freely; some speakers find them rather marginal. And morphologically tensed clausal complements to these predicates are limited, in that they can contain verbs in the future tense or the conditional only, and not the past tense.

A third distinction between the finite and non-finite types of *i*-clauses is that those in (61) and (62) do *not* coordinate freely with ordinary tensed clauses; this contrasts with the situation shown in (54), with a finite *i*-clause. Sadler (1988: 40) points out that examples like (65) are 'at best marginal, and fully ungrammatical for some speakers':

(65)   ??Disgwyliodd Emrys   [i   Mair fynd   i Gaerdydd] ac
         expect.PAST.3S Emrys   to   Mair go.INF to Cardiff   and
         [y byddai   Siôn yn   mynd i Abertawe].
         PRT be.COND.3S Siôn PROG go.INF to Swansea
         ??'Emrys expected Mair to go to Cardiff and that Siôn would be going to
         Swansea.'

The coordination in (65) is degraded, exactly parallel to the English example in (55): a true non-finite clause essentially cannot be coordinated with a finite clause.

Fourth, in terms of anaphora, these *i*-clauses have the properties of normal *non-finite* clauses: a pronominal subject cannot be bound by a nominal element in the matrix clause, but must be disjoint in reference, as shown in (66), whereas an anaphor such as *ei hun*, 'himself', *can* be bound by a nominal element in the matrix clause, as shown in (67) (data from Tallerman 1998: 92):

(66)   Dymunai   Aled$_i$ [iddo   **fo$_j$/*fo$_i$** fynd].
         wish.COND.3S Aled   to.3MS he   go.INF
         'Aled would want him to go.'

(67)   Dymunai   Aled [iddo   '-i   **hun**   ddarllen y   llyfr].
        wish.COND.3s Aled   to.3MS   3MS   REFL   read.INF the book
        'Aled would want himself to read the book.'

The binding domain for the subject of the lower clause must therefore be the main clause. These data contrast clearly with the finite *i*-clauses seen in (56) and (57).

Fifth, negation operates differently in the finite and the non-finite *i*-clauses (Sadler 1988: 41). The complements to verbs such as *disgwyl* 'expect' and *dymuno* 'want/wish' can be negated with the usual negator of non-finite verbs, *peidio*, here in its soft mutation form, *beidio* (see section 7.1 regarding the trigger for such mutation):[9]

(68)   Disgwyliodd   Aled [i   Elen **beidio** â   darllen y   llyfr].
        expect.PAST.3s Aled   to   Elen NEG   with read.INF the book
        'Aled expected Elen not to read the book.'

It seems clear, then, that we have two types of *i*-clauses with overt subjects. Those seen in section 3.4.1 are genuinely syntactically finite, while those in the present section are genuinely non-finite. The syntactic behaviour of each set contrasts in all respects, and the interpretation is different in each case. A reasonable assumption is that the differences are brought about by distinct properties of the matrix predicates which select each type of *i*-clause. We return to this in section 3.6.4.

One question which we have not yet addressed concerns the status of *i* itself in the infinitival clauses seen in this section. In order to deal with this, we first need to consider the distribution of *i* in subjectless infinitivals. Section 3.5 discusses one variety of these, namely the infinitival complements to control predicates.

3.5   Control predicates

In this section we examine controlled infinitival complements, some of which are also introduced by a functional *i* element. However, there is good evidence that this is not the same morpheme as the *i* found in either type of *i*-clause (sections 3.4.1 and 3.4.2). An initial indication of this comes

---

[9] A tensed negative complement clause is a possible alternative:

(i)   Disgwyliodd   Aled [**na   fyddai**   Elen yn   darllen y   llyfr].
       expect.PAST.3s Aled   NEG   be.COND.3s Elen PROG read.INF the book
       'Aled expected that Elen would not read the book.'

from the significant lexical variation in the way subjectless infinitivals are introduced.

Looking first at subject control verbs, we find that some select a bare infinitival complement, while others select a complement introduced by *i*. For instance, recall from section 3.4.2 that verbs in the *dymuno* 'wish' and *disgwyl* 'expect' class select *i*-clausal complements. These same verbs are also optional control predicates, but it is noteworthy that in the control usage, there is no *i* before the non-finite verb in the embedded clause:

(69)   Dymunai   nifer   dda [(*i) ymfudo   i'r   Unol Daleithiau].
        wish.COND.3s number good   to emigrate.INF to.the united states
        'A good number would wish to emigrate to the United States.'

There are also many other subject control predicates, such as *bwriadu* 'intend', *penderfynu* 'decide', *cofio* 'remember', *addo* 'promise', *gobeithio* 'hope', *ceisio* 'try' and *trafferthu* 'be bothered', all of which take a bare infinitival complement with no *i*; (70) illustrates:

(70)   Maen   nhw wedi penderfynu [mynd yn   gynnar].
        be.PRES.3P they PERF decide.INF   go.INF PRED early
        'They have decided to go early.'

A minority of subject control verbs take complements which do contain *i*, such as *cytuno* or *bodloni* 'agree', *ymdrechu* 'endeavour', *llwyddo* 'succeed', *ymegnïo* 'strive' and *ymroi* 'devote oneself':

(71)   Mae   'r ysgol yn   llwyddo   [i gael   canlyniadau da].
        be.PRES.3s the school PROG succeed.INF to get.INF results   good
        'The school succeeds in getting good results.'

A rough generalization seems to be that if the predicate has a transitive form, then in its control usage it takes no *i*; if the predicate has no transitive form, then as a control verb, it does take *i*. Note, for example, that *gobeithio*, 'hope', which takes no *i*, can take a direct object in Welsh: *gobeithio'r gorau* (lit. 'hope the best' = 'hope for the best'). However, there is also a considerable amount of idiolectal variation as to whether or not *i* occurs at the start of the infinitival clause following a control predicate.

Turning next to the class of subject control adjectives, we find that these display further lexical variation in the complement clause. Many select infinitival complements introduced by *i* (e.g. *awyddus* 'keen', *galluog* 'able', *parod* 'willing, ready, prepared', *hapus* 'happy'); others select complements introduced by *o*, homophonous with the preposition meaning 'of' (e.g. *balch* 'glad', *hoff* 'fond', *penderfynol* 'determined', *euog* 'guilty'); and yet others select bare infinitivals, for instance *bodlon* 'willing, happy', *braf* 'nice', *pwysig* 'important', *peryglus* 'dangerous' and *da* 'good':

(72)   Mae   Garan yn   barod [i ddechrau ar unwaith].
       be.PRES.3S Garan PRED ready to begin.INF at once
       'Garan is ready to start at once.'

(73)   Dw   i 'n   benderfynol [o ddarllen y   llyfr 'na].
       be.PRES.1S I PRED determined of read.INF the book there
       'I'm determined to read that book.'

(74)   Byddai   'n   dda [cael   ei   farn].
       be.COND.3S PRED good get.INF 3MS opinion
       'It would be good to get his opinion.'

Once again, there is considerable idiolectal variation; for example, Jones &
Thomas point out (1977: 241) that *bodlon*, 'willing', can also take an infinitival
clause introduced by *i*. Web searches also clearly reveal much speaker variation regarding complements to adjectives, specifically over whether or not *i* is
needed in the infinitival clause.

Nouns also occur with subjectless infinitival complements, with the same
type of variation in how the embedded clause is introduced. Most take a
clausal complement with *i*; for instance *addewid* 'promise', *cytundeb* 'agreement', *penderfyniad* 'decision' and *gallu* 'ability':

(75)   Roedd   y cytundeb [i werthu 'r cwmni] 'n   rhyfedd.
       be.IMPF.3S the agreement to sell.INF the company PRED strange
       'The agreement to sell the company was surprising.'

Some nouns, often as an alternative, take an *o*-clausal complement, such as
siawns 'chance', *posibilrwydd* 'possibility', *tebygrwydd* 'likelihood, probability'
and *profiad* 'experience'. An *o*-clause in these contexts is generally the equivalent of an English participial -*ing* clause:

(76)   Mae   hwn yn   lleihau   eich tebygrwydd [o ddatblygu
       be.PRES.3S this PROG reduce.INF 2P   likelihood   of develop.INF
       canser].
       cancer
       'This reduces your likelihood of developing cancer.'

A few nouns select a bare infinitival complement:[10]

(77)   Roedd   Mair eisiau   [cael   swydd newydd].
       be.IMPF.3S Mair want(n.) get.INF job   new
       'Mair wanted to get a new job.'

Looking next at object control verbs, the majority select infinitival clauses
which include *i*, as shown for *calonogi* 'encourage' in (78):

[10] Despite the English translation, *eisiau* (colloquial Welsh *isio*), 'want', in (58) and
   (77) is in fact probably best regarded as a noun: see note 13 in chapter 1 and also
   section 2.6.3.

(78)   Maen   nhw 'n   calonogi   grwpiau [i   wneud   cais].
        be.PRES.3P they PROG encourage.INF groups   to make.INF application
        'They encourage groups to make an application.'

Other object control verbs selecting *i* in the infinitival clause include *argyhoeddi* 'convince', *perswadio* 'persuade', *cynghori* 'advise', *dysgu* 'teach', *cefnogi* 'encourage, support' and *cymell* 'urge'. A few object control verbs, such as *gofyn* 'ask', *caniatáu* 'allow' and *gwarafun* 'forbid' select an *i*-noun phrase complement in the matrix clause but no *i* in the infinitival clause (see Tallerman 1998: 88):[11]

(79)   Maen   nhw wedi gofyn   i 'r   ymgeiswyr [(*i) ddod   i mewn].
        be.PRES.3P they PERF ask.INF to the applicants   to come.INF in
        'They have asked the applicants to come in.'

As usual, however, there is speaker variation in these cases, and some speakers use *i* at the start of the infinitival clause, as well as having what we might call a dative *i*-phrase in the matrix clause: see also section 8.3.2.2.

In sum, there is considerable variation in the way control infinitival complements are introduced: some are simply bare infinitivals, while others contain an *i* element, and others still, an *o* element. The choice is largely lexically determined, with a certain amount of idiolectal variation occurring. With these facts in mind, section 3.6 considers the status and syntactic behaviour of *i* and other functional elements introducing infinitival complements.

3.6   The syntax of *i* in infinitival complements

3.6.1   *An apparent paradox in the distribution of* i

A major issue for generative analyses of Welsh infinitival complements has been how to account for the distribution of *i*. The ostensible paradox for a Principles & Parameters approach was first noted by Borsley (1986). As presented at the time, the issue was that what appeared to be a *single* element *i* precedes not only overt subjects in the infinitival *i*-clauses (sections

---

[11] We can tell that the *i*-noun phrase is in the matrix clause from examples like (i), where the same predicate selects a (finite) *wh*-clause: the *i*-phrase is above the start of the embedded question:

(i)   Rhaid   gofyn   **iddyn nhw** [pa   oriau maen   nhw 'n
        necessity ask.INF to.3P them   which hours be.PRES.3P they PRED
        barod   i weithio].
        prepared to work.INF
        'We must ask them what hours they are prepared to work.'

3.4.1 and 3.4.2) but also the empty category subject PRO, in the infinitival complements to the control predicates illustrated in section 3.5. If *i* is associated with Case-licensing, such a distribution is problematic. A general assumption was that *i* assigned abstract Case under government to the lexical and pronominal subjects of infinitival *i*-clauses – in other words, it was regarded as parallel to *for* in English examples such as [*For Kim to be absent*] *would be odd*. But the paradox is that *i* also precedes PRO, which, under then standard assumptions, was an ungoverned and Caseless element.

In terms of more recent work on PRO within a Principles & Parameters framework, Borsley's paradox can be expressed somewhat differently. PRO is typically considered to have null abstract Case, rather than no Case at all (Sigurðsson 1991, Chomsky & Lasnik 1993, Vanden Wyngaerd 1994, Martin 2001), and the government relationship itself is eliminated in more recent work. Nonetheless, PRO and lexical/pronominal subjects crucially do not have the same distribution. In Welsh, the two subject types are certainly not interchangeable in all other positions, yet both apparently occur following an element *i* in infinitival complements.

However, Tallerman (1998) demonstrates that there is in fact no paradox, once the syntactic distinctions in the various classes of infinitival complements are properly taken into account. What appears to be a single *i* element should actually be considered as two lexically and syntactically distinct items. In *i*-clauses (section 3.4), *i* is an element generated in the T head. But in subjectless infinitivals of all types, *i* is a complementizer: this is true of control clauses, section 3.5, as well as raising complements, section 3.7. As we show in section 3.6.3, each *i* element has different syntactic properties. Before that, we establish that *i* is not merely an ordinary preposition.

3.6.2   Evidence that functional i is not a preposition

So far, we have shown that *i* occurs in three different clause types: in sections 3.4.1 and 3.4.2 we saw that it occurs in *i*-clauses (both the finite type and the non-finite type), preceding a lexical/pronominal subject, and in section 3.5, we showed that *i* also occurs in (some, though not all) control infinitival clauses. Section 3.7 illustrates the use of *i* in the complements to raising predicates. As noted earlier, there is considerable evidence that the *i* found in *i*-clauses is not the same morpheme as the *i* which introduces some infinitival complements to control and raising predicates.

Is it possible that the *i* found in infinitival complements might be an ordinary preposition? There are two similarities between the preposition *i* and the *i* in infinitival *i*-clauses: both trigger soft mutation, and both have an inflectional paradigm. However, while the preposition inflects to agree with its pronominal *object*, infinitival *i* inflects to agree with the (c)overt pronominal *subject* of the infinitival clause: see, for example, (56), (66) and (67) above.

Furthermore, the preposition forms a constituent with its object, but what we can call INFLECTIONAL *i* (i.e. the element found in *i*-clauses, section 3.4) does not form a constituent with the subject, as shown by Borsley (1986: 76), Hendrick (1988: 181) and Sadler (1988: 38). So for instance, though pied-piping of preposition *i* plus its object is very common, the inflectional *i*-plus-subject sequence, in contrast, cannot undergo pied-piping in *wh*-questions (compare (62) above):

(80)   *I **bwy** disgwyliodd   Aled ddarllen y   llyfr?
         to who expect.PAST.3S Aled read.INF the book
         ('Who did Aled expect to read the book?')

Note that the sequence *i bwy* 'to whom' is itself not ill-formed, and indeed often occurs with the preposition *i*. It seems, then, that we can dismiss the idea that inflectional *i* might be a preposition, at least in clauses with an overt subject. The fact that *i* does not form a constituent with the subject also indicates that it is unlikely to be simply a dummy Case marker; see Rouveret (1990: 60, 1994: 281).

What, though, of *i* in control clauses (section 3.5)? The idea that this *i* might be a preposition is briefly mentioned by Rouveret (1994: 292, note 49). If true, this would be one way of resolving Borsley's paradox, since it would distinguish between control *i* and inflectional *i* (section 3.4): the former would be P and would select a CP complement, while the latter could be analysed as C, selecting a TP complement. The fact that each has different Case assignment properties could then fall out from their distinct syntactic status. There are, indeed, prepositional verbs whose P takes a CP complement, for instance a *wh*-clause:

(81)   Maen   nhw 'n   meddwl   **am**   [beth i'w   wneud yn y
         be.PRES.3P they PROG think.INF about what to.3MS do.INF in the
         dyfodol].
         future
         'They're thinking about what to do in the future.'

But subject control verbs which select *i* cannot take this construction (Tallerman 1998: 83):

(82)   *Gwnaethon nhw gytuno   **i** [beth i'w   ddarllen].
         do.PAST.3P   they agree.INF to what to.3MS read.INF
         ('They agreed what to read.')

The grammatical alternative uses the true preposition *ar*, 'on', which does take a CP complement:

(83)   Gwnaethon nhw gytuno **ar** [beth i'w   ddarllen].
        do.PAST.3P   they agree.INF on   what to.3MS read.INF
        'They agreed on what to read.'

This shows that control *i* does not behave like a true preposition with a CP complement.

A second indication that control *i* is not a preposition comes from the following set of data. First we have an optional control verb, *hiraethu am* 'long for'; as in (81), *am* 'for' can be regarded as a preposition taking a CP complement in (84):

(84)   Hiraethai   Wyn [**am** ddychwelyd].
        long.COND.3s Wyn for return.INF
        'Wyn longed to return.'

Alternatively, the verb may select an *i*-clause complement with an overt subject, in which case the *am* of the prepositional verb in the matrix clause is retained (Awbery 1976: 127):

(85)   Hiraethai   Wyn **am** [**i** Ann ddychwelyd].
        long.COND.3s Wyn for to Ann return.INF
        'Wyn longed for Ann to return.'

Thus, we have both the preposition *am* and the functional element *i*. Compare what happens with a predicate that selects *i* in its control usage, (86), but can also select an *i*-clause with an overt subject, as in (87). Here we find that control *i* cannot co-occur with inflectional *i*, as (87) shows:

(86)   Mae   Aled yn   awyddus **i** fynd.
        be.PRES.3s Aled PRED keen   to go.INF
        'Aled is keen to go.'

(87)   Mae   Aled yn   awyddus (***i**) [**i** Rhys fynd].
        be.PRES.3s Aled PRED keen   to to Rhys go.INF
        'Aled is keen for Rhys to go.'   (cf. (64))

So a true preposition can co-occur with inflectional *i*, as in (85), but control *i* cannot – which indicates that it is not a preposition at all.

In sum, we have shown that neither control *i* nor the inflectional *i* found in *i*-clauses is a preposition. The other two major possibilities are that *i* is a complementizer, or that it is a functional head lower down within the clause, such as I, or one of the heads replacing a unitary I, such as T. Both of these possibilities have been proposed in earlier work: see, for instance, Sadler (1988: 38), Rouveret (1990, 1994) and Harlow (1992). Typically, though, it is assumed in this earlier work that *all* instances of *i* are categorially identical, so that *i* in *i*-clauses with lexical and pronominal subjects is the same entity as *i* in the subjectless complements to control and raising predicates.

Conversely, as noted above, Tallerman (1998) argues that all instances of *i* are *not* the same: *i* in control and raising infinitival clauses is a complementizer, while inflectional *i* (section 3.4) is a lower functional head within the clause. Section 3.6.3 examines the evidence for such a distinction.

3.6.3   Two distinct i elements in infinitival clauses: complementizer i versus inflectional i

Here we consider four arguments for distinguishing COMPLEMENTIZER *i*, found in certain raising and control complements, from INFLECTIONAL *i*, an element in T in clauses with overt (or null pronominal) subjects, as seen in section 3.4. Tallerman (1998) provides additional evidence.

First, consider the variation displayed by control predicates in lexical choice of complementizer (section 3.5). Subject control verbs either select *i* (e.g. *cytuno* 'agree', *llwyddo* 'succeed') or what is arguably a null complementizer, Ø (e.g. *addo* 'promise', *gobeithio* 'hope'); object control verbs normally take *i* (e.g. *perswadio* 'persuade', *calonogi* 'encourage'), but some take Ø (e.g. *gofyn* 'ask', *gwarafun* 'forbid'), and there is also some idiolectal variation. Control adjectives select one of three complementizers, *i*, *o*, or Ø, again with idiolectal and also lexical variation; and control nouns also select from the same set of complementizers, *i*, *o*, or Ø. Amongst raising predicates, there is again lexical selection amongst *i*, *o*, and Ø (see section 3.7 below).

Now compare inflectional *i*. Here, there is no lexical or idiolectal variation. The *i* morpheme is simply obligatory in all the pre-subject contexts shown in section 3.4, even if the subject itself is the null pronominal, *pro*. The variation seen in the control contexts is typical of a complementizer – compare the use of *that* in English – while the stable distribution of inflectional *i* is quite distinct.

Second, none of the three complementizers *i*, *o*, or Ø licenses an overt subject in the clause it selects, and none of them inflects to agree with a pronominal subject in that clause. We illustrate with the adjective *balch*, 'pleased, glad'. This can occur in a control context, (88), in which case it selects complementizer *o*. The same adjective can select a non-finite inflectional *i*-clause, as in (89): compare the behaviour of complementizer *o* in (88) and (90) with inflectional *i* in (89). Complementizer *o* does not license an overt subject, as (90) shows – and this is despite the fact that *o* does have an inflectional paradigm, so might be expected to behave like *i* in terms of Case-licensing:

(88)   Mae   Aled yn   falch   o weld   Mair.
        be.PRES.3s Aled PRED pleased of see.INF Mair
        'Aled is pleased to see Mair.'

(89)   Mae   Aled yn falch **i Gwyn/ iddo** weld Mair.
be.PRES.3S Aled PRED pleased to Gwyn/ to.3MS see.INF Mair
'Aled is pleased for Gwyn/for him to see Mair.'

(90)   *Mae   Aled yn falch **o Gwyn/ ohono** weld Mair.
be.PRES.3S Aled PRED pleased to Gwyn/ of.3MS see.INF Mair
('Aled is pleased for Gwyn/for him to see Mair.')

If both inflectional i and o were in the same position (e.g. both complementizers), why would only i license an overt subject? Why can o not inflect here? Note that the finiteness of the embedded clause is not a possible factor, since in each case, this clause is non-finite.

In fact, no complementizers in contemporary Welsh inflect, so it is entirely predictable that, as complementizers, i and o do not inflect either. A possible explanation for this within a Principles & Parameters framework is that the subject with which they would potentially agree is lower down in the clause, and the complementizer has no structural relationship with it. In order to agree with a complementizer, the subject would need to be sited in the specifier position of a structural complement to C. But in a verb-initial language, subjects are unlikely to be sited so high in the clause. The lack of inflection on complementizers can also be explained in terms of a generalization concerning agreement proposed in section 6.3. It is shown there that a head inflects to agree with an immediately following pronominal element, i.e. an overt pronoun or *pro*. Since no pronominal follows the complementizers i or o, they do not inflect.

The very fact that the complementizer i does not inflect provides a third piece of evidence to distinguish it from inflectional i. The adjective *awyddus* 'keen' selects complementizer i in its control usage, (91), but *awyddus* can also take an inflectional i-clause, as in (92) (see also (64)), in which case i inflects to agree with the following subject:

(91)   Mae   Aled$_i$ yn awyddus [$_C$ **i**] PRO$_i$ fynd.
be.PRES.3S Aled PRED keen   to   go.INF
'Aled is keen to go.'

(92)   Mae   Aled$_i$ yn awyddus [$_{Agr-S}$ **iddo**] *pro$_j$*/**pro*$_i$ fynd.
be.PRES.3S Aled PRED keen   to.3MS   go.INF
'Aled$_i$ is keen for him$_j$/*him$_i$ to go.'

Inflectional i in (92) agrees with the null subject *pro*, as shown, or alternatively an overt third person singular pronominal subject, *fo*, could be used, giving *iddo fo fynd*. Note that there is also a contrast in the possibilities for anaphoric reference between (91) and (92). In (92), the embedded pronominal subject – either overt or null – is disjoint in reference from the matrix subject. On the other hand, the embedded subject PRO in (91) is co-referential with the matrix subject. The binding facts are thus parallel to those of the English translations.

Under then-current assumptions, Tallerman (1998) analysed inflectional *i* as being generated in T, and raising to Agr-S, the head of a subject agreement projection, as indicated in (92).[12] Tallerman proposed that the abstract Case of subjects is checked in the Spec, Agr-S position; subjects raise covertly, at LF, to check Case under the spec/head relation. Crucially, unless the subject is PRO, the Agr-S head must contain overt material: the proposal is that non-null Case must be checked in the specifier of a lexically-supported Agr-S. A number of distinct elements can lexically support Agr-S by raising to that position: finite verbs and auxiliaries, the infinitive *bod* in *bod*-clauses, and both types of inflectional *i* in *i*-clauses. In all of these clause types, an overt (or covert pronominal) subject is licensed. These are also the only clauses containing heads which display agreement with a pronominal subject; see sections 6.1 and 6.3 below.

The null Case associated with PRO, on the other hand, can only be checked by Agr-S which is *not* lexically supported: in controlled infinitival clauses such as (91), no element raises to the Agr-S head, and no agreement is displayed.

Inflectional *i* – but not complementizer *i* (or *o*) – decides the finiteness of the clause it occurs in, and, as we saw in section 3.4, is associated with either an anterior or a non-finite interpretation (3.4.1 versus 3.4.2). This is unsurprising if inflectional *i* is generated in T. Complementizers in Welsh, on the other hand, do not affect the tense or finiteness of the clause they select; for instance, the main clause complementizers *mi/fe* (see section 2.1.2) co-occur with any of the three synthetic verbal paradigms, future, past or conditional (section 1.4.3).[13] Here, then, we have a fourth piece of evidence for distinguishing complementizers from inflectional *i*.

We conclude that whereas control (and raising) predicates select one of three complementizers, *i, o,* or Ø, the inflectional *i* in *i*-clauses is a distinct element, which we have proposed to be in T. (See also Tallerman (1997) on infinitival clauses in Breton.) The next section turns to the nature of finiteness in Welsh.

---

[12] In more recent work within a Principles & Parameters or Minimalist framework, Agr projections have generally been eliminated (though see Roberts 2005). The analysis proposed by Tallerman (1998) relies crucially on an Agr-S projection, but this could be updated in various ways. For instance, one possibility would be to utilize a split-CP analysis (cf. Rizzi 1997), with complementizer *i* perhaps in the Force head position, and finite verbs, *bod* in *bod*-clauses, and inflectional *i* all in the lower Fin head position. This would also account for the fact that all these elements are associated with finiteness; see section 3.6.4 below.

[13] There are some dialectal restrictions on the co-occurrence of *mi* and *fe* with certain forms of *bod* 'be'; see section 2.1.2 for details.

3.6.4   Finiteness and clause structure

In early generative accounts, it was often suggested that word order in Welsh (and other Celtic languages) varies according to the finiteness of the clause, with finite clauses having VSO word order and infinitival clauses having SVO word order; see, for instance, Sproat (1985), Stephens (1990) and Harlow (1992: 105). However, we have seen in section 3.4 that 'infinitival' does not correlate with 'non-finite' in Welsh: *i*-clauses are of two types, of which one is finite (section 3.4.1) and the other non-finite (section 3.4.2). As a consequence, there is also no correlation between finiteness and word order in Welsh.

A more satisfactory way of looking at the clause structure of Welsh abstracts away from 'VSO', 'SVO' or 'AuxSVO' word order. *All* full clauses – i.e. clauses with subjects – in fact have the same basic structure, in the sense that the initial position always contains an element which inflects to agree with a following pronominal subject. The five possibilities for the clause-initial element are thus:

(93)   Clause-initial inflectional elements
    a. finite verb
    b. finite auxiliary
    c. *bod* (section 3.3)
    d. 'finite' inflectional *i* (section 3.4.1)
    e. 'non-finite' inflectional *i* (section 3.4.2)

Looked at this way, there is no inherent distinction in word order between matrix and dependent clauses: the subject always immediately follows the inflectional element, whatever the clause type. Since each of the clause-initial elements in (93) inflects to agree with the subject, an obvious analysis in a Principles & Parameters type of framework is that all these elements are generated in, or pass through, the T head. The T head is a plausible locus of finiteness in the clause; however, see note 12: an alternative within a split-CP analysis would be Fin (see also Roberts 2005: 123). Thus it is predictable that finite verbs and auxiliaries, *bod* in *bod*-clauses and both types of inflectional *i* are all associated with finiteness. Note that all of these heads agree with an immediately following pronominal element; see section 6.3.

Interestingly, we cannot equate 'finiteness' in Welsh either with 'morphologically tensed' or with 'exhibits subject agreement'. Both *bod*-clauses and the *i*-clause complements to epistemic and declarative predicates (section 3.4.1) are *finite*, but neither of these clause types bears morphological tense. And both the syntactically finite *and* the syntactically non-finite inflectional *i*-clauses (sections 3.4.1 and 3.4.2) display subject agreement. Put another way,

Table 3.1 *Summary of properties of Welsh clause types*

	Bears morphological tense	Displays subject agreement	Finite
auxiliaries	yes	yes	yes
lexical verbs	yes	yes	yes
impersonal verbs	yes	no	yes
infinitival *bod*	no	yes	yes
finite *i*-clauses	no	yes	yes
non-finite *i*-clauses	no	yes	no
verbal infinitives	no	no	no

morphological tense is not a necessary condition for finiteness, and subject agreement is not a sufficient condition for finiteness. Moreover, note that impersonal verbs are morphologically tensed, but do not display subject agreement (section 8.3.3). The situation is summarized in Table 3.1.

Since *i* in *i*-clauses is associated with two different tense interpretations, it is likely that T has two distinct sets of features: in finite *i*-clauses, T is [+ anterior, + finite], whereas in non-finite *i*-clauses, T is [– past, – finite], so accounting for the 'possible future' interpretation seen, for instance, in (61) and (62) in section 3.4.2. Presumably, these distinctions are dependent on the class of predicate in the matrix clause: epistemic and declarative predicates select a finite *i*-clause, while expectational and volitional predicates select a non-finite *i*-clause.

It is clear that the locus of the major distinction in Welsh clause structure is not at the front of the clause – as we have seen, this always contains an element that inflects to agree with a (c)overt pronominal subject. Instead, the main differentiation comes in the post-subject position, where the question is, does the clause contain any aspectual projection(s) or not (see section 2.5)? The appearance of aspect markers, such as *yn* 'progressive' and *wedi* 'perfect', is not dependent on the clause having morphological tense: aspectual projections are licensed not only by tensed forms of *bod* but also by infinitival *bod*; see, for instance, (28), (31) and (33) in section 3.3. Both of these are 'AuxSVO' clause types. However, there is no straightforward correlation between the availability of aspect markers and the superficial word order either, since AuxSVO clauses containing an auxiliary other than *bod* do *not* license an aspectual head. So in (94), where the finite auxiliary is a form of *gwneud*, 'do', the perfect aspect marker *wedi* cannot occur:

(94)   Gwnaeth Rhys (*wedi) astudio   Ffrangeg.
        do.PAST.3S Rhys   PERF   study.INF French
        'Rhys studied French.'

We conclude, then, that although labels indicating superficial word order such as 'VSO', 'AuxSVO' etc. may be useful mnemonics, nothing especially follows from them, and they predict little about the structure or properties of specific clauses.

3.7   Raising predicates

3.7.1   A class of raising predicates

In section 3.6, we noted that one of the long standing issues for analyses of Welsh infinitival clauses concerns the role and status of *i*. If the *i* element which introduces some control infinitival complements were the same as the inflectional *i* element in *i*-clauses with an overt subject, it would then be hard within the Principles & Parameters approach to explain the distribution of PRO versus overt subjects in the two clause types. Borsley (1986, 1989a) notes that the same apparent paradox also occurs in the analysis of raising predicates. Some raising complements are introduced by *i*, so the question arises as to how *i* can license not only the trace of the raised subject nominal, but also the overt subject found in inflectional *i* clauses – two kinds of subject which are supposedly in complementary distribution. In section 3.6, we gave an account handling the parallel problem of *i* in control clauses: we argued that control *i* (and also *o* and Ø) are complementizers, and have a different structure and syntax to inflectional *i*, an element in T. In this section we show that a similar account is also available for raising clauses.

The lexical variation occurring in the complements to raising predicates is analogous to that found in the complements to control predicates (section 3.5): there are three possibilities for clause-initial elements, namely *i*, *o* and Ø. Some raising predicates, such as *digwydd* 'happen', *dechrau* 'begin', *gorffen* 'finish' and *stopio* 'stop' select a bare infinitival complement. Others select a clause with an initial *i*, such as *para* (literary *parhau*) and *dal*, both 'continue', also *tueddu* 'tend' and *i fod* 'be supposed to'. Raising adjectives generally select an *o*-clause: examples are *bownd* and *rhwym* 'bound', *sicr* and *siŵr* 'sure, certain', *tebyg/tebygol* 'likely' and *tueddol* 'inclined, likely'; however, *lwcus* 'lucky' selects an *i*-clause. The examples in (95) to (102) illustrate these possibilities.

A good indication that these all contain raising predicates is that the subject in the matrix clause in each case receives its thematic role from the predicate in the lower clause, as is particularly clearly seen with the inanimate subjects in some of these examples. Further discussion can be found in Jones & Thomas (1977: 243–52).

(95)   Ar ei ffordd adref mae   Steff yn **digwydd** [gweld Lowri].
        on 3MS way   home be.PRES.3S Steff PROG happen.INF see.INF Lowri
        'On his way home Steff happens to see Lowri.'

(96)   Mae   'r wal wedi **dechrau** [disgyn].
        be.PRES.3S the wall PERF begin.INF fall.INF
        'The wall has begun to fall.'   (Jones & Thomas 1977: 245)

(97)   Mae   'r hen adeiladau 'n   **dal**   [i sefyll].
        be.PRES.3S the old buildings PROG continue.INF to stand.INF
        'The old buildings are still standing.'

(98)   Mae   cawl twym yn   **tueddu** [i chwythu allan trwy
        be.PRES.3S soup hot   PROG tend.INF to blow.INF out   through
        glawr y   prosesydd].
        lid   the processor
        'Hot soup tends to blow out through the lid of the liquidizer.'

(99)   Mae   protocol Kyoto **i fod** [i ddod   i rym yr
        be.PRES.3S protocol Kyoto to be.INF to come.INF to force the
        wythnos hon].
        week   DEM.FS
        'The Kyoto protocol is supposed to come into force this week.'

(100)   Mae   'r blodau 'n   **para** [i flodeuo].
        be.PRES.3S the flowers PROG continue.INF to flower.INF
        'The flowers continue to blossom.'

(101)   Mae   'r math hwn   o frwdfrydedd yn   **rhwym** [o
        be.PRES.3S the sort DEM.MS of enthusiasm PRED bound of
        greu   ymateb].
        create.INF response
        'That sort of enthusiasm is bound to create a response.'

(102)   Mae   gweithwyr yn   **lwcus** [i ennill   US$140 y   mis].
        be.PRES.3S workers   PRED lucky to earn.INF US$140 the month
        'Workers are lucky to earn US$140 a month.'

Such lexical variation in the way the embedded clauses are introduced implies
that, once again, the clause-initial elements (*i/o/Ø*) are complementizers, just
as in the case of control predicates.

    Standard evidence can be used to argue for the existence of a class of raising
predicates in Welsh. First, the subject of an idiom in the lower clause can be
raised to appear as the subject of the matrix clause, as shown in (103) and (104)
(see Tallerman 1998: section 6):

(103)   Mae   *gwaed y ceiliog* yn   **tueddu** i fod   *yn y cyw.*
        be.PRES.3S blood the cockerel PROG tend.INF to be.INF in the chick
        'The cockerel's blood tends to be in the chick.'
        (i.e. 'Like father, like son.')

(104)   Mae   *natur y   cyw*   yn   **debyg** o fod   *yn y   cawl.*
be.PRES.3S nature the chicken PRED likely of be.INF in the soup
'The nature of the chicken is likely to be in the soup.'
(i.e. 'An apple never falls far from the tree.')

The idiom in the first example is *Mae gwaed y ceiliog yn y cyw* (= is blood the cockerel in the chick, i.e. 'The blood of the cockerel is in the chick'), and in (103), its subject has been raised. Assuming that the idiom is stored whole in the lexicon, such examples are evidence that the matrix subject is the underlying subject of the lower clause.

Secondly, the weather expletive *hi*, which receives its interpretation from the weather predicate in the lower clause, can also occur as the subject of the raising adjective here:

(105)   Mae   *hi* 'n   **rhwym** [o fwrw   glaw].
be.PRES.3S she PRED bound of throw.INF rain
'It's bound to rain.'

The occurrence of weather *hi*, 'it', in the matrix subject position is evidence that this is not a position in which a thematic role is assigned.

Thirdly, consider raising predicates such as *tebyg*, 'likely', which optionally select a *finite* complement as an alternative. Here, an extraposition expletive – also *hi* – can occur in the matrix subject position: again, since the expletive is not theta-marked, this shows that the subject position in the *tebyg* clause is a non-theta position:

(106)   Mae   *hi* 'n   **debyg** [bydd   glaw trwm yn yr haf].
be.PRES3S she PRED likely be.FUT.3S rain heavy in the summer
'It's likely that there'll be heavy rain in the summer.'

Evidently, then, Welsh does have a class of raising predicates.

Note also that the *i* element which precedes the infinitival verb in some raising complements does not license an overt subject in the lower clause, since raising of the subject is obligatory: compare (100) and (107):

(107)   *Mae   'n   para   [i **'r blodau** flodeuo].
be.PRES.3S PROG continue.INF to the flowers flower.INF
('It continues the flowers to blossom.')

Interestingly, though, not all raising predicates require obligatory raising. For instance, *ymddangos* 'appear' allows the embedded subject either to stay in situ or to raise:

(108)   a. Mae   'n   ymddangos [bod   cwningod yn yr ardd].
be.PRES.3S PROG appear.INF be.INF rabbits   in the garden
'There appear to be rabbits in the garden.'

   b. Mae   cwningod yn   ymddangos [bod   yn yr ardd].
      be.PRES.3S rabbits   PROG appear.INF be.INF in the garden
      'Rabbits appear to be in the garden.'

3.7.2   Complementizers in raising clauses

Note that the overt complementizer elements *i* and *o* only occur when
the predicate selects an infinitival complement – in other words, when it
appears in a raising context. So *tebyg*, 'likely', in (104) selects an *o*-clause, but
the *finite* clause selected by the same adjective in (106) has no complementizer.
This is predictable under the assumption that the complementizers themselves
select a [-finite] complement (Tallerman 1998: 129). Such a premise also
accounts for the variation in (109) and (110):

(109)   Roedd   y   bws yn   siŵr [**o** fynd   yn   gynnar].
         be.IMPF.3S the bus PRED sure of go.INF PRED early
         'The bus was sure to go early.'

(110)   Dw   i 'n   siŵr [**i** 'r bws fynd   yn   gynnar].
         be.PRES.1S I PRED sure to the bus go.INF PRED early
         'I'm sure that the bus went early.'

In (109) we have raising *siŵr*, which selects an *o* infinitival clause; *o* itself
selects a [-finite] complement. But in (110), the same adjective, *siŵr*, selects a
finite complement, which now requires the inflectional *i*, associated with the
licensing of non-pronominal and pronominal subjects.

Note further that, as complementizers, neither *o* nor *i* occurs in an inflected
form, as shown for complementizer *i* in (111); compare the parallel situation
seen in the case of control predicates in (88) and (90), where complementizer
o did not inflect:

(111)   a. *Mae   'r blodau 'n   para   [**iddyn** (nhw) flodeuo].
            be.PRES.3S the flowers PROG continue.INF to.3P they flower.INF
            ('The flowers continue to blossom.')
         b. *Mae   'n   para   [**iddyn** (nhw) flodeuo].
            be.PRES.3S PROG continue.INF to.3P they flower.INF
            ('They continue to blossom.')

In contrast, (112) contains inflectional *i* (section 3.4.1), which, as expected,
does inflect to agree with a pronominal subject:

(112)   Dw   i 'n   siŵr [**iddo** (fo) fynd   yn   gynnar].
         be.PRES.1S I PRED sure to.3MS he go.INF PRED early
         'I'm sure he went early.'

Exactly the same explanation is available for this set of facts as was proposed in section 3.6 for control predicates. Raising predicates select one of three complementizers, *i/o/Ø*, just like control predicates. These do not inflect, since they are not immediately followed by an overt/covert pronominal: given the structural assumptions made in section 3.6, the subject is too low down in the clause in the overt syntax to have a structural relationship with the complementizer. Conversely, inflectional *i* in (112) is a functional head in T, and this inflects to agree with a following subject pronominal:

(113)   Dw i'n siŵr [$_{TP}$ [$_T$ iddo] [fo [fynd yn gynnar]]].

In sum, raising predicates, like control predicates, display lexical variation between complementizers Ø, *i*, and *o*, but (in their raising/control incarnations) such predicates never select inflectional *i*, which is an element in T. Again, it is clear that Borsley's paradox in fact does not arise. There is no conflict between complementizer *i/o* and inflectional *i*, which are simply different morphemes sited in different positions, and selecting distinct kinds of complements.

4

Wh-constructions

There are three major patterns of marking Welsh *wh*-constructions (including *wh*-questions, relative clauses, focus structures etc.). These can be illustrated with patterns found in *wh*-questions. The first pattern found with *wh*-questions involves a *wh*-element in clause-initial position, with the grammatical function of that element being identified by a gap with no agreement in the corresponding syntactic position. This is illustrated in (1). Here, the *wh*-word *beth* 'what' is in initial position; there is a gap where the direct object would normally be; and there is no agreement marking the direct object on the verb or anywhere else.

(1)   Beth glywaist   ti   ___ wedyn?
       what hear.PAST.2s you ___ then
       'What did you hear then?'

A second possibility, found in other environments, is that the grammatical function of the *wh*-element is identified by a resumptive pronoun. In (2), we find the pronoun *fe* 'him' in the object position of the preposition. There is agreement on the relevant head (as with *ganddo* in this example) if that head can show agreement, but the pattern is found also with non-agreeing heads.

(2)   Pwy gest   ti 'r llythyr 'na ganddo fe?
       who get.PAST.2s you the letter DEM with.3MS him
       'Who did you get that letter from?'

A third possibility involves a gap accompanied by rich agreement on a relevant head (either an object clitic, a possessive clitic or an inflection on a preposition). This is illustrated in (3), where the preposition *ganddi* 'with' shows feminine singular inflection, and there is no overt resumptive pronoun.

(3)   Pa ferch gest   ti 'r llythyr 'na ganddi?
       which girl get.PAST.2s you the letter DEM with.3FS
       'Which girl did you get that letter from?'

An important question of interpretation is whether these are really sub-cases of the gap pattern in (1), or whether the rich agreement is associated with a null pronoun, and hence these are cases of the resumptive pattern in (2).

Table 4.1. *Summary of patterns of marking* wh-*constructions.*

context	gap, no agreement	pronoun	gap, with agreement
subject	+	−	−
object of synthetic verb	+	−	−
object of periphrastic verb	+*	−	+
object of inflecting preposition	+†	+	+
object of uninflecting preposition	+†	+	n/a
possessor noun phrase	−	+	+
adjunct	+	n/a	n/a

Note:
*colloquial and informal written only
†substandard, but possible for younger speakers

The availability of the different patterns of *wh*-marking for different syntactic positions is summarized in Table 4.1.

This chapter sets out the patterns of data found in each of the main types of *wh*-construction: *wh*-questions (section 4.1), relative clauses (section 4.2), focus constructions (section 4.3), copular constructions (section 4.4), infinitival questions and relative clauses (section 4.5) and comparatives and correlatives (section 4.6). As well as setting out the data, these sections will consider the distribution of the different patterns, arguing that these patterns can be reduced essentially to two strategies for forming *wh*-constructions in Welsh. A gap (movement) strategy is available for *wh*-constructions formed on subject, direct object and adjunct positions, and, in colloquial Welsh, for the object of a preposition. Conversely, a resumptive-pronoun strategy is available for *wh*-constructions formed on the object of a preposition and a possessor noun phrase. Different authors have taken different approaches to the gap-with-agreement type, particularly in the case of *wh*-constructions formed on the object of a periphrastic verb. This chapter will present the different interpretations and the evidence offered in support of them.

Section 4.7 deals with differences between literary and colloquial Welsh with respect to the use of particles in relative clauses and other *wh*-constructions. Section 4.8 looks at some special properties associated with negative *wh*-constructions. In section 4.9, we turn to long-distance *wh*-constructions, of the type 'Who did you say that you saw?', and, in particular, we consider the evidence that these involve movement of the *wh*-element cyclically via intermediate positions.

4.1   *Wh*-questions

Wh-questions contain one of the *wh*-words, *pwy* 'who(m)', *be*(*th*) 'what', *ble* / *lle* 'where', *sut* / *shwt* 'how', *pam* 'why', *pryd* 'when', *sawl* 'how many', *faint* 'how many' or a *wh*-phrase such as *pa fyfyrwyr* 'which students' or *pa mor aml* 'how often'. The *wh*-word is in clause-initial position in the question. *Wh*-words may remain in situ only in multiple *wh*-questions (see section 4.1.10).

4.1.1   *The basic pattern*

Basic examples of questions formed on subject and object position are given below:[1]

(4)   Pwy gafodd   y   wobr?
       who get.PAST.3s the prize
       'Who got the prize?'

(5)   Beth glywaist   ti   wedyn?
       what hear.PAST.2s you afterwards
       'What did you hear afterwards?'

The *wh*-phrase is in initial position. The verb undergoes soft mutation in colloquial Welsh when preceded by a *wh*-phrase (*cafodd* > *gafodd* and *clywaist* > *glywaist* in the examples above). In literary Welsh, a particle (*a*) is used, preceding the verb in subject *wh*-questions as in (6), and in the case of *wh*-questions formed on the object of a synthetic verb, as in (7). The mutation effect is the same:

(6)   Pwy a   gafodd   y   wobr?
       who PRT get.PAST.3s the prize
       'Who got the prize?'

(7)   Beth a   glywaist   wedyn?
       what PRT hear.PAST.2s afterwards
       'What did you hear afterwards?'

The particle *a* is often termed a 'relative pronoun' in traditional descriptions (e.g. Thorne 1993: 171) and early generative approaches (Awbery 1977: 157). This terminology is not justified, given that *a* may co-occur with *wh*-pronouns in (6) and (7), and that, in archaic literary style, it co-occurs in relative clauses with overt relative pronouns *yr hwn, yr hon, y rhai* 'the one(s)'; see (60) below.

---

[1] Examples such as (4) formed on the subject position in the third person singular are normally in principle ambiguous between a subject-*wh* reading and an object-*wh* reading, in this case, the rather improbable 'Whom did the prize get?'

Since *pwy* and *yr hwn* etc. are pronouns, *a* cannot also be a pronoun. Furthermore, there are a number of environments typical for relative pronouns where *a* is not found. For instance, it never forms a constituent with a fronted preposition.

4.1.2   Antiagreement in subject wh-*questions*

If a *wh*-question is formed on subject position, the verb does not agree with the extracted subject. Instead, it appears in a default third-person singular form, as in (8). The agreeing form, in (9), is ungrammatical.

(8)   Pa   fyfyrwyr **enillodd**   y   wobr?
       which students win.PAST.3S the prize
       'Which students won the prize?'

(9)   *Pa   fyfyrwyr **enillon**   y   wobr?
       which students win.PAST.3P the prize
       ('Which students won the prize?')

As we shall see from focus examples below, there is in fact no agreement at all, whether for person, number or gender, between a *wh*-moved subject and the verb. This effect is found in a number of other languages (for instance, in the other Celtic languages, in Berber and in Turkish), and has been termed the Antiagreement Effect (Ouhalla 1993). Compare Berber, where a *wh*-moved subject requires a special verbal form (participle), as in (10), rather than an agreeing verb, in (11).

(10)   Man   tamghart ay   yzrin   Mohand?
        which woman   COMP see.PART Mohand
        'Which woman saw Mohand?'   (Ouhalla 1993: 479)

(11)   *Man   tamghart ay   t-zra   Mohand?
        which woman   COMP 3FS-see.PAST Mohand
        ('Which woman saw Mohand?')   (Ouhalla 1993: 479)

Within the context of Welsh agreement, the effect partially follows from the general rule of Welsh agreement that heads agree with personal pronouns but not with non-pronominal noun phrases (see section 1.4.3 and chapter 6, especially section 6.1). In (8), the extracted subject *pa fyfyrwyr* 'which students' is a non-pronominal noun phrase, hence the appearance of the default third-person form is expected. If we assume that *wh*-words such as *pwy* 'who' belong to the same class as non-pronominal noun phrases (that is, noun phrases other than personal pronouns), agreement is not expected with these either. An approach in which Welsh agreement is a surface phenomenon applying between a verb and a following pronoun, such as that proposed in chapter 6, will also account for such data, assuming that the gap left by *pwy* is not pronominal. Some further issues that arise with respect to agreement in focus constructions are discussed in section 4.3.2 below.

4.1.3   Ungrammaticality of resumptive pronouns in subject and object position

Overt resumptive pronouns are impossible in subject and direct-object position in all varieties of Welsh:

(12)   *Pa   fyfyrwyr enillon   **nhw** 'r   wobr?
        which students win.PAST.3P they the prize
        ('Which students won (did they win) the prize?')

(13)   *Beth glywaist   ti   **e** wedyn?
        what hear.PAST.2S you it then
        ('What did you hear (it) then?')

The unavailability of resumptive pronouns in subject position seems to be more or less universal in language. There are two versions of this constraint: some languages which allow resumptive pronouns in *wh*-constructions disallow them in any subject position. Such languages include Polish (Bondaruk 1995), Slovene and Serbian and Croatian. Within Celtic, Irish operates a version of this, banning resumptive pronouns in subject position only in the main clause of a *wh*-construction (the 'Highest Subject Restriction'):

(14)   *an fear a   raibh   **sé** breoite
        the man PRT be.IMPF.3S.DEP he ill
        ('the man that (he) was ill')   (McCloskey 1990: 210)

The Highest Subject Restriction also operates in Palestinian / Levantine Arabic and in Hebrew (Alexopolou 2006: 100–2; Shlonsky 1992). Welsh lies somewhere in between, disallowing resumptive pronouns in subject position in main clauses and in those embedded clauses where a gap is possible. For further details, see section 4.9.1 below.

The unavailability of resumptive pronouns in object position, however, contrasts with Irish, where they are possible:

(15)   an fear ar   bhuail   tú **é**
        the man PRT strike.PAST.3S you him
        'the man that you struck (him)'   (McCloskey 1990: 206)

The Welsh pattern is shared with a number of non-Celtic languages, for instance, Berber and Turkish (Ouhalla 1993: 491–3) and Czech (Toman 1998).

The unavailability of resumptive pronouns in these positions has been analysed by a number of authors within Principles and Parameters frameworks (see McCloskey 1990 for Irish, Ouhalla 1993 for Berber, and, for Welsh, Rouveret 1994: 386–7, 407–10 and Willis 2000) as following from a requirement that pronouns must be free from binding by a *wh*-element (A′-free) within a certain domain, probably subject to variation between languages (the A′-Disjointness Requirement).

4.1.4 *Verb forms in* wh-*constructions*

Most verbs simply undergo soft mutation in *wh*-questions. The verb *bod* 'be' is more complicated, and has a special form used with subject *wh*-constructions in the present tense, *sy* in colloquial Welsh, *sydd* in literary Welsh:

(16)   Beth sy   'n   digwydd?
        what be.PRES.REL PROG happen.INF
        'What's happening?'

As would be expected from the Antiagreement Effect, it is used for subjects of all persons, genders and numbers. In the imperfect, the verb *bod* takes the form *oedd*, as in (17).

(17)   Beth oedd/   *roedd   yn   digwydd?
        what be.IMPF.3S be.IMPF.3S PROG happen.INF
        'What was happening?'

Note that, in *wh*-constructions formed on subject position, only *oedd* is possible as the imperfect of *bod*, never *roedd*. This contrasts with non-*wh*-environments, where there is variation between the two forms (compare section 2.1.2). Outside of the present and imperfect, *bod* behaves like other verbs.

In *wh*-constructions other than those formed on subject position, the verb *bod* varies in form in the imperfect in colloquial Welsh between forms with an initial *r-* and those without. As with this in non-*wh*-contexts, there is some degree of free variation. Representative colloquial forms, omitting much dialect variation, are given in Table 4.2. The distinctive forms will be referred to as 'relative' forms and glossed as REL.

4.1.5 *Object* wh-*questions in periphrastic clauses*

In those object *wh*-questions where the verb is periphrastic, an object-agreement clitic precedes the verb. This clitic may be dropped in speech, but its mutation effect often remains. Thus, in (18), there is a masculine third-person singular agreement clitic *ei* proclitic to the non-finite verb. This clitic

Table 4.2. *Forms of* bod *'be' in* wh-*constructions in colloquial Welsh.*

		present	imperfect
subject *wh*-constructions	3s	*sy*	*oedd*
other *wh*-constructions	1s	*dw*	*(r)oeddwn*
	2s	*(r)wyt*	*(r)oeddet*
	3s	*mae*	*(r)oedd*
	1p	*(r)ydyn*	*(r)oedden*
	2p	*(r)ydych*	*(r)oeddech*
	3p	*maen*	*(r)oedden*

may be dropped, but, in neutral colloquial Welsh, the non-finite verb still undergoes mutation (*bwyta* > *fwyta*).

(18)   Beth ydych   chi 'n   (ei)   fwyta?
        what be.PRES.2P you PROG (3MS) eat.INF
        'What are you eating?'

In non-*wh*-environments, object-agreement clitics allow either an overt object pronoun or a null object in the position after the verb (see sections 1.4.5, 3.1.2 and 5.2.2):

(19)   Mae   Ifan yn   ei   fwyta (e).
        be.PRES.3s Ifan PROG 3MS eat.INF (it)
        'Ifan is eating it.'

In *wh*-constructions, however, an overt object pronoun is ungrammatical (the clitic *ei* is optional here in colloquial Welsh):

(20)   *Beth ydych   chi 'n   ei   fwyta   e?
        what be.PRES.2P you PROG 3MS eat.INF it
        ('What are you eating?')

In very colloquial Welsh, both object-agreement clitic and its mutation effect may be absent:

(21)   Be' 'dych   chi 'n   byta?
        what be.PRES.2P you PROG eat.INF
        'What are you eating?'

The object-agreement clitic normally agrees in person and number with the *wh*-object, as in (22), where the *wh*-object *pa rai* 'which ones' is plural, and the clitic *eu* is likewise plural.

(22)   Pa   rai   wyt   ti   wedi (eu) clywed   o'r blaen?
        which ones be.PRES.2s you PERF (3P) hear.INF   before
        'Which ones have you heard before?'

This rule is not always observed in speech, and a masculine third-person clitic or its mutation alone is sometimes found regardless of person and number.

Where the auxiliary is *bod* 'be', it is preceded by the particle *yr* in literary Welsh:

(23)   Beth yr ydych   yn   ei   fwyta?
        what PRT be.PRES.2P PROG (3MS) eat.INF
        'What are you eating?'

In colloquial Welsh, this particle may appear in the form of an initial *r-* added to the front of the auxiliary, as in the forms in Table 4.2:

(24)   Beth rydych   chi 'n   (ei) fwyta?
        what be.PRES.2P you PROG (3MS) eat.INF
        'What are you eating?'

In this type of *wh*-question, however, the forms without *r-*, as in (18), are more usual in speech.

To sum up, there is a great deal of variation, with a sociolinguistic continuum of stylistic variation from the most literary form with particle *yr* and object-agreement clitic *ei* to the most colloquial form with neither. Hence, 'What are you eating?' may be expressed in any of the following ways from most literay at the top to most colloquial at the bottom:

(25)   Beth yr ydych   yn   ei   fwyta?   LITERARY WELSH
        Beth   rydych   chi   'n   ei   fwyta?
        Beth   ydych   chi   'n   ei   fwyta?
        Beth   ydych   chi   'n   fwyta?
        Be'   'dych/'dach chi   'n   byta?   COLLOQUIAL WELSH
        what PRT be.PRES.2P you PROG 3MS eat.INF
        'What are you eating?'

A further complication arises from clauses containing modals such as *gallu* 'be able', *cael* 'be allowed', *dylai* 'should' or *medru* 'be able, know how to'. Colloquial Welsh requires a soft mutation of the verb here (*galla* > *alla*):

(26)   Beth alla   i (ei) wneud?
        what can.PRES.1s I (3MS) do.INF
        'What can I do?'

The literary norm traditionally allowed both particles *a* and *y* here, with a preference for *a* (see Richards 1938: 86–9 and Thorne 1993: 178 for relevant examples with various *wh*-constructions):

(27)   Beth a allaf   ei   wneud?
        what PRT can.PRES.1s 3MS do.INF
        'What can I do?'

(28)   Beth y   gallaf   ei   wneud?
        what PRT can.PRES.1S 3MS do.INF
        'What can I do?'

In current literary practice, there seems to have been a shift towards using $y(r)$ in this context. Current grammars accept both options for literary Welsh (Thorne 1993: 178).

4.1.6   Analysing subject and object wh-questions

4.1.6.1 Subject wh-questions

As we have seen, subject wh-questions exhibit the Antiagreement Effect and disallow resumptive pronouns. The absence of agreement, coupled with the absence of any overt pronoun in subject position, means that these clearly do not involve a resumptive strategy. In transformational frameworks, the wh-word originates in the normal postverbal subject position and moves directly to the front (to [Spec, CP] in Principles and Parameters), leaving a gap (trace, t):

(29)   [Pa   fyfyrwyr] enillodd   t   y   wobr?
        which students   win.PAST.3S   the   prize
        'Which students won the prize?'

If we assume that all wh-words and wh-phrases count as non-pronominal, then the verb is appearing with a non-pronominal subject, and hence shows no morphological agreement.

4.1.6.2 Wh-questions formed on the object position of non-finite verbs

There are good reasons for treating the clitics that precede non-finite verbs as object-agreement markers rather than as object pronouns. Principally, these clitics are taken to be object-agreement markers because they co-occur with normal object pronouns after the verb, as in (18) above (see section 5.2.2.2 for further details). Given that we have analysed ei as an object-agreement marker, its presence does not automatically imply that there is a resumptive pronoun in object position.

Opinion is divided over the correct analysis of sentences like (18). The two possibilities are:

(i)   they involve a null resumptive pronoun; or
(ii)   they involve a gap (trace, copy) left by movement of the wh-word.

According to account (i), the wh-object in (18) does not move: it originates in clause-initial position and is linked to the object position via a null pronoun (*pro*) in that position, forming a chain *beth*$_i$ . . . *pro*$_i$. The object-agreement clitic *ei* is needed to license a null object pronoun (*pro*), identifying it as masculine third-person singular:

(30)   [$_{CP}$ Beth$_i$ ydych   chi 'n   (ei$_i$)   [VP fwyta *pro*$_i$]] ?
        what   be.PRES.2P you PROG (3MS)   eat.INF
        'What are you eating?'

This is effectively the approach advocated in the seminal work of Awbery (1977) and a number of authors since (for instance, Manning 1996, Rouveret 2002: 124, Sadler 1988).

According to account (ii), *beth* originates in object position, and moves to sentence-initial position leaving a gap (trace, *t*). Agreement is a reflex of this movement. Such an account is proposed by Willis (2000) within a Principles and Parameters framework. He assumes that this movement is a staged process via an intermediate position at the left edge of the verb phrase ([Spec, AgrOP] in that framework, [Spec, vP] in more recent versions of the theory, required because movement may not cross a phase boundary without stopping at the phase edge). Movement through this position triggers the appearance of an object-agreement clitic. This is exemplified in (31). Here *beth* 'what' starts in the object position of *bwyta* 'eat'. It moves first to the left edge of its verb phrase ([Spec, vP]), triggering the appearance of the object-agreement clitic *ei* (and / or its mutation effect *bwyta* > *fwyta*), then moves on to the clause-initial position ([Spec, CP]).

(31)   [$_{CP}$ Beth$_i$ ydych   chi 'n   [$_{vP}$ t$_i$ (ei$_i$) [$_{vP}$ fwyta   t$_i$]]]?
        what   be.PRES.2P you PROG   (3MS)   eat.INF
        'What are you eating?'

See section 4.9.6.2 for further evidence for this intermediate position.

There are two arguments in favour of the former (resumptive) approach. First, as we have seen, the particle *y(r)* is found in literary Welsh in object *wh*-questions with auxiliary *bod* 'be'. This particle is not found in subject *wh*-questions or in object *wh*-questions with a synthetic verb, both of which indisputably use a gap strategy. On the other hand, *y(r)* is found in literary Welsh in *wh*-constructions that clearly have resumptive pronouns in them (see below). Therefore, it is claimed, positing a null resumptive pronoun in (18) allows a simple generalization: in literary Welsh, *a* is used when there is a gap, and *y(r)* is used when there is a resumptive pronoun.

Secondly, the object-agreement clitic is normally associated with a pronominal element, either an overt object pronoun, or a null pronominal in object position. Positing a null object pronoun in (18) allows this generalization to be maintained, without us having to posit any other mechanism for the appearance of the object-agreement clitic.

Nevertheless, there are a number of arguments that point to the reverse conclusion. First, despite the parallelism between *wh*-constructions and ordinary cases involving object-agreement clitics, there is one area where the parallelism breaks down. The null object pronoun normally alternates fairly freely with an overt pronoun with no particular emphasis on the overt pronoun in colloquial Welsh. However, as we saw above in (20), in the case of *wh*-objects, an overt postverbal object pronoun is never possible. This contrasts with the situation with other types of *wh*-construction where overt resumptive pronouns are found (see sections 4.1.7 and 4.1.8 below). The unavailability of an overt pronoun is not easily explained if these are analysed as resumptive.

Secondly, in colloquial Welsh, the object-agreement clitic may assume a default masculine third-person singular form. This is very difficult for a resumption account, since it is hard to see how a masculine third-person singular form could license anything other than a masculine third-person singular null object.

The construction in (21), with no object-agreement clitic and no mutation on the nonfinite verb, is also difficult for a resumption account. There is no object-agreement clitic here, hence no possibility of a null object. So, it seems that we are forced to posit a gap strategy for these cases.

Finally, it is clearly wrong to say that, in literary Welsh, *a* is always associated with a gap strategy, and *y(r)* is always associated with a resumptive strategy. A number of authors (Rouveret 1994, Manning 1996, Willis 2000) have demonstrated that this simple correlation does not work (cf. also the 'anomalous relatives' of Awbery 1977). If it were correct, we would be forced to say that there is a gap in (27), but a resumptive null object in (28). It also faces problems with adjunct *wh*-constructions. See section 4.7 below for further discussion.

The arguments against positing resumption in *wh*-questions formed on the object position in periphrastic clauses seem stronger than those in favour. We tentatively conclude that these make use of a gap strategy.

4.1.7   *Prepositional* wh-*questions*

Traditionally, the object of a preposition is questioned by moving the entire prepositional phrase containing the *wh*-word to the front (pied-piping), as in (32). The verb undergoes soft mutation in colloquial Welsh in the usual way (*cest* > *gest*).[2]

---

[2] Note that the absence of agreement morphology on the preposition *gan* indicates that *pwy* 'who' is treated as non-pronominal for agreement purposes.

(32)   Gan bwy gest   ti   'r   llythyr 'na?
        with who get.PAST.2S you the letter DEM
        'Who did you get that letter from?'

In literary Welsh, the particle *y(r)* is used, and the verb does not mutate:

(33)   Gan bwy y   cefaist   y   llythyr hwnnw?
        with who PRT get.PAST.2S the letter DEM.MS
        'Who did you get that letter from?'

An alternative pattern, with only the *wh*-word in initial position and a stranded preposition at the end of the clause, is also found in current colloquial Welsh, although it is frowned upon by prescriptivists. This type of construction is required in some other *wh*-environments, notably in relative clauses (see section 4.2.3). If the preposition can inflect, it does so:

(34)   Pwy gest   ti   'r   llythyr 'na **ganddo?**
        who get.PAST.2S you the letter DEM with.3MS
        'Who did you get that letter from?'

The inflected preposition may be followed by an overt resumptive pronoun:

(35)   Pwy gest   ti   'r   llythyr 'na ganddo **fe?**
        who get.PAST.2S you the letter DEM with.3MS him
        'Who did you get that letter from?'

(36)   Beth wyt   ti   amdano **fo?**
        what be.PRES.2S you for.3MS it
        'What are you after?', 'What do you want?'   (*TMC* 183)

If the *wh*-phrase is plural, so is the agreement on the preposition:

(37)   Pa   rai gest   ti   'r   llythyr 'na ganddyn nhw?
        which ones get.PAST.2S you the letter DEM with.3P them
        'Which ones did you get that letter from?'

Some prepositions, for instance, *efo* 'with', have no inflected forms, using a single invariant form with all possible objects. With these prepositions, an overt pronoun is obligatory in neutral registers:

(38)   Beth wyt   ti   'n   chwarae efo **fo?**
        What be.PRES.2S you PROG play.INF with it
        'What are you playing with?'

Use of uninflected stranded prepositions is attested, both with prepositions that can inflect, and with those that cannot. However, it is considered non-standard. The preposition *o* 'of' has inflected forms. In (39), however, it is left stranded in clause-final position without an inflection. This example is considered non-standard. The stylistically neutral equivalent is (40), with pied-piping of the entire prepositional phrase.

(39)   %Lle   'dach   chi 'n   dod   o?
   where   be.PRES.2P you PROG come.INF from
   'Where do you come from?'

(40)   O   le   'dach   chi 'n   dod?
   from   where   be.PRES.2P you PROG come.INF
   'Where do you come from?' (lit. 'From where do you come?')

The pattern in (39), with preposition stranding and no inflection, appears to be a twentieth-century innovation resulting from language contact, modelled on preposition stranding as found in English.

These patterns suggest that, with the exception of the type in (39), movement of the object of a preposition to clause-initial position is not possible in Welsh. The two strategies for forming *wh*-questions of this type both avoid such movement. The pied-piping option in (32) and (40) avoids it by moving the entire prepositional phrase rather than merely the object of the preposition, as shown in (41). The preposition-stranding option avoids it by using either a richly inflected preposition licensing a null object pronoun, as in (34), shown in (42), or an overt object pronoun, as in (35)–(37), shown in (43). Both of these can be considered variants of a resumptive strategy:

(41)   [Gan bwy]$_i$ gest   ti 'r   llythyr 'na   t$_i$?
   with   who   get.PAST.2s you the letter   DEM
   'Who did you get that letter from?'

(42)   [Pwy]$_i$ gest   ti 'r   llythyr 'na   ganddo   *pro$_i$*?
   who   get.PAST.2s you the letter   DEM with.3MS
   'Who did you get that letter from?'

(43)   [Pwy]$_i$ gest   ti 'r   llythyr 'na   ganddo   fe$_i$?
   who   get.PAST.2s you the letter   DEM with.3MS him
   'Who did you get that letter from?'

4.1.8   *Possessor* wh-*questions*

Possessor *wh*-questions normally involve pied-piping of the entire noun phrase containing the possessor *wh*-word. There are no special possessor *wh*-words corresponding to English 'whose'. The ordinary *wh*-words *pwy* 'who' and *beth* 'what' appear, with no case marking, following the head noun in the same pattern as that found with other possessors (see section 5.5). An example is given in (44).[3]

---

[3] Again, note that the absence of an agreement clitic (*ei*) before *car* confirms the conclusion that *pwy* does not count as pronominal for agreement purposes.

(44)　　Car pwy welaist　ti?
　　　　car who see.PAST.2S you
　　　　'Whose car did you see?'

Again, movement of a possessor from within a noun phrase seems to be impossible, necessitating movement of the entire noun phrase. The resumptive strategy is marginal with *wh*-questions, although a resumptive pattern is found here in other types of *wh*-construction. An example is (70) in section 4.2.4 below.

4.1.9　　*Adjunct* wh-*questions*

Adjunct *wh*-questions are formed using the various adjunct *wh*-words, such as *sut* 'how', *pryd* 'when', *pam* 'why', *lle / ble* 'where', and *pa mor* + adjective 'how + adjective'. In colloquial Welsh, both soft mutation and absence of mutation are found after these. *Lle / ble* 'where' tends not to trigger a following soft mutation. With the others, there seems to be fairly complex variation, partly influenced by what verb follows. Examples are given in (45)–(47).

(45)　　Sut　**gwyddost / wyddost** ti　　hyn?
　　　　how know.PRES.2S　　　you DEM.NS
　　　　'How do you know that?'

(46)　　Pryd　**cest / gest**　ti　dy benblwydd?
　　　　when get.PAST.2S you 2s birthday
　　　　'When did you have your birthday?'

(47)　　Pa　　mor aml　**byddwch / fyddwch** chi 'n　torri　'r　lawnt?
　　　　which so　often be.FUT.2P　　　you PROG cut.INF the lawn
　　　　'How often do you mow the lawn?'

In literary Welsh, the particle *y(r)* appears in all these cases, with no mutation on the verb:

(48)　　Sut　y　gwyddost　hyn?
　　　　how PRT know.PRES.2S DEM.NS
　　　　'How do you know that?'

(49)　　Pryd　y　cefaist　　dy benblwydd?
　　　　when PRT get.PAST.2S 2s birthday
　　　　'When did you have your birthday?'

(50)　　Pa mor aml　y　byddwch yn　torri　'r　lawnt?
　　　　WH so　often PRT be.FUT.2P PROG cut.INF the lawn
　　　　'How often do you mow the lawn?'

4.1.10   Multiple wh-*questions and superiority*

Unlike most other Celtic languages (Irish, Scottish Gaelic), multiple *wh*-questions are possible in Welsh. One *wh*-word moves to clause-initial position, and the rest remain in situ.

(51)   a. Pwy sy   'n   gadael pryd?
            who be.PRES.REL PROG leave.INF when
            'Who's leaving when?'
        b. Pwy ydy   pwy?
            who be.PRES.3s who
            'Who's who?'

Which *wh*-word moves depends on a superiority hierarchy that appears to be much the same as in English. Consequently, superiority effects obtain. In (52) and (53), the subject *wh*-word must take precedence over the object *wh*-word in determining which moves to initial position.

(52)   Pwy sy   'n   gwneud beth?
        who be.PRES.REL PROG do.INF   what
        'Who's doing what?'

(53)   *Beth mae   pwy yn   ei   wneud?
        what be.PRES.3s who PROG 3MS do.INF
        ('What's who doing?')

4.2   Relative clauses

Relative clauses are structurally quite similar to *wh*-questions. However, in most relative clauses, there is no overt relative pronoun. Relative clauses have the same form as the material following the *wh*-word in a *wh*-question. As with *wh*-questions, relative clauses are marked by soft mutation of the verb, and, in some contexts, by rich agreement or a resumptive pronoun at the relativization site.

4.2.1   Subject and object relatives

An example of a subject restrictive relative is given in (54), and an object relative in (55).

(54)   y dyn gafodd   y   wobr
        the man get.PAST.3s the prize
        'the man who got the prize'

(55)   y   ffrwydrad glywais   i wedyn
        the explosion hear.PAST.1s I then
        'the explosion that I heard then'

In both these cases, an overt pronoun is excluded at the relativization site:

(56)   *y   dyn gafodd   e 'r   wobr
        the man get.PAST.3s   he the prize
        ('the man who he got the prize')

(57)   *y   ffrwydrad glywais   i e wedyn
        the explosion hear.PAST.1s I it then
        ('the explosion that I heard it then')

In the literary language, the particle *a* is used in both cases, immediately preceding the verb.

Wh-question words may not normally be used as relative pronouns:

(58)   *y   dyn pwy gafodd   y   wobr
        the man who get.PAST.3s the prize
        ('the man who got the prize')

Adjunct relatives constitute an exception. The *wh*-words *lle* 'where', *pryd* 'when' and *pam* 'why' are grammatical in these (for further details of adjunct relatives, see section 4.2.5 below):

(59)   yr ardal lle   gafodd   ei   fagu
        the district where get.PAST.3s 3MS raise.INF
        'the district where he was brought up'

In archaic literary style, an overt demonstrative pronoun, such as *yr hwn* 'that one (masc.)', may be used as a relative pronoun:

(60)   y dyn   yr hwn   a   gafodd   y   wobr
        the man the DEM.MS PRT get.PAST.3s the prize
        'the man who got the prize'

This usage was largely modelled on foreign languages, and has mostly fallen out of use (for details, see Richards 1938: 75).

In Principles and Parameters approaches, subject and object relatives are usually taken to involve a null operator, the null equivalent of the *wh*-words such as *who* or *which* in relative clauses in English and other languages. The null operator receives an overt realization, as a relative pronoun, in the case of the adjunct relatives in (59). The null operator moves from subject or object position to the front of the relative clause creating a chain (A'-chain) with the relevant operator-variable interpretation ('the man x, such that x got the prize'):

(61)   y   dynion [_CP Op_i gafodd   t_i y   wobr]
         the men   get.PAST.3S   the prize
         'the men who got the prize'

The Antiagreement Effect found in *wh*-questions is also found in relative clauses. Again, if the null operator is defined as being non-pronominal in specification, then this is expected, since verbs in Welsh never agree with non-pronominal subjects, only with pronominal ones.

4.2.2   Object of non-finite verbs

The patterns with relatives formed on the object position of a structure involving an auxiliary are essentially the same as those found with *wh*-questions. Examples are given in (62). The verb may be accompanied by an object-agreement clitic, (62a). This clitic may be dropped, leaving its mutation effect behind (62b), or both clitic and mutation may be absent entirely, (62c). Of these options, (62a), with strict agreement, is closest to the literary language; (62c) is the most colloquial.

(62)   a. y   car mae 'r   lladron wedi ei   ddwyn ___
         b. y   car mae 'r   lladron wedi   ddwyn ___
         c. y   car mae 'r   lladron wedi   dwyn ___
            the car is   the thieves PERF (3MS) steal.INF
            'the car that the thieves have stolen'

An overt resumptive object pronoun is not possible:

(63)   *y   car mae   'r lladron wedi ei   ddwyn e
          the car be.PRES.3S the thieves PERF 3MS steal.INF it
          ('the car that the thieves have stolen it')

In the literary language, a particle is inserted at the front of the relative clause, *y(r)* if the auxiliary is *bod*, and either *a* or *y(r)* if the auxiliary is modal (*gallu* 'be able', *cael* 'be allowed' etc.). The patterns are essentially the same as with *wh*-questions (section 4.1.5 above). The reasons given above for concluding that *wh*-questions formed on the object of a periphrastic verb involve a gap strategy rather than resumption apply here too.

4.2.3   Object-of-preposition relatives

With relatives formed on the object position of prepositions, the normal pattern involves leaving the preposition in clause-final or near-final position. There is obligatory agreement between the preposition and the antecedent of the relative:

(64)   y   fenyw   werthodd   Ieuan y   ceffyl iddi
         the woman sell.PAST.3S Ieuan the horse to.3FS
         'the woman that Ieuan sold the horse to'

Note that, in contrast to *wh*-questions, pied-piping of the prepositional phrase is not possible, presumably because overt *wh*-words, such as *pwy* 'who', are not available in relative clauses:

(65)   *y   fenyw   i   bwy   werthodd   Ieuan y   ceffyl
         the woman to who sell.PAST.3S Ieuan the horse
         ('the woman that Ieuan sold the horse to')

An overt resumptive pronoun is possible:

(66)   y   myfyrwyr werthodd   Ieuan y   ceffyl iddyn **nhw**
         the students sell.PAST.3S Ieuan the horse to.3P them
         'the students that Ieuan sold the horse to'

The literary pattern, as in *wh*-questions, involves the particle *y(r)*; there is no mutation of the verb and there is generally no overt resumptive pronoun, although agreement on the preposition remains:

(67)   y   wraig   y   gwerthodd Ieuan y   ceffyl iddi
         the woman PRT sell.PAST.3S Ieuan the horse to.3FS
         'the woman that Ieuan sold the horse to'

As with *wh*-questions, the availability of an overt resumptive pronoun suggests that these involve a resumptive strategy, with the pronoun being null in cases such as (64), where an inflected preposition is used with no overt pronoun following. We thus have the structure in (68).

(68)   y   fenyw   [$_{CP}$ Op$_i$ werthodd   Ieuan y   ceffyl [$_{PP}$ iddi *pro$_i$* / hi$_i$]]
         the woman   sell.PAST.3S Ieuan the horse to.3FS   *pro* / her
         'the woman that Ieuan sold the horse to'

4.2.4   Possessor relatives

Possessor relative clauses require a resumptive strategy. The verb mutates and the possessor is represented by a possessor-agreement clitic on the noun:

(69)   y   dyn   welais   i   **ei**   chwaer
         the man see.PAST.1S I   3MS   sister
         'the man whose sister I saw'

An overt resumptive pronoun is possible:

(70)   y   dyn welais   i   ei   chwaer **e**
        the man see.PAST.1S I   3MS   sister him
        'the man whose sister I saw'

In literary Welsh, the particle $y(r)$ is used and there is no soft mutation of the verb:

(71)   y   dyn **y**   gwelais   ei   chwaer
        the man PRT   see.PAST.1S 3MS   sister
        'the man whose sister I saw'

There is general agreement that these involve a resumptive pronoun after the noun. This may be null, as in (69) or (71) or overt, as with *e* 'him' in (70). The structure is therefore:

(72)   y   dyn [$_{CP}$ Op$_i$ welais   i   [$_{DP}$ ei   chwaer *pro$_i$* / *e$_i$*]]
        the man   see.PAST.1S I   3MS   sister *pro* / him
        'the man whose sister I saw'

4.2.5   *Adjunct relatives*

With generic nouns denoting places, times, reasons etc., the *wh*-word may be omitted, as in (73). With other nouns, as is the case in (74), the *wh*-word is compulsory. The pattern of mutations with *wh*-words is the same as in *wh*-questions described above.

(73)   y   flwyddyn ges   i   'ngeni
        the year   get.PAST.1S I   1S.be.born.INF
        'the year I was born'

(74)   yr   ysbyty lle   ces   i   'ngeni
        the hospital where get.PAST.1S I   1S.be.born.INF
        'the hospital where I was born'

In literary Welsh, the first of these requires the particle $y(r)$ and the verb does not mutate:

(75)   y   flwyddyn y   cefais   fy   ngeni
        the year   PRT get.PAST.1S 1S   be.born.INF
        'the year I was born'

Non-restrictive adjunct relatives always require an overt *wh*-word:

(76)   y   flwyddyn honno,   pryd gafodd   Dylan Thomas ei   eni
        the year   DEM.FS   when get.PAST.3S Dylan Thomas 3MS   be.born.INF
        'that year, when Dylan Thomas was born'

(77)   *y flwyddyn honno, gafodd   Dylan Thomas ei   eni
        the year   DEM.FS get.PAST.3s Dylan Thomas 3MS be.born.INF
        ('that year, when Dylan Thomas was born')

Given that these relatives contain no possible resumptive element, it is reasonable to suppose that they involve a gap strategy:

(78)   y   flwyddyn [$_{CP}$ Op$_i$ ges   i [$_{VP}$ 'ngeni]   t$_i$]
        the year   get.PAST.1s I   1s-be.born.INF
        'the year I was born'

4.3   Focus

Mild contrastive focus is expressed by moving the focused constituent to the front of the clause. What follows this constituent is structurally identical to a *wh*-question. Examples of the basic types are given in (79)–(83). These essentially follow the syntax of *wh*-questions, with the focused element occupying the same position as the *wh*-word in a *wh*-question. Constructions of this type are extremely common in spoken Welsh.

(79)   Fo   sy   'n   ennill.
        he.STRONG be.PRES.REL PROG win.INF
        '*He*'s winning.' 'He's the one who's winning.'

(80)   Dim ond hyn   gollais   i.
        only   DEM.NS lose.PAST.1s I
        'I lost *only that*.' 'That's all I lost.'

(81)   Hwnna dw   i 'n   (ei) leicio.
        DEM.MS be.PRES.1s I PROG 3MS like.INF
        'I like *that one*.' 'That's the one I like.'

(82)   Dim ond hyn   a   hyn   o alcohol mae   'r corff yn
        only   DEM.NS and DEM.NS of alcohol be.PRES.3s the body PROG
        gallu   ymdopi â   fo.
        be.able.INF cope.INF with it
        'The body can cope with *only so much alcohol*.' 'There's only so much alcohol that the body can cope with.'

(83)   Yno (y)   mae   'r gwaith.
        there (PRT) be.PRES.3s the work
        'That's where the work is.'

Only a single constituent may be focused in this way.

4.3.1   *Propositional adverbs*

A number of adverbs also appear in the clause-initial focus position. These are all propositional adverbs, and include *efallai* 'perhaps', *hwyrach* 'probably', *braidd* 'hardly' and *prin* 'hardly':

(84)   Hwyrach (y)   bydd   rhaid   i   chi aros.
        probably (PRT) be.FUT.3s necessity to you wait.INF
        'You'll probably have to wait.'

These adverbs never trigger mutation of the verb, even in colloquial Welsh. Their syntax shows similarities with that of *wh*-constructions. First, unlike ordinary clause-initial adverbs, they do not co-occur with an affirmative particle *fe* or *mi*. Contrast *hwyrach* 'probably' in (85) with *yfory* 'tomorrow' in (86).

(85)   *Hwyrach fe   fydd   rhaid   i   chi aros.
        probably   PRT be.FUT.3s necessary to you wait.INF
        ('You'll probably have to wait.')

(86)   Yfory   fe   fydd   rhaid   i   chi aros.
        tomorrow PRT be.FUT.3s necessary to   you wait.INF
        'Tomorrow you will have to wait.'

Secondly, when embedded, these adverbs allow a focus complementizer, such as *mai* in (87), with neutral interpretation, whereas other adverbs do not (on focus complementizers, see section 4.3.4 below). Contrast (87), which has a neutral (non-focus) interpretation, with (88), which is grammatical only with a focus interpretation.

(87)   Mae   Ieuan yn   dweud mai   hwyrach bydd
        be.PRES.3s Ieuan PROG say.INF COMP.FOCUS probably be.FUT.3s
        rhaid   i   ni aros.
        necessity to us wait.INF
        'Ieuan says we'll probably have to wait.'

(88)   *Mae   Ieuan yn   dweud mai   yfory   bydd
        be.PRES.3s Ieuan PROG say.INF COMP.FOCUS tomorrow be.FUT.3s
        rhaid   i   ni aros.
        necessity to us wait.INF
        ('Ieuan says that tomorrow we'll have to wait.')
        (grammatical interpretation: 'Ieuan says that it's tomorrow that we'll have to wait.')

These distributional facts point to one of two conclusions, either:

(i)   although semantically they do not form part of a *wh*-structure (since they are neither *wh*-elements nor do they bear focus, and they cannot plausibly be said to have moved), these elements occupy the same structural position as *wh*-words and focused constituents;

(ii)   structures such as (84) contain two clauses: a reduced main clause *hwyrach*, which takes the remainder of the sentence as a complement clause.

4.3.2   Agreement in focus constructions

Focus constructions allow a wider range of types of possible fronted constituent than *wh*-questions and, in particular, relative clauses, and hence tell us slightly more about the system. Two aspects are particularly worthy of note. The first of these concerns agreement with focused personal pronouns. We have already seen that there is no number agreement between *wh*-subject and verb in a subject *wh*-construction. Focus constructions show us that there is no person agreement either. When a pronoun is focused, the verb remains in the default third-person singular form, as in (89).

(89)   Fi   (ddy)wedodd / *(ddy)wedais hyn.
        I.STRONG say.PAST.3S   / *say.PAST.1S   DEM.NS
        'It was me who said that.'

This aspect of the syntax of *wh*-constructions does not self-evidently follow from general principles of Welsh agreement. Recall (from section 1.4.3) that verbs and other agreeing heads in Welsh show morphological agreement only with personal pronouns. Since *fi* 'I' in (89) is a pronoun, we might expect the verb to agree with it, but it does not.

One possible account (see section 6.4) relates absence of subject–verb agreement in (89) to properties of strong and weak pronouns (see section 1.4.5). In (89), the pronoun appears in the strong form *fi*, as required if it is under focus, whereas in immediately postverbal position only the weak (clitic) form is possible, that is, *dywedais i* 'I said' not *dywedais fi*. On such an account, strong pronouns would be treated as non-pronominal for purposes of agreement and would be required to move to a focus position. Weak pronouns conversely would be treated as pronominal with no movement requirement. Once the strong form is chosen, default third-person agreement automatically results, together with movement of the strong pronoun to initial position. This amounts to revising our generalization about agreement to say that verbs and other agreeing heads in Welsh show morphological agreement only with weak personal pronouns.

Another way of accounting for this is to say that agreement in Welsh is a surface phenomenon dependent on a head being adjacent to a following pronoun (Borsley 2005). On this account, we find third-person agreement in (89) because the pronoun does not end up adjacent to the agreeing head (verb). Note that this again amounts to saying that an element must be adjacent to a head in order to trigger agreement.

Roberts (2005: 64) suggests something similar when he proposes that the trace of a pronoun focused to initial position acts like a non-pronominal noun phrase and agreement is with the trace and not with the moved element. This makes sense within a Principle and Parameters framework, where the trace is a *wh*-trace, which is non-pronominal. Being non-pronominal, it triggers default third-person agreement. It makes less sense within the more recent Copy Theory of Movement, where traces are actually copies of the moved element, and where a fronted pronoun would presumably leave a pronominal copy. For full discussion of these issues, see chapter 6.

Person agreement also fails when the direct object of a periphrastic verb is fronted. So, in (90), *fi* is the pronominal object of the verb, but the object-agreement clitic preceding the verb can only be the default form, the masculine third-person singular, and never first-person, as in (91):

(90)   Fi   wyt   ti   'n   **(ei)**   olygu?
        I.STRONG be.PRES.2S you PROG (3MS) mean.INF
        'You mean me? / Is it me that you mean?'

(91)   *Fi   wyt   ti   'n   **(fy)**   ngolygu?
        I.STRONG be.PRES.2S you PROG (1S)   mean.INF
        ('You mean me? / Is it me that you mean?')

This poses problems for the view that *wh*-constructions formed on the object position of a periphastic verb are resumptive. If there is a null resumptive pronoun after the verb in (90), then the clitic *ei* makes it clear that this resumptive pronoun is masculine third-person singular. If so, it is hard to see how it can be linked to a first-person singular pronoun in focus position.

4.3.3   *Fronting of verbal phrases and minor constituent types*

The second important aspect of this construction is that a range of other constituent types may be fronted. Locative prepositional phrases, nonfinite verbal phrases, and predicate phrases may be fronted freely with no particular contrastive focus:

(92)   [_PP Yn syth   i   'w gwely] (yr)   aeth   hi.
            PRED straight to 3FS bed (PRT) go.PAST.3S she
        'Straight to bed she went.'

(93)   [$_{AspP}$ Wedi [$_{VP}$ mynd   adre   'n   gynnar]] (y)   mae   Siân.
        PERF   go.INF   home PRED early   (PRT) be.PRES.3S Siân
        'Gone home early has Siân.'

(94)   [$_{AP}$ Go   debyg] (y)   mae   ei   wraig yn   edrych.
        quite similar (PRT) be.PRES.3S 3MS wife   PROG look.INF
        'Quite similar his wife looks.'

These are all much more idiomatic in Welsh than their direct English translations.

Fronted verbal phrases exist in a number of forms. In (93), a verbal phrase is fronted complete with aspect particle (aspect phrase). Note that the unmarked ('progressive') aspect marker *yn* disappears when fronted:

(95)   (*Yn) Gadael   am ddeg 'dyn   ni.
        PROG leave.INF   at   ten   be.PRES.1P we
        'We're leaving at ten.'

In colloquial Welsh, fronting of an aspect phrase triggers soft mutation on the following verb, *bydd* > *fydd* in (96); but this construction uses the particle *y(r)* in literary Welsh, in (97).

(96)   Wedi cyrraedd   **fydd**   hi erbyn hyn.
        PERF   arrive.INF   be.FUT.3S she by   now
        'She will have arrived by now.'

(97)   Wedi cyrraedd   **y**   bydd   hi erbyn hyn.
        PERF arrive.INF PRT be.FUT.3S she by   DEM.NS
        'She will have arrived by now.'

The verb phrase complements of the auxiliaries *gwneud* 'do' and *ddaru* (past-tense auxiliary) may be fronted:

(98)   ... [$_{VP}$ sleifio   yma yn sgîl Bob Owen] wnaeth   hi ...
        sneak.INF here behind Bob Owen do.PAST.3S she
        '... she sneaked here behind Bob Owen ...'   (*TMC* 11)

(99)   [$_{VP}$ Cerdded i   lawr] ddaru chi, Mrs Gruffydd?
        walk.INF to down PAST   you Mrs Gruffydd
        'You walked down, did you, Mrs Gruffydd?'   (*TMC* 150)

The construction with *ddaru* is not available in literary Welsh since *ddaru* is not used as a past-tense auxiliary in literary Welsh. The particle with *gwneud* 'do' is *a* in literary Welsh:

(100)   . . . credent   . . . mai   [_{VP} myned i achub cam gwledydd
         believe.IMPF.3P COMP.FOCUS   go.INF to save.INF wrong countries
         bychain] a   wnaeth   Prydain Fawr.
         small.P PRT do.PAST.3S Britain Great
         '. . . they believed . . . that Great Britain had gone to defend small countries.'
                                                                    (*TMC* 159)

Clearly, these cases are further examples of the gap strategy, since there is no evidence that they involve any kind of resumptive element. We must therefore recognize that *wh*-dependencies involving a gap are permitted with the complement of a auxiliary.

4.3.4   Embedded focus constructions

Focus constructions may be embedded using one of the focus complementizers, northern and literary *mai* or southern *taw* (see Tallerman 1996):

(101)   Dw   i 'n   siwr mai / taw   hi gaiff   y   wobr.
         be.PRES.1S I PRED sure COMP.FOCUS she get.FUT.3S the prize
         'I'm sure that she's the one who'll get the prize.'

Mai and *taw* do not differ in their syntax in any way. Henceforth, *mai* will be used for illustrative purposes.

Although focus constructions resemble relative clauses in many ways, the fact that they may occur in subordinate clauses, with the same syntax as in main clauses, raises a problem. It is normally assumed that *wh*-words occupy the leftmost clausal position – within a Principle and Parameters framework, the specifier of CP. Since the CP-layer is headed by a complementizer (C), it should be impossible for a complementizer to precede a *wh*-element. This, among other things, is what excludes the English sentence in (102). There is no structural position for the complementizer *that*, since *who came to dinner* is already a complete clause (complementizer phrase).

(102)   *I know that [_{CP} who came to dinner].

In (101), therefore, we have the problem that a focused element, apparently in [Spec, CP], is preceded by the complementizer *mai*. Tallerman (1996) proposes that *mai* is a complementizer that itself introduces a full clause (CP) and therefore allows a structure with two CPs. This would make it analogous to apparently recursive CP-structures in English, such as (103).

(103)   She said [_{CP} that [_{CP} under no circumstances could she learn Irish]].

Here, the subject – verb inversion of *could* and *she* implies that the verb is in C, and that *under no circumstances* is in [Spec, CP]. Given this, a second C-position must be available for *that*. Roberts (1997) proposes a related analysis, but treats the upper CP as being ForceP and the lower one as FocP.

A further problem with *mai* is that, in colloquial Welsh, it may be used to convey focus in a clause headed by the conditional complementizer *os* 'if', as in (104). Although co-occurrence of *os* and *mai* is normal in speech, it is frowned upon prescriptively, in favour of more conservative usage where *os* expressed both conditional meaning and focus.

(104)   Os mai   hi gaiff   y   wobr . . .
          if   COMP.FOCUS she get.FUT.3s the prize
          'If *she* gets the prize . . .'

Furthermore, focus may co-occur with *wh*-movement in embedded questions involving *pam* 'why':

(105)   Esboniodd   Aled pam mai   Ewrop fydd   yn   rheolu
          explain.PAST.3s Aled why COMP.FOCUS Europe be.FUT.3s PROG rule.INF
          'r   21ain ganrif.
          the 21st   century
          'Aled explained why *Europe* will be ruling the 21st century.'

Constructions like (105) seem to motivate a more complex CP-layer, with separate projections for the different complementizers, the *wh*-elements and the focus elements.

4.4   Copular constructions

Some features of *wh*-dependencies are also apparent in a copular construction involving *yw* (literary and southern *yw*, northern *ydy* / *ydi*, archaic literary *ydyw*), a special form of *bod* 'be'. This construction, known traditionally as the 'impure nominal sentence' (*brawddeg enwol amhur*), is illustrated in (106)–(108). *Yw* may not appear clause initially, but must be preceded by some element. Semantically, the construction may convey an identificational meaning or may be predicational.

4.4.1   *Fronting in identity copular constructions*

In (106), *Caerdydd* 'Cardiff' and *prifddinas Cymru* 'the capital of Wales' are identifed as having identical reference. Either element may be

interpreted as the new information, and hence (106) may answer either of the
wh-questions in (107) or (108). The more natural interpretation is with
Caerdydd as topic and *prifddinas Cymru* as new information, that is, answering (107), in which case there is a falling intonation on *Cymru* followed by an
intonational break. Alternatively, there is no intonational break, and a falling
intonation on *Caerdydd*, in which case *Caerdydd* is interpreted as new information, in answer to (108).

(106)   Prifddinas Cymru yw   Caerdydd.
        capital   Wales be.PRES.3s Cardiff
        'Cardiff is the capital of Wales.'

(107)   Beth yw   Caerdydd?
        what be.PRES.3s Cardiff
        'What is Cardiff?'

(108)   Pa   ddinas yw   prifddinas Cymru?
        which city   be.PRES.3s capital   Wales
        'Which city is the capital of Wales?'

The order may be reversed, as in (109), with the same possibilities for
interpretation.

(109)   Caerdydd yw   prifddinas Cymru.
        Cardiff be.PRES.3s capital   Wales
        'The capital of Wales is Cardiff.'

4.4.2   *Fronting in predicative copular constructions*

When the construction with *yw* is interpreted as having predicational
meaning, it is the counterpart to ordinary predicative 'be' structures. For
instance, corresponding to neutral (110), we have focus-fronting structures,
with fronting of the predicate noun phrase *dinas hardd* 'beautiful city' in (111),
and fronting of the subject *Caerdydd* 'Cardiff' in (112). This is the ordinary
focus construction as discussed in section 4.3 above, but with fronting of a
predicate noun phrase. When a predicative noun phrase or adjective phrase is
fronted, *bod* 'be' always takes on the *yw*-form. In both cases, the fronted
element bears contrastive focus.

(110)   Mae   Caerdydd yn   ddinas hardd.
        be.PRES.3s Cardiff PRED city   beautiful
        'Cardiff is a beautiful city.'

(111)   Dinas hardd   yw   Caerdydd.
        city beautiful be.PRES.3s Cardiff
        'Cardiff is a beautiful city.'

(112)   Caerdydd sy   'n   ddinas hardd.
         Cardiff be.PRES.REL PRED city   beautiful
         'It's Cardiff that's a beautiful city. / *Cardiff* is a beautiful city.'

In (112), the verb is *sy(dd)*, as is normal in a *wh*-construction formed when a subject is moved. The existence of the pattern in (112), which instantiates the order fronted subject – be – predicate, means that this order may not be instantiated using *yw*. That is, (113) is ungrammatical, even though the superficially similar construction with an identificational meaning in (109) above is grammatical.

(113)   *Caerdydd yw   dinas hardd.
         Cardiff   be.PRES.3S city   beautiful
         ('Cardiff is a beautiful city.')

Note that, in predicative contexts, *yw* is used only when a noun phrase or an adjective phrase is fronted, whereas in identificational contexts *yw* is the only possibility. This means that examples can be constructed where the form of the verb distinguishes predicational from identificational meaning. This is the case in (114) and (115).

(114)   Yng Nghaerdydd yw   'r lle i fod.
         in Cardiff   be.PRES.3S the place to be.INF
         'In Cardiff is the place to be.'

(115)   Yng Nghaerdydd mae   'r lle i fod.
         in Cardiff   be.PRES.3S the place to be.INF
         'The place to be is *in Cardiff*.'

In (114), the verb is *yw*, hence the meaning is identificational: 'in Cardiff' and 'the place to be' are identified as having the same reference, hence the meaning is that the whole city is the place to be. In (115), the verb is *mae*, hence the meaning is predicational: '(being) in Cardiff' is stated to be a property that the place to be has, hence the place to be is some location (bar, club, etc.) within Cardiff. For further exemplification and discussion, see Zaring (1996).

4.4.3   *Affinities with* wh-*constructions*

Copular constructions with *yw* show a number of affinities with *wh*-constructions. First, an anaphor such as *ei hun* 'himself' in (116) may have the following subject as an antecedent. This is parallel to *wh*-questions, such as (117), where reconstruction of anaphoric relations is possible and *ei hun* 'himself' may be interpreted as referring to *Ifan*. Contrast this with ordinary verb-initial clauses such as (118), where an anaphor inside the subject cannot be coreferential with the following object.

(116)   [Ei elyn   gwaethaf ei   hun] yw   Ifan.
          3MS enemy worst   3MS self   be.PRES.3S Ifan
          'Ifan is his own worst enemy.'

(117)   [P'un   o 'i   luniau ei   hun] mae   Ifan yn   (ei)
          which-one of 3MS pictures 3MS self   be.PRES.3S Ifan PROG (3MS)
          leicio   fwya?
          like.INF most
          'Which of his own pictures does Ifan like best?'

(118)   *Prynodd   [ei   awdur ei   hun] y   llyfr.
          buy.PAST.3S 3MS author 3MS self   the book
          ('*Its own author bought the book.')

Secondly, these constructions must be embedded in the same way as focus
constructions, using the focus complementizer *mai* (compare section 4.3.4
above). Embedding of the identificational copular sentence in (109) is illustrated in (119).

(119)   Mae   pawb   yn   gwybod [mai   Caerdydd yw
          be.PRES.3S everyone PROG know.INF COMP.FOCUS Cardiff   is
          prifddinas Cymru].
          capital   Wales
          'Everyone knows that the capital of Wales is Cardiff.'

Thirdly, in tenses where it begins with a mutable consonant, the copula undergoes soft mutation, as in focus and other *wh*-constructions:

(120)   Y   brif broblem **fydd**   sicrhau   bod   ein cefnogwyr
          the main problem be.FUT.3S ensure.INF be.INF 3P supporters
          yn   pleidleisio.
          PROG vote.INF
          'The main problem will be ensuring that our supporters vote.'

This mutation is common to both the colloquial and literary language, and the
literary norm does not permit a particle here (Richards 1938: 11). A literary
example is given in (121).

(121)   . . . ond methiant **fu**   pob dadl   a   phob her.
                but failure   be.PRET.3S every argument and every challenge
          '. . . but every argument and every challenge became a failure.'   (*WJ* 31)

These similarities have led linguists to analyse the precopular element in
these constructions as having undergone fronting to the same position
as focused elements and *wh*-elements, namely [Spec, CP]. For a full exposi-
tion of such an analysis, see Rouveret (1996). For further discussion see
section 8.1.

4.5   Non-finite *wh*-constructions

Tough-constructions are shown in (122)–(123). Note that the object-agreement clitic in (122) is optional in less formal varieties.

(122)   Mae   'r llyfr yn   anodd i   ('w) ddarllen.
         be.PRES.3S the book PRED hard   to 3MS read.INF
         'The book is hard to read.'

(123)   Roedden nhw 'n   neis iawn i   siarad   efo   nhw.
         be.IMPF.3P they PRED nice very to talk.INF with them
         'They were very nice to talk to.'   (*DHMH* 25)

Embedded infinitival questions are illustrated in (124)–(125). Main clause infinitival questions are also possible.

(124)   Wn   i ddim beth i   ('w) ddarllen.
         know.PRES.1S I NEG what to (3MS) read.INF
         'I don't know what to read.'

(125)   Wn   i ddim at bwy i   anfon   y   llythyr.
         know.PRES.1S I NEG to who to send.INF the letter
         'I don't know to whom to send the letter.'

In (126), we have an *i*-clause with a finite (perfective) interpretation of a kind not found in English (see discussion of finite *i*-clauses in non-*wh*-environments in section 3.4.1).

(126)   Dw   i 'n   cofio   nawr pam / sut i 'r cynllun
         be.PRES.1S I PROG remember.INF now why / how to the plan
         gael   ei   wrthod.
         get.INF 3MS reject.INF
         'I remember now why / how the plan was rejected.'

Pam 'why' displays some unexpected properties in nonfinite environments. It may appear in an infinitival *wh*-question with a *bod*-clause as its complement (on *bod*-clauses in non-*wh*-environments, see section 3.3), in this case resembling the syntax of the propositional adverbs discussed in section 4.3.1 above:

(127)   Pam ei bod hi mor bwysig?
         why 3FS be.INF it so important
         'Why is it so important?'

Furthermore, it is the only *wh*-word that may co-occur with a focused element (see example (105) above).

Infinitival relatives are illustrated in (128)–(132). In general, these form the same types of structures as we found with finite *wh*-constructions above. That is, we find both optional object-agreement clitics, as in (129), and resumptive pronouns, as in (130) and (131).[4]

(128)   Dw   i 'n   chwilio   am rywun   i gyfieithu   'r llyfr.
        be.PRES.1S I PROG search.INF for someone to translate.INF the book
        'I'm looking for someone to translate the book.'

(129)   Dw   i 'n   chwilio   am rywbeth   i ('w) ddarllen.
        be.PRES.1S I PROG search.INF for something to (3MS) read.INF
        'I'm looking for something to read.'

(130)   'Dyn   ni angen rhywbeth i siarad amdano   (fe).
        be.PRES.1P we need something to talk.INF about.3MS (it)
        'We need something to talk about.'

(131)   Dw   i angen rhywun i fyw gydag e.
        be.PRES.1S I need someone to live with him
        'I need someone to live with.'

(132)   Mae   heddiw yn ddiwrnod braf i fynd   allan am dro.
        be.PRES.3S today PRED day   nice to go.INF out for walk
        'Today's a nice day to go out for a walk.'

Pied-piping is possible (and preferred) in infinitival *wh*-questions formed on the object of a preposition (see (125) above) but is not possible in the equivalent infinitival relatives, as illustrated in (133). This follows from the fact that non-adjunct *wh*-words are true interrogative pronouns, and may only appear in interrogative contexts (see (59) above).

(133)   *'Dyn   ni angen rhywbeth am   beth i siarad.
         be.PRES.1P we need something about which to talk.INF
         ('We need something about which to talk.')

Infinitival relatives are also possible with finite (perfective) *i*-clauses (see section 3.4.1), normally with a superlative or similar adjective in the antecedent, illustrated in (134)–(135). Note especially, that this type forms adjunct relatives freely, as in (135), in contrast to English.

(134)   Mae   e wedi canu   ar bob albwm i ni ei wneud erioed.
        be.PRES.3S he PERF sing.INF on every album to us 3MS do.INF ever
        'He's sung on every album we've ever done.'

(135)   y tro cyntaf erioed iddo fod yn hwyr
        the time first ever to.3MS be.INF PRED late
        'the first time ever that he'd been late'

As well as illustrating the full extent of *wh*-constructions in Welsh, nonfinite *wh*-constructions are significant for two reasons. In general, an extension

---

4 On the use of *angen* 'need' in these examples, see chapter 1 note 13, and section 2.6.3.

of the standard analysis of *wh*-constructions is possible. That is, we propose the availability of the different strategies, with the same distribution as elsewhere. So, a *tough*-construction formed on object position involves a gap strategy with a null operator, just like a finite relative clause:

(136)   Mae   'r   llyfr yn   hawdd [Op$_i$ i ('w)   ddarllen t$_i$].
         be.PRES.3S the book PRED easy   to (3MS) read.INF
         'The book is easy to read.'

In (136), the object-agreement clitic takes the form *'w*, rather than *ei*, because it follows the preposition *i* 'to' (see section 5.2.2 for details).

One formed on the object of a preposition involves a resumptive pronoun, whether overt or null, again paralleling a finite relative clause:

(137)   Roedden nhw 'n   neis iawn [Op$_i$ i siarad efo nhw$_i$].
         be.IMPF.3P they PRED nice very   to talk.INF with them
         'They were very nice to talk to.'

The optionality of the object-agreement clitic in non-finite *wh*-constructions formed on the object position of the non-finite verb in (136) is important in that it provides further support for the claim, discussed in section 4.1.6.2 above, that the object position of a non-finite / periphrastic verb is accessible to the gap strategy and does not involve resumption. In the version of (136) containing the object-agreement clitic *'w*, it is conceivable that the postverbal object position of *ddarllen* 'read' is being occupied by a null object pronoun. However, null objects are not licensed in the absence of an object-agreement clitic. Hence, in the version of (136) lacking the clitic, there is clearly no postverbal null object pronoun, and hence we cannot suggest that there is a null resumptive pronoun in object position. The only conclusion left is that there is a gap left by *wh*-movement.

There is another consideration here that undermines the suggestion that there is a consistent link between verbal particles and the type of *wh*-strategy chosen. Non-finite *wh*-constructions take the same form in literary and in colloquial Welsh, with the single exception that the object-agreement clitic in (136) is obligatory in literary Welsh. Importantly, the particles *a* and *y(r)*, characteristic of literary Welsh, are not present in non-finite constructions in any variety, since these particles are associated with finite contexts only. This means that we can conclude that these particles are not a necessary condition for the formation of a *wh*-dependency. Hence, the idea that these particles respectively license a gap and a resumptive pronoun (see discussion below, section 4.7) is not tenable, because it cannot extend to non-finite *wh*-structures of the type discussed in this section.

4.6   Other *wh*-constructions: comparatives and correlatives

A number of other *wh*-constructions are parallel to those that have been examined already, notably comparative and equative clauses and correlatives. Comparatives are illustrated in (138)–(140). Note expecially that comparatives require the relative form of the auxiliary (*sy*(*dd*)) when the comparative is formed on subject position in (138). Comparatives normally use the literary form of the *wh*-clause. Literary forms, with particles and literary mutations, are given in (139) and (140). On the object clitic in (140), see section 4.9.6 below.

(138)   Mae   mwy o bobol yn   mynd i   wylio   pêl-droed ar
         be.PRES.3s more of people PROG go.INF to watch.INF football   on
         y   penwythnos na(g) **sy**   'n   mynd i 'r   eglwys.
         the weekend   than be.PRES.REL PROG go.INF to the church
         'More people go to watch football at the weekend than go to church.'

(139)   Mae   hyn   yn   haeddu   mwy o sylw   nag a
         be.PRES.3s DEM.NS PROG deserve.INF more of attention than PRT
         gafodd   hyd yn hyn.
         get.PAST.3s until.now
         'This deserves more attention than it has had up till now.'

(140)   Mae   hyn   yn   cymryd mwy o amser nag y   byddech
         be.PRES.3s DEM.NS PROG take.INF more of time   than PRT be.COND.2P
         chi 'n   ei   ddisgwyl.
         you PROG 3MS expect.INF
         'This takes more time than you'd expect.'

'As'-clauses with *fel* 'as' behave in the same way.

The correlative construction using *po* 'the' plus a superlative adjective is illustrated in (141). Note the crosslinguistically rare use of the superlative rather than the comparative in this construction in Welsh.

(141)   Po   fwyaf o amser dreuliwch   chi ar y   llinell, mwyaf fydd
         CORREL most of time   spend.PRES.2P you on the line   most be.FUT.3s
         y   gost.
         the cost
         'The more time you spend on the line, the more the cost will be.'

4.7   Particles in literary Welsh

As we have seen at various points in this chapter, literary Welsh differs from colloquial Welsh fairly systematically in the realm of *wh*-constructions. Where colloquial Welsh marks *wh*-dependencies using soft mutation of the verb, literary Welsh uses the particles *a* and *y(r)*. Much of the research on Welsh *wh*-constructions has focused on the literary variety, hence much work has been devoted to trying to derive the distribution of the two particles. It must be emphasized that literary Welsh is not anyone's native language and exists primarily in written form (see section 1.3).

The main data to be accounted for are summarized in Table 4.3, which lists the choice of particle in literary Welsh for each of the types of main-clause finite *wh*-structures that have been considered in this chapter. A popular approach, in the generative tradition stemming from Awbery (1977), has been to attempt to correlate the choice of particle with the choice of strategy (gap versus resumption). On this approach, choice of *a* entails use of a gap strategy, whereas use of *y(r)* entails use of resumption.

This approach is based on the traditional distinction between direct (*rhywiog*) and indirect (*afrywiog*) *wh*-structures. These terms have been used in two distinct ways in the literature:

(i)   direct: 'a *wh*-dependency formed on the subject position or on the object position of a synthetic verb';
       indirect: 'a *wh*-dependency formed on any other position'.
(ii)   direct: 'a *wh*-dependency formed using the particle *a*';
       indirect: 'a *wh*-dependency formed using the particle *y(r)*'.

The first definition is that adopted by Richards (1938). Most recent work (P. W. Thomas 1996: 495) has adopted the second definition, sometimes apparently in the belief that the two definitions are equivalent. On either definition, there seems to be a broad correlation between particle and type, with direct *wh*-dependencies using *a* and a gap, and indirect ones using *y(r)* and resumption.

This all works up to a point. If we consider *wh*-dependencies in finite *wh*-questions and relative clauses, then the correlation holds for some of the major types: subjects and objects of synthetic verbs clearly use the gap strategy and have *a* in literary Welsh; and objects of prepositions and possessor noun phrases clearly use the resumptive strategy and have *y(r)* in literary Welsh.

However, a number of authors (Rouveret 1994, Manning 1996, Willis 2000) have demonstrated that this straightforward mapping does not extend to a number of problematic cases. A cursory glance at Table 4.3 shows that the correlation is not good for minor types of dependency found mostly in focus constructions. In particular, we note the following problems:

Table 4.3. *Choice of particle in* wh-*constructions in literary Welsh.*

type of dependency	particle	strategy
subject	*a*	gap
object of synthetic verb	*a*	gap
object of periphrastic verb (with aux. *bod* 'be')	*y(r)*	gap?
object of periphrastic verb (with modals)	*a / y(r)*	gap?
object of preposition	*y(r)*	resumptive, (gap)
possessor noun phrase	*y(r)*	resumptive
adjunct	*y(r)*	gap
locative prepositional phrase complement	*y(r)*	gap
aspectual complement of *bod* 'be'	*y(r)*	gap
verb phrase complement of *gwneud* 'do'	*a*	gap
predicate complement of copula *bod* 'be'	zero	gap

(i)   A number of arguments were presented above (section 4.1.6.2) suggesting that *wh*-constructions involving the object of a periphrastic verb using auxiliary *bod* may employ a gap. However, these use *y(r)*, contrary to the generalization that *y(r)* is associated with a resumptive strategy. In order to maintain the generalization, it would be necessary to suggest that these involve a resumptive pronoun licensed by object-agreement clitics, as a number of authors have indeed proposed. This would entail providing alternative interpretations of the data presented above that point to the use of a gap strategy in this context.

(ii)   *Wh*-constructions involving the object of a non-finite verb dependent on a modal may use either particle, but the choice does not seem to reflect a difference in strategy. To maintain the proposed generalization, it would be necessary to demonstrate some syntactic differences associated with the choice of particle.

(iii)   All types of adjunct *wh*-constructions and focus constructions using locative prepositional phrase complements ('locative inversion') involve a gap, but use *y(r)*.

(iv)   When the aspectual phrase complement of auxiliary *bod* fronts, there is a gap with *y(r)*.

Providing motivated rules for choice of particle in literary Welsh is therefore not at all straightforward, and the attempt to link choice of particle with choice of *wh*-strategy cannot be regarded as successful.

4.8   Negative *wh*-constructions

In colloquial Welsh, the verb in a *wh*-construction may be negated in the usual way using *ddim* (for further details of negation in Welsh, see section 8.2):

(142)   Pwy sy   ddim yn   gwybod am   y   gân
         who be.PRES.REL NEG   PROG know.INF about the song
         adnabyddus hon?
         well.known DEM.FS
         'Who doesn't know of this well-known song?'

(143)   Beth wyt   ti ddim yn   hoffi am   dy waith?
         what be.PRES.2S you NEG   PROG like.INF about 2s work
         'What don't you like about your work?'

(144)   Pam wyt   ti ddim yn   dod   nos   'fory?
         why be.PRES.2S you NEG   PROG come.INF night tomorrow
         'Why aren't you coming tomorrow night?'

These behave essentially like their affirmative counterparts.

Alternatively, the subordinating negative complementizer *na(d)* may be used, both in colloquial and in literary Welsh. Examples are given in (145)–(147). In colloquial Welsh, it is used principally for the less accessible positions, hence the adjunct *wh*-question with *nad* in (147) is more acceptable than the subject *wh*-question in (145), for which (142) would normally be preferred. In literary Welsh, *na(d)* may be used freely for all positions.

(145)   Pwy nad   yw   'n   gwybod am   y   gân
         who COMP.NEG   be.PRES.3S PROG know.INF about the song
         adnabyddus hon?
         well.known DEM.FS
         'Who doesn't know about this well-known song?'

(146)   Beth nad   wyt   ti   'n (ei) hoffi am   dy waith?
         what COMP.NEG be.PRES.2S you PROG (3MS) like.INF about 2s work
         'What don't you like about your work?'

(147)   Pam nad   wyt   ti 'n   dod   nos   yfory?
         why COMP.NEG   be.PRES.3S you PROG come.INF night tomorrow
         'Why aren't you coming tomorrow night?'

When *na(d)* is used to negate a *wh*-construction, the resumptive strategy is more freely available than in affirmative cases. In both literary and colloquial Welsh, an overt resumptive pronoun is possible in object position. Example (148) shows an overt resumptive pronoun as the object of a periphrastic verb.

(148)   lot o ryw   eiria' Saesneg nad   oeddwn   i 'n
         lot of some-kind-of words English COMP.NEG be.IMPF.1S I PROG
         'u dallt   nhw
         3P understand.INF them
         'a lot of English words that I didn't understand'   (WJ 134)

With synthetic verbs, *nas* may be used instead of *na(d)* in literary Welsh, where
-*s* is a fossilized third-person object clitic:

(149)   a. Beth nas   trafodwyd   yn ystod y   cyfarfod?
            what COMP.NEG.3 discuss.PAST.IMPERS during   the meeting
            'What wasn't discussed during the meeting?'
         b. cynlluniau nas   trafodwyd   yn ystod y   cyfarfod
            plans   COMP.NEG.3 discuss.PAST.IMPERS during   the meeting
            'plans that were not discussed during the meeting'

An overt resumptive pronoun is also possible in object position:

(150)   teimladau . . . nas   cysylltodd   **hwynt** â   hi o'r blaen
         feelings   COMP.NEG.3 connect.PAST.3S them with her before
         'feelings . . . that he had not associated (them) with her before.'   (TMC 72)

The object may also be represented by inflected forms of the negative preposition / pronoun *mo* (on *mo* as a pseudo-quantifier, see section 8.2.3):

(151)   a. pobl na   welai   **mohonynt** yn   aml
            people COMP.NEG see.IMPF.3S NEG.3P   PRED often
            'people that she did not see often'   (TMC 109)
         b. y llawr cerrig na   olchwyd   **mohono** ers
            the floor stones COMP.NEG wash.PAST.IMPERS NEG.3MS since
            dyddiau lawer
            days   many
            'the stone floor that had not been washed for many a day'   (WJ 124)

Negative *wh*-constructions with *na(d)* formed on subject position tend to be
restricted to the literary language. Here, in contrast to affirmative clauses,
subject – verb agreement is obligatory, hence, in (152), the plural form of the
verb, *ydynt*, is required.

(152)   a. Pa rai nad   ydynt   yn   addas?
            which ones COMP.NEG be.PRES.3P PRED suitable
            'Which ones are not suitable?'
         b. gweithiau nad   ydynt   ar gael yn awr
            works   COMP.NEG be.PRES.3P available now
            'works that are not available now'   (Thorne 1993: 176)

These facts are often interpreted as indicating that, in negative *wh*-clauses
involving *na(d)*, a resumptive strategy is more widely available than in

the equivalent affirmative clauses, and that, in *wh*-dependencies formed on object position, both gap and resumptive strategies are available in negative clauses.

4.9   Long-distance *wh*-constructions

4.9.1   Wh-constructions formed on embedded subject position

4.9.1.1   The gap strategy

Welsh allows long-distance *wh*-dependencies. The example in (153) shows a *wh*-question formed on an embedded subject:

(153)   Pwy (r)ydyn   nhw 'n   meddwl sy   'n   prynu   pethau
         who be.PRES.3P they PROG think.INF be.PRES.REL PROG buy.INF things
         yn eu siopau nhw?
         in 3P shops   them
         'Who do they think buys things in their shops?'

A number of features of this construction are noteworthy. First, auxiliary *bod* 'be' in the embedded clause of (153) takes the relative form *sy(dd)*. We saw above (section 4.1.4) that *bod* 'be' requires special relative forms if it is in a clause with *wh*-extraction from subject position. This example demonstrates that this applies in embedded as well as in main clauses.

Where the auxiliary in the embedded clause is the imperfect of *bod* 'be', the form must be *oedd* rather than *roedd*, as in (154). Obligatory use of *oedd* in a subject *wh*-extraction contrasts with variability between *oedd* and *roedd* in other syntactic contexts. Again, therefore, we see the same effects in embedded contexts as in main clauses.

(154)   Pwy (r)oedden nhw 'n   meddwl oedd / *roedd yn   prynu
         who be.IMPF.3P they PROG think.INF be.IMPF.REL   PROG buy.INF
         pethau yn eu siopau nhw?
         things in 3P shops   them
         'Who did they think bought things in their shops?'

Note, that, in both (153) and (154), the verb in the main clause is in the non-relative form, not being subject to these restrictions.

Second, the Antiagreement Effect holds in embedded subject *wh*-constructions in Welsh, just as in main-clause ones. In (155), the auxiliary in the embedded clause takes the singular form *fyddai*, even though the antecedent of the relative *y prif bwyntiau* 'the main points' is plural. This seems to be confirmation that there is no (null) resumptive pronoun in (153)–(155), and that these therefore instantiate a long-distance gap strategy.

(155)   y   prif bwyntiau rydyn   ni   'n   meddwl **fyddai**   o
        the main points   be.PRES.1P we   PROG think be.COND.3S of
        ddiddordeb i   chi
        interest   to you
        'the main points that we think would be of interest to you'

This is in contrast to some other languages that have the Antiagreement Effect, such as Irish, where it is manifested only in main clauses.

Third, the verb mutates in an embedded clause in a *wh*-construction, just as it does in a main clause *wh*-environment. In (156), the embedded verb is soft-mutated *fyddai*. In a non-*wh*-context, unmutated (*y*) *byddai* would be the only option.

(156)   Pwy ydych   chi 'n   credu **fyddai**   'n   hoffi   bwyta
        who be.PRES.2P you PROG think be.COND.3S PROG like.INF eat.INF
        'r   aeron?
        the   berries
        'Who do you think would like to eat the berries?'

Fourth, restrictions on tensed complement clauses are voided in *wh*-constructions. There is very limited acceptance of tensed affirmative complement clauses in the present and imperfect tenses in non-*wh*-environments, as given in (157) and (158) (see section 3.3.1). However, the parallel *wh*-questions in (159) and (160) are fully grammatical for all speakers.

(157)   *Maen   nhw 'n   meddwl   mae   Ifan yn   prynu bara
        be.PRES.3P they PROG think.INF be.PRES.3S Ifan PROG buy.INF bread
        yn y   siop.
        in the shop
        ('They think that Ifan buys bread in the shop.')

(158)   %Roedden nhw 'n   meddwl   roedd   Ifan yn   prynu bara
        be.IMPF.3P they PROG think.INF be.IMPF.3S Ifan PROG buy.INF bread
        yn y   siop.
        in the shop
        'They thought that Ifan bought bread in the shop.'

(159)   Pwy ydyn   nhw 'n   meddwl   sy   'n   prynu bara
        who be.PRES.3P they PROG think.INF be.PRES.REL PROG buy.INF bread
        yn y   siop?
        in the shop
        'Who do they think buys bread in the shop?'

(160)   Pwy oedden   nhw 'n   meddwl   oedd   yn   prynu bara
        who be.IMPF.3P they PROG think.INF be.IMPF.REL PROG buy.INF bread
        yn y   siop?
        in the shop
        'Who do they think bought bread in the shop?'

Voiding of this restriction also occurs in other (that is, non-subject) embedded *wh*-constructions too:[5]

(161)   Ble   wyt   ti   'n   feddwl   mae   o   'n   mynd?
        where be.PRES.2S you PROG think.INF be.PRES.3S he PROG go.INF
        'Where do you think he's going?'

(162)   Beth wyt   ti   'n   feddwl   mae   hyn   yn
        what be.PRES.2S you PROG think.INF be.PRES.3S DEM.NS PROG
        ei   olygu?
        3MS mean.INF
        'What do you think this means?'

4.9.1.2   *That*-trace effects

That-trace effects, where extraction of an embedded subject is in some languages blocked by the presence of a complementizer, are difficult to test for in Welsh. The examples of subject extractions in this section from colloquial Welsh do not contain a complementizer in the embedded clause anyway. In literary Welsh, the particle *y(r)* could be added in some cases, but it is unclear whether this should be counted as a complementizer for the purposes of testing for *that*-trace effects.

There is, however, a related restriction, that might be termed a *mai*-trace effect. Extraction of the fronted element in an embedded copula clause is possible only if the focus complementizer *mai* is omitted. This is shown in (163). In (164), the equivalent non-*wh*-construction, *mai* is possible, although it may be omitted in colloquial Welsh.

(163)   Pa   ddinas wyt   ti   'n   meddwl   (*mai)   yw
        which city   be.PRES.2S you PROG think.INF (COMP.FOCUS) be.PRES.3S
        prifddinas Cymru?
        capital   Wales
        'Which city do you think is the capital of Wales?'

(164)   Dw   i   'n   meddwl mai   Caerdydd yw
        be.PRES.1S I PROG think.INF COMP.FOCUS Cardiff   be.PRES.3S
        prifddinas Cymru.
        capital   Wales
        'I think that Cardiff is the capital of Wales.'

4.9.1.3   The resumptive strategy

The resumptive strategy may also be used for embedded subject *wh*-constructions. An example of a relative clause of this type is given in (165).

---

[5] Infinitives in long-distance *wh*-contexts often undergo soft mutation, hence *meddwl* 'think' and *credu* 'believe' become *feddwl* and *gredu* in various of the examples here and below. For a fuller account, see section 4.9.6.

In this case, as in non-*wh*-environments, the verb in the embedded clause must be an infinitive. This infinitive, *fod* 'be' in (165), is interpreted as present or imperfect.

(165)   Synnodd   yn   fawr wrth weld   y   llanc,   y
be.surprised.PAST.3S PRED big   at   see.INF the young-man PRT
tybiai   ef **ei   fod**   yn   aelod   o 'r Clwb, yn
suppose.IMPF.3S he 3MS be.INF PRED member of the club   PROG
dal   i sefyllian y tu allan.
hold.INF to loiter.INF outside
'He was greatly surprised to see the young man, who he thought was a
member of the Club, still loitering outside.'   (*WJ* 138)

An overt subject pronoun is possible here after *ei fod* in the embedded clause. Use of the resumptive strategy is somewhat literary, and a gap strategy would be preferred in colloquial Welsh:

(166)   y llanc,   roedd   e 'n   tybio   oedd   yn
the young.man be.IMPF.3S he PROG suppose.INF be.IMPF.REL PRED
aelod . . .
member
'the young man, who he thought was a member . . .'

4.9.1.4   Interpretation

Both gap and resumptive strategies co-exist here, although the gap strategy is more usual in colloquial Welsh. The gap strategy maintains the same characteristics as in main-clause *wh*-structures, in particular exhibiting no subject – verb agreement and triggering the usual effects on the embedded verb (special relative forms of *bod* 'be' and soft mutation, see section 4.1.4).

4.9.2   Wh-constructions formed on embedded object positions

Wh-constructions formed on embedded object positions are exemplified in (167)–(169). These essentially manifest the same properties as main-clause *wh*-constructions formed on this position. An object-agreement clitic occurs optionally in the embedded clause.

(167)   Beth wyt   ti 'n   gredu   y bydd   e 'n **ei**   wneud?
what be.PRES.2S you PROG believe.INF PRT be.FUT.3S he PROG 3MS do.INF
'What do you think he'll do?' (literary)

(168)   Beth wyt   ti 'n   gredu   fydd   e 'n **(ei)**   wneud?
what be.PRES.2S you PROG believe.INF be.FUT.3S he PROG (3MS) do.INF
'What do you think he'll do?' (colloquial)

(169) llygaid y boi roedd   e 'n   meddwl **ei** fod   e 'n
       eyes   the boy be.IMPF.3S he PROG think.INF 3MS be.INF he PROG
       nabod
       know.INF
       'the eyes of the boy that he thought he knew'   (*DE* 12)

As with main-clause *wh*-constructions of this type, overt resumptive pronouns are marginal:

(170) ??Beth wyt   ti   'n   gredu   y   bydd   e   'n   ei
       what be.PRES.2S you PROG believe.INF PRT be.FUT.3S he PROG 3MS
       wneud **e**?
       do.INF it
       'What do you think he'll do?'

(171) *Beth wyt   ti   'n   feddwl   gawn   ni e?
       what be.PRES.2S you PROG think.INF get.FUT.1P we it
       ('What do you think we'll get?')

It appears that *wh*-constructions formed on this position require a gap strategy, like their main-clause counterparts.

4.9.3   Wh-*constructions formed on other embedded positions*

Long-distance *wh*-dependencies may be formed on adjunct positions, again using a gap strategy and no resumptive element (compare also the locative complement in (161) above):

(172) a. Pam (r)wyt   ti   'n   meddwl   eu bod   nhw 'n   gadael
          why be.PRES.2S you PROG think.INF 3P be.INF they PROG leave.INF
          nawr?
          now
          'Why do you think they are leaving now?'

       b. Nodiodd   tua   'r llofft, lle   gwyddai   fod   yr
          nod.PAST.3S towards the loft   where know.IMPF.3S be.INF the
          arweinydd wrth ei   waith fel saer.
          leader   at   3MS work as carpenter
          'He nodded upstairs, where he knew that the leader was at his work as
          a carpenter.'   (*WJ* 108)

Embedded complements of other types work the same way, as, for instance, the prepositional-phrase complement in (173).

(173) P'run   ynta i 'r eglwys ynta i 'r capel rydach   chi
       which-one either to the church or   to the chapel be.PRES.2P you
       'n   meddwl   yr ewch   chi?
       PROG think.INF PRT go.FUT.2P you

'Is it to church or to chapel that you think you'll go?'
'Do you think you'll go to church or to chapel?'   (*TMC* 14)

4.9.4   Resumptive embedded wh-*constructions*

Wh-constructions formed on embedded objects of prepositions and embedded possessor noun phrases use the resumptive strategy as might be expected:

(174)   Pwy wyt   ti   'n   meddwl ein bod   ni 'n   chwilio
who be.PRES.2S you PROG think.INF 1P be.INF we PROG search.INF
amdanyn **nhw**?
for.3P   them
'Who do you think we are looking for?'

(175)   y dyn mae   pawb   yn   meddwl bod   ei fam
the man be.PRES.3S everyone PROG think.INF be.INF 3MS mother
e 'n   gweithio i 'r   heddlu
he PROG work.INF for the police
'the man whose mother everyone thinks works for the police'

Other relatively inaccessible positions also use the resumptive strategy, for instance, the subject of a non-finite *i*-clause in (176).

(176)   y bobl   hoffwn   i iddyn nhw ddod
the people like.COND.1S I to.3P them come
'the people that I'd like to come'

The resumptive strategy may also be used freely to void many island effects (see below).

4.9.5   Islands and subjacency

Nonresumptive *wh*-constructions in embedded contexts manifest subjacency violations due to island effects in a crosslinguistically familiar way. This is best seen from adjunct relatives, which indisputably use a non-resumptive strategy. In (177), the noun phrase *y si y byddai hi'n dod* 'the rumour that she'd come' acts as a complex-noun-phrase island leading to the ungrammaticality of the relative clause.

(177)   *Yfory   yw   'r dydd y lledodd [y si   y
tomorrow be.PRES.3S the day PRT spread.PAST.3S the rumour PRT
byddai   hi 'n   dod   ___.]
be.COND.3S she PROG come.INF
('Tomorrow is the day that the rumour spread that she'd come.')

In this example, the tense difference between the main clause (present) and the embedded clause (future) ensures that the only possible interpretation is with *yfory* 'tomorrow' understood as modifying, and hence extracted from, the embedded clause. However, such extraction is ruled out because it would have to involve movement out of the complex noun phrase.

With resumptive *wh*-constructions, the situation is less clear-cut. Island constraints can be overcome in some circumstances where there is some kind of rich agreement. So, in (178a), an example of an adjunct island, there is a possessive clitic *ei* in *ei eiriau* 'his words'; in (178b), also an adjunct island, there is rich agreement on the preposition *arni* 'on (third sing. fem.)'. Although there are no overt resumptive pronouns (that is, no *ef* 'he, it' in (178a), and no *hi* 'she, it' in (178b), such examples are not normally found if there is no agreement element (clitic or inflection), so it is reasonable to suppose that they involve a null resumptive pronoun licensed by rich agreement.

(178) a. yr un y   buasai   pob athro   Ysgol Sul   a
       the one PRT be.PLUPERF.3S every teacher school Sunday PRT
       gawsai   yn hollti   blew wrth chwilio am ystyr
       have.PLUPERF.3S PROG split.INF hairs in   look.INF for meaning
       ei   eiriau
       3MS words
       '. . . the one [Bible] that every Sunday School teacher that he'd had
       had split hairs looking for the meaning of its words.'   (*WJ* 66)
       b. B'le   mae   'r enfys   honno, tybed, yr adroddais
       where be.PRES.3S the rainbow DEM.FS wonder PRT read.PAST.1S
       gyntaf y   llinellau wrth syllu   arni?
       first   the lines   at   stare.INF on.3FS
       'Where is that rainbow, I wonder, which I first read the lines
       staring at (it)?'   (*COG* 13)

In the same way, in (179), a complex-noun-phrase island, there is an object-agreement clitic in *i'w cuddio* 'to hide them', with plausibly a null object pronoun after it, although, again, no overt resumptive (*nhw* 'them') in the example.

(179) Y   mae   gan bob un ohonom ei   feddyliau cudd, y   rhai
       PRT be.PRES.3S with every one of.1P   3MS thoughts hidden the ones
       hynny y   gwnawn   ymdrech deg i   'w cuddio â
       DEM.P PRT make.FUT.1P effort   fair to 3P hide.INF with
       gwên-wneud   wrth sôn   am   rywun   neu rywbeth   diflas.
       smile-make.INF by   talk.INF about someone or   something boring
       'Every one of us has his secret thoughts, those that we make a fair
       attempt to hide with a put-on smile by talking about someone or
       something boring.'   (*WJ* 36)

On the other hand, Tallerman (1983) reports that, although resumptives do save most types of *wh*-island violation, they do not save extractions from relative clauses, citing examples such as (180). The grammaticality judgements on such cases nevertheless remain quite subtle, and further research is necessary.

(180)   *Dyma 'r   ffenest   darais   i 'r   bachgen   dorrodd   hi ddoe.
         that-is the window   hit.PAST.1s I the boy   break.PAST.3s it yesterday
         ('That's the window that I hit the boy who broke it yesterday.')

                                                   (adapted from Tallerman 1983: 198)

4.9.6   Successive cyclicity

As we have seen, within transformational frameworks, the gap strategy is interpreted as reflecting movement of a *wh*-element (either a *wh*-word or its null equivalent) from some argument or adjunct position to a clause-initial position within the highest clause, [Spec, CP]. Within such a framework, examination of the details of Welsh *wh*-movement provides a number of pieces of evidence to suggest that the *wh*-element moves cyclically, stopping off at a number of intermediate positions: a clause-initial position within each subordinate clause, and another intermediate position immediately before each nonfinite verb. The former position is interpreted within a Principles and Parameters framework as the specifier of CP, the latter as the specifier of vP. This section considers the evidence for each of these in turn.

4.9.6.1   Movement via [Spec, CP]

This section considers the evidence that *wh*-constructions using the gap strategy involve cyclic movement via an intermediate [Spec, CP] position at the beginning of each clause. For instance, in (181), the adjunct *wh*-word *pam* 'why' moves first to the beginning of its own clause, before moving on to the front of the main clause.

(181)   Pam$_i$ (r)wyt   ti   'n   meddwl   [$_{CP}$ t$_i$ eu bod   nhw 'n   gadael   nawr t$_i$]?
         why   be.PRES.2s you PROG think. INF   3P be.INF they PROG leave.INF now
         'Why do you think they are leaving now?'

The first evidence for this comes from the fact that *wh*-constructions using the gap strategy obey island constraints, whereas those using agreement, interpreted as the resumptive strategy, in the main do not. This is normally taken to imply that, in the gap strategy, *wh*-movement is blocked in contexts where an intermediate [Spec, CP] position either does not exist or is filled by some other element.

For instance, the complex-noun-phrase island in (182) makes no appropriate position available at the left edge of the noun phrase (since noun phrases are not clauses); in *wh*-islands, in (183), the intermediate position is filled by some *wh*-element (null or overt) associated with the embedded *wh*-construction. In both cases, the *wh*-element is forced to move too far in a single movement: over a noun phrase (DP) in (182), and over a clause boundary (CP) in (183).

(182)   ??I ba   barti$_i$ glywaist   ti [$_{DP}$ 'r   si   [$_{CP}$ t$_i$ y   byddai
        to which party hear.PAST.2s you   the rumour   COMP be.COND.3s
        hi 'n   dod   t$_i$]]?
        she PROG come.INF
        ('To which party did you hear the rumour that she'd be coming?')

(183)   *I ba   barti$_i$ oedd   hi 'n   gwybod [$_{CP}$ pam$_j$ oeddet
        to which party be.IMPF.3s she PROG know.INF   why be.IMPF.2s
        ti 'n   dod   t$_i$t$_j$]?
        you PROG come.INF
        ('To which party did she know why you were coming?')

In the resumptive strategy, the resumptive pronoun rather than the gap left by movement identifies the base position, hence locality restrictions on movement do not apply, there being no movement and no need for intermediate landing sites. The equivalent cases are illustrated in (184) and (185).

(184)   Pa   ddinas glywaist   ti 'r   si   y   byddwn ni 'n
        which city   hear.PAST.2s you the rumour that be.FUT.1P we PROG
        ymweld â   **hi**?
        visit.INF with it
        'Which city did you hear the rumour that we'll visit (it)?'

(185)   Pa   ddinas wyt   ti 'n   gwybod [$_{CP}$ pryd nes   i
        which city   be.PRES.2s you PROG know.INF   when do.PAST.1s I
        ymweld â   **hi**?]
        visit.INF with it
        'What city do you know when I visited (it)?'

A second piece of evidence for cyclic movement is that the finite verb in an embedded clause may mutate in a *wh*-construction, even where it would not mutate in a non-*wh*-environment. Compare non-*wh* (186), with the *wh*-question in (187). Mutation of the embedded verb *caiff* to *gaiff* is possible in (187), but not in (186).

(186)   Dw   i 'n   meddwl (y) caiff   Nia y   wobr.
        be.PRES.1s I PROG think.INF (PRT) get.FUT.3s Nia the prize
        'I think Nia will get the prize.'

(187)   Pwy_i ddywedaist ti [_{CP} t_i gaiff   t_i y   wobr]?
      who say.PAST.2S you   get.FUT.3S   the prize
      'Who did you say will get the prize?'

Within a Principles and Parameters type of framework, it is plausible to suggest that this mutation is some kind of agreement process triggered by the movement of the *wh*-word through the intermediate CP in (187).

Finally, we have seen that auxiliary *bod* 'be' has special relative forms, most notably the special present-tense relative form *sy(dd)*. This appears in embedded clauses from which subjects have been extracted. The change in the verb form to *sy(dd)* in (188) (=(153)), as compared with the equivalent non-*wh*-context with tenseless *bod* in (189), could be interpreted as reflecting an agreement process triggered by movement via the specifier of CP.

(188)   Pwy_i (r)ydyn   nhw 'n   meddwl [_{CP} t_i **sy**   t_i 'n   prynu
      who be.PRES.3P they PROG think.INF   be.PRES.REL   PROG buy.INF
      pethau yn eu siopau nhw]?
      things in 3P shops them
      'Who do they think buys things in their shops?'

(189)   Maen   nhw 'n   meddwl **bod**   myfyrwyr yn   prynu pethau
      be.PRES.3P they PROG think.INF be.INF students   PROG buy.INF things
      yn eu siopau nhw.
      in 3P shops them
      'They think that students buy things in their shops.'

4.9.6.2   Movement via [Spec, vP]

In some varieties, a non-finite verb mutates if there is extraction across it. Sometimes a masculine third-person singular object clitic also appears as an overt trigger of this mutation before the verb. Examples are given in (190) and (191), with mutation of *meddwl* 'think' to *feddwl*.

(190)   Pwy_i oedd   e 'n [_{vP} t_i (ei) feddwl [_{CP} t_i oedd   e t_i]]?
      who be.IMPF.3S he PROG   (3MS) think.INF   be.IMPF.3S he
      'Who did he think he was?'

(191)   Roedd   hi 'n   dipyn hŷn   nag o'n   i wedi 'i
      be.IMPF.3S she PRED a.little older than be.IMPF.1S I PERF 3MS
      feddwl   i   ddechrau arni.
      think.INF to start.INF on.3FS
      'She was a bit older than I'd thought to start with.'   (*DHMH* 38)

In neither of these cases is the extracted element the direct object of the verb that acquires an object clitic. This means that it is hard to see how the clitic and mutation could be resumptive in nature, that is, licensing a null resumptive object pronoun. The conclusion must be that the clitic and mutation are triggered by the movement operation itself. The non-finite verb must therefore be sensitive to whether or not an element has been moved past it. An obvious way to achieve this is to propose that movement of a *wh*-element is required to stop off at the left edge of the verb phrase, [Spec, vP] in recent frameworks, triggering the mutation as a marker of agreement as it goes.

4.10   Conclusion

This chapter has considered various issues in the syntax of Welsh *wh*-constructions, focusing in particular on colloquial Welsh. We have seen that a basic distinction between gap and resumptive strategies is essential to analysing them, and that this distinction recurs in a variety of *wh*-constructions, including *wh*-questions, relative clauses, comparatives and non-finite *wh*-questions and relatives. This distinction is nevertheless not straightforward to establish and apply in practice, since resumptive pronouns may be null, thus making them difficult to distinguish from true gaps, and we have therefore considered what evidence can be used to establish which strategy is used for a given context. Much of the literature on *wh*-constructions has focused on the factors which determine the choice of preverbal particle. We have seen, however, that, in colloquial Welsh, *wh*-contexts are marked by soft mutation of the clause-initial verb rather than preverbal particles. Even in literary Welsh, where the particles are used, there is no straightforward correlation between the choice of particle and the *wh*-strategy employed. Finally, we have highlighted some of the more crosslinguistically interesting aspects of Welsh *wh*-constructions, for instance, restrictions on resumptive pronouns in subject and object position and the compelling evidence found in Welsh for successive cyclic *wh*-movement via the intermediate positions [Spec, vP] and [Spec, CP].

5

Noun phrases

5.1 Introduction: major features of the Welsh noun phrase

The Welsh noun phrase is head-initial. Although determiners, numerals and quantifiers regularly precede the head noun, all other elements, including adjectives, possessor noun phrases, demonstratives and relative clauses, normally follow. A few adjectives precede the head noun, but these represent the marked case. The basic order of elements within the noun phrase is therefore:

(1)   Determiner – Numeral – Noun – Adjective – Possessor/Demonstrative –
        Complement – Relative clause

Some examples illustrating the basic ordering patterns are given in (2) to (4).

(2)   y   tair   cath ddu
        the three.F cat black
        'the three black cats'
        (determiner – numeral – noun – adjective)

(3)   straeon newydd Nia am   fôr-forynion
        tales   new   Nia about mermaids
        'Nia's new tales about mermaids'
        (noun – adjective – possessor – complement)

(4)   syniad cyffrous i sefydlu   theatr newydd
        idea   exciting to establish.INF theatre new
        'an exciting idea to establish a new theatre'
        (noun – adjective – complement)

The word order in these examples, and indeed generally within the noun phrase, is fairly rigid, with some degree of freedom only for the relative order of adjectives and for rightward extraposition of heavy elements. This chapter sets out the various elements that may occur in each of the positions in the noun phrase, and in doing so raises some issues of more general interest.

The first major point of interest concerns the rather complex patterns of initial-consonant mutation within the noun phrase. The system is based essentially on gender. Welsh has a two-way grammatical gender opposition in nouns (masculine and feminine), with gender oppositions effectively neutralized in the plural. Except in the case of sex-based gender, gender assignment is arbitrary, and, although some morphological generalizations can be made, gender cannot easily be determined from the form of a noun. Various instances of soft mutation are triggered by the presence of feminine (singular) gender within the noun phrase. For instance, in (5), both the head noun after the definite article and the postnominal adjective undergo soft mutation (*cath* > *gath* and *du* > *ddu*) triggered by the fact that *cath* 'cat' is a feminine noun.

(5)   y   gath ddu   (*cath, du*)
        the cat black
        'the black cat'

The status of this grammatically conditioned mutation will be discussed in the course of this chapter. Most other mutations within the noun phrase are triggered by individual lexical items and are of less general interest.

Next, restrictions on the syntax of possessor noun phrases are of crosslinguistic interest. Possessor noun phrases are placed after the head noun and any adjectives, as in (3) above and in (6). There is no morphological genitive case marking on the possessor noun phrase. Marking of definiteness within the noun phrase is restricted. The possessor may be marked as definite, as it is in (6), in which case the whole noun phrase is interpreted as definite. If the possessor is indefinite, as in (7), the whole noun phrase is interpreted as indefinite. However, the head noun itself cannot be marked as definite, as the ungrammaticality of (8) demonstrates. This means that the definiteness value of the whole phrase is taken from the marking on the possessor and not from the marking on the head noun.

(6)   mab y   brenin
        son the king
        'the son of the king'

(7)   mab brenin
        son king
        'a son of a king, a king's son'

(8)   *y   mab y   brenin
        the son the king
        'the son of the king'

The possessor construction contrasts with the syntax of attributive noun phrases such as *llyfrau Cymraeg* 'Welsh books' in (9). Here the attributive noun phrase may not show definiteness marking, whereas the head noun of the entire phrase (*siopau* 'shops') may do so.

(9)   y   siopau llyfrau Cymraeg
       the shops books Welsh
       'the Welsh book shops (i.e. the shops that sell Welsh books)'

The first of these constructions shows marked parallels, but also some differences, with construct-state constructions in Hebrew, Arabic and other Semitic languages.

Finally, the order of postnominal adjectives within the noun phrase is relevant for the question of how postnominal adjectives are analysed in different languages. Postnominal-adjective languages are sometimes divided into those where the relative order of adjectives is the same as that found in English, and those where it is the mirror image of English (Cinque 1994: 99–100, Fassi Fehri 1999: 107–9, Longobardi 2001: 576). As this chapter will demonstrate, Welsh does not fit easily into a typology that recognizes only these two types, and both orders are found in different environments: English-like order in (10), and mirror-image order in (11).

(10)   cwpan mawr gwyrdd Sieineaidd
       cup   big   green Chinese
       'a big green Chinese cup'   (Rouveret 1994: 213)

(11)   caneuon newydd gwych eraill
       songs   new   great other.P
       'other great new songs'   (Willis 2006a: 1826)

This chapter is organized to consider each of the major elements within the noun phrase in the order in which they occur in Welsh. We begin by looking at determiners and related elements, moving thereafter to consider numerals and quantifiers, adjectives, demonstratives and, finally, possessors. The final section raises issues about the structure of the noun phrase overall.

5.2   Determiners and related elements

There are three types of item that could be considered determiners in Welsh: the definite article, possessive clitics, and some quantifiers that cannot co-occur with a definite article. Each of these occurs in absolute initial position within the noun phrase; there is no possibility of any element preceding; and these elements may not co-occur with each other. They are considered in turn in this section.

5.2.1   The definite article

Welsh has a definite article *y(r)*, but no indefinite article. Bare nouns are interpreted as indefinite or generic. As in English, the definite article may be used generically to denote a class of entities with a singular count noun, but not with a mass noun or a plural noun. In (12), *y teigr* 'the tiger' ('*r teigr* after a vowel) denotes the species of tigers, rather than any specific individual tiger.

(12)   Ers   blynyddoedd maith, mae   **'r teigr** yn   cael   ei
       since years   long   be.PRES.3S the tiger PROG get.INF 3MS
       hela   gan botswyr.
       hunt.INF by   poachers
       'For many years, the tiger has been hunted by poachers.'

It also occurs in various idiomatic expressions unrelated to definiteness, for instance, with illnesses (13a), generic location (13b) or rates (13c).

(13)   a. Mae   **'r frech goch** arno   fe.
         be.PRES.3S the rash red   on.3MS him
         'He's got measles.'
      b. Mae   Megan yn ei   blwyddyn olaf **yn yr ysgol**.
         be.PRES.3S Megan in 3FS year   last in the school
         'Megan is in her last year at school.'
      c. Mae   Ifan yn   treulio   **pedair awr   y   dydd** yn
         be.PRES.3S Ifan PROG spend.INF four.F hour the day   PROG
         gwylio   teledu.
         watch.INF TV
         'Ifan spends four hours a day watching TV.'

The definite article *y(r)* is a clitic. It is enclitic to the preceding word and takes the form '*r* /r/ if that word ends in a vowel; otherwise it is proclitic to the first word of the noun phrase, taking the form *yr* /ər/ if that word begins with a vowel, otherwise *y* /ə/. Relevant examples are given in (14)–(16). For further details, see Hannahs & Tallerman (2006).

(14)   o   'r tŷ   / ardd
       from the house / garden
       'from the house / garden'

(15)   o   flaen y tŷ
       from front the house
       'in front of the house'

(16)   o   flaen yr ardd
       from front the garden
       'in front of the garden'

Although the article does not itself inflect for gender, it triggers soft mutation on a following feminine singular noun, hence *cath* 'cat' becomes *gath* after the article in (17).

(17)   y   <u>gath</u>   (*cath*)
        the cat
        'the cat'

There is no mutation on a following masculine noun, nor on a plural noun of either gender. Exceptionally, this rule is also applied to the feminine noun *pobl* 'people', which is grammatically plural:

(18)   y   <u>bobl</u>   eraill   (*pobl*)
        the people other.P
        'the other people'

The article triggers idiosyncratic mutations on cardinal numerals. The numeral 'two' mutates after the article, whether masculine (*dau*) or feminine (*dwy*). Other numerals do not mutate, at least in the literary language, irrespective of the gender of the head noun, which remains morphologically singular (see section 5.3 below):

(19)   y   <u>ddau</u> aderyn   (*dau*)
        the two.M bird.S
        'the two birds'

(20)   y   tair /   pedair / pum cath
        the three.F four.F   five cat.S
        'the three / four / five cats'

This last rule is sometimes ignored in colloquial Welsh, and the mutable numerals *tair* 'three (fem.)', *pedair* 'four (fem.)', *pum* 'five' and *de(n)g* 'ten' are sometimes found soft-mutated after the article before a feminine noun. This is regarded as nonstandard.

Ordinal numerals, which, with the exception of *cyntaf* 'first', precede the noun, mutate regularly according to gender after the article; contrast feminine cases with mutated *drydedd* etc. in (21) with masculine cases with unmutated *trydydd* etc. in (22).

(21)   y   <u>drydedd</u> / <u>bedwaredd</u> / <u>bumed</u> wobr   (*trydedd, pedwaredd, pumed*)
        the third.F   fourth.F   fifth.F   prize
        'the third / fourth / fifth prize'

(22)   y   trydydd / pedwerydd / pumed tro
        the third.M   fourth.M   fifth.M time
        'the third / fourth / fifth time'

For mutations triggered by the numerals themselves, see section 5.3.1.

Table 5.1. *Possessive proclitics ('genitive prefixed pronouns').*

	singular	plural
first person	*fy* + nasal mutation	*ein* + radical / aspiration
second person	*dy* + soft mutation	*eich* + radical
third person	masc. *ei* + soft mutation	*eu* + radical / aspiration
	fem. *ei* + aspirate mutation	
	/ aspiration	

The mutation triggered by the feminine article is generally analysed as being the result of an agreement process. That is, the article actually has two forms, feminine $y(r)^{SM}$, a soft-mutation trigger, and masculine and plural $y(r)$, not a mutation trigger. The relevant form is chosen in agreement with the head noun, and it either triggers or fails to trigger a mutation on the immediately following word.

The exceptional non-mutation with numerals in (20) does not follow easily from this analysis, although the tendency to regularize the mutations with feminine numerals suggests that the rules in these cases are indeed synchronically exceptional. A possibility for these cases is that, in (20), the article actually agrees with the plural numeral rather than the feminine head noun. Consequently, $y(r)$ is chosen rather than $y(r)^{SM}$, and no mutation is triggered on the numeral.

5.2.2   Possessive clitics

A pronominal possessor is expressed by attaching a clitic to the front of the noun phrase. These are traditionally referred to as 'genitive prefixed pronouns' (*rhagenwau genidol blaen*), but, as we shall see, this term is misleading. If mutation effects are taken into account, there are four possibilities in the singular and three in the plural, listed in Table 5.1. On aspiration before a vowel, see section 1.4.4.

Preposed possessive clitics are proclitic to the next word in the noun phrase, usually the noun. An example is given in (23).

(23)   fy nghar
        1s car
        'my car'

In literary Welsh, if the previous word ends in a vowel (except a diphthong ending in /ʊ/) without a prosodic break, they are enclitic to the previous word,

Table 5.2. *Possessive enclitics ('genitive infixed pronouns').*

	singular	plural
first person	*'m* + radical / aspiration	*'n* + radical / aspiration
second person	*'th* + soft mutation	*'ch* + radical
third person	masc. *'i* + soft mutation	*'u* + radical / aspiration
	(*'w* after *i* 'to')	(*'w* after *i* 'to')
	fem. *'i* + aspirate mutation	
	/ aspiration	
	(*'w̦* after *i* 'to')	

and somewhat different enclitic forms are used (traditionally termed 'genitive infixed pronouns', *rhagenwau genidol mewnol*), as given in Table 5.2.

In the first- and second-person singular, the enclitics are restricted to use after certain particles, prepositions and conjunctions (for instance, *a* 'preverbal particle', *â* 'with', *i* 'to' and *a* 'and') in literary Welsh, and are not in general use in colloquial Welsh. Instead, the proclitics are used in their place. In the other persons, these clitics are in general use.

These clitics may co-occur with a dependent personal pronoun following the noun in the position where non-pronominal possessors normally appear. Compare (24) with pronominal possessor and (25) with a non-pronominal possessor.

(24)   fy nghar **i**
        1s car   me
        'my car'

(25)   car **Megan**
        car Megan
        'Megan's car'

In speech, an overt pronoun in postnominal position conveys no particular emphasis.

In literary Welsh and in the speech of older speakers, there are obviation effects (Watkins 1977a, b). That is, a postnominal pronoun must be omitted if it would be coreferential with the subject of the clause. Thus, for older speakers, (26) is ungrammatical with the relevant coreferential interpretation in which John is looking for his own cap. Instead, it can only be interpreted with John looking for someone else's cap.

(26)   %Mae John$_i$ yn   chwilio   am ei   gap **ef**$_j$.
        be.3s John PROG search.INF for 3SM cap him
        'John$_i$ is looking for his$_i$ (own) cap.'   (Watkins 1977a: 359)

However, there is tendency in the colloquial Welsh of younger speakers for the postnominal pronoun to be included regardless of obviation.

A postnominal pronoun may be used alone, as illustrated in (27), although this is considered non-standard.

(27) Car **fi**   'dy   hwnna.
      car me.STRONG   be.PRES.3S   DEM.MS
      'That's my car.'   (adapted from B. M. Jones 1990a: 68)

Note that, in this case, an independent form of the pronoun is used (*fi* in (27)), rather than the dependent form found in co-occurrence with a clitic (*i* in (24)). Watkins (1977b: 157) regards this usage as characteristic only of child language. Although this pattern certainly seems to be normal in the language of children aged 3–7 (B. M. Jones 1990b), it is not restricted to child language, and widespread use is reported for adult speech (A. Roberts 1988: 112, B. M. Jones 1990a). The innovation of the pattern in (27), lacking a clitic, effectively represents an extension of the pattern found with non-pronominal noun phrases in (25) to pronouns.

As already noted in section 3.1.2, nouns and non-finite verbs take the same set of proclitics, the system for expressing pronominal possessors in noun phrases being almost entirely parallel to that used for expressing pronominal objects of non-finite verbs. In fact, this similarity is one of the main reasons for the traditional treatment of non-finite verbs as verb-nouns (see section 3.1). The same clitics are used for both, with essentially the same distributional restrictions and the same mutations. Compare the non-finite-verb syntax in (28) with the nominal examples seen in this section so far, especially (23) and (24).

(28) Mae   Megan wedi fy ngweld (i).
      be.PRES.3S Megan PERF 1s see.INF me
      'Megan has seen me.'

Such parallels are attested in such other languages as Hungarian, Tzutujil and Yup'ik (see also below) (Abney 1987: 16–19, 27–33).

Traditionally, the prenominal element *fy* in cases like (24) was treated as the main pronoun, with the postnominal element *i* 'me' being considered 'auxiliary': this analysis is implicit in the traditional term for the postnominal pronoun as auxiliary or affixed (cf. Williams 1980: 50). This analysis was supported by the observation that, in literary Welsh, the prenominal element is compulsory, whereas the postnominal one is optional. The parallelism between noun phrases and non-finite verb phrases was accounted for by defining the prefixed pronouns as genitive: it could then reasonably be claimed that both the object of a non-finite verb and a possessor noun phrase were marked as genitive in Welsh (as in Scottish Gaelic and conservative varieties of Irish), and that this genitive case marking appeared overtly when the possessor or object was pronominal.

On the other hand, within the generative tradition going back to Awbery (1976: 23) and Sadler (1988), the dominant position is that the main pronominal element is actually the postnominal one. The prenominal element *fy* in (24) is then analysed as being a determiner (or simply an agreement head) that marks agreement with the possessor. This would make Welsh similar to such languages as Hungarian and Turkish, where nouns agree with their possessors. For instance, in the Hungarian examples in (29), the noun *kalap-* 'hat' occurs with a different ending depending on the person and number of the possessor:

(29)   a. a   mi   kalapunk
           the we.NOM hat.1P
           'our hat'   (Hungarian, Szabolcsi 1994: 186)
        b. a   te   kalapod
           the you.NOM hat.2s
           'your hat'   (Hungarian, Szabolcsi 1994: 186)

Furthermore, in Hungarian, since the inflection on the noun shows the person and number of the possessor unambiguously, the pronominal possessor itself may be omitted, hence (30) is an unemphatic alternative to (29a).

(30)   a   kalapunk
        the hat.1P
        'our hat'   (Hungarian, Szabolcsi 1994: 187)

The agreement-marker analysis of Welsh pronominal possessors effectively says that Welsh is like Hungarian. Nouns agree with their possessors, although the form of this agreement in Welsh is a clitic rather than an inflection. This view has the advantage that it analyses the possessive noun phrase *Megan* in (25) as having the same status as the postnominal pronoun *i* in (24): both are 'real' possessor noun phrases. The fact that the prefixed clitics occur only when the possessor is pronominal is not problematic, since this follows from the general principle that all agreement in Welsh appears only when a head agrees with a pronoun rather than a non-pronominal noun phrase (see sections 1.4.3 and 6.1).

This analysis also makes the relationship between pronominal possessors and pronominal objects less mysterious. In (28), it is clear that we would want to consider *i* 'me' to be the direct object, even though it is optional, with *fy* agreeing with it. This is because Welsh is a VSO language, and, with a lexical object in an equivalent construction, the object would necessarily follow the non-finite verb:

(31)   Mae   Megan wedi gweld Dafydd.
        be.PRES.3s Megan PERF see.INF Dafydd
        'Megan has seen Dafydd.'

If *Dafydd* is the object in (31), then *i* must be the object in (28), and *fy* must be an agreement marker. In order to maintain parallelism between noun phrase and non-finite verb phrase, we are therefore committed to claiming that *i* is the possessor noun phrase in (24) and that *fy* is an agreement marker in both (23) and (24).

Finally, clitics show ongoing erosion in both nominal and verbal contexts. We have already seen an example of the loss of the (prehead) clitic in a nominal context in (27). In (32), we see the loss of the pre-verbal clitic in a non-finite verbal context. Note that, in the absence of a pre-verbal clitic, the postverbal pronoun must appear in the independent form (*fi*) rather than the dependent form (*i*) (cf. (27) above). This pattern is considered non-standard, but is in widespread use.

(32)   Mae   Megan wedi gweld fi.
         be.PRES.3S Megan PERF see.INF me.STRONG
         'Megan has seen me.'

If the proclitic is an agreement marker in both nominal and non-finite verbal contexts, then this erosion is a straightforward case of the loss of agreement marking and is parallel in the two cases.

5.2.3   Other determiners

As well as the definite article *y(r)*, three other items, *pob* 'all, every', *pa* 'which' and *sut* 'what kind of' seem to pattern as determiners. These must occupy initial position within the noun phrase, and may not co-occur with a definite article or with each other. They must precede numerals:

(33)   pob   dwy   flynedd
         every two.F year.NUM
         'every two years'

Although they do not co-occur easily with quantifiers, when they do, they precede:

(34)   a. pa   sawl   mis
            which several month
            'how many months'
         b. pob   dim rheol
            every any rule
            'every single rule'

Finally, like the definite article, they may not co-occur with a possessor noun phrase, in (35), or a possessive clitic, in (36):

(35)   a. *pob   llyfr Dafydd
             every book Dafydd
             ('Dafydd's every book')
         b. *pa   lyfrau Dafydd
             which book   Dafydd
             ('which of Dafydd's books')

(36)   a. *fy   mhob llyfr
             1s   every book
             ('my every book')
         b. *fy   mha   lyfrau
             1s   which books
             ('my which books, which books of mine')

5.2.4   Early postdeterminers

Although historically a noun meaning 'sort, kind', the item *rhyw* 'some (kind of)' (along with *unrhyw* 'any') now occupies an early position within the noun phrase. It follows determiners, but precedes numerals and quantifiers, and consequently can be classified as an 'early postdeterminer':

(37)   a. pob   rhyw dri   mis
             every some three.M month
             'every three months or so'
         b. rhyw ychydig fisoedd yn ôl
             some few   months   ago
             'a (some) few months ago'
         c. Doedd   y   gynulleidfa ddim yn   cymryd [rhyw lawer
             NEG.be.IMPF.3S the audience   NEG   PROG take.INF some much
             o   sylw].
             of attention
             'The audience wasn't paying much attention.'

Holl 'all (definite)', *un* 'same' and *unig* 'only' belong here too:[1]

(38)   yr unig dri   bachgen
         the only three.M boy
         'the only three boys'

---

[1] *Un* causes mutation irrespective of the gender of the head noun when it means 'same, of the same kind' (*Mae gan Nia yr un gar â fi* 'Nia has the same (kind of) car as me', *car > gar*). It causes mutation on feminine nouns only when used as a numeral 'one', a quantifier 'any' or to mean 'same, one and the same' (*Mae Nia a Dafydd yn rhan-nu'r un car* 'Nia and Dafydd share the same / one car', no mutation on *car* because *car* is masculine). The mutation difference suggests that we are dealing with at least two different items with the form *un* here. There also exist two other items: *un* used 'pronominally' in place of a head noun as in *yr hen un* 'the old one' or *yr un un* 'the same one'; and as part of *yr un* 'no, any', a negative polarity item used in negative and related contexts (see Borsley & Jones 2005: 124–6).

Unig is also used as a prenominal adjective, in which case it occupies the position between a numeral and the noun, and has a different meaning, as, for instance, in *tri unig blentyn* 'three only children'.

5.3   Numerals

Nouns following a numeral are singular in form, as in (39). Numerals may also be followed by the preposition *o* 'of' followed by a plural noun phrase, as in (40).

(39)   deg llun
        ten picture.s
        'ten pictures'
(40)   deg o luniau
        ten of pictures
        'ten pictures'

One noun, *blwyddyn* 'year', has two special 'numerative' forms used only after numerals, *blynedd* 'years' and *blwydd* 'years of age':

(41)   a. tair   blynedd
           three.F year.NUM
           'three years'
        b. tair   blwydd   (oed)
           three.F year.NUM   (age)
           'three years old'

5.3.1   Mutations with numerals

Only the numerals 2–4 agree in gender with the head noun: *dau* (masc.) ~ *dwy* (fem.) 'two'; *tri* (masc.) ~ *tair* (fem.) 'three'; *pedwar* (masc.) ~ *pedair* (fem.) 'four'. The numeral *un* 'one' does not have separate masculine and feminine forms but instead triggers soft mutation of a following feminine noun in the same way that the article does, hence *un ferch* 'one girl' (mutation of *merch*), but *un mab* 'one son' (no mutation of *mab*). The numerals 'two', 'three' and 'six' trigger lexically idiosyncratic mutation on the following element, usually the head noun. *Dau* 'two (masc.)' and *dwy* 'two (fem.)' trigger a soft mutation; *tri* 'three (masc.)' and *chwe* 'six' trigger aspirate mutation: *dau dŷ* 'two houses' (mutation of *tŷ*), *dwy ferch* 'two girls' (mutation of *merch*), *tri thŷ* 'three houses' (mutation of *tŷ*), *chwe thŷ* 'six houses' (mutation of *tŷ*). The soft mutations after *dau* and *dwy* are stable, but the aspirate mutations after *tri* and *chwe* are observed only sporadically in spoken colloquial Welsh (Thomas & Thomas 1989: 49). Ball (1988b: 76–7) and Ball & Müller (1992:

251–3) report the frequency of aspirate mutation in this context as low as 15% in the spoken Welsh of speakers from Cwmtawe (Swansea valley).

Other numerals trigger mutations only with certain nouns. In the standard, *blynedd* 'years' and *blwydd* 'years old' undergo (regular) soft mutation after *un* 'one' and *dwy* 'two', and (exceptional) nasal mutation after *pum* 'five', *saith* 'seven' and all numerals higher than this. The nasal mutation is frequently extended to *chwe* 'six', and, less frequently, to *tair* 'three' and *pedair* 'four', especially with *blwydd* (*tair mlwydd, pedair mlwydd*). The patterns are illustrated for *blynedd* 'years' in (42).

(42) a. un flwyddyn   (soft mutation, *blwyddyn*)
       one year.s
       'one year'
    b. dwy flynedd   (soft mutation, *blynedd*)
       two.F year.NUM
       'two years'
    c. tair blynedd   (no mutation, *blynedd*)
       three.F year.NUM
       'three years' (also non-standard: nasal mutation, *tair mlynedd*)
    d. pedair blynedd   (no mutation, *blynedd*)
       four.F year.NUM
       'four years' (also non-standard: nasal mutation, *pedair mlynedd*)
    e. pum mlynedd   (nasal mutation, *blynedd*)
       five year.NUM
       'five years'
    f. chwe blynedd   (no mutation, *blynedd*)
       six year.NUM
       'six years' (also non-standard: nasal mutation, *chwe mlynedd*)
    g. saith mlynedd   (nasal mutation, *blynedd*)
       seven year.NUM
       'seven years'

Nasal mutation of *blynedd* after *chwe* 'six' is normally regarded as nonstandard (D. G. Jones 1988: 141, Thorne 1993: 58, S. J. Williams 1980: 44), and does not represent majority usage, but has sometimes been regarded as the literary norm (P. W. Thomas 1996: 310) or as normal in spoken Welsh (King 1993: 119–20). With *blwydd*, nasal mutation after *chwe* (*chwe mlwydd* 'six years old') is about as frequent as non-mutation.

Composite numerals involving *un* 'one' sometimes have a soft mutation rather than a nasal mutation (by analogy with the non-composite *un flwyddyn* 'one year'), hence non-standard *un flynedd ar ddeg* 'eleven years' for standard *un mlynedd ar ddeg*. Conversely, some speakers apply a nasal mutation to *blwydd* after *un* 'one' even when not part of a composite numeral (*un mlwydd oed* 'one year old'), although the norm is soft mutation here (*un flwydd oed*).

A similar pattern of nasal mutation with *diwrnod* 'day' is now restricted to highly literary Welsh.

Saith 'seven' and *wyth* 'eight' sometimes trigger soft mutation in northern varieties, for instance, *saith bunt* 'seven pounds', more frequently *saith punt*.

For details of the mutation triggered by the definite article on a following numeral, see section 5.2.1 above.

5.3.2   Agreement patterns with a numeral

We have seen that the head noun in a numeral phrase must be singular, except in the construction illustrated in (40). In the main, the internal syntax of the noun phrase treats a numeral phrase as singular, although it is plural for external rules such as pronominalization or anaphora. Welsh adjectives in some cases show agreement with their head noun, although this agreement is nearly always optional (see section 5.4.2 below). However, adjectives in numeral phrases must be singular, and they behave as singular for mutation purposes, undergoing soft mutation following a feminine noun:

(43)   tair   merch **ifanc** / *ifainc
        three.F girl.S young young.P
        'three young girls'

(44)   y   tair   noson   **gyntaf**   (*cyntaf*)
        the three.F night.S first
        'the first three nights'

It can be seen that adjectives are actually singular from the fact that the singular rule applies even to *arall* 'other', an adjective that is consistently found in its plural form *eraill* in plural noun phrases not containing a numeral:

(45)   y   tri /   pedwar / pum llun   arall   / *eraill
        the three.M / four.M five picture other.S / other.P
        'the three / four / five other pictures'

Demonstratives, however, are normally plural with numerals:

(46)   y   tri   / pedwar / pum llun   hyn
        the three.M / four.M five picture.S DEM.P
        'these three / four / five pictures'

Singular demonstrative forms are sometimes found here in written Welsh. P. W. Thomas (1996: 313) regards these as the result of (hypercorrect) over-application of logic to these cases. They are not found in speech.

A special case is the numerative form *blynedd*. Although *blwyddyn* 'year' is feminine singular, and hence triggers and undergoes various soft mutations,

Table 5.3. *Frequency of soft mutation of adjectives after* blynedd *'year'*.

Numeral	% non-mutation with *cyntaf*	Sample size	% non-mutation with *diwethaf*	Sample size
2	15	254	52	1268
3	56	329	75	983
4	59	73	84	459
5–10, 20	69	222	83	1820

the numerative form *blynedd* does not consistently behave as feminine singular for mutation purposes. As with other nouns in numeral phrases, adjectives with *blynedd* must be singular:

(47)   tair   blynedd   arall /   *eraill
        three.F year.NUM   other.S   other.P
        'another three years'

However, either soft mutation, as expected from a feminine noun, or absence of mutation, as expected if *blynedd* were plural, may be found on a following adjective:

(48)   y   tair   blynedd   cyntaf / gyntaf
        the   three.F year.NUM first
        'the three first years'

Table 5.3 shows the pattern of data found with the adjectives *cyntaf* 'first' and *diwethaf* 'last', based on searches of Internet Welsh. With *dwy* 'two' soft mutation is frequent, but there is a cline of decreasing use of soft mutation, with higher numerals tending to use a non-mutated form. Despite the difficulties inherent in using Internet Welsh, the clear patterning over a large quantity of data suggests that, with higher numerals, *blynedd* is treated as grammatically plural, rather than as feminine singular, since adjectives do not mutate after plural nouns. *Llawn* 'full' also occurs moderately frequently in phrases such as *tair blynedd llawn* 'three full years' and, here too, non-mutation is the majority pattern; *cyfan* 'whole' tends to mutate. For the historical reasons behind these patterns, see section 9.11.

5.3.3   The syntax of complex numerals

Welsh has two systems for constructing numerals higher than ten. A decimal system forms numbers of the form number of tens followed by *deg* 'ten' followed by the number of units, for instance, *chwe deg naw* (literally 'six ten nine') 'sixty-nine'. A vigesimal system forms complex numbers based on *deg* 'ten', *pymtheg* 'fifteen' and *ugain* 'twenty':

(49)   a. un ar bymtheg
            one on fifteen
            'sixteen'
        b. un ar ddeg ar hugain
            one on ten   on twenty
            'thirty-one'
        c. naw a   thrigain
            nine and sixty (three-twenty)
            'sixty-nine'

All numerals above ten can be formed using either system. On the history of the decimal system and the factors conditioning the choice between the systems, see G. Roberts (2000). For further details of the traditional system as found in the Welsh Bible, see Hurford (1975: 136–201).

The decimal numerals follow the syntax of numerals below ten, allowing either a bare singular noun to follow, or, more commonly, *o* 'of' and a plural noun, compare examples (39) and (40) above.

The vigesimal numerals are more complicated. Three patterns are found. In (50), the whole numeral precedes a singular noun; in (51), the numeral is split, with the simple low numeral preceding the noun, and the rest following; in (52), the whole numeral is followed by *o* 'of' and a plural noun. Of these, (50) is somewhat colloquial.

(50)   tair   ar ddeg gwlad
          three.F on ten   country
          'thirteen countries'

(51)   tair   gwlad   ar ddeg
          three.F country on ten
          'thirteen countries'

(52)   tair   ar ddeg **o** wledydd
          three.F on ten   of countries
          'thirteen countries'

The split construction in (51) poses the most problems. In particular, what is the position and status of the second part of the numeral? Adjectives may precede or follow this second part according to scope, generally following if the adjective is understood to refer to a property of the group as a whole, as in (53), and preceding if understood as applying to each member individually, as in (54) (cf. the English translations in each case):

(53)   y   pedwar aelod   ar ddeg **gwreiddiol**
        the four.M member on ten   original
        'the original fourteen members'

(54)   pedair ysgol **gynradd** ar ddeg
        four.F school primary on ten
        'fourteen primary schools'

5.3.4   Noun phrases headed by numerals

A cardinal number may appear without a head noun in phrases such as:

(55)   Mae   **tri**   yn   cael   eu holi   gan yr heddlu.
        be.PRES.3S three.M PROG get.INF 3P question.INF by the police
        'Three are being questioned by the police.'

The numeral may be accompanied by a determiner and/or adjectives: *y pedwar* 'the four', *y tair olaf* 'the last three (fem.)'. As with numerals before nouns, adjectives in these phrases must be singular. Some adjectives have distinct feminine forms, and these feminine forms may be used here if the numeral is feminine. If the phrase is feminine, adjectives often undergo soft mutation (P. W. Thomas 1996: 312) (*mwyaf* > *fwyaf* and *coch* > *goch*), but non-mutation is frequently encountered:

(56)   a. %y   tair   **fwyaf**   (*mwyaf*)
           the three.F biggest
           'the biggest three'
        b. %pedair **goch**   (*coch*)
           four.F red
           'four red ones'

After *dau* 'two', an adjective mutates in the same way as a noun (*gwyn* > *wyn*):

(57)   dau **wyn**   (*gwyn*)
        two.M white
        'two white ones'

As we have seen, *tri* 'three' and *chwe* 'six' trigger aspirate mutation on a following noun in more formal styles. With a following adjective, P. W. Thomas (1996: 307) suggests a distinction whereby, if a following adjective is mutated, as in (58), it is interpreted as a noun, and, if it does not mutate, as in (57), it is interpreted strictly as an adjective.

(58)   y   tri   chyntaf
        the three.M first
        'the three firsts (first prizes, first-class degrees)'

(59)   y   tri   cyntaf
the   three.M   first
'the first three (persons, things)'

However, such a distinction is not maintained consistently in usage, and *y tri chyntaf* is used, in more formal styles, to mean simply 'the first three'.

Unlike singular adjectives (see below), ordinal numerals may form a noun phrase standing alone with the definite article:

(60)   Mae   'r   cyntaf / gyntaf / ail   yn   well.
be.PRES.3S the first.M / first.F / second PRED better
'The first / second is better.'

They may also follow the pattern of adjectives, using the pronominals *un* 'one' and *rhai* 'ones': *yr un cyntaf* 'the first one', *yr ail un* 'the second one'.

With a phrase such as *y tair fwyaf* 'the biggest three' in (56a), there are three possible structures that could be assigned:

(i)   the numeral is the head;
(ii)   the adjective is the head;
(iii)   a null noun is the head.

There are various pieces of evidence that bear on this question. First, consider the soft mutation of *mywaf* 'biggest' to *fwyaf* and *coch* 'red' to *goch* in (56). *Tair* and *pedair* are not soft-mutation triggers, so where does this mutation come from? One possibility is that there is a null feminine head noun which, like all feminine nouns, triggers a mutation on a following adjective (compare (5) above). A second possibility is that *tair* 'three' is the head, and, when it is a head, it is treated as a feminine noun, triggering soft mutation on a following adjective. The data seem to rule out the possibility that the adjective is the head, since there would be no possible source for the mutation in this case, since *tair* is not a mutation trigger itself.

Next, in (57), *dau* 'two' is a soft mutation trigger, but a null masculine noun head would not be, so, if the structure is as in (61), with a null head noun, we have to say that the null noun is transparent to the mutation caused by *dau*, allowing it to be realized on *gwyn* > *wyn*. This is not inconceivable, since, as we shall see in chapter 7, some null elements block mutation, while others are transparent to it or trigger it.

(61)   dau   [$_N$ ø]   wyn
two.M   white
'two white ones'

If either the numeral or the adjective were treated as the head, this pattern would follow since, in the absence of any null elements, *dau* would trigger a soft mutation on the following word. Thus, example (61) points in a rather different direction from the examples in (56).

Thirdly, singular adjectives cannot normally function as head of a noun phrase in Welsh (see section 5.4.5 below). 'The blue one' is *yr un glas*, not **y glas*. If the adjective were the head, this construction would be an exception to this generalization. Similarly, the ungrammaticality of **y glas* may lead us to conclude that Welsh does not allow a singular null noun. This restriction has also been used to account for the fact that a possessor cannot stand alone as a noun phrase (Rouveret 1994: 184–7), and a pronominal element such as *un* 'one' or *rhai* 'ones' must be inserted:

(62)   Dyma   'ch esgidiau chi, ond wn   i ddim ble   mae
         here-are 2P shoes   you but know.PRES.1S I NEG where be.PRES.3S
         *(fy rhai) i.
         *(1S ones) me
         'Here are your shoes, but I don't know where mine are.'
                                          (adapted from Rouveret 1994: 186)

If so, this points against the null-noun analysis.

Finally, the only part of the construction that is compulsory is the numeral, as evidenced in (55), and the numeral alone may fulfil the function of the whole phrase. This sort of data would normally be taken as evidence that the numeral is the head (cf. Corbett 1993).

Taken together, these pieces of evidence allow us to exclude the possibility that the adjective is the head, except where it is nominalized, as in (58). They do not allow us to decide conclusively between the other two possibilities, but, on the face of it, an analysis whereby the numeral is a nominal head in these constructions seems the most promising.

5.3.5   *Numeral* + o *'of'* + *plural noun*

The pattern numeral + *o* 'of' + plural noun is used predominantly for higher numbers and where the noun refers to individuated entities. Contrast *pump o geiniogau* 'five pennies (coins)' with *pum ceiniog* 'five pence (amount of money)' (P. W. Thomas 1996: 314). It is also used with nouns that have no singular, such as *pobl* 'people'.

The numeral agrees in gender with the noun:

(63)   tair   o ferched
         three.F of girls
         'three girls'

The numeral may be modified by *arall* 'other' (singular in form only), but not by an ordinary adjective:

(64)   tri   arall   o ffilmiau
        three.M other.s of films
        'another three films'

(65)   *tri   newydd o ffilmiau
        three.M new   of films
        'three new films'

The noun may be modified by any adjective, which may be plural if the adjective can show plural inflection:

(66)   tri   o bobl   eraill   / newydd
        three.M of people other.P   new
        'three other / new people'

5.3.6   Numeral-like quantifiers

A number of items may appear after determiners, apparently in the same syntactic position as numerals. They must precede any prenominal adjectives. Some of them may co-occur with a preceding definite article or with a definite noun phrase, particularly in combination with a relative clause:

(67)   y   sawl   eglwys sydd   yn y   ddinas
        the several church be.PRES.REL in the city
        'those (several) churches that are in the city'

The quantifier closest in its syntax to a numeral is *llawer* 'much, many', which may be followed either by a bare noun, as in (68), or by *o* 'of' plus a noun, as in (69). Like numerals, it requires singular nouns and adjectives in the former case:[2]

(68)   llawer gwlad   arall   / *eraill
        many country.s other.s /   other.P
        'many other countries, many another country'

---

[2] If there is no head noun and a count noun is understood, then *llawer* is regularly followed by a plural adjective, a pattern not possible with numerals:

(i)   llawer eraill   / arall
       many other.P / other.s
       'many others'

Note also the regular use of a plural adjective in such cases as (69), where a singular adjective would be required following a numeral, compare (64).

Table 5.4. *Restrictions on the syntactic environments in which quantifiers may occur.*

	mass (*bwyd* 'food', *arian* 'money')	singular count (*ci* 'dog', *myfyriwr* 'student')	plural count (*cŵn* 'dogs', *myfyrwyr* 'students')
y naill 'the one (. . . or other)'	−	+	+
peth 'some, a little (mass)'	+	−	−
rhai 'some (count)'	−	−	+
sawl 'several (count)'	−	+	− (+)†
(*yr*) *un* 'any'	−	+	+

Note:
† *Sawl pobl* 'several people' is an exception.

(69) llawer (eraill)   o wledydd
      many (other.P) of country.P
      'many (other) countries'

Ychydig '(a) few, little' and *dim* 'no' also appear in both patterns, but following nouns and adjectives are singular (mass nouns) or plural (count nouns) according to sense:

(70) ychydig (o) wledydd   eraill
      few   (of) country.P other.P
      'few other countries'

Other quantifiers occur mostly only in one or other of these environments. Table 5.4 shows quantifiers that may appear in the pattern quantifier + bare noun. Some of these show sensitivity to the distinction between mass and count nouns. These may all be followed by *o* 'of' if the following noun phrase is definite, but, unlike numerals, not if it is indefinite:

(71) *peth o elw
       some of profit
      ('some profit')

(72) peth o 'r elw
      some of the profit
      'some of the profit'

These can all be used without an accompanying noun ('pronominally'):

(73) Daeth   peth hefyd o   Iwerddon.
      come.PAST.3S some too   from Ireland
      'Some [of it, mass noun] came from Ireland too.'

Of this group, *sawl* 'several' behaves most like a numeral, being followed, like numerals, only by a singular count noun, and requiring a singular adjective:

(74)   sawl   plentyn / *plant
        several child.s / child.p
        'several children'

(75)   sawl   arall   / *eraill
        several other.s / other.p
        'several others'

It differs from numerals only in disallowing the pattern with *o* + indefinite plural noun. The others (except *peth* 'some', which has a mass interpretation only) allow a following bare plural noun and plural adjectives:

(76)   rhai gwledydd eraill
        some country.p other.p
        'some countries'

A further group of quantifiers occurs only with *o* + noun phrase. The noun may be a plural count noun or a singular mass noun in all cases:

(77)   *digon* 'enough'
        dwsin 'a dozen'
        faint 'how much, how many'
        gormod 'too much, too many'
        lot 'a lot of' (colloquial)
        mwy 'more'
        rhagor 'more'
        rhywfaint 'some sort of'
        tipyn 'a little (mass only)'
        ychwaneg 'more'

These can all also be used alone without a following noun.

In some cases, the quantifier itself may be modified by another item (cf. also *llawer mwy, llawer rhagor* 'much more', *cryn ddwsin* 'a good dozen', *prin digon* 'scarcely enough'):

(78)   a. Rydyn   ni wedi cael   [**hen** ddigon o amser] i ddatrys
           be.PRES.1P we PERF get.INF old enough of time   to solve.INF
           y   broblem hon.
           the problem DEM.F
           'We've had plenty enough time to solve this problem.'
        b. Rwyt   ti wedi colli [**cryn** dipyn o bwysau].
           be.PRES.2S you PERF lose.INF quite bit of weight
           'You've lost quite a bit of weight.'

5.3.7   Late postdeterminers

Another group of items, *amryw* 'various', *cyfryw* 'such', *cyffelyb* 'similar', *fath* 'such, sort of', *ffasiwn* 'such a' and *gwahanol* 'various', occur after determiners:

(79)   o dan y   fath amgylchiadau
        under the such circumstances
        'under such circumstances'

In so far as they can co-occur at all with numerals and quantifiers, they follow:

(80)   y   tair   gwahanol iaith
        the three.F various   language
        'the three different languages'

Their late position with the pre-nominal part of the noun phrase justifies the term 'late predeterminer' for them. Two of these items, *cyffelyb* and *gwahanol*, may also behave syntactically as ordinary adjectives, appearing in postnominal position.

Fath, derived historically from the noun *math* 'sort', is now probably an independent item, bearing fixed soft mutation. Like feminine numerals, *cyfryw*, *cyffelyb* and *gwahanol* do not normally undergo mutation after the feminine article (but do mutate in other contexts):

(81)   a. y cyfryw wybodaeth
           the such   information.F
           'such information'
        b. y gwahanol bobl
           the various   people
           'the various people'

These items are therefore distinguished from ordinary adjectives by their position and by their failure to mutate according to the gender of the head noun. Like other pre-nominal adjectives, they trigger soft mutation on the following element.

5.3.8   How much structure?

An important issue in the syntax of numerals and quantifiers is how much structure to posit: does a phrase such as *tri o blant* 'three children' in (82) contain a full noun phrase (*blant*) within the larger noun phrase (*tri o blant*), or is it a single noun phrase like the alternative *tri phlentyn* 'three children', literally 'three child' (singular)? If the former, then the syntax of a numeral or a quantifier in (82) is essentially the same as that of a noun denoting a measure or container as in (83). A related question is whether the syntax of a numeral or quantifier is the same when the *o*-phrase is definite, as in (84), and when it is indefinite, as in (82).

(82)   tri   / digon   o blant
        three.M / enough of children
        'three / enough children'

(83)   potel o win
        bottle of wine
        'a bottle of wine'

(84)   tri   o 'r plant
        three.M of the children
        'three of the children'

Hurford (2003) discusses this issue, treating phrases like (82) and (83) as parallel, and hence treating *plant* (*blant*) in (82) as a fully independent noun phrase:

(85)   [$_{NP}$ tri [$_{PP}$ o [$_{NP}$ blant]]]

He argues that this has the advantage of giving a straightforward status to *o* as an ordinary preposition in all cases. Gender agreement between the numeral and the noun is not a problem, since this happens in other languages, such as German, in cases where there is unquestionably an independent noun phrase:

(86)   eine   von den   Frauen
        one.F of   the.DAT women
        'one of the women'   (German, Hurford 2003)

Against this, it may be noted that the possibilities for modification of numerals are much more restricted than measure/container nouns. Numerals may be modified by *arall* 'other' but not by other adjectives, whereas measure or container nouns may be modified freely by adjectives in the same environment:

(87)   cwpanaid haeddiannol o de
        cup   deserved   of tea
        'a well-deserved cup of tea'

5.4   Adjectives and demonstratives

In general, adjectives and demonstratives follow the noun they modify. Demonstratives follow adjectives, but otherwise pattern as adjectives in that they must co-occur with a definite article:

Table 5.5. *Forms of demonstratives in Welsh.*

	proximal	distal	'new' distal
masc. dem. / pron.	*hwn*	*hwnnw*	*hwnna*
fem. dem. / pron.	*hon*	*honno*	*honna*
neut. pron. (dem.)	*hyn*	*hynny*	*hynna*
plural demonstrative	*hyn*	*hynny*	*hynna*
plural pronoun	*rhain*	*rheini*	*rheina*

(88)   yr adeilad newydd hwn   / hwnnw / 'ma / 'na
        the building new   DEM.M / DEM.M / DEM / DEM
        'this / that new building'

There is essentially a binary demonstrative system with a contrast between proximal *hwn* / *'ma* (*yma*) 'this' and distal *hwnnw* / *'na* (*yna*) 'that'. *Acw* 'yonder' is a marginal third member of the system. The difference between *hwn* and *'ma* 'this' and *hwnnw* and *'na* 'that' is stylistic, with the latter being rather colloquial. *Hwn* and *hwnnw* show agreement for gender and number with the head noun. A paradigm of the main forms is given in Table 5.5.

Both *hwn* and *hwnnw* may be used pronominally. There are neuter forms *hyn* 'this' and *hynny* 'that', which may be used pronominally and also with some singular nouns (*y pryd hynny* 'that time').

Usage of *hwn* versus *hwnnw* does not correspond closely to English *this* versus *that*. The *hwnnw*-series seems to be unmarked, and is often used for textual cohesion where English would use *this*:

(89)   Ers hynny, mae darlledu wedi dod yn rhan ganolog o'n bywydau
        cymdeithasol a diwylliannol, ac o bosib, mae **hynny**'n fwy gwir am Gymru
        na'r rhan fwyaf o rannau eraill y Deyrnas Unedig.
        'Since then, broadcasting has become a central part of our social and
        cultural lives, and possibly **this** is more true of Wales than most of the
        other parts of the United Kingdom.'

In informal Welsh, the distal *hwnnw* has tended to encroach upon the semantic range of the proximal *hwn*, and another series *hwnna* is used as a 'new' distal form meaning physically distant from the speaker, primarily, but not exclusively, pronominally. In the dialects, various other forms, for instance *hwncw* < *hwn acw* 'that one over there', for pronominal demonstratives also exist.

The use of *'ma* 'this' and *'na* 'that' pronominally, without a head noun, is very restricted. *'Na* is used as an expletive subject corresponding to English *there* in colloquial Welsh (see section 2.6). Expressions such as *fel 'na* 'like that'

may be interpreted by some speakers as containing *'na* 'that', although historically they are contractions of *fel hyn yna* 'like this there'.

5.4.1   Mutations on adjectives

After a feminine noun, an adjective undergoes soft mutation if
possible:

(90)   gardd   <u>brydferth</u>   (*prydferth*)
        garden beautiful
        'a beautiful garden'

If there is a string of adjectives, each one undergoes soft mutation:

(91)   gardd   <u>fawr</u> <u>breifat</u>   (*mawr, preifat*)
        garden large private
        'a large private garden'

However, a local mutation takes precedence over a more distant one. For
instance, with conjoined adjectives, the aspirate mutation caused by *a* 'and'
takes precedence over the soft mutation caused by a feminine noun. Hence, in
(92), we have the aspirate-mutated form *phrysur* 'busy', as required by *a*, rather
than soft-mutated *brysur*.

(92)   gardd   <u>fawr</u> a   <u>phrysur</u>   (*mawr, prysur*)
        garden large and busy
        'a large and busy garden'

If the adjective is itself modified by a preceding element, the modifier bears
the mutation (if it can) and the adjective undergoes whatever mutation effect
the modifier requires. In (93), *tra chymhleth* 'quite complex' undergoes soft
mutation as a whole, *gorchest* 'achievement' being feminine, and so *tra*
becomes *dra*. *Cymhleth* itself does not undergo soft mutation, but rather
undergoes the aspirate mutation triggered by *tra*.

(93)   gorchest   [$_{AP}$ <u>dra</u>   <u>chymhleth</u>]   (*tra, cymhleth*)
        achievement   quite+SM complex+AM
        'quite a complex achievement'

In (94), there is no mutation. Although *swydd* 'job' is feminine, *eithaf*
'extremely' begins with a vowel, and hence cannot show the soft mutation triggered by *swydd* on the adjective phrase. On the other hand, *eithaf* is not a
mutation trigger, and hence *pwysig* 'important' escapes mutation.

(94)   swydd   [$_{AP}$ eithaf pwysig]
        job   quite important
        'an extremely important job'

Note that the principle that the most local mutation takes precedence within the Welsh noun phrase contrasts with the situation in Irish, where more distant mutations may take precedence. Compare (95), where the mutation triggered by the possessive pronoun (eclipsis, *cuid* > *gcuid*) takes precedence over the mutation that would be triggered by the numeral alone (lenition, *cuid* > *chuid*).

(95)   ár   dhá   gcuid
        our two   part
        'our two parts'   (Irish, Green 2006: 1966)

Notwithstanding (93) and (94), there are a few cases where the gender mutation may 'skip' elements, for instance, a possessive noun phrase. In (96), *cynffon* 'tail' is feminine. *Mochyn* 'pig' functions as a possessor, and does not mutate. Nevertheless, *cynffon* triggers a soft mutation on *cyrliog* 'curly' because it is feminine.

(96)   cynffon mochyn gyrliog
        tail   pig   curly
        'a curly pig's tail'

Similarly, in (97), *cyntaf* 'first' undergoes soft mutation (*cyntaf* > *gyntaf*) because *wythnos* 'week' is feminine (and singular after a numeral), despite the fact that part of the numeral intervenes.

(97)   y   tair   wythnos ar ddeg gyntaf
        the three.F week   on ten first
        'the first thirteen weeks'

5.4.2   Number and gender agreement

Some adjectives have morphologically distinct plural forms, and some have distinct feminine singular forms. These forms may be used as attributive adjectives, as illustrated in (98) and (99). In most cases, as in (98), adjective agreement is optional and the general form may also be used. Number agreement is, however, compulsory with *arall* 'other' (plural *eraill*).

(98)   llygaid gleision / glas
        eyes   blue.P   / blue.GENERAL
        'blue eyes'

There is a great deal of variation between different adjectives and between dialects. Some forms, such as feminine *bechan* 'small' or plural *ifainc* 'young', are in common use, hence gender agreement in (99) is more or less compulsory.

(99)   siop <u>fechan</u> / *<u>fychan</u>   (*bechan, bychan*)
        shop small.F   small.GENERAL
        'a small shop'

Other forms, for instance, feminine *gwleb*, plural *gwlybion* (corresponding to general *gwlyb* 'wet'), are rare, formal or restricted to fossilized expressions.

In predicative position, adjectives never agree in gender or number with their noun:

(100)   Mae   ei   lygaid yn <u>las</u>   /   *<u>leision</u>.   (*glas, gleision*)
        be.PRES.3S 3MS eyes PRED blue.GENERAL   blue.P
        'His eyes are blue.'

5.4.3   Position of adjectives relative to the noun

Although most adjectives follow the noun they modify, there are a few adjectives that always or often precede. A non-exhaustive list of adjectives that always or typically precede the noun is given in (101).

(101)   *dewis* 'chosen'
        dirprwy 'deputy'
        diweddar 'late, deceased'
        gwir 'true, genuine, real'
        hen 'old'
        hoff 'favourite'
        mân 'minor, insignificant'
        prif 'main'
        unig 'only (child)'

Pre-nominal adjectives, except when comparative or superlative, trigger soft mutation of the following word, normally the noun.

In highly literary Welsh, more or less any adjective can precede the noun. Even in moderately literary Welsh, comparative and superlative adjectives often precede. Hence, we find both *gwell ateb* 'a better answer' with adjective – noun order, alongside more frequent *ateb gwell* with noun – adjective order (see also Tallerman 1999).

A number of adjectives have distinct meanings when used pre-nominally and postnominally. For instance, *unig* means 'only' in pre-nominal position (*unig blentyn* 'an only child') but 'lonely' in postnominal position (*plentyn unig* 'a lonely child').

Pre-verbal adjectives tend to be non-gradable. Of the adjectives that are used regularly in pre-nominal position, most either have no predicative use or else are used predicatively only in a meaning that is not available to them in pre-nominal position. It is not generally possible to modify a pre-nominal adjective:

(102)   *yr hen iawn afon
          the old very river
          'the very old river'

Pre-nominal adjectives occur in a fairly fixed order. P. W. Thomas (1996: 319) provides the following ordering for the field between the numeral and the noun:

(103)   *gwir/diweddar*   *- prif* *- hoff-*   *cas/mân*   *- hen*   *- uchel*
          'true'/'deceased' 'main' 'favourite' 'nasty'/'minor' 'old'   'high'

5.4.4   *Order of postnominal adjectives*

Although there is some degree of flexibility in the relative order of postnominal adjectives, some rules and tendencies can be noted. Two fairly rigid rules are that *arall* 'other' is normally last in a series of adjectives (except that *posib* 'possible' may follow with the relevant interpretation, and some heavy adjective phrases may follow); and that, apart from this, comparative and superlative adjectives must be last. The first restriction is illustrated in the contrast between (104) and (105).

(104)   adeilad mawr gwag arall
          building big   empty other
          'another big empty building'

(105)   ??adeilad mawr arall gwag
          building big   other empty
          ('another big empty building')

The restriction on comparative and superlative adjectives is illustrated in (106) and (107).

(106)   y   llyfr Cymraeg newydd gorau
          the book Welsh   new   best
          'the best new Welsh book'

(107)   *y   llyfr Cymraeg gorau newydd
          the book Welsh   best   new
          ('the best new Welsh book')

Note that the resulting order of adjectives is the reverse of that required in English.

With other adjectives, order is less rigid, but there are nevertheless tendencies. An important issue (see section 5.6 below) is whether the Welsh order is the same as that found in English. Sproat & Shih (1991: 586–7) investigate adjectives of size, colour, shape and provenance in Irish, and conclude that the default order is SIZE > SHAPE > COLOUR > PROVENANCE. They note that Welsh is identical to Irish in this respect, and that both are identical to English. This conclusion is widely accepted in the literature (see Cinque 1994: 100 fn. 20, Rouveret 1994: 212–13, Fassi Fehri 1999: 108, 147–8, Sichel 2000: 571, Longobardi 2001: 578).

Although this is true as far as it goes, there are two provisos. First, adding in adjectives of age (*ifanc* 'young', *newydd* 'new') and quality (*da* 'good', *gwych* 'great', *neis* 'nice') makes the comparison far more complicated. A comparison of default orders with these included is given in (108) and (109). The English order is based on that of Sproat & Shih (1991: 565), with the addition of adjectives of age at their appropriate place (see also Cinque 1994: 96 for a very similar hierarchy for Italian). The Welsh hierarchy is based on P. W. Thomas (1996: 318), adapted so as to make direct comparison with English possible.

(108)   English
        QUALITY > SIZE > AGE > SHAPE > COLOUR > PROVENANCE
        good   *big*   *new* *long*   *red*   *English*

(109)   Welsh
        SIZE > SHAPE/COLOUR > PROVENANCE > AGE > QUALITY
        mawr   *hir* / *coch*   *Saesneg*   *newydd da*

Both adjectives of age and adjectives of quality come early in the sequence in English, but late in Welsh. In any case, their order with respect to each other is reversed between the two languages, with quality preceding age in English but following it in Welsh. Examples of contrasting neutral word orders are given in (110).

(110)   a. caneuon newydd gwych   (AGE > QUALITY)
           songs   new   great
           'great new songs'
        b. athro   ifanc   hoffus   (AGE > QUALITY)
           teacher young   likeable
           'a likeable young teacher'   (Willis 2006a: 1817)

Furthermore, where one adjective is felt to be more integral to the sense of the head noun, or where one adjective takes scope over the other, Welsh has 'mirror-image' ordering compared to English, since scope relations are defined according to distance from the noun, rather than according to the hierarchies in (108) and (109):

(111)   a. brics   coch mawr   (COLOUR > SIZE)
           bricks red   big
           'big red bricks'

b. ryg Twrcaidd coch   (PROVENANCE > COLOUR)
   rug Turkish   red
   'a red Turkish rug'

For further details of adjective ordering in Welsh, see Willis (2006a).

5.4.5 Noun phrases headed by adjectives

Plural adjectives, irrespective of whether they are morphologically distinct from the singular, may be used with a definite article to form a noun phrase denoting a group of people:

(112) a. yr ifainc
           the young.P
           'the young'
       b. y   Gleision
           the blue.P
           'the Blues'
       c. y   diwaith
           the unemployed.GENERAL
           'the unemployed'

There seem to be two criteria for deciding whether these are adjectives or nouns.

First, in some of these cases, the plural form is obsolete in its adjectival use with a head noun. Consider the adjective *deallus* 'intellectual'. If the plural suffix *-ion* is added, the result is a noun, *deallusion* 'intellectuals'. This plural form can never be used independently as an adjective after a plural noun. Thus, we find only the general form *deallus* with a plural noun: *penderfyniadau deallus* 'intelligent decisions', not **penderfyniadau deallusion*. This seems to be a good reason for regarding *deallusion* synchronically as a noun distinct from the corresponding adjective from which it derived historically.

Secondly, singular adjectives cannot normally be used alone with the article, and, instead, *un* 'one' must be used as a pronominal head:[3]

(113) *y glas
        the blue
        ('the blue one')

(114) yr un glas
        the one blue
        'the blue one (masculine)'

---

[3] As in English, a colour adjective may be used alone in a nominalization, particularly to refer to the colour itself, for instance, *yn y coch* '(financially) in the red'.

For individuated plural referents, the plural conterpart *rhai* 'ones' may be used:

(115)   y   rhai   ifainc
         the ones   young.P
         'the young ones'

If the phrase has a female or grammatically feminine referent, the adjective mutates:

(116)   yr   un   *las*   (*glas*)
         the one blue+SM
         'the blue one (feminine)'

Thus, where the singular of an adjective can be used alone with an article, we are justified in regarding it as a noun. This is the case with pairs such as *y claf* 'the ill person, patient' (plural *y cleifion*) and *y tlawd* 'the poor person, pauper' (plural *y tlodion*).

5.4.6   The 'genitive of respect'

Complex adjective phrases may be formed along the pattern [adjective – prefixed possessive clitic – noun], where the clitic is co-referential with the head noun of the entire noun phrase, and the adjective is predicated of the noun within the adjective phrase. An example is given in (117).

(117)   dynes   [$_{AP}$ fyr   [$_{NP}$ ei   thymer]]
         woman   short   3SF temper
         'a short-tempered woman'

This construction has generally been known as the 'genitive of respect', a not entirely appropriate term given the absence of case marking on Welsh nouns. The terminology is based on classical languages, and was first applied to Welsh by Morris-Jones (1913). The two most salient aspects of the construction are that a feminine head noun still triggers a mutation on the adjective embedded within the adjective phrase, as with *fyr* 'short' (not *byr*) in (117). However, it cannot agree in gender, hence *fyr* (general form), not *fer* (feminine). Second, an overt postnominal pronoun is not possible, even though such a pronoun is otherwise possible with pronominal possessors:

(118)   cyfaill   oer   ei   galon   (*ef)
         friend   cold 3SM heart   (*him)
         'a cold-hearted friend'

5.5   Possessor noun phrases and related constructions

Possessor noun phrases follow the noun. Welsh has no morphological case inflection on nouns, so possession is signalled by word order alone. The possessor follows adjectives, as illustrated in (119), and complex numerals, as in (120).

(119)   a. car newydd Siôn
                car new   Siôn
                'Siôn's new car'
            b. tŷ   arall Mair
                house other Mair
                'Mair's other house'

(120)   dau   gar ar hugain Siôn
            two.M car on twenty Siôn
            'Siôn's twenty-two cars'

For an example of a simple possessor noun phrase without a modifying adjective, see (25) above.

5.5.1   The 'construct-state' effect

As noted in the introduction to this chapter, possessor constructions manifest restrictions on the expression and interpretation of definiteness. Only the final possessor may bear a definite article or be in any way definite. Hence, we find (121), where the definite article modifies *meddyg* 'doctor'. If the final possessor is marked as definite, the entire noun phrase is interpreted as definite.

(121)   siop mab chwaer y   meddyg
            shop son sister   the doctor
            'the shop of the doctor's sister's son'

There are no gender mutations on possessor noun phrases. Even though *siop* is feminine, the initial consonant of the possessor does not undergo mutation, hence we have unmutated *mab* 'son' rather than the mutated form *fab*.

A definite article before any of the other nouns in (121) would be ungrammatical:

(122)   a. *y   siop mab chwaer meddyg
                the shop son sister   doctor
            b. *y   siop y   mab y   chwaer y   meddyg
                the shop the son the sister   the doctor
                ('the shop of the doctor's sister's son')

These restrictions do not hold if the possessor noun phrase is replaced by a prepositional phrase headed by *o* 'of', as is possible in 'picture' nouns and event nominals. Compare (123) with (124).

(123)   llun   [y   brenin newydd]
         picture the king   new
         'the picture of the new king'

(124)   y   llun   o ['r brenin newydd]
         the picture of the king   new
         'the picture of the new king'

These restrictions on definiteness parallel those found in construct-state nominals in Semitic languages, and are also paralleled in the other Celtic languages. A Hebrew construct-state example is given in (125).

(125)   (*ha-) beyt   ha- mora
         (the) house the- teacher
         'the teacher's house'   (Hebrew, Ritter 1988)

In (125), only the possessor noun phrase *ha-mora* may contain a definite article, and the head noun *beyt* appears in a special construct-state form. Contrast this with the non-construct-state case in (126), where either noun may be freely marked with the definite article, and the head noun *bayit* appears in its normal form.

(126)   (ha-) bayit šel (ha-) mora
         the- house of the- teacher
         'the/a house of the/a teacher'   (Hebrew, Ritter 1988)

Although the constructions are similar in the two languages, there are some differences. In Welsh, there is no special construct-state form for the head noun. Furthermore, word order is different. The possessor in Welsh follows adjectives, as in (119), whereas in Hebrew and other Semitic languages with construct-state constructions, the possessor precedes adjectives:

(127)   beyt ha- mora   ha- yafe
         house the- teacher the- pretty
         'the teacher's pretty house'   (Hebrew, Ritter 1988)

5.5.2 *Possessor noun phrases versus attributive noun phrases*

As we have seen, possessor noun phrases never mutate, even after a feminine noun. Attributive noun phrases, on the other hand, are treated like adjectives, mutating after a feminine noun. Note therefore the contrast between (128) and (129). In (128), a possessor construction, *siop* 'shop' is feminine, but the possessor *mab y meddyg* 'the doctor's son' does not mutate to become *fab y meddyg*. In (129), an attributive-noun construction, *lyfrau* does mutate (from *llyfrau*) because *siop* is feminine:

(128)   siop [mab y   meddyg]
          shop son   the doctor
          'the doctor's son's shop'

(129)   siop [lyfrau]
          shop books
          'a book shop'

Unlike possessor noun phrases, attributive noun phrases precede adjectives:

(130)   siop lyfrau fawr
          shop books big
          'a large book shop'

5.5.3   The mixed construction

Another construction seems to combine the properties of the preceding two. This is illustrated in (96), repeated here as (131).

(131)   [[cynffon mochyn] gyrliog]
              tail   pig   curly
          'a curly pig's tail'

Here, the head noun *cynffon* 'tail' is modified by an indefinite noun or noun phrase, in this case, *mochyn* '(a) pig'. Like a possessor noun phrase, *mochyn* does not mutate even though *cynffon* 'tail' is feminine, and the adjective *cyrliog* 'curly' does mutate as expected to *gyrliog*. On the other hand, like an attributive noun phrase, *mochyn* is placed close to the head noun, preceding the adjective *cyrliog* 'curly'. It seems therefore that it has some properties of a possessor noun phrase, and some properties of an attributive noun phrase.

5.6   Possible analyses of noun-phrase structure

5.6.1   Noun-raising approaches

It is widely assumed (Rouveret 1994, Roberts 2005; see also Guilfoyle 1988:195 and especially Duffield 1996 for similar analyses of Irish) that the noun–adjective order of Welsh is the result of leftward movement of the noun.

This section sets out the main features of this type of approach. N-raising analyses propose that the noun phrase contains a minimum of three projections within it: a noun phrase (NP) contained within a functional phrase (NumP, number phrase, for Rouveret 1994; QP, quantifier phrase, for Roberts 2005), within a determiner phrase (DP). The definite article, possessive clitics and a few other elements are determiners in the head of D (see, however, sections 2.5.2 and 3.1.2 for some problems associated with treating the possessive clitics as D-heads). Adjectives are left-adjoined to the top of the lowest projection, NP. Nouns move from the head of N to Q, bypassing any adjectives adjoined to it. This results in the noun – adjective order observed in Welsh, and in such other languages as Irish, French and Italian. The structure of a simple noun phrase with noun – adjective order is illustrated in (132).

(132)

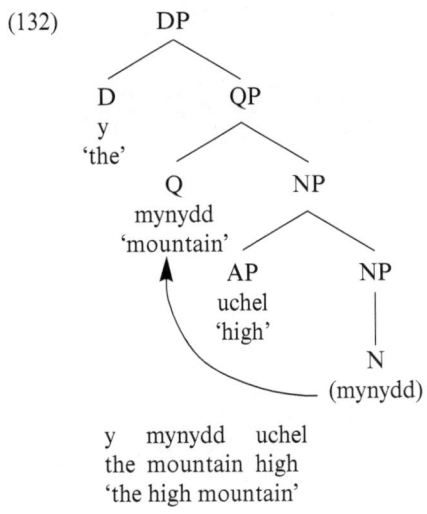

y   mynydd   uchel
the mountain high
'the high mountain'

This approach is sometimes justified by reference to the claim that Welsh adjective order is the same as that in English. If this were true, it would allow an analysis whereby the noun-phrase syntax of English and Welsh was the same, except that Welsh had a movement operation absent in English. However, as we have seen, Welsh often manifests 'mirror-image' adjective orders as compared with English, as exemplified in (104)–(107) and (110). Another problem concerns acquisition: children acquiring Welsh do not go through a stage of producing adjective – noun orders, even when they otherwise lack functional categories (Aldridge *et al.* 1997), contrary to what this analysis predicts. Problems with mutation for this analysis are discussed below. For discussion of other problems, see Sadler (2000: 76–92).

5.6.2   *Non-movement approaches*

An alternative approach, put forward by Sadler (2000) and Willis (2006a) involves no movement of the noun. Instead, adjectives are right-adjoined within the noun phrase. Assuming the same three-level structure as was assumed above, this type of analysis would propose trees like (133). The non-movement approach is evidently simpler, so should be preferred in the absence of good evidence to the contrary. The main evidence against this approach is that it is forced to assume either that complements of nouns are right-adjoined to the top of the noun phrase (DP) (Sadler 2000) or that they move to this position (Willis 2006a) in order to achieve the observed noun – possessor – complement order (see Roberts 2005: 90 for discussion).

(133)

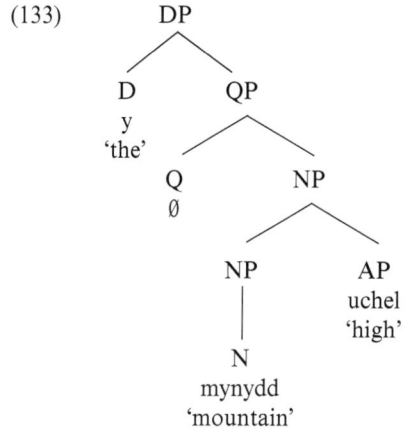

5.6.3   *Adjective mutation: phonology or morphosyntax?*

There are essentially three approaches that can be taken to analysing the mutations triggered by feminine singular nouns on following adjectives:

(i)   the mutation has a lexical trigger and is phonological: at the end of every feminine noun there is a floating autosegment which re-attaches itself to the following word, and is interpreted by the phonological component as an instruction to change (that is, soft mutate) the initial segment of that word (Lieber 1983) [the phonological approach];

(ii)   the mutation has a morphosyntactic trigger: a feminine noun triggers a mutation on the first phrase that it immediately precedes and c-commands (that is, a following sister or its descendants) (Roberts 2005; see also Green 2006 for whom a mutation trigger selects the mutated morphological form of its complement) [the morphosyntactic approach]. This approach can be coupled either with a noun-raising analysis of the structure of noun phrases or with a non-movement analysis;

(iii)   the mutation is essentially an agreement operation: feminine adjectives agree with their head nouns, and the mutation is a morphological manifestation of this agreement [the agreement approach].

All three approaches would handle a standard case such as (90), where a single non-complex adjective immediately follows a feminine noun. The test for them comes from more complex cases, which will be considered in turn here.

5.6.3.1 Multiple adjectives

As we have seen, in a string of adjectives, each undergoes mutation after a feminine noun. According to the phonological approach, (i) above, both feminine nouns and feminine adjectives bear a floating autosegment that triggers mutation on the following word. Hence, in a sequence of adjectives, the mutation on all but the first adjective is actually triggered by the preceding adjective:

(134)   gardd^{SM} fawr^{SM} breifat^{SM} (*mawr, preifat*)
         garden large   private
         'a large private garden'

In (134), each word triggers a mutation on the following one (the floating autosegment is henceforth marked as ^{SM}). Note, however, that, according to this analysis, the mutation on *breifat* is caused by the preceding adjective, whereas the mutation on *fawr* is caused by the preceding noun. This in itself might be considered an undesirable feature of the analysis.

On the morphosyntactic approach, (ii) above, there are two possible analyses, depending on whether the movement approach is assumed, as in (132), or else a non-movement approach is assumed, as in (133). If we assume, following the movement approach, that the head noun raises from the right of the adjectives to the left, we have the structure in (135). There, *gardd* is a mutation trigger. It triggers mutation on a phrasal sister, NP. This triggers a mutation on the /m/ of *mawr > fawr*. If we assume that all adjectives adjoin to NP, then, arguably, each separate NP is subject to mutation, since they are all maximal projections of the same phrase. Hence a mutation is triggered on the initial consonant of the second instance of the NP, namely the /p/ of *preifat*, and multiple mutations arise.

(135)

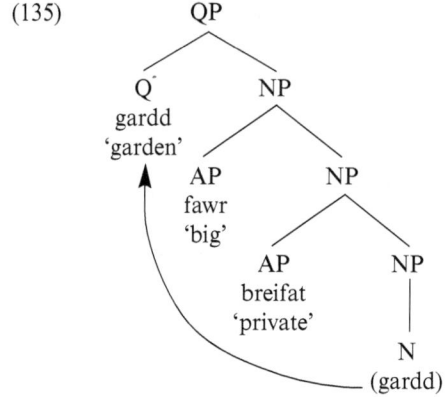

If we pursue a non-movement approach, the relevant subtree is (136). We need to assume that a feminine NP triggers a soft mutation on a following sister. The adjectives are adjoined, so each adjunction forms a new NP, hence each new NP is a mutation trigger, triggering mutation on each adjective that is added to the structure.

(136)

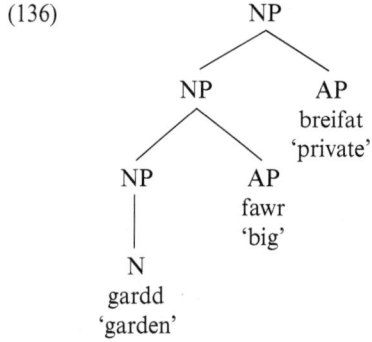

Finally, on the agreement approach, (iii) above, the adjectives agree with their head, and the mutation is a reflex of that agreement.

5.6.3.2 Phrasal adjectives

With phrasal adjectives, such as *tra chymhleth* 'quite complex' and *eithaf pwysig* 'extremely important', where the adjective is modified by a preceding element, a mutation appears on the modifier if the head noun is feminine singular, and the adjective itself mutates or fails to mutate according to the requirements of the modifier and not the requirements of the head noun; compare (93) and (94).

This poses no problems for the phonological approach, where the floating autosegments trigger mutations on the immediately following words, and pay no attention to what the head of a phrase is:

(137)   gorchest[SM]   dra[AM] chymhleth
         achievement quite complex
         'quite a complex achievement'

On the morphosyntactic approach, illustrated in (138), *gorchest* 'achievement' will be a soft-mutation trigger, triggering mutation on its complement NP, the first element of which is the /t/ of *tra,* hence *dra.* This mutation will be triggered successfully irrespective of whether the N-raising or the non-movement approach is adopted.

(138)

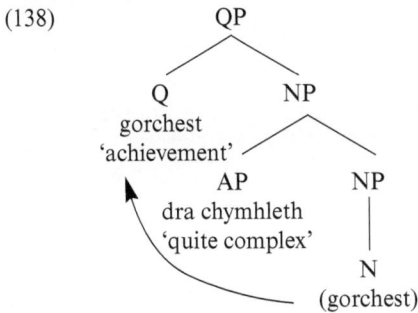

Only on the agreement approach is there a problem: the adjective phrase *tra chymhleth* would agree in gender with *gorchest.* Since agreement is normally between heads, it would be expected that the agreement would be manifested on the adjective and not on its modifier, hence we would expect *cymhleth* to mutate to *gymhleth,* but it does not. This looks like a good reason to reject this analysis outright.

5.6.3.3 Attributive noun phrases

Attributive noun phrases, as in (139), are extremely difficult for the phonological approach, and probably pose insurmountable problems. In (139), *siop* 'shop' is feminine, and hence triggers a soft mutation on both the attributive noun phrase *lyfrau Cymraeg* and the adjective *leol.*

(139)   eich siop [lyfrau Cymraeg] leol   (*llyfrau, lleol*)
         2P   shop books Welsh   local
         'your local Welsh book shop'

For the morphosyntactic approaches, these examples are unremarkable, and pose no special problems, being treated exactly like the corresponding cases where the attributive noun happens to be a single word.

According to the phonological approach, each word which bears a mutation will itself be a mutation trigger on the immediately following word. In (139), *siop* is feminine, so has a floating autosegment that successfully triggers the correct mutation on *llyfrau* > *lyfrau* 'books'. Since *lyfrau* undergoes mutation, it itself bears a floating autosegment triggering a mutation on the following word. However, this produces the wrong result, triggering mutation on *Cymraeg* rather than on *lleol* > *leol*. The problem, essentially, is that, being purely phonological, the approach is unable to distinguish that, in this case, the following word is part of the attributive noun phrase *lyfrau Cymraeg*, and that it is this phrase as a whole that needs to trigger mutation.

5.6.3.4   Distinguishing attributive noun phrases from possessor noun phrases

Finally, we have seen that feminine singular nouns trigger soft mutation on an attributive noun phrase, but not on a possessor noun phrase or on an adjunct.

For the phonological approach, the problem is to prevent mutation from applying in (140), and to explain its optionality in (141).[4] In these examples, *siop* 'shop' and *noson* 'night' are feminine, so they have a floating autosegment that should trigger a mutation on the following word.

(140)   siop^{SM} mab y   meddyg
         shop son the doctor
         'the doctor's son's shop'

(141)   y   noson^{SM} cynt / gynt
         the night   before
         'the night before'

These examples are also problems for a morphosyntactic approach. Although it is plausible to suggest that a possessor noun phrase occupies a different syntactic position from an attributive noun phrase, we need to ensure that the difference in position leads to a difference in mutation. Standard N-raising analyses posit that possessors are specifiers of NP, whereas attributive adjectives are adjoined to NP. A typical structure is illustrated in (142), representing (140).

---

[4] According to P. W. Thomas (1996: 199), when *cynt* resists mutation in this context, it means 'previous', and, when it undergoes mutation, it means 'of yore, of old'. By this rule, the only form for (141) should be *y noson cynt*, since 'the previous night' is the only plausible interpretation. This having been said, *y noson gynt* is in practice found with this interpretation.

(142)

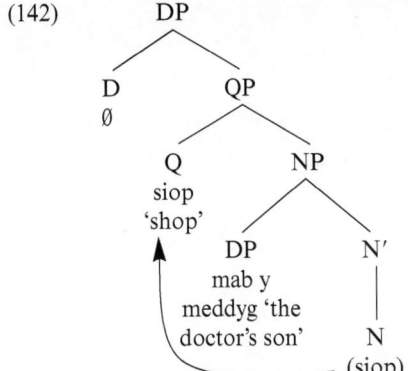

The structural difference would have to be exploited to trigger mutation in the latter case, but not in the former. However, it is not clear exactly what would block a head's mutation effect from appearing on *mab*, the first word of the specifier of the complement of *siop*.

Non-N-raising analyses would fare much better, since they could posit a radically different structural position for the possessor noun phrase. Following Sadler (2000) and Willis (2006a), the structural difference between an attributive noun phrase and a possessor noun phrase would be that illustrated in (143) and (144). In (143), the attributive noun phrase *lyfrau Cymraeg* 'Welsh books' right-adjoins to NP, and is therefore the sister of *siop* (NP1), and is a potential target of mutation. In (144), the possessor noun phrase occupies a much higher position, either right-adjoined to the top of the entire phrase (DP), or else in a rightward-projecting specifier of this phrase. Consequently, it is not the sister of *siop*, and is outside the domain for targeting mutation.

(143)

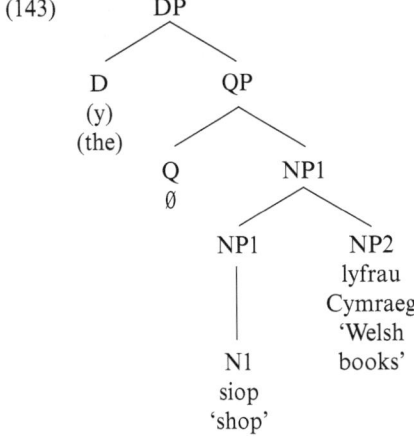

(144)

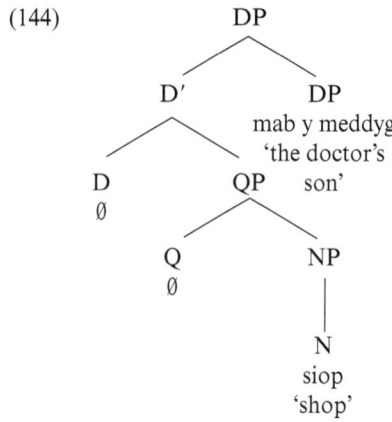

The situation with *y noson cynt* in (141) is similar: the non-mutating case can be analysed with *cynt* right-adjoined to the entire noun phrase (DP), and the mutating case with *cynt* as an ordinary adjective.

The agreement approach also deals easily with such data: the non-mutating items are nominal or adverbial, and the fact that they show no agreement with the head noun is not surprising, since nouns and adverbs do not normally agree with nouns.

5.6.4   *Conclusions about possible analyses*

We have seen that the phonological approach faces problems with phrasal attributive nouns, and cannot distinguish between an attributive noun phrase and a possessor noun phrase for mutation purposes. It is also questionable whether it provides a satisfying account of mutations on multiple adjectives. The noun-raising morphosyntactic approach accounts successfully for much of the data, but faces substantial difficulty in distinguishing attributive noun phrases from possessor noun phrases. The agreement approach cannot account for mutations on phrasal adjectives with premodifiers. Only the non-movement morphosyntactic approach provides a satisfactory account of all the mutation phenomena discussed here.

5.7   Conclusion

This chapter has considered the main features of the Welsh noun phrase. Many of these are the features expected in a consistently head-initial language. However, as we have seen, a number of aspects present quite considerable difficulties of analysis. Adjective ordering turns out to be a quite complex phenomenon not amenable to simple generalization. Mutation patterns within the noun phrase are also not easy to account for. We have considered the implications of both for various different types of approach. We have also seen a number of characteristics and constructions that suggest comparison with other languages, most notably the 'construct-state' construction with close parallels in Semitic languages.

Appendix: Mutation triggers in the noun phrase

Soft mutation

Determiners

y(r)	feminine definite article (except before numerals higher than two)
y(r)	masculine definite article before *dau* 'two' only
	feminine noun triggers mutation on following adjectives or attributive noun phrases
pa	'which'
rhyw	'some'
sut	'what kind of'
unrhyw	'any'

Numerals

un	'one' (mutation in feminine only)
dau	'two' (masc.)
dwy	'two' (fem.)
ail	'second'
	ordinal numerals higher than second trigger mutation on a feminine noun

Quantifiers, postdeterminers etc.

ychydig	'a few'
unig	'only'
holl	'all'
ambell	'occasional'
amryw	'various'
y naill	'the one (. . . or other)'
(yr) un	'any' (feminine only)
amryw	'various'
fath	'such'
cyfryw	'such'
cyffelyb	'such'
ffasiwn	'such a'
gwahanol	'various'

Adjectives
   prenominal adjectives

Modifiers of adjectives in pre-adjectival position
cwbl	'completely'
cymharol	'comparatively'
eithriadol	'extremely'
go	'quite'
gweddol	'fairly'
gwir	'truly'
hollol	'completely'
lled	'fairly'
rhy	'too' etc. (but note that *digon* 'enough', *eithaf* 'extremely', *hanner* 'half, semi-' etc. require absence of mutation) other pre-adjectival modifiers

Clitic agreement markers
dy	second-person singular proclitic
'th	second-person singular enclitic
ei	masculine third-person singular proclitic
'i / 'w	masculine third-person singular enclitic (but note that accusative *'i* with finite verbs requires absence of mutation / aspiration)

Aspirate mutation

Numerals
tri	'three'
chwe	'six'

Clitic agreement markers
ei	feminine third-person singular proclitic
'i / 'w	feminine third-person singular enclitic

Modifiers of adjectives
tra	'quite'

Nasal mutation

Numerals
tair	'three' on *blynedd, blwydd year* etc. (non-standard)
pedair	'four' on *blynedd, blwydd* etc. (non-standard)
pum	'five' on *blynedd, blwydd* etc.

chwe	'six' on *blynedd, blwydd* etc. (non-standard)
saith and higher numerals	'seven' on *blynedd, blwydd* etc.

Clitic agreement markers

fy	first-person singular proclitic

Aspiration

Clitic agreement markers

'm	first-person singular enclitic
ein	first-person plural proclitic
'n	first-person plural enclitic
eu	third-person plural proclitic
'u / *'w*	third-person plural enclitic

6

More on agreement

In this chapter we look more closely at agreement. We saw in section 1.4.3 that finite verbs and most prepositions show agreement in the form of an inflection, the former agreeing with a following pronominal subject and the latter agreeing with a following pronominal object. In chapters 3 and 5 we noted that non-finite verbs and nouns show agreement in the form of a clitic, the former with a following pronominal object and and the latter with a following pronominal possessor. We also observed in chapter 3 that the element *i* which introduces non-finite clauses shows agreement in the form of an inflection with a following pronominal subject and that *bod*, the non-finite form of the verb 'be', shows agreement in the form of a clitic with a following pronominal subject. In all cases there is no agreement with a non-pronominal NP. Table 6.1 summarizes the basic facts about agreement. It is generally accepted that these various kinds of agreement are different manifestations of a single phenomenon. We argue here that all involve a head and a pronoun which follows it on the surface, and we consider how this fact can best be captured.

Table 6.1. *Summary of Welsh agreement patterns.*

Head	Agreement form	Agreement trigger
Finite verbs	inflection	following pronominal subject
Prepositions	inflection	following pronominal object
Clause-initial *i*	inflection	following pronominal subject
Non-finite verbs	clitic	following pronominal object
Bod	clitic	following pronominal subject
Nouns	clitic	following pronominal possessor

6.1   The basic data

We begin by illustrating all six kinds of agreement and highlighting the reasons for thinking that they are different forms of a single phenomenon.

As we have said, finite verbs agree with a following pronominal subject. The following colloquial paradigm from section 2.1.1 illustrates:

(1)   a. gweles   i   d. gwelon   ni
        see.PAST.1S I   see.PAST.1P we
        b. gwelest   ti   e. gweloch   chi
        see.PAST.2S you.S   see.PAST.2P you.P
        c. gwelodd   e/ hi   f. gwelon   nhw
        see.PAST.3S he she   see.PAST.3P they

As noted in section 2.1.1, subjects are commonly omitted in literary Welsh but rarely omitted in the colloquial language. We assume that there is a phonologically null pronoun when there is no overt pronoun. As also noted in section 2.1.1, the third person singular form is used with a non-pronominal subject, either singular or plural. The following illustrate:

(2)   Gwelodd y bachgen/bechgyn ddraig.
        see.PAST.3s the boy   boys   dragon
        'The boy/boys saw a dragon.'

(3)   *Gwelon   y bechgyn ddraig.
        see.PAST.3P the boys   dragon
        ('The boys saw a dragon.')

Thus, there is agreement with a pronoun but not with a non-pronominal noun phrase.

We turn now to prepositions. Most prepositions have inflectional paradigms showing agreement with a following pronominal object. The following is a typical paradigm:

(4)   a. arnaf i   e. arnon ni
          on.1S me   on.1P us
          'on me'   'on us'
        b. arnat ti   f. arnoch chi
          on.2S you.S   on.2P you.P
          'on you (S)'   'on you (P)'
        c. arno   fo   g. arnyn nhw
          on.3MS him   on.3P them
          'on him'   'on them'
        d. arni   hi
          on.3FS her
          'on her'

Notice that, unlike finite verbs, inflecting prepositions have separate masculine and feminine third-person singular forms. There is often no overt prepositional object in literary Welsh but the object is normally overt in colloquial

Welsh. The basic uninflected form of the preposition *ar* appears with a non-pronominal object. Thus, we have (5) and not (6).

(5)   ar y   bachgen/yr eneth/y bechgyn
       on the boy   the girl   the boys
       'on the boy / the girl / the boys'

(6)   a. *arno   'r   bachgen
          on.3MS the boy
       b. *arni   'r   eneth
          on.3FS the girl
       c. *arnyn y   bechgyn
          on.3P the boys

Again, then, we have agreement with a pronoun but not with a non-pronominal noun phrase.

Next consider the element *i*, which introduces non-finite clauses, which we discussed in section 3.4. Like the homophonous preposition, it has a defective paradigm, only showing agreement with a following third person pronoun. We might assume that agreement features are present but not realized in the case of first and second person forms. The following illustrate:

(7)   a. Disgwyliodd Emrys [i mi fynd   i Fangor].
          expect.PAST.3S Emrys to me go.INF to Bangor
          'Emrys expected me to go to Bangor.'
       b. i ti   fynd   i Fangor.
          to you.S go.INF to Bangor
          '. . . you (S) to go to Bangor.'
       c. iddo fo   fynd   i Fangor.
          to.3MS him go.INF to Bangor
          '. . . him to go to Bangor.'
       d. iddi hi fynd   i Fangor.
          to.3FS her go.INF to Bangor
          '. . . her to go to Bangor.'
       e. i ni fynd   i Fangor.
          to us go.INF to Bangor
          '. . . us to go to Bangor.'
       f. i chi fynd   i Fangor.
          to you.P go.INF to Bangor
          '. . . you (P) to go to Bangor.'
       g. iddyn nhw fynd   i Fangor.
          to.3P them go.INF to Bangor
          '. . . them to go to Bangor.'

With a third-person form, the pronominal subject is often not overt in literary Welsh but is normally overt in the colloquial language. There is no agreement with a following non-pronominal subject, as (8) and (9) show:

(8)   Disgwyliodd Emrys i 'r bachgen/eneth/bechgyn fynd   i Fangor.
          expect.PAST.3S Emrys to the boy   /girl /boys   go.INF to Bangor
          'Emrys expected the boy/girl/boys to go to Bangor.'

(9)   a. *iddo 'r bachgen fynd i Fangor.
             to.3MS the boy   go.INF to Bangor
             ('. . . the boy to go to Bangor.')
          b. *iddi 'r eneth fynd i Fangor.
             to.3FS the girl   go.INF to Bangor
             ('. . . the girl to go to Bangor.')
          c. *iddyn y bechgyn fynd i Fangor.
             to.3P the boys   go.INF to Bangor
             ('. . . the boys to go to Bangor.')

Once more, then, there is agreement with pronouns but not with a non-pronominal noun phrase.

Consider next nouns. As we saw in section 5.2.2, they are preceded by a clitic when they are followed by a pronominal possessor. The following illustrate:

(10)   a. fy nhad i
             1S father me
             'my father'
          b. dy dad   di
             2S father you.S
             'your (S) father'
          c. ei   dad   o
             3MS father him
             'his father'
          d. ei   thad   hi
             3FS father her
             'her father'
          e. ein tad   ni
             1P father us
             'our father'
          f. eich tad   chi
             2P   father you.P
             'your (P) father'
          g. eu tad   nhw
             3P father them
             'their father'

As noted in 5.2.2, the pronominal possessor is often not overt in literary Welsh and may also be non-overt in the colloquial language. When there is no overt possessor pronoun following the noun, the clitics look rather like an English possessive determiner. However, their co-occurrence with a pronoun in the normal possessor position shows that they are functionally more like the suffixes on finite verbs and prepositions than like the English possessive determiners. There is no clitic with a non-pronominal possessor, as the following show:

(11)   tad   y   bachgen/bechgyn
         father the boy   boys
         'the boy's/boys' father'

(12)   a. *ei   dad   y   bachgen
            3MS father the boy
            ('the boy's father')
         b. *eu tad   y   bechgyn
            3P father the boys
            ('the boys' father')

Again, then, we see agreement with pronouns but not with non-pronominal noun phrases.

   Non-finite verbs behave in much the same way as nouns. They are preceded by the same clitics when there is a pronominal object.

(13)   a. Gwnaeth Emrys fy ngweld i.
            do.PAST.3S Emrys 1S see.INF me
            'Emrys saw me.'
         b. Gwnaeth Emrys dy weld   di.
            do.PAST.3S Emrys 2S see.INF you.S
            'Emrys saw you.'
         c. Gwnaeth Emrys ei   weld   o.
            do.PAST.3S Emrys 3MS see.INF him
            'Emrys saw him.'
         d. Gwnaeth Emrys ei   gweld   hi.
            do.PAST.3S Emrys 3FS see.INF her
            'Emrys saw her.'
         e. Gwnaeth Emrys ein gweld   ni.
            do.PAST.3S Emrys 1P see.INF us
            'Emrys saw us.'
         f. Gwnaeth Emrys eich gweld   chi.
            do.PAST.3S Emrys 2P   see.INF you.P
            'Emrys saw you.'
         g. Gwnaeth Emrys eu gweld   nhw.
            do.PAST.3S Emrys 3P see.INF them
            'Emrys saw them.'

As noted in 3.1.2, the pronominal object is often not overt in literary Welsh and it may also be non-overt in colloquial Welsh. There is no clitic with a non-pronominal object.

(14)   Gwnaeth Emrys weld   y   bachgen/bechgyn.
         do.PAST.3S Emrys see.INF the boy   /boys
         'Emrys saw the boy/boys.'

(15)   a. *Gwnaeth Emrys **ei** weld y bachgen.
       do.PAST.3S Emrys 3MS see.INF the boy
       ('Emrys saw the boy.')
    b. *Gwnaeth Emrys **eu** gweld y bechgyn.
       do.PAST.3S Emrys 3P see.INF the boys
       ('Emrys saw the boys.')

Once more, then, there is agreement with pronouns but not with non-pronominal noun phrases.

Finally, consider what we have called *bod*-clauses. As noted in section 3.3, these are subordinate clauses in which the non-finite form *bod* occurs where one might expect a present or imperfect form. Here, a clitic appears when there is a following pronominal subject.

(16)   a. Dywedodd Gwyn fy mod (i) yn ddiog.
       see.PAST.3S Gwyn 1S be.INF I PRED lazy
       'Gwyn said I was lazy.'
    b. dy fod (di) yn ddiog.
       2S be.INF you.S PRED lazy
       '. . . you (S) were lazy.'
    c. ei fod (o) yn ddiog.
       3MS be.INF he PRED lazy
       '. . . he was lazy.'
    d. ei bod (hi) yn ddiog.
       3FS be.INF she PRED lazy
       '. . . she was lazy.'
    e. ein bod (ni) yn ddiog.
       1P be.INF we PRED lazy
       '. . . we were lazy.'
    f. eich bod (chi) yn ddiog.
       2P be.INF you.P PRED lazy
       '. . . you (P) were lazy.'
    g. eu bod (nhw) yn ddiog.
       3P be.INF they PRED lazy
       '. . . they were lazy.'

The subject is often not overt in literary Welsh but is normally overt in the colloquial language. There is no clitic with a non-pronominal subject.

(17)   Dywedodd Gwyn bod y bachgen/yr eneth/y bechgyn yn ddiog.
       see.PAST.3S Gwyn be.INF the boy /the girl /the boys PRED lazy
       'Gwyn said the boy/the girl/the boys was/were lazy.'
(18)   a. *Dywedodd Gwyn ei fod y bachgen yn ddiog
       see.PAST.3S Gwyn 3MS be.INF the boy PRED lazy
       ('Gwyn said the boy was lazy.')
    b. *ei bod yr eneth yn ddiog
       3FS be.INF the girl PRED lazy
       ('the girl was lazy.')

    c. *eu bod y bechgyn yn   ddiog.
      3P be.INF the boys   PRED lazy
      ('the boys were lazy.')

Yet again, there is agreement with pronouns but not with non-pronominal noun phrases.

    There is one further situation in which a clitic may appear. It is illustrated by the following:

(19)   Fe 'u cerais   i nhw.
          PRT 3P love.PAST.1S I them
          'I loved them.'

Here an 'accusative' enclitic *'u* attached to a preverbal particle is associated with the object of a finite verb. The enclitics that are used here are similar but not identical to those discussed in 5.2.2 which appear with nouns and non-finite verbs. Unlike the other phenomena that we have looked at, this phenomenon is confined to a very literary variety of Welsh. It also differs formally from the other phenomena in two ways. Firstly, it is optional. Literary Welsh also allows the following with no clitic:

(20)   Fe gerais   i nhw.
          PRT love.PAST.1S I them
          'I loved them.'

Secondly, the clitic is not associated with the nearest following noun phrase, which is the subject *i* and not the object *nhw*. For these reasons, it seems to us that this is a separate phenomenon and we will say no more about it in this chapter.

    With the exception of clitics associated with objects of finite verbs, the agreement phenomena outlined above are clearly very similar to each other. They show the following similarities:

(21)   a. All involve agreement with pronouns, which are often not overt in the literary language, but not full noun phrases.
         b. All are obligatory (except in quite colloquial Welsh).
         c. In all cases the pronoun follows the realization of agreement.

The obvious conclusion is that they all manifestations of a single phenomenon. This was first noted by McCloskey & Hale (1984: 520)[1], and a number of researchers have come to the same conclusion, including Sadler (1988: 104), who remarks that agreement morphemes and clitics are 'essentially the same phenomenon', Roberts & Shlonsky (1996: 184), who conclude that Welsh has

---

[1] McCloskey & Hale's main concern is Irish, but they also look briefly at Welsh in section 6.5.

a 'single agreement system', Pollard & Sag (1994: section 9.3), and Rouveret (1994). Obviously if this is right, a unified account is desirable. We return to this question in later sections.

6.2   Coordination and focus sentences

Before we can consider what sort of analysis might be appropriate for Welsh agreement, there are two further bodies of data that we need to introduce. The first involves coordination and the second involves focus sentences.

6.2.1   Coordination

In all the data we have considered so far, we have a simple, non-coordinate NP in the position associated with agreement. Naturally it is also possible to have a coordinate NP in these positions. As noted by Morris-Jones (1931: 84), Rouveret (1994: section 5.1) and Sadler (1999), when a coordinate NP appears in a position associated with agreement, the agreement is apparently with the first conjunct, if this is a pronoun. The following, in which the coordinate NPs are bracketed, show this for finite verbs, prepositions, nouns and non-finite verbs:

(22)   Gwelais   [i a   Megan] geffyl.
         see.PAST.1s I and Megan horse
         'Megan and I saw a horse.'

(23)   arnaf [i   a   Megan]
         on.1s me and Megan
         'on me and Megan'

(24)   fy nhad [i   a   Megan]
         1s father me and Megan
         'my and Megan's brother'

(25)   Gwnaeth Emrys fy ngweld [i   a   Megan].
         do.PAST.3s Emrys 1s see.INF me and Megan
         'Emrys saw me and Megan.'

As we discuss in section 10.2.2.3, agreement with a single conjunct is a feature of many languages. Often, however, it is optional, and agreement with the whole coordinate structure is also possible. In Welsh, agreement with the whole coordinate structure is not possible even if both conjuncts are pronouns. Thus, (26b) is not possible as an alternative to (26a). ((26c) shows that *gwelon* appears with a first person plural pronoun subject.)

(26)   a. Gwelaist   [ti   a   fi] geffyl.
            see.PAST.2S you.s and I   horse
            'You and I saw a horse.'
         b. *Gwelon   [ti   a   fi] geffyl.
            see.PAST.1P you.s and I   horse
            ('You and I saw a horse.')
         c. Gwelon   ni geffyl.
            see.PAST.1P we horse
            'We saw a horse.'

One response to these data would be to suggest that coordinate structures have the person, number and gender features of the first conjunct so that agreement is really with the entire coordinate structure. However, there is evidence from anaphora that coordinate structures have their own person, number and gender features distinct from those of the first conjunct. Consider the following:

(27)   a. Gwelais   [i a   Megan] ein hunain.
            see.PAST.1S I and Megan 1S self
            'Megan and I saw ourselves.'
         b. Gwelaist [ti   a   Megan] eich hunain.
            see.PAST.2S you.s and Megan 2P   self
            'You and Megan saw yourselves.'
         c. Gwelodd   [e a   Megan] eu hunain.
            see.PAST.3S he and Megan 3P self
            'He and Megan saw themselves.'

In each of these examples the verb apparently agrees with the first conjunct of the following coordinate subject but the reflexive agrees with the whole coordinate subject. This might lead one to suggest that coordinate noun phrases have two sets of person, number and gender features relevant to different kinds of agreement. It seems simpler, however, to assume that they have just one and that what looks like agreement with the first conjunct is just that.

6.2.2   Focus sentences

We turn now to focus sentences. As we saw in chapter 4, there is no agreement in a focus sentence with a focused pronominal subject. Thus, while agreement is required in (28a), an unmarked VSO clause, it is impossible in (28b).

(28)   a. Gwelon/   *gwelodd nhw geffyl.
            see.PAST.3P/see.PAST.3S they horse
            'They saw a horse.'
         b. Nhw welodd/   *welon   geffyl.
            they see.PAST.3s/see.PAST.3P horse
            'It's they who saw a horse.'

One way to describe these data is to say that agreement only occurs when a pronoun follows on the surface. On a transformational approach, the pronoun in (28b) follows the verb prior to movement, but this seems to be irrelevant to the account of agreement.

There are, however, focus sentences which appear to involve agreement with a preceding pronoun. Consider the following:[2]

(29)   Hi   soniodd   Gwyn amdani.
         she talk.PAST.3S Gwyn about.3FS
         'It's her that Gwyn talked about.'

(30)   Nhw wnes   i eu gweld.
         they do.PAST.1S I 3P see.INF
         'It's them that I saw.'

In (29) it appears that the preposition *amdani* agrees with the preceding pronoun *hi*, and in (30) we appear to have agreement between the clitic *eu* and the preceding pronoun *nhw*. In both cases, the pronoun can be replaced by a non-pronominal NP.

(31)   Y   ferch soniodd   Gwyn amdani.
         the girl   talk.PAST.3S Gwyn about.3FS
         'It's the girl that Gwyn talked about.'

(32)   Y   dynion wnes   i eu gweld.
         the men   do.PAST.1S I 3P see.INF
         'It's the men that I saw.'

It looks, then, as if these sorts of examples are doubly problematic for the idea that agreement involves a following pronoun on the surface. The agreement in (29)–(32) is with a preceding element and it is not necessarily a pronoun. However, in the case of examples like (29) and (31) it is clear that there is no problem at all for the idea that agreeing elements agree with a following pronoun. As noted in section 4.1.7, it is generally assumed that a stranded inflected preposition is followed by a phonologically null resumptive pronoun. We can assume that the preposition agrees with this pronoun. What about examples like (30) and (32)? As was noted in section 4.1.6.2, it is sometimes assumed that examples like these have an empty resumptive pronoun in object position. Obviously, if they do, then they too will involve

---

[2] For many speakers the example with a pied-piped preposition in (i) would be preferable to (29):

(i)   Amdani   hi soniodd   Gwyn.
        about.3FS her talk.PAST.3S Gwyn
        'It's about her that Gwyn talked.'

agreement with a following pronoun. However, as was also pointed out in section 4.1.6.2, there are some reasons for thinking that such examples involve a *wh*-trace. On this analysis, such examples obviously do not involve agreement with a following pronoun. Rather the agreement must be a special phenomenon separate from the agreement phenomena that are our main concern here.

We also seem to have a special kind of agreement in passives. Consider, for example, the following:

(33)   Mi gafodd   Gwyn **ei**   daro   gan Emrys.
         PRT get.PAST.3S Gwyn 3MS hit.INF with Emrys
         'Gwyn was hit by Emrys.'

Here the non-finite verb is preceded by a clitic (in bold) agreeing with the subject. One might be tempted to suggest that the clitic marks agreement with an NP-trace following the non-finite verb. However, there is no clitic in certain other cases where there would be a postverbal trace on standard transformational assumptions. The following is a raising sentence of the kind discussed in section 3.7, and on transformational assumptions the bracketed complement would have an NP-trace in subject position following the non-finite verb *dechrau*.

(34)   Mae   Gwyn wedi dechrau [*t* darllen y   llyfr].
         be.PRES.3S Gwyn PERF begin.INF   read.INF the book
         'Gwyn has begun to read the book.'

Thus, it looks as if passives also involve a special kind of agreement.

It seems, then, that we probably have two special kinds of agreement. However, the main types of agreement, which we are concentrating on here, involve a following pronoun on the surface.

6.3   Generalizations

Before we consider the implications of the main agreement phenomena, we need to provide a more precise description. As we will see, there are two possible generalizations here.

At the beginning of this chapter we summarized the facts of agreement, and we said among other things that nouns show agreement – in the form of clitics – with a following pronominal possessor. However, we noted in section 5.2.2 that the generative tradition has generally analysed clitics as determiners. On this view, it is not the noun that agrees with the following pronominal possessor but the preceding D. Rouveret (1994, chapter 4) proposes that pre-verbal clitics such as those seen in (13) above are also realizations of D. However, as noted in section 2.5.2 and section 3.1.3, the associated idea that non-finite verb phrases are embedded in a DP is problematic. Hence, the idea that a pre-verbal clitic is a realization of D is dubious. An obvious alternative is that they are the realization of some other functional element, and in fact Roberts (2005, chapter 3) proposes that they are realizations of an Agr head. On this view, it is not the non-finite verb that agrees with the following pronominal object but the preceding Agr head. It looks, then, as if clitics may involve the following configuration, where the functional head is D or Agr, the lexical head N or non-finite V and the pronoun may be null:

(35)   Functional Head [Lexical Head . . . Pronoun]

Clitics also appear before *bod*. Rouveret (1994) proposes that these are a realization of C. This, of course, is another functional head. Within P&P theory it is natural to assume that inflections too are the realization of a functional head, and this position is developed by Rouveret (1994, chapter 2), who proposes that inflections on both finite verbs and prepositions are the realization of agreement heads. Thus, within P&P, all instances of the agreement that we are concerned with here will involve the structure in (35).

What about more concrete frameworks such as LFG and HPSG? Here it is natural to assume that inflections are the realization of features on the heads to which they are attached, and that they involve the following configuration, where the head is a finite verb, a preposition, or clause-initial *i* and the pronoun may be null:

(36)   Head . . . Pronoun

In more concrete frameworks, as in P&P, one might assume that clitics are the realization of functional elements. Alternatively, however, one might assume that they are just morphological elements which realize agreement on nouns, non-finite verbs and *bod*. Pollard & Sag (1994: 357) assume that they are prefixes on nouns and non-finite verbs.[3] It is fairly clear, however, that they are not ordinary prefixes since they can be separated from the associated noun by an adjective or numeral, as in the following:

(37)   a. ei   dri   llyfr   (o)
             3MS three book   him
             'his three books'
         b. ei   hen lyfr   (o)
             3MS old book   him
             'his old book'

---

[3] McCloskey & Hale (1984: 512) make the same assumption.

One might propose, however, that they are what Anderson (1992) calls phrasal affixes, affixes which are attached not to a word but to a phrase. On this view, agreement involves the configuration in (36) in all cases.

If agreement is the realization of features on finite verbs, prepositions, *i*, nouns, non-finite verbs and *bod*, it will involve adjacent elements in most cases. This is true with finite verbs, prepositions, *i*, non-finite verbs and *bod*. The one apparent exception is nouns, where examples like the following occur with an intervening adjective:

(38)   ei   gar newydd o
         3MS car new   him
         'his new car'

Recall, however, that we suggested in section 5.6.2 that attributive adjectives may form a constituent with the preceding noun. On this view, *gar newydd* is a constituent in (38) and one might suggest that it is this constituent which agrees with the pronoun. If this is right, agreement may involve the following configuration:

(39)   Head Pronoun

Ultimately how we describe the agreement facts depends on what assumptions we make about inflections, clitics and attributive adjectives. If both inflections and clitics are the realization of functional heads, agreement involves the structure in (35) and we have the following generalization:

(40)   An agreeing element agrees with the first following noun phrase if and only if the latter is a pronoun.

On the other hand, if inflections are the realization of features on the head to which they are attached and clitics are the realization of features on the following head, and if attributive adjectives form a complex head with the preceding noun, we may have the following generalization:

(41)   An agreeing element agrees with an immediately following noun phrase if and only if the latter is a pronoun.

In other words, we may be able to say that the agreeing element and the noun phrase with which it agrees are always adjacent. There are two points that we should emphasize about these generalizations. First, there is no suggestion that the noun phrase with which a head agrees is some kind of argument. It may be, but it is not always, given that agreement may be with the first conjunct of a coordinate structure. Second, the generalizations do not refer to some abstract level of structure. Rather, given that there is no agreement with a focused subject in a focus sentence, as shown by (28a), either (40) or (41) holds on the surface, which one depending on the view we take of inflections, clitics and attributive adjectives.

6.4   Implications

We can now consider the implications of the agreement data. One thing that seems fairly clear is that the data are problematic for a grammatical function-based approach to agreement of the kind that is assumed in Lexical Functional Grammar. Concentrating for the moment on the basic data outlined in section 6.1, we might have the situation shown in Table 6.2. This assumes that possessors are subjects. If they were assumed to represent some other grammatical function, e.g. possessor, the situation would be more complex. The important point is that some heads agree with a subject and some agree with an object. Hence, there are essentially two sorts of agreement, and it is accidental that they have various properties in common. The facts would be no more complex if finite verbs agreed with an object or non-finite verbs with a subject. We would just have two rather different sorts of agreement. There seems to be no possibility of formulating a single generalization here. The coordination data just make the situation worse. Here the relevant noun phrase is neither a subject nor an object of the agreeing head but just part of a subject or object.

Table 6.2. *Agreement and grammatical functions (GF).*

Head	GF of relevant noun phrase
Finite verb	Subject
Preposition	Object
Prepositional complementizer *i*	Subject
Noun	Subject
Non-finite verb	Object
Bod	Subject

The basic data are no problem for the HPSG approach to Welsh agreement outlined in Pollard & Sag (1994: chapter 9). As noted in section 2.4.1, Borsley (1989a, 1995) proposes an HPSG analysis in which subjects of finite verbs are the realization not of the single member of the SUBJ list of the verb, but of an extra member of the COMPS list. Borsley also proposes an analysis of noun phrases in which possessors are the realization of an extra member of the COMPS list of the noun. Building on these ideas, Pollard & Sag propose that heads in Welsh agree with the first member of their COMPS list. Both the subject of a finite clause and the possessor in a noun phrase are first members of a COMPS list of the relevant head, and so are the objects of a non-finite verb and a preposition. Borsley (1999) and Borsley & Jones (2005) propose that the subject of an *i*-clause is also the first member of the COMPS list of *i*, the predicate being the second member. Thus, the basic data are no problem for this approach. However, the coordination data are problematic. The first conjunct of a coordinate structure is obviously not the first member of the COMPS list of the relevant head but just part of the first member.

What of transformational approaches? There are two analyses to consider here, those of Rouveret (1994, chapter 2) and Roberts (2005, chapter 2). Rouveret proposes that pronouns are NumPs containing Num and an NP complement and that agreement involves the incorporation of Num to a higher head leaving the NP behind, as follows:[4]

(42) $\ldots X \ldots [_{\text{NumP}} \text{Num NP}] \implies \ldots \text{Num}_i X \ldots [_{\text{NumP}} t_i \text{NP}]$

Roberts proposes that Welsh agreement involves the minimalist operation Agree. This is an operation involving an expression and the nearest c-commanding head with an appropriate feature or features. The basic data are probably no problem for these approaches. Whether the coordination data are a problem depends on the analysis of coordination, which is not a simple matter. It seems, however, that the focus sentence data are problematic for standard transformational approaches. In Rouveret's analysis, incorporation is a case of head-movement, and although Chomsky (1999) suggests that some kinds of head-movement may apply in PF, he explicitly assumes that incorporation is a syntactic process. In Roberts' analysis, Agree is also a syntactic process. Thus, in both analyses, agreement is the product of a process which applies before movement to focus position. Hence, one might expect it to be possible for a verb to agree with a pronominal subject which is subsequently moved to focus position. In other words, one might expect a derivation of the following form:[5]

(43) $[\text{welon}_i [\text{nhw } t_i \text{ geffyl}]] \implies [\text{nhw}_j [\text{welon}_i [t_j t_i \text{ geffyl}]]]$

But this would give rise to the ungrammatical version of (28b), repeated here as (44).

(44)   *Nhw welon   geffyl.
        they   see.PAST.3P horse
        'It's they who saw a horse.'

---

[4] Rouveret also assumes that NP moves to Spec NumP. Strictly speaking then, he has structures of the following form:

(i) $\ldots \text{Num}_i X \ldots [_{\text{NumP}} \text{NP}_j t_i t_j]$

However, this is of no importance in the present context.

[5] We are assuming here that movement leaves a trace. However, within Minimalism it leaves a copy of the moved constituent, which is deleted in PF.

It looks, then, as if the fact that there is no agreement with a focused subject noun phrase is problematic for a transformational approach.

There are certain ways in which one might try to reconcile a transformational approach with the impossibility of agreement with a focused pronominal subject. One possibility would be to propose that it is not the focused subject that is moved but a non-pronominal empty operator. However, it is not just noun phrases that can be focused, as shown by the following:

(45)   a. [$_{PP}$ Ym Mangor] welais   i Megan.
                in   Bangor   see.PAST.1s I Megan
                'It was in Bangor that I saw Megan.'
         b. [$_{VP}$ Darllen y llyfr] wnaeth   Gwyn.
                read   the book do.PAST.3s Gwyn
                'It was read the book that Gwyn did.'

This suggests that it is the focused constituent that is moved. Hence, the idea that an empty operator is moved seems untenable.

Another possibility is to assume that movement is not from the position with which agreement is associated but from some other position. This approach is in fact adopted in Rouveret (2002: 149–50), who assumes structures like the following, in which the trace of the fronted subject *nhw* is in Spec vP and not the standard subject position, Spec TP:

(46)   [$_{CP}$ nhw$_j$ C^0 [$_{AgrSP}$ welodd$_i$ AgrS^0 [$_{TP}$ t$_i$ T^0 [$_{VP}$ t$_j$ t$_i$ geffyl]]]]

Some complex machinery is necessary here. Whatever normally forces the subject to move to Spec TP must not operate. Within Minimalism it is assumed that movement to the standard subject position is triggered by a so-called EPP feature on T^0. It is not clear how one could ensure that such a feature is absent in the present case. It seems to us, then, that this is not a very promising approach.

Finally, one might exploit the contrast between strong and weak pronouns highlighted in section 1.4.5, and propose that strong pronouns do not trigger agreement and must be fronted, while weak pronouns trigger agreement and may not be fronted.[6] The following examples, where the pronouns are in bold, might suggest that this is plausible:

(47)   a. **Fi** welodd   y   ceffyl.
                I   see.PAST.3s the horse
                'It was I that saw the horse.'

---

[6] A related distinction between strong and weak pronouns is a feature of French and other Romance languages. See e.g. Cardinaletti & Starke (1999).

b. *Gwelais   **fi** 'r   ceffyl.
   see.PAST.1S. I the horse
   ('I saw the horse.')

(48)   a. Gwelais   **i** 'r   ceffyl.
      see.PAST.1S I the horse
      'I saw the horse.'
     b. ***I** welodd   y   ceffyl.
      I see.PAST.3S the horse
      ('It was I that saw the horse.')

(47) shows that the strong form *fi* cannot appear as an in-situ subject but must be fronted, while (48) shows that the weak form *i* can appear as an in-situ subject but cannot be fronted. One might suggest that strong pronouns do not trigger agreement because they are not genuine pronouns. This, however, will not provide a complete account of their distribution, since – unlike ordinary non-pronominal noun phrases – they cannot appear as subject of a finite verb even if it does not show agreement and is a default third-person singular form.

(49)   *Gwelodd fi 'r   ceffyl.
       see.PAST.3S I the horse
       ('I saw the horse.')

It seems that the restriction on strong pronouns is that they cannot appear on the surface in a position which could be associated with agreement, whether or not it actually is associated with agreement. As for weak pronouns, it seems that the restriction is that they must appear on the surface in a position that is associated with agreement. This approach seems more promising than the other two. However, it crucially involves two superficial constraints.

We have now considered three responses to the fact that there is no agreement with a focused pronominal subject. Notice that they share an important property: all involve the assumption that agreement takes place before movement but that for one reason or another there is no evidence for this. On the face of it, it would be simpler to accept that agreement takes place after movement. The idea seems to be implicitly accepted by McCloskey & Hale (1984: 490), McCloskey (1990: 221), and Roberts (2005: 64). All suggest that there is no agreement with a focused subject because traces are non-pronominal. Obviously the properties of traces are only relevant if agreement applies after movement.

Thus, it is plausible to propose that the main kinds of Welsh agreement involve a superficial level of structure and refer either to linear order or to some structural relation closely related to linear order. A satisfactory analysis must ensure agreement either with the first following noun phrase or with an immediately following noun phrase if and only if it is a pronoun. To ensure that agreement is with a first conjunct if it is pronominal, it must not 'see' coordinate structures. Finally, to ensure that there is no agreement with a focused subject, unbounded dependency gaps must be non-pronominal.

6.5   A Linearization-based HPSG approach

It may be that various approaches can accommodate the idea that Welsh agreement involves linear order at a superficial level. For example, it may be possible to provide an analysis of this kind within the version of P&P developed in Ackema & Neeleman (2004), in which a number of types of agreement are analysed in terms of PF. Here, however, we will outline an analysis of the data within Linearization-based HPSG following Borsley (2005).

In much HPSG work, e.g. Pollard & Sag (1994), order is a reflection of constituent structure, but for Linearization-based HPSG, developed in Pollard *et al.* (1993), Reape (1994) and especially Kathol (2000), it is defined in terms of a separate system of order domains. For Linearization-based HPSG, phrasal constituents have both a list of daughters and a list of domain elements. The former are signs, linguistic expressions with syntactic, semantic and phonological properties, and, if phrasal, their own internal structure. The latter include syntactic, semantic and phonological information, but do not include information about internal structure. The domain elements of a constituent may be 'compacted' to form a single element in the order domain of the mother or they may just become elements in the mother's order domain. In the latter case, the mother has more domain elements than daughters, and some members of the order domain are not sisters.

Among other things, the distinction between daughters and domain elements permits an analysis of certain extraposition phenomena. Consider, for example, the following Welsh examples:

(50)   a. Mae   chwant mynd adref arna' i.
             be.PRES.3S desire go.INF home on.1s me
             'I desire to go home.'
         b. Mae   chwant arna' i   fynd   adref.
             be.PRES.3S desire on.1s me go.INF home
             'I desire to go home.'

(50a) has a subject containing an abstract noun *chwant* and an infinitival complement *mynd adref*, while in (50b) the complement is extraposed. Within Linearization-based HPSG, we can propose that these sentences have the same three daughters but that the second has one more domain element. For HPSG, the syntactic and semantic properties of an expression are encoded as the value of a feature SYNSEM and the daughters and domain elements are encoded as the value of the features DTRS and DOM respectively. If we use bracketed orthography to represent both daughters and domain elements, we might propose the following schematic analyses:

(51)   a.
$$\begin{bmatrix} \text{SYNSEMS} \\ \text{DTRS} < [\textit{mae}], [\textit{chwant mynd adref}], [\textit{arnaf i}] > \\ \text{DOM} < [\textit{mae}], [\textit{chwant mynd adref}], [\textit{arnaf i}] > \end{bmatrix}$$
        b.
$$\begin{bmatrix} \text{SYNSEMS} \\ \text{DTRS} < [\textit{mae}], [\textit{chwant fynd adref}], [\textit{arnaf i}] > \\ \text{DOM} < [\textit{mae}], [\textit{chwant}], [\textit{arnaf i}], [\textit{fynd adref}] > \end{bmatrix}$$

Alternatively, we might use the standard tree format to represent constituent structure. Adopting this format, we might give slightly fuller analyses as follows (where we adopt the standard HPSG assumption that noun phrases are NPs):

(52)   a.

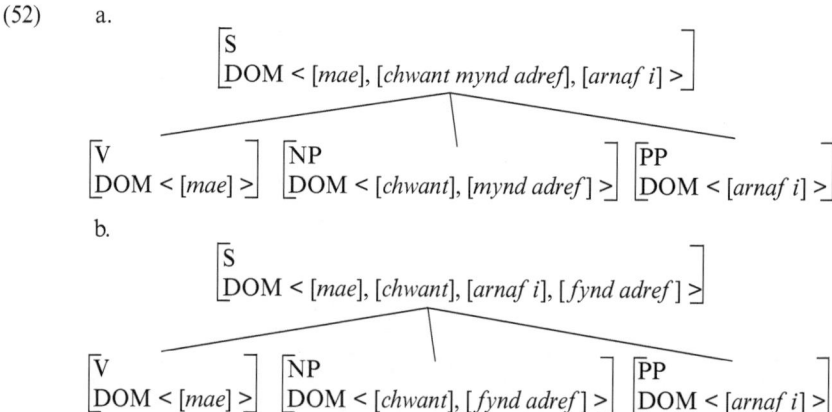

b.

We will use this form of representation in the following discussion.

We return now to the agreement data. The basic data are a fairly simple matter. They involve analyses in which there is a one-to-one correspondence between daughters and domain elements. The example in (53) will have the schematic analysis in (54).

(53)   Gwelais   i geffyl.
        see.PAST.1S I horse
        'I saw a horse.'

(54)

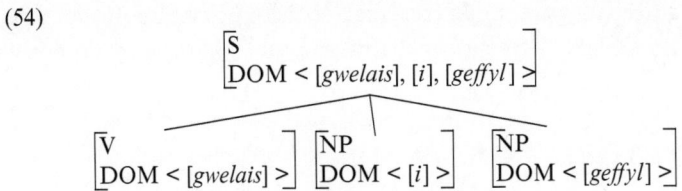

The PP in (4a), repeated as (55), will have the analysis in (56), while the clause in (7c), repeated as (57), will have the analysis in (58).

(55)   arnaf i
          on.1s me
          'on me'

(56)

$$\begin{bmatrix} \text{PP} \\ \text{DOM} < [\textit{arnaf}], [i] > \end{bmatrix}$$

$$\begin{bmatrix} \text{V} \\ \text{DOM} < [\textit{arnaf}] > \end{bmatrix} \quad \begin{bmatrix} \text{NP} \\ \text{DOM} < [i] > \end{bmatrix}$$

(57)   iddo   fo   fynd   i   Fangor
          to.3MS him go.INF to Bangor
          '. . . him to go to Bangor'

(58)

$$\begin{bmatrix} \text{CP} \\ \text{DOM} < [\textit{iddo}], [\textit{fo}], [\textit{fynd i Fangor}] > \end{bmatrix}$$

$$\begin{bmatrix} \text{C} \\ \text{DOM} < [\textit{iddo}] > \end{bmatrix} \quad \begin{bmatrix} \text{NP} \\ \text{DOM} < [\textit{fo}] > \end{bmatrix} \quad \begin{bmatrix} \text{VP} \\ \text{DOM} < [\textit{fynd i Fangor}] > \end{bmatrix}$$

In all these cases a head agrees with an element which immediately follows in the topmost order domain.

What about examples where agreement takes the form of a clitic? If clitics are phrasal affixes, (10a), repeated here as (59), will have the schematic analysis in (60):

(59)   fy nhad i
          1s father I
          'my father'

(60)

$$\begin{bmatrix} \text{NP} \\ \text{DOM} < [\textit{fy nhad}], [i] > \end{bmatrix}$$

$$\begin{bmatrix} \text{N} \\ \text{DOM} < [\textit{fy nhad}] > \end{bmatrix} \begin{bmatrix} \text{NP} \\ \text{DOM} < [i] > \end{bmatrix}$$

If attributive adjectives are right-adjoined to the preceding noun, the more complex example in (38), repeated here as (61), will have the analysis in (62):

(61)   ei   gar newydd o
        3MS car new   him
        'his new car'

(62)

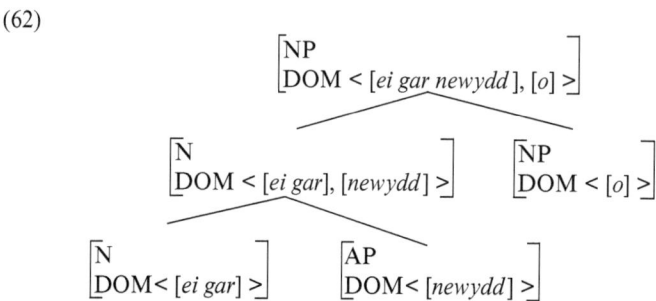

In both cases agreement is with an immediately following element within the order domain of NP. These examples would have somewhat different structures and order domains if clitics were analysed as functional heads, but we won't explore this possibility.

We turn now to the coordination data. Here the distinction between daughters and domain elements is crucial. We assume that coordinate structures are not compacted. This means that a typical two conjunct coordinate structure will give two domain elements in the order domain of the constituent of which it is a daughter. On this approach, coordinate structures are invisible at the level that is relevant to agreement. Given this assumption, (22), repeated here as (63), will have the analysis in (64):

(63)   Gwelais   i a   Megan geffyl.
        see.PAST.1S I and Megan horse
        'Megan and I saw a horse.'

(64)

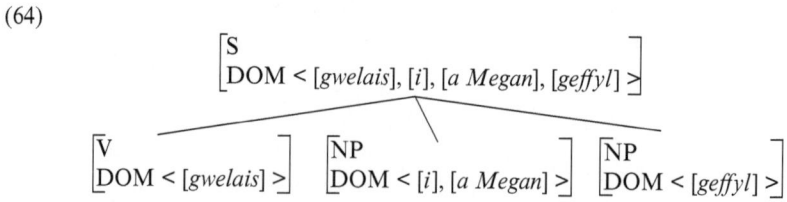

Here, S has three daughters but four domain elements. As in (54), the verb agrees with the element which immediately follows it within the order domain of S. It looks, then, as if it is fairly easy to accommodate the coordination data.

To accommodate the focus sentence data we need an appropriate treatment of unbounded dependency gaps. Pollard & Sag (1994, chapter 4) assume that they involve an empty category of the following form:

(65) $\begin{bmatrix} \text{LOCAL}[1] \\ \text{SLASH}\{[1]\} \end{bmatrix}$

Here the value of the LOCAL feature, which encodes the main syntactic and semantic properties of an expression, is the single member of the set which is the value of the SLASH feature. Interacting with certain constraints, this ensures that information about the main syntactic and semantic properties of the gap is available higher in the tree. Hence, when there is a filler higher in the tree, it will have these syntactic and semantic properties. We can ensure that a nominal gap is non-pronominal with a constraint which says that if [1] in (65) is NP then it is non-pronominal. Given standard HPSG assumptions, this will ensure that a filler is also non-pronominal. This will always be the case if strong pronouns are non-pronominal, as suggested in the last section. If we assume that they are, the grammatical version of (28b) repeated here as (66) will have the analysis in (67):

(66)   Nhw welodd   geffyl.
        they see.PAST.3s horse
        'It's they who saw a horse.'

(67)

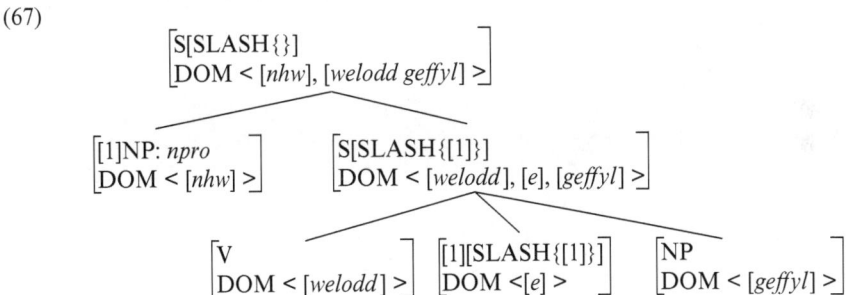

If there are any reasons for analysing strong pronouns as pronominal, standard assumptions would need to be modified to allow a filler to be pronominal when the value of SLASH is non-pronominal.

Assuming the structures proposed here, the facts can be handled with a few quite simple constraints. We have already proposed a constraint requiring a nominal gap to be non-pronominal. We probably need three more. If we use the term agreeing head for heads which can show agreement, the main constraint can be formulated as follows:

(68)   An agreeing head agrees with an immediately following domain element if and only if the latter is a weak pronoun.

This will rule out the examples in (3), (6), (9), (12), (15), (18) and the ungrammatical version of (28b) (i.e. (44)), and (47b), in which an agreeing element agrees with something other than a weak pronoun. We also need a constraint to ensure that a weak pronoun immediately follows an agreeing element. This will rule out an example like (48b). Finally, we need a constraint to ensure that strong pronouns do not immediately follow an agreeing head even if it does not show agreement. This will rule out an example like (49) (and also examples like (47b)).

Returning to the main theme, it seems that it is not too difficult to provide an account of the Welsh agreement facts within Linearization-based HPSG. As noted at the outset, it may be possible to provide a similar analysis within other frameworks. The important point is that there are grounds for thinking that Welsh agreement, unlike agreement in many languages, involves a superficial level of structure. In the next chapter, we will argue that the same is true of mutation. Thus, superficial levels of structure are of some importance in Welsh syntax.

6.6   Reflexives

We have been concerned in the preceding sections with a set of agreement phenomena which involve pronouns and not non-pronominal noun phrases. In all the examples we have considered, the pronouns have been ordinary, non-reflexive pronouns. It is natural to wonder what happens with reflexives. Do they also trigger agreement? This question is of some interest because it has been claimed by Rizzi (1990) and Woolford (1999) that anaphors, including reflexives, do not appear in positions associated with agreement. Welsh reflexives have had very little attention. We cannot give a definitive answer to this question. The facts are quite complex, and there seems to be significant variation among speakers. However, we can make a number of relevant observations.

Firstly, it is clear that there are examples where a reflexive does not trigger agreement in the way that an ordinary pronoun does. The following naturally occurring examples have a reflexive as object of a non-finite verb, and the non-finite verb is not preceded by a clitic, as would be expected if reflexives triggered agreement.

(69)   a. . . . mae   e 'n   hoffi   profi   **'i   hun**.
            be.PRES.3S he PROG like.INF prove.INF 3MS REFL
            'He likes to prove himself.'   (*DE* 18)

b. Roedden   ni   wedi dysgu   'n **hunain** i   hoffi   lager . . .
be.IMPF.1P we PERF teach.INF 1P REFL   to like.INF lager
'We had taught ourselves to like lager.'   (*DE* 34)

Similarly, the following examples have a reflexive as object of a preposition and the preposition is not inflected.

(70) a. ei   syniad hi   o   **'i   hunan**
3FS idea   she of 3FS REFL
'her idea of herself'   (*DE* 57)
b. Roedden nhw 'n   hunanol am   ei gilydd,   ac   am
be.IMPF.3P they PRED conceited about each-other and about
eu hunain hefyd . . .
3P REFL   too
'They were conceited about each other and about themselves too.'
(*DE* 215)

If reflexives triggered agreement we would expect the third-person singular feminine form of the preposition *o*, namely *ohoni* in (70a) and the third-person plural form of the preposition *am*, namely *amdanyn* in (70b).

The picture is complicated by examples with reflexives in possessor position. Examples like the following are quite dubious:

(71)   *?Rhaid iddo   sefyll   ar draed **ei hunan**.
need   to.3MS stand.INF on feet   3P SELF
('He needs to stand on his own feet.')

The following with a clitic (in bold) is preferable:

(72)   Rhaid iddo   sefyll   ar **ei**   draed ei hunan.
need   to.3MS stand.INF on 3MS feet   3P SELF
'He needs to stand on his own feet.'

One might conclude from this that a reflexive triggers agreement when it is in possessor position. However, there is an alternative position which deserves to be explored. It is possible that (72) involves agreement with a phonologically null pronoun and that the reflexive is not an argument reflexive but an emphatic reflexive. It is also possible that (71) is dubious because an argument reflexive may not be embedded inside an NP.

There are other sorts of example in which a reflexive co-occurs with agreement. Consider the following naturally occurring examples:

(73) a. Dyw   e ddim yn   gorfod   trio   'i   roi **ei   hun**
be.PRES.3S he NEG PROG necessity try.INF 3MS put 3MS REFL
yn sefyllfa   Davies.
in situation Davies
'He doesn't have to try to put himself in Davies's situation.'   (*DE* 20)

b. . . . yn   ei   blethu   **'i** **hun** yn y   byd.
    PROG 3MS integrate.INF 3MS REFL in the world
'. . . integrating himself in the world'   (*DE* 38)

(74)   a. ynof **fy hun**
    in.1S 1S REFL
    'in myself'   (*DE* 15)
b. syniadau 'r   llall amdano   **'i** **hun**
    ideas   the other about.3MS 3MS REFL
    'the other's ideas about himself'   (*DE* 33)

The examples in (73) might suggest that a reflexive that is object of a non-finite verb sometimes triggers agreement, and those in (74) might suggest that the same is true with a reflexive that is object of a preposition. Again, however, it could be that the agreement is with a phonologically null pronoun and that the reflexives are emphatic. One thing that suggests that this approach may be right is the fact that we find examples with both an overt pronoun and a reflexive, for example the following:

(75)   Ac   roedd   hi 'n   dal   i wenu . . . iddi hi
    and be.IMPF.3S she PROG continue.INF to smile   to.3FS she
    'i   **hun**.
    3FS   REFL
    'And she was still smiling to herself.'   (*DE* 111)

The question, of course, is whether all examples in which a reflexive appears to trigger agreement can be analysed as involving a phonologically null pronoun and an emphatic reflexive. We will not try to answer this question here.

It is possible, then, that Welsh is compatible with the claim that anaphors do not appear in positions associated with agreement. However, establishing whether this is so will require a much fuller investigation than we have been able to undertake.

6.7   Conclusions

This chapter has explored the main agreement phenomena of Welsh. It has argued that they are different manifestations of a single phenomenon and it has considered their theoretical implications. It has presented evidence that these phenomena involve linear order at a superficial level, and it has shown that this idea can be implemented within HPSG. Finally it has looked briefly at the interaction of reflexives with agreement.

7

Syntax and mutation

7.1   Mutation environments: some basic data

We saw in section 1.4.4 that Welsh, in common with the other Celtic languages, displays several sets of morphophonological alternations in the initial segments of words, known as consonantal mutations. In the vast majority of instances, mutation is triggered by the preceding lexical item, so that a simple list of mutation triggers is sufficient to describe the environments for the mutation. Typical triggers include prepositions, proclitics on V and N (see section 6.1), various determiners, numerals, conjunctions, complementizers and numerous other small, 'closed class' grammatical words. To illustrate these straightforward cases, the preposition *i* 'to' is a trigger for soft mutation, giving *i Fangor* 'to Bangor', whilst the third person feminine singular proclitic *ei* triggers aspirate mutation, giving *ei chath* (< *cath*) 'her cat'. Note that mutation is assigned not to a head, but to the first word of the constituent immediately following the trigger, whatever the status of this constituent. For instance, 'her five cats' is *ei phum cath*, with aspirate mutation (*pum* > *phum*) at the start of the phrase *pum cath* (lit. 'five cat'), but no mutation on the head, *cath*. If the first word following the mutation trigger happens not to have a mutable initial consonant, then the constituent bears no signs of the mutation: thus we get *ei beic* 'her bike', with no mutation, as /b/ cannot undergo aspirate mutation.

In some cases, however, the triggering environment for a mutation is grammatical (morphosyntactic) rather than lexical. Two major instances of this type both involve the relationship between attributive adjectives and the nouns they modify. Recall from section 5.4 that the unmarked word order is NA, but that AN also occurs. Firstly, any pre-nominal adjective triggers soft mutation on the following item (typically the head noun): for instance, *hen gath* (< *cath*) 'old cat'; see Tallerman (1999) for an analysis of this mutation in terms of marked word order. Secondly, a feminine singular noun such as *merch*, 'girl', triggers soft mutation on the following adjective, but all following adjectives which modify such a head also bear soft mutation, e.g. *merch dal gref* (< *tal*, *cref*) '(a) tall, strong girl'; see section 5.4 for discussion of this construction.

One instance of grammatically triggered soft mutation, however, is of particular theoretical interest, since it appears under various syntactic conditions of a rather complex nature. In the remainder of this chapter we investigate the syntax of this latter kind of mutation. The factors which trigger what we term 'syntactic soft mutation' have been the subject of some debate in the generative literature over a period of twenty-five years. Some of the core data are shown in (1) to (6), where the mutated item is underlined and its radical form (i.e. the citation form) is given in parentheses:

(1) Prynodd   y   ddynes feic.   (*beic*)
     buy.PAST.3s the woman bike
     'The woman bought a bike.'

(2) Gwnaeth y   dyn [werthu beic].   (*gwerthu*)
     do.PAST.3s the man sell.INF bike
     'The man sold a bike.'

(3) Dechreuodd Huw [olchi   'r llestri].   (*golchi*)
     begin.PAST.3s Huw wash.INF the dishes
     'Huw began to wash the dishes.'

(4) Dymunodd Aled [i Mair fynd   adref].   (*mynd*)
     want.PAST.3s Aled to Mair go.INF home
     'Aled wanted Mair to go home.'

(5) Mae   yn yr ardd gi.   (*ci*)
     be.PRES.3s in the garden dog
     'There's a dog in the garden.'

(6) Roedd   yna gath yn y   gegin.   (*cath*)
     be.IMPF.3s there cat in the kitchen
     'There was a cat in the kitchen.'

In (1), a VSO clause, the direct object of the finite verb bears soft mutation (SM). In (2), an AuxSVO clause, the VP *gwerthu beic* (sell.INF bike) bears the SM, which shows up on the initial word in the phrase, giving *werthu*. Example (3) would be treated as biclausal within a Principles and Parameters (P&P) framework: *dechreuodd*, 'began', is a raising verb, and here, the entire embedded clause *golchi'r llestri* (wash.INF the dishes) bears the mutation, which as usual shows up on its initial segment: *golchi > olchi*. In (4) we have an embedded infinitival *i*-clause (see section 3.4), and the mutation (*mynd > fynd*) appears on the initial segment of the predicate of that clause, *fynd adref* (go.INF home). In examples (5) and (6), the subject is separated from the associated verb, and such a subject bears SM (see section 2.6.2 regarding the properties of *yna*, which differ from those of English expletive *there*). Other data will be discussed as we examine the syntactic environments in more detail. From the examples in (1) to

(6), it can be seen that the constituent bearing the mutation does not have one single grammatical function, nor does it belong to one single syntactic category. At the very least, we can already see that objects, subjects, VPs and infinitival clauses are all possible targets for syntactic SM.

In this chapter we will discuss the various attempts that have been made within generative grammar to account for the occurrence of syntactic SM. A satisfactory analysis must obviously be able to accurately predict the appearance of the mutation: in exactly what context(s) does it occur, and when, if ever, is the mutation blocked? It is worth noting that most work in the Welsh grammatical tradition has not worried unduly about obtaining a concise statement of the environments for the mutation. The classic work (written in Welsh) is Morgan (1952), but more recent grammars, such as Thorne (1993) and P. W. Thomas (1996), present a very similar set of contexts.[1] For instance, in traditional terms, the mutation in (1) to (3) would be regarded as 'mutation of the direct object of a finite verb' (where 'direct object' can broadly be interpreted as 'complement') while the mutation in (4) to (6) would be regarded as 'mutation following a parenthesis' – the Welsh term is *sangiad* – i.e., an intervening phrase of some kind before the constituent bearing the SM. We will see, however, that a unified statement of the syntactic SM in (1) to (6) is indeed possible, and that this generalization also correctly predicts the appearance of mutation in a number of other – superficially disparate – instances.

We now turn to the analyses of syntactic SM. Two distinct approaches appear in the generative literature; these are characterized by Borsley (1997) as the phrase-based approach and the case-based approach. In section 7.2 we outline the basics of the phrase-based approach, and in section 7.3 we discuss the earliest case-based approaches. Section 7.4 examines a more recent proposal by Roberts (2005), which is case-based in a rather different (and looser) sense; for that reason, we term this approach 'case-linked'. Section 7.5 presents a critique of that proposal; see also Tallerman (2006). In section 7.6 we discuss a recent phrase-based analysis (Borsley 1999) in more detail, and conclude that this approach provides a satisfactory account of the data. Section 7.7 examines some wider theoretical issues concerning syntactic SM, and a brief final section 7.8 asks whether there is any common ground between recent analyses.

---

[1] A notable exception is King (2003: 21–2), who states the generalization that SM follows the subject of a clause. This has the effect of unifying the environments in (1) to (4), which even in some of the recent generative literature (for instance, Roberts 2005) must be treated as encompassing two distinct contexts for mutation. However, King does not suggest a context which covers all the data in (1) to (6).

7.2   Phrase-based approaches to syntactic SM

The phrase-based approach originates in an informal suggestion by T. J. Rhys Jones (1977: 328, 338). His observation is that syntactic SM is triggered by a preceding noun phrase; see also King (2003: 21–2). Within generative grammar, the proposal which we can call the NP trigger hypothesis was taken up by Harlow (1981: 238–9): 'Initial consonants undergo soft mutation when immediately preceded by an NP.' In (1), for instance, the subject *y ddynes*, 'the woman', immediately precedes the constituent bearing the SM; likewise in (2), the trigger for mutation is the subject of the clause. In the biclausal example (3), the trigger for SM is again the subject of the matrix clause, *Huw*, although the SM appears on the initial element of the embedded clause. The mutation in (4) also occurs in the embedded clause, but this time the embedded subject, *Mair*, triggers the SM on the following predicate. From data seen so far, then, the trigger is a noun phrase, in fact a subject.

However, Harlow also notes (1981: 251, n. 18) that it may actually be the case that any maximal projection (XP) is a trigger for syntactic SM. Subsequent work showed this latter generalization to be preferable, and the phrase-based approach in its most recent form has become known as the XP trigger hypothesis (XPTH): see Harlow (1989), Tallerman (1987, 1990), Borsley (1997, 1999), Borsley & Tallerman (1996), Tallerman (2006). The essential idea is that syntactic SM occurs on a constituent which is immediately preceded by a phrasal category, XP. Phrases (XPs) are thus seen as the trigger for syntactic SM.

Two types of evidence favour the XPTH rather than the earlier NP trigger hypothesis. The first is purely empirical: a wide class of XPs which don't contain any noun phrase appear to trigger syntactic SM. For instance, consider (7) and (8):

(7)   Gwnaeth [$_{XP}$ gweithio 'n   galed] <u>bres</u>   i   'r   bobl.   (*pres*)
       do.PAST.3s   work.INF PRED hard   money   for   the   people
       'Working hard made money for the people.'

(8)   Gwelais   i [$_{AdvP}$ yn   sydyn] <u>blismyn</u>   yn   y   stryd.   (*plismyn*)
       see.PAST.1s I   PRED   sudden   policemen   in   the   street
       'I suddenly saw policemen in the street.'

In (7), the phrase marked XP is a VP or a full clause, depending on the theoretical assumptions made (see section 7.6 for some discussion); in neither case does it contain a noun phrase. In (8), the trigger is an adverbial phrase.[2]

---

[2] The direct object *plismyn* would undergo SM whether or not the adverbial were present, since it would in any case immediately follow the subject noun phrase, itself a trigger for SM.

And in (6) above, the trigger *yna*, 'there', appears to be a PP in Welsh; see Borsley & Tallerman (1996: 12). Such data clearly favour the XPTH over the NP trigger hypothesis. Other phrasal categories which constitute triggers for SM under the XPTH will be shown in later sections.

Theoretical considerations also indicate that the XPTH is preferable to the earlier formulation. In (5), the constituent which bears the SM (*gi*, 'dog') is immediately preceded by the PP *yn yr ardd* 'in the garden'. It might be assumed that the noun phrase, *yr ardd*, 'the garden', is the trigger for the mutation. However, an argument against this is advanced by Borsley & Tallerman (1996: 8–10), on the basis of a strong – and probably universal – constraint on muta-tion processes known as the Trigger Constraint, proposed by Lieber (1983) and Zwicky (1984). Borsley & Tallerman (1996: 8) formulate the constraint as follows:

(9)   A mutation trigger must immediately precede and c-command its target.

In an example like (5), with the partial structure in (10), a noun phrase is embedded within a PP. This means that the noun phrase precedes but does *not* c-command the target, given any reasonable structural assumptions:

(10)   Mae   [$_{PP}$ yn [$_{NP}$ yr   ardd]]   gi.   (*ci*)
        be.PRES.3S   in   the garden dog
        'There's a dog in the garden.'

It is, though, fair to assume that the PP itself does c-command the con-stituent that mutates, *ci* (see section 7.6 below for one proposed structure), in which case the Trigger Constraint is satisfied. Such an analysis supports the XPTH rather than the earlier NP trigger hypothesis. It is clear that trig-gers in general do conform to the Trigger Constraint, which is probably a sub-case of the more general 'adjacency hypothesis' proposed by Emonds (1985: 8).[3] Maintaining the Trigger Constraint also eliminates a further problem, namely the theoretically undesirable position of having more than one trigger for a single instance of mutation. Consider (11), from Borsley & Tallerman (1996: 9):

(11)   Prynodd   [$_{NP}$ tad   [$_{NP}$ y   bachgen]]   fuwch.   (*buwch*)
        buy.PAST.3S   father   the boy   cow
        'The boy's father bought a cow.'

---

[3] Emonds' adjacency hypothesis states that 'No language-particular rule of any kind makes use of a string variable . . . Given a complete and accurate definition of "adjacent", no child can ever learn a dependency particular to some but not all natural languages which is stated in terms of elements related at a distance' (1985: 8).

Without the c-command restriction of the Trigger Constraint, both of the bracketed noun phrases would be triggers, since both immediately precede the target, *buwch*. Given (9), though, only the outer noun phrase is a possible trigger, since only this phrase c-commands the target (the facts are identical if the noun phrases are regarded as DPs; see chapter 5 above).

In the XPTH, then, we appear to have a constrained and empirically quite successful statement of the environment for syntactic SM. Nonetheless, there are various classes of exceptions. The first concerns empty category noun phrases. In terms of classical P&P theory (e.g. Chomsky 1982), two of these bear abstract Case (small *pro* and the trace of *wh*-movement) whilst two are Caseless (PRO and the trace of NP-movement). Harlow (1981: 250, n.15) points out that only empty noun phrases which are Case-marked are triggers for syntactic SM. This means that the null subject of a finite clause, *pro*, which occurs in literary Welsh, is a trigger, as is the Case-marked *wh*-trace, seen in subject position in a focus construction in (13):

(12)   Prynodd   *pro* <u>feic</u>.   (*beic*)
        buy.PAST.3S   bike
        'He/she bought a bike.'

(13)   Y   ddynes   brynodd   *wh-t* <u>feic</u>.   (*beic*)
        the woman   buy.PAST.3S   bike
        'It was the woman who bought a bike.'

Compare the empty categories PRO and NP-trace, postulated as the subjects of control and raising infinitival clauses respectively, within the P&P framework. These do not trigger SM (see Borsley 1984, Harlow 1989, Tallerman 1990):

(14)   Mae   Elen   yn   disgwyl   [PRO prynu/*brynu   beic].
        be.PRES.3S Elen PROG expect.INF   buy.INF/(+SM) bike
        'Elen is expecting to buy a bike.'

(15)   Mae   Elen$_j$ wedi dechrau   [t_j gyrru/*yrru   bws].
        be.PRES.3S Elen PERF begin.INF   drive.INF/(+SM) bus
        'Elen has started to drive a bus.'

So in (14), the constituent following PRO, namely *prynu beic*, does not bear SM (**brynu beic*), and (15) is exactly parallel, giving *gyrru bws* after the trace, not **yrru bws*. Example (4), with an overt embedded subject which does trigger SM on the following predicate, contrasts with both of these.

Not only do the Caseless empty categories fail to *trigger* SM, they also do not *block* an immediately preceding overt XP from triggering SM. In general, we would expect such blocking to occur, just as the Trigger Constraint predicts: if some element intervenes between a mutation trigger and a potential target, the mutation is blocked. For instance, as noted in section 7.1, in *ei phum cath* 'her five cat(s)', *ei* (3FS) triggers aspirate mutation, giving *phum* (< *pum*), but *ei* cannot trigger aspirate mutation on *cath* because it does not immediately precede that noun. There is evidence that empty elements in general also block mutation from occurring across them. For instance, in (16), the third-person plural proclitic *eu* may be phonetically absent, but if it is, the subject XP *Aled* does not then trigger SM on the following verb: the verb form is *gwerthu* and not *werthu:

(16)   Gwnaeth   Aled   (eu)   gwerthu/*werthu   nhw.
        do.PAST.3S Aled   3P   sell.INF / sell.INF(+SM) them
        'Aled sold them.'

From such examples, we can conclude that empty elements normally block an immediately preceding XP from triggering SM. But in the case of PRO and the NP-trace, no such blocking effects appear. The following examples again show infinitival complements to control and raising predicates, but this time with VSX constituent order in the main clause, so that the embedded clauses immediately follow the matrix subject, *Elen*:

(17)   Disgwyliodd   Elen   [PRO <u>brynu</u>   beic].   (*prynu*)
        expect.PAST.3S Elen   buy.INF bike
        'Elen expected to buy a bike.'

(18)   Dechreuodd   Elen_j   [t_j <u>yrru</u>   bws].   (*gyrru*)
        begin.PAST.3S Elen   drive.INF bus
        'Elen started to drive a bus.'

In (17) and (18), the subject of each matrix clause, *Elen*, is the XP trigger for SM. This XP is not adjacent to the constituent bearing the mutation in the embedded clause – that is, assuming the presence of the empty category subjects of the infinitival clause. It seems, then, that PRO and NP-trace are simply inert in terms of mutation. We return to the issue of Caseless nominals in sections 7.6 and 7.7 below.

Turning now to other classes of exceptions, a number of potential targets for syntactic SM actually do not undergo the mutation. The first class is rather trivial, and concerns items which (often for historical reasons) do not bear SM. For instance, the second-person singular proclitic *dy* cannot undergo SM. Similarly, prepositions such as *gan* and *gyda* (both meaning 'with') do not undergo SM, most probably because they already appear in a fossilized SM form in all contexts (see Borsley & Tallerman (1996: 6) for some discussion).

A more interesting class of exceptions involves clauses. Firstly, consider the embedded clause in (19). This immediately follows a trigger for SM, the matrix subject *i*, 'I', but displays no mutation, even though *pwy*, 'who', can itself bear SM in other contexts:

(19)   Gwn   i [cp pwy/*bwy   ddaeth   yn ôl].
        know.FUT.1S I   who/(+SM) come.PAST.3S back
        'I know who came back.'

Morgan (1952: 441) states that *wh*-items at the start of complement clauses do not mutate, and regards the tendency for some authors to use the mutation in such examples as hypercorrection. It has been suggested (Harlow 1989: 307–8, Tallerman 1990: 404–6, Borsley & Tallerman 1996: 6–7) that clauses (CPs) themselves do not bear SM. However, the situation is not entirely clear-cut, and Tallerman (2006: 1770) shows that embedded *wh*-clauses may bear SM. For instance:

(20)   Os gwyddoch   chi [ba   swyddfa sy   'n   delio   â
        if know.FUT.2P you which office   be.PRES.REL PROG deal.INF with
        'r   broblem . . .]   (*pa*)
        the problem
        'If you know which office is dealing with the problem . . .'

Secondly, if an adverbial constituent is adjoined to the clause, the clause bears no SM, even though it follows an XP:

(21)   [Yn   sydyn] [cp dechreuodd   y   môr ferwi].
        PRED sudden   begin.PAST.3S the sea boil.INF
        'Suddenly, the sea began to boil.'

However, the situation is actually quite complex. We have already seen in (17) and (18) that what would be considered full clauses within a P&P framework do indeed bear SM. Clearly, it is quite hard to maintain both a straightforward account of the presence of mutation in (17) and (18), and the absence of mutation in (19) and (21): see Borsley (1984) for some discussion. We return to this issue in section 7.6.

We have seen in this section that the phrase-based approach ties together a number of contexts for syntactic SM in a satisfactory way, and makes strong predictions which are generally consistent with the requirements of an apparently universal constraint on mutation, the Trigger Constraint. The phrase-based approach seems, then, to score well on empirical adequacy. In the next section, we outline the roots of the case-based approach.

7.3   Early case-based approaches to syntactic SM

The case-based approach within generative grammar has its roots in Lieber (1983) and Zwicky (1984). A completely distinct variant of this approach has more recently been proposed by Roberts (1997, 2005). Case-based approaches take a very different line from that of phrase-based analyses, since they link syntactic soft mutation with accusative case, and for that reason, case-based approaches are often grouped together under the designation 'direct object mutation' (DOM) analyses.

At its most transparent, the idea that syntactic SM is accusative case-marking would account for the SM on the direct object in (1). Such an approach has quite a lot in common with the Welsh grammatical tradition, which, as noted earlier, regards the mutation as marking the object (or other complement) of a finite verb. However, it is not possible to maintain the case proposal in its simplest form, because, as Roberts (2005: 171, n.19) notes, 'DOM is neither necessary nor sufficient for objecthood.' Since some confusion on this point often arises in discussions of Welsh outside the specialist literature, we devote some space here to illustration of the facts.

To illustrate that DOM is not *necessary* for objecthood (in other words, the fact that a noun phrase can be an object and yet not bear SM), consider first the AuxSVO clause in (22), which has a periphrastic verb. The finite element is the initial auxiliary, and the lexical verb, *prynu* 'buy', is non-finite; the direct object immediately follows. In this construction, the object does not normally bear syntactic SM, so that **feic* in (22) is ungrammatical:

(22)   Roedd   y   ddynes   yn   prynu   beic/*feic.
be.IMPF.3S the woman PROG buy.INF bike/bike(+SM)
'The woman was buying a bike.'

The lack of mutation on the object in (22) contrasts with the mutation seen on the VSO object in (1). A reasonable null hypothesis for a case-based account would seem to be that if SM is the realization of accusative case, then it ought to mark the objects of both finite and non-finite verbs, but clearly this is not what happens. Traditional accounts of syntactic SM and modern generative case-based accounts alike attempt to handle the contrast between (1) and (22) by claiming that the two kinds of objects each have a different case. For Zwicky (1984) (and in line with the view taken by traditional grammar) the objects of finite verbs are accusative, whilst the objects of non-finite verbs are genitive. Roberts (2005) suggests that the latter are not genitive but nominative. However, it is clear that Welsh has no morphological case, as seen in section

1.4.5. There are therefore no independent correlations with the proposed 'case' distinctions,[4] and terms such as 'accusative' and 'genitive / nominative' are in effect nothing more than diacritics describing the presence versus absence of mutation on the object in (1) versus (22).

A second type of object which does not bear SM is illustrated in (23):

(23)   Casglwyd   deg punt/*ddeg punt.
        collect.PAST.IMPERS ten   pound/(+SM)
        'Ten pounds was collected.'

Here, the object of an impersonal verb fails to mutate. As noted by Comrie (1977), evidence from object cliticization shows that the single argument of an impersonal verb really is an object – and not a subject, unlike the single argument of a passive verb in English; see section 8.3.3 below. In literary Welsh, objects (but not subjects) can be realized as an enclitic on the pre-verbal particle, so the appearance in (24) of a third person plural object clitic *'u* indicates that an impersonal verb takes an object argument:[5]

---

[4] Ian Roberts suggests to us that there are in fact independent correlations between case and mutation, namely that subjects and possessors do not mutate, whereas direct objects and complements of some prepositions do. He also suggests that such a split is precisely like that between nominative/genitive on the one hand and accusative on the other in a case-rich language like Latin. However, note that subjects can in fact mutate, provided they are in an appropriate context: see (5), (6) and (39). Possessors do not mutate, but this is predicted under the XPTH since they are not immediately preceded by an XP; see Borsley & Tallerman (1996). The complements of some prepositions do indeed bear SM, but this is lexically triggered, not a subcase of syntactic SM; in any case, the complements of other prepositions bear different mutations (aspirate or nasal), or no mutation at all, so prepositions can hardly be relevant. We conclude that there are, indeed, no independent correlations between case and mutation.

[5] The object cliticization test also shows that the mutated constituent in examples such as (i) could not plausibly be considered an object, despite the translation. (There is no direct equivalent to a 'have' verb in Welsh; see section 10.2.2.4.) What we have in (i) is in fact a displaced subject, parallel to that in (5). Compare (ii) and (iii): in (iii), there is no possibility of representing the argument *beic* as a third-person singular object enclitic, *'i*:

(i)   Mae   gen   i   <u>feic.</u>   (*beic*)
        be.PRES.3S with.1S me bike
        'I've got a bike.'

(ii)   Byddai   'n   well gen   i   <u>feic.</u>   (*beic*)
        be.COND.3S PRED better with.1S me bike
        'I'd prefer to have a bike.'

(iii)   *Fe 'i   byddai 'n   well gen   i   (ef).
        AFF 3S be.COND.3S PRED better with.1S me it
        ('I'd prefer to have it.')

(24)   Fe 'u casglwyd.
        AFF 3P collect.PAST.IMPERS
        'They were collected.'

There are two further clear indications that DOM is not necessary for objecthood. As Zwicky (1984: 399) also notes, the objects of VSO clauses do not bear DOM when they are fronted, as in the cleft construction in (25), nor when they are sentence fragments, (26):

(25)   **Beic/*feic** brynodd y ddynes.
        bike/(+SM) buy.PAST.3S the woman
        'It was a bike that the woman bought.'

(26)   Beth brynodd y ddynes? **Beic/*feic**.
        what buy.PAST.3S the woman bike/(+SM)
        'What did the woman buy? A bike.'

Such data cast further doubt on the idea that DOM is linked with objecthood per se, or indeed that it realizes accusative case. It is usual, in languages with morphological case, for a fronted argument to bear the same case as it would have in a clause-internal position. The German example in (27) shows that the fronted object bears accusative case:

(27)   **Ihn**   hab'   ich gesehen.
        him(+ACC) have.PRES.1S I   seen.PAST.PART
        'I've seen *him*.'

If DOM realizes accusative case in Welsh, then the fact that the fronted object in (25) bears no SM requires some explanation. Note that the XPTH, on the other hand, straightforwardly predicts the absence of SM in examples like (25) and (26): neither extracted nor sentence fragment objects are immediately preceded by any XP.

Next we illustrate the fact that DOM is not *sufficient* for objecthood. Zwicky's claim is that 'SM is an exponent of the Acc[usative] case' (1984: 392). However, any narrowly case-based approach – i.e. one which relates case directly to grammatical function – is problematic in light of data such as (2) through (6) in section 7.1. Taking (5) and (6) first, the constituent bearing the SM is arguably the subject in each example, as noted above, and there is no independent reason to think that such subjects are accusative – though this is exactly how they are treated by Roberts (2005); see section 7.5 below. (Compare also the examples in footnote 5, which show that displaced subjects fail the object cliticization test.) Obviously, within a strict case-based approach, one could suggest an entirely different analysis of the mutation on displaced subjects. But since such mutation does seem to form a natural class with other kinds of syntactic SM, and since it is treated as such within a phrase-based approach, which handles (5) and (6) straightforwardly, it would seem desirable for a case-based approach also to include these data in the general environment for syntactic SM.

Data such as (2) through (4) are more problematic. In (2) and (4), the target for SM is a VP. In (3), the constituent bearing SM is an infinitival complement clause within a P&P model; in other frameworks, such as Head-driven Phrase Structure Grammar (HPSG), it would again be regarded as a VP: see section 7.6. Neither a VP nor a clause is a case-bearing element, so, as noted by Tallerman (1987) and Harlow (1989: 299–301), the case proposal cannot easily be sustained in light of such data. Furthermore, Borsley (1997: 46–7) also points out that infinitival complements occur in a position where a noun phrase cannot occur, suggesting that case is not licensed in that context. For instance, compare (28), which has an infinitival complement to a matrix control predicate, with (29). Note that the phrase *ddisgrifio'r llun* bears SM in (28), so is clearly in a context where syntactic SM is triggered. Using an ordinary nominal phrase *disgrifiad o'r llun* 'description of the picture' in that same context in (29), however, gives an ungrammatical result (with or without the mutation).

(28)   Gobeithiodd Emrys <u>ddisgrifio</u>   'r   llun.   (*disgrifio*)
         hope.PAST.3S Emrys describe.INF the picture
         'Emrys hoped to describe the picture.'

(29)   *Gobeithiodd Emrys ddisgrifiad o 'r   llun.
         hope.PAST.3S Emrys description of the picture
         (*'Emrys hoped a description of the picture.')

The idea that syntactic SM realizes accusative case is obviously problematic in light of the contrast between (28) and (29).[6]

So far, we have seen that syntactic SM occurs not only on objects, but also on subjects, VPs and infinitival complement clauses. Other kinds of constituents can also be targets for syntactic SM, providing further evidence that DOM is not sufficient for objecthood. A final example in this section (first used in Borsley & Tallerman 1996: 37–8) shows a PP predicate that bears the mutation:[7]

(30)   Roedd   **ei   thŷ   hi** [$_{PP}$ <u>dafliad</u> carreg i   lawr y   ffordd]. (*tafliad*)
         be.IMPF.3S 3FS house her   throw stone to down the road
         'Her house was a stone's throw down the road.'   (*AN* 95)

---

[6] As noted in section 3.5, *gobeithio*, 'hope', can in some contexts take a direct object in Welsh, e.g. *gobeithio'r gorau* (lit. 'hope the best' = 'hope for the best').

[7] The PP contains a pre-head specifier constituent, which, as it is the beginning of the PP, bears the mutation.

Since PPs are also not case-marked, such examples provide further evidence against the idea that this mutation is a realization of accusative case. Significantly, a noun phrase predicate is not possible in this same environment (i.e. immediately following the subject in a copular clause) unless accompanied by the predicate marker *yn* (section 8.1.1). The fact that a bare nominal phrase cannot occur here indicates that again, this is not a case-licensing context:

(31)   Roedd   Alys *(yn)   feddyg.
        be.IMPF.3S Alys   PRED doctor
        'Alys was a doctor.'

However, the XPTH once again clearly predicts the mutation in (30), since the PP predicate bearing the mutation immediately follows an XP, the subject of the clause, shown in bold.

It is clear from the data examined in this section that syntactic SM occurs on constituents which are not plausibly regarded as objects: the appearance of mutation is, then, not a sufficient test for objecthood. Conversely, it is not necessary for objecthood: fronted objects and sentence fragment objects of finite verbs, as well as objects of non-finite verbs and impersonal verbs, all fail to bear syntactic SM. In its simplest form, the proposal that the so-called DOM equates with accusative case – or with objecthood – is not supported by the evidence. However, subsequent research on syntactic SM from a case-linked perspective avoids making any direct connection between objecthood, accusative case and syntactic SM, and it is to this work that we turn next.

7.4   Roberts' case-linked approach

Recent work by Roberts (1997, 2005) builds on Zwicky's proposals for syntactic SM, in that Roberts also regards the mutation as an indication of accusative case (ACC). Note, though, that Roberts (2005) does not propose any direct connection between DOM and objecthood, and for that reason we can consider his account as case-*linked* rather than strictly speaking case-*based*. Roberts points out (2005: 171, n.19) that crosslinguistically, accusative case *in general* is neither a necessary nor a sufficient condition for objecthood: 'ACC is doubly dissociated from the notion of direct object, as is well known. Quirky case-marked objects and objects of passive and unaccusative verbs . . . are objects but not ACC. Subjects of ECM [i.e. exceptional case marked] clauses are ACC but not objects.' By proposing a more tenuous link with case, Roberts' proposals get round the problem for a strictly case-based account which was mentioned in section 7.3, namely that various constituents which cannot be case-bearing do bear SM; see also (54) below. However, such proposals also seem to lack the immediate conceptual attraction of an approach which says that DOM is directly linked with case and objecthood – though as we have seen, such a position cannot be maintained.

First, we provide a brief sketch of the mechanics of syntactic SM according to Roberts (2005: ch. 2.3). In line with all recent analyses of verb-initial word order in the Celtic languages within the P&P framework, Roberts assumes an underlying verb phrase, which the verb raises out of when it is finite, but which it remains within when non-finite. Under Roberts' proposals, a finite verb V moves to v and then up to higher functional head positions, namely Num and Pers in his account. Roberts' account crucially links the mutation of the object with the raising of the finite lexical verb: specifically, the trigger for syntactic SM in this account is the finite v, which within Minimalism licenses accusative Case and is adjacent to the object in Spec VP. Thus, Roberts argues that 'DOM is a phonological reflex of v and hence – plausibly – of accusative Case' (2005: 70). The relevant part of the structure for a simple VSO sentence such as (1) is as follows (after Roberts 2005: 70):

(32)

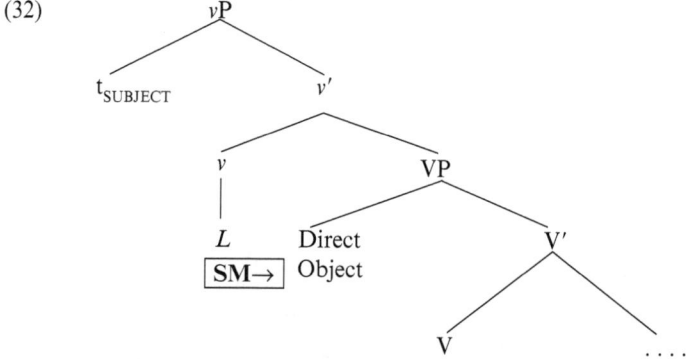

The object, sited in Spec, VP, is head-governed by v (Roberts 2005: 73), and it is this specifier position which receives the ACC Case. ACC is realized as soft mutation. Roberts' precise idea is that v contains a floating autosegmental feature for the mutation, L (meaning lenition, i.e. soft mutation), activated only when V moves through v. Roberts also notes that 'the phonological mutation process takes place at PF [Phonetic Form] and so is sensitive to post-movement configurations only' (2005: 71).

Any account must make the essential distinction between VSO clauses such as (1) and AuxSVO clauses such as (22): the object of the finite verb in (1) bears syntactic SM, while the object of the non-finite verb in (22) does not. Roberts' proposal is that the object of the non-finite verb is lower down in the clause – it is not in Spec, VP, and so cannot be a target for DOM, triggered by *v*. Roberts comments (2005: 106) that 'there is simply no occurrence of *v* (or none close enough . . .)'. In fact, he proposes that the objects of non-finite verbs bear NOM and not ACC Case.

Conversely, the subject typically fails to mutate because it is generally higher in the clause: it is merged in Spec, *v*P, and subsequently raises. Hence, the subject is sited above *v*, and is not a target for the mutation. (We will see in section 7.5 how Roberts handles such data as (5) and (6), where the subject is low down in the clause and does mutate.)

Roberts also addresses the fact, illustrated in (25), that extracted objects of finite verbs do not bear DOM. He proposes (2005: 78) that the mutation feature *L* is attached at PF, i.e. after the movement of objects, which is in the overt syntax. No trigger therefore precedes the fronted object. However, it is not clear that this explanation can be extended to account for the lack of SM on sentence fragment objects, as in (26).

So much, then, for constituents which are objects but which do not bear SM. What about constituents which are not objects but which do bear syntactic SM? We have seen that complements to control and raising predicates do bear the mutation, under the appropriate conditions: see (3), (17) and (18). We repeat two relevant examples:

(33)   Disgwyliodd Elen [<u>brynu</u>   beic].   (*prynu*)
           expect.PAST.3s Elen buy.INF bike
           'Elen expected to buy a bike.'

(34)   Dechreuodd Elen [<u>yrru</u>   bws].   (*gyrru*)
           begin.PAST.3s Elen drive.INF bus
           'Elen started to drive a bus.'

The bracketed phrases are not direct objects (they are not nominal). However, this is one aspect of mutation on which all major accounts agree, including Welsh traditional grammar: in terms of syntactic SM, these constructions are treated as exactly parallel to ordinary VSO clauses, such as (1), where the object bears the mutation. For Roberts, this parallelism is expressed by the fact that the bracketed phrase (which he regards as a participial) 'is the structural complement of [the mutation trigger] *v*' (2005: 81). A similar account can be maintained for examples like (2), in which a predicate bears the mutation. Clearly, then, it is crucial to dissociate objecthood in the narrowest sense from the occurrence of DOM. Note, though, that (4) is problematic for Roberts, as we discuss in section 7.5. One remaining issue within the P&P framework concerns the empty category subjects of the complement clauses in (33) and (34); we turn to this in section 7.7.2.

We have now seen how Roberts (2005) deals with some of the basic examples of syntactic SM. Obviously, the most important issue for any account of the mutation concerns its empirical adequacy. In section 7.5 we show that Roberts' case-linked account breaks down in this respect, since it fails to predict the occurrence of syntactic SM in numerous contexts where it is in fact found. Section 7.7 examines theoretical issues arising from the case-linked account.

7.5   Problems with the case-linked account

Problematic aspects of a case-based approach in general are discussed by Borsley (1997). Tallerman (2006) provides a critique of the specific case-linked analysis in Roberts (2005), which, as we saw in the previous section, predicts that syntactic SM occurs only where a finite verb raises to v. In this section we assess some of the main drawbacks to Roberts' approach.

7.5.1   *Empirical issues*

First, consider the objects of periphrastic verbs. We have already shown that these do not normally bear syntactic SM; consider (22), repeated here as (35):

(35)   Roedd   y   ddynes yn   prynu   beic/*feic.
        be.IMPF.3S the woman PROG buy.INF bike/bike(+SM)
        'The woman was buying a bike.'

We also saw in section 7.4 that Roberts' analysis predicts – correctly for (35) – that the object here cannot be a target for DOM, since it is not in the Spec, VP position where it would be the structural complement of v. Now consider (36):

(36)   Roedd   y   ddynes yn   prynu [yn 2008] feic newydd sbon. (*beic*)
        be.IMPF.3S the woman PROG buy.INF in 2008 bike new   brand
        'The woman was buying in 2008 a brand new bike.'

What examples like (36) show is that if a phrasal category of some kind intervenes between the non-finite verb and its object, then that object does indeed bear syntactic SM – obligatorily. This is entirely unexpected under Roberts' account, and cannot in any way be integrated within the DOM analysis.

Secondly, consider the objects of impersonal verbs (see section 8.3.3 for a discussion of the syntax of these constructions). Again, in the basic construction, such objects cannot bear SM, as we saw in (23). However, on the face of things, this absence of mutation seems unexpected: impersonal clauses have a finite verb which raises, and thus do contain the triggering head v, and this does indeed take the phrase containing the object as its complement. Roberts, however, atttributes the lack of mutation in such examples as (23) to ACC being deactivated in passive constructions generally (Roberts 2005: 79). He suggests that v contains a voice feature PASS(ive), which is in complementary distribution with the mutation feature L. So v is not a possible trigger for SM in passive constructions: 'the lack of DOM in impersonal passives is exactly what we would expect if DOM is a reflex of ACC-licensing' (Roberts 2005: 80). Nonetheless, impersonal constructions are still problematic for Roberts. Firstly, the idea that impersonals are passives (and are thus unable to have accusative complements) is shown by Blevins (2003) to be incorrect; see section 8.3.3 below. Second, the proposal that ACC is deactivated in impersonals is difficult to sustain, because the clear evidence is that the argument in impersonals truly is an object, as we saw in (24). Differentiating impersonal objects from ordinary objects in this way in fact amounts to a stipulation.[8]

Furthermore, the mutation facts in impersonal clauses are also problematic for Roberts. Although there is no mutation in (23), if a phrasal category intervenes before the object, then the object must indeed bear SM:[9]

(37)   Casglwyd   [ganddynt] <u>dd</u>eg punt.   (*deg*)
        collect.PAST.IMPERS with.3P   ten pound
        'Ten pounds was collected by them.'   (Morgan 1952: 431)

Here, a PP *ganddynt* (lit. 'with them') immediately precedes the object, so the mutation is predicted by the XPTH. Within Roberts' framework for DOM, however, there is no possible account of the mutation in (37), because if ACC is deactivated, then v cannot be a mutation trigger.

---

[8] Roberts (2005: 80) proposes that the single arguments of impersonal verbs are actually licensed as NOM, despite the evidence from cliticization presented in section 7.3 which shows that they are true objects. Roberts comments that the evidence from cliticization 'is not compelling'. Whether or not this is true, impersonals are still seriously problematic for the case-linked account, not least because their arguments do indeed manifest SM under the appropriate conditions; see (37).

[9] The absence of mutation in (23) is predictable under a phrase-based account if the subject position is occupied by the empty category PRO; see Borsley & Tallerman (1996: 12–14) for such an account. In frameworks such as HPSG or Lexical Functional Grammar, there is no need to posit an empty category subject in impersonal sentences at all, so again, the absence of SM is predicted by the XPTH, since there is no phrasal category immediately preceding the object.

Thirdly, consider predicates that take more than one complement (see Tallerman 2006): such verbs have a subject, an object, and a third argument, typically a PP. The third argument is shown in brackets:

(38)   Taflodd   Aled b<u>êl</u> [<u>ddwy</u> droedfedd tuag at   Mair].   (*pêl, dwy*)
        throw.PAST.3S Aled ball two   foot   towards Mair
        'Aled threw a ball two feet towards Mair.'

Roberts' analysis correctly predicts that the direct object in such cases mutates: in (38), the object *bêl* (< *pêl*) bears SM. However, Roberts' account predicts that *only* the direct object – which is in Spec, VP – is in a position to receive DOM triggered by *v*. But in fact *both* complements bear syntactic SM, hence the mutation on the bracketed argument in (38). Under Roberts' account, unless the third argument is a structural complement to *v*, it is not in a position to receive DOM. Of course, the result will depend on the exact analysis of three-argument verbs: see Borsley (1997: 35, 44). However, whatever structure is assumed, crucially only one constituent can be the structural complement to Roberts' mutation trigger *v*. There is, then, no account of the fact that *both* the second and third arguments bear syntactic SM.[10]

Let us pause briefly at this point to consider how a phrase-based account would handle the data seen so far in this section. Taking the last example first, three-argument predicates such as (38) are straightforward. The subject, *Aled*, is a phrasal category, so under the XPTH it triggers SM onto the following direct object, *bêl*, and in turn the object triggers SM onto the following PP. The mutation on both complements is predicted. Similarly, in both (36) and (37), the constituent bearing the mutation is immediately preceded by a phrasal category, so the SM is again predicted by the phrase-based account. So far, then, it appears that the XPTH is superior in empirical terms to a case-linked account.

Fourthly, consider subjects: normally, these do not bear syntactic SM. Under the XPTH, this is because (given VSO/AuxSVO word order) subjects

---

[10] Ian Roberts has suggested to us that the first four problematic cases in this section, namely those seen in (36), (37), (38) and (39), may all be instances of a single phenomenon, stated as follows: extraposed elements undergo SM. However, while (36) and (39) clearly display a rather marked word order (especially (39)), and could thus plausibly be considered examples of extraposition, example (37) is unmarked, and (38) – crucially – displays the only ordering possible. It would be misleading to argue that such an example is derived by extraposition. Example (38) is thus inescapably problematic for Roberts' account, as noted in the text, since it contains not one but two instances of SM, yet (in Roberts' terms) only one triggering *v* element. Moreover, even if these were all instances of extraposition, they still remain unaccounted for under the case-linked account, whereas they fall out straightforwardly from the XPTH.

do not usually immediately follow any XP, but instead follow a finite verb or auxiliary. For Roberts, the absence of mutation is attributed to the fact that the subject is generally higher in the clause than *v*, which is the trigger for DOM: see (32). However, in some contexts, subjects do bear SM. Roberts (2005: 82–4) briefly discusses examples parallel to (5) and (6), where a subject is not in its canonical (high) position in the clause, and where it bears the mutation. He suggests that in such instances, the subject remains lower down; in fact, it is crucially in the 'accusative' Spec, VP position, where DOM is triggered by *v*. Note that this is possible because of the dissociation between grammatical function and case in Roberts' framework: displaced subjects are allowed to be ACC. The problem for Roberts' account comes from other examples of displaced subjects which cannot be treated in the same way. An example from formal Welsh is shown in (39), where the postposed subject is in brackets, and its initial element, which bears SM, is underlined:

(39)   Mae   'n   dy arwain [*gwmwl* niwl a   cholofn dân].   (*cwmwl*)
        be.PRES.3S PROG 2S lead.INF cloud   mist and column fire
        'A cloud of mist and a column of fire are guiding you.'

(Morgan 1952: 432)

In the unmarked word order, we would find *Mae [cwmwl niwl a cholofn dân] yn dy arwain* with no SM on the bracketed subject. Given the position of the subject in (39), it cannot be in Spec, VP – the position where, under Roberts' proposals, mutation is triggered by *v*. The subject is positioned to the *right* of the entire verb phrase here, and so is well below *v*.[11] So the explanation Roberts proposes with respect to examples like (5) and (6) is not available. For Roberts, then, the SM on the displaced subject in (39) cannot be predicted.

Within the XPTH account, on the other hand, the SM on extraposed subjects is predicted, providing we make the reasonable assumption that the subject is not wholly contained within the verb phrase. Tallerman (2006: 1761) suggests the following structure, where the subject is adjoined to VP:

(40)

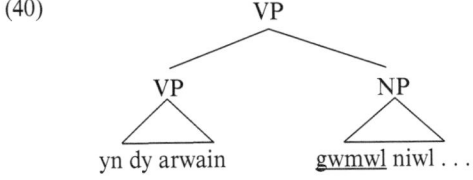

---

[11] Roberts actually considers the phrase consisting of the aspect marker and the non-finite verb to be an AspP, with the non-finite verb heading a participial phrase. There is in any case no triggering *v*.

Since the VP *yn dy arwain* precedes and c-commands the displaced subject, the SM is predicted under the XPTH. Within the HPSG framework, the assumption would be a flat structure, where the VP and the displaced subject are simply sisters; see also section 7.6.

Fifthly, we return to the issue of infinitival clauses. As noted in section 7.4, Roberts discusses the SM found on the infinitival complements in (33) and (34): such constituents are predicted to take DOM under his proposals, as they are complements to *v*. However, as noted earlier, infinitival *i*-clauses such as (4) are problematic for Roberts, and these do not feature in his analysis of syntactic SM. Consider the data in (41) to (43), from Tallerman (2006: 1764). (See chapter 3 above on the structure of *i*-clauses.)

(41)   Dymunodd   Aled [i **Mair** <u>fynd</u>   adref].   (*mynd*)
       want.PAST.3S Aled to Mair go.INF home
       'Aled wanted Mair to go home.'

(42)   Synnodd   y   ffaith [i **ni** <u>orffen</u>]   bawb.   (*gorffen*)
       surprise.PAST.3S the fact   to us finish.INF everyone
       'The fact that we'd finished surprised everyone.'

(43)   Wrth [i **Aled** <u>ddod</u>   allan], aeth   Mair i   mewn.   (*dod*)
       as   to Aled come.INF out   go.PAST.3S Mair in
       'As Aled came out, Mair went in.'

Under the XPTH, the mutation in (41) to (43) is entirely predictable. The elements in bold (the subjects of the embedded clauses) are of course XPs, and are thus triggers for SM. Such examples would appear to fall together with the examples of syntactic SM seen in (33) and (34), and they are treated in the same way by the XPTH, but in Roberts' DOM analysis, no parallel treatment is available. The mutation in (41) to (43) is completely unexpected under Roberts' account, because the constituent bearing SM (the predicate of the embedded clause – the non-finite verb and its postmodifiers) is *not* a complement to any finite *v*. The problem for Roberts is that the mutated constituent is well within the non-finite embedded clauses, out of reach of any triggering *v* head.

Note finally that the embedded *wh*-clauses discussed in section 7.2 in the context of exceptions to the XPTH are also problematic for Roberts. Recall that such clauses appear to bear SM somewhat idiosyncratically. Roberts (2005: 82) suggests that *wh*-clauses cannot bear SM at all, because head-government from outside CP will be blocked by minimality. Clearly, this restriction is too strong in the case of examples like (20).

In sum, purely with respect to data coverage, we have seen in this section that the case-linked approach to syntactic SM taken by Roberts (2005) is seriously flawed. Illustrating with a number of different constructions, we have shown many instances of syntactic SM which cannot be accounted for under the DOM analysis. Obviously, a proponent of the DOM account could suggest an entirely separate treatment for the problematic data seen in this section. For instance, an account could be given for much of the problematic data along the lines of the traditional statement of 'mutation following a parenthesis' mentioned in section 7.1. However, the 'parenthesis' of traditional grammar is simply an intervening phrase before the mutated constituent, which, of course, is exactly equivalent to the XPTH itself. It is worth emphasizing that any satisfactory account of syntactic SM should treat these 'parenthetical' contexts in exactly the same way as the standard contexts for 'direct object mutation' (as in (1) to (3) above). This, the XPTH does.

7.5.2   The question of head government

One remaining issue concerns a further advantage claimed by Roberts for his analysis. Under the phrase-based approach, syntactic SM appears to be a quite distinct mutation process, having little in common with many remaining instances of mutation in the grammar, which are (mostly) simply lexically triggered. Roberts suggests that his account would allow syntactic SM to be analysed as head government (by v), in line with many other instances of mutation occurring under government by a head. For instance, the head P in a PP typically triggers mutation onto its complement; various elements that could be regarded as determiners trigger mutation onto an NP complement (assuming a DP analysis); and a number of complementizers (C) trigger mutations on the initial segment of their clausal complements. In fact, Roberts (2005: 73–4, 92–3) proposes that mutation *in general* can be characterized as head government.[12]

Since most mutation is lexically triggered, and the trigger c-commands the target, it is not surprising that most instances of mutation can be seen as head government. The head-complement configuration is characteristic of the relation between mutation triggers and targets in Welsh (and, indeed, in the other Celtic languages), but it is certainly not the only configuration in which mutation occurs; see also chapter 5. There are other contexts for mutation which do not seem amenable to the head government account. For instance,

---

[12] Roberts (2005: 74) discusses whether or not the notion of head government can be reduced to some other relation in the grammar. For instance, 'It may be . . . that the effect of head-government can be reduced to phonological properties of the putatively governing head.' Roberts declines to say whether or not head government itself is the crucial configuration in the triggering of (much) consonantal mutation, but it is clear that if it is not, then the effects of head government will need to be captured in some other way.

(44) illustrates another purely grammatical environment: superlatives used adverbially bear SM:

(44)   Dere   draw <u>gyntaf</u>   y   gelli   di.   (*cyntaf*)
        come.IMPER.2S over quick.SUPERL PRT can.FUT.2S you
        'Come over as quickly as you can.'   (Thorne 1993: 28)

In such contexts, there is no head that could act as the mutation trigger; in fact, there appears to be no trigger at all. See also chapter 5 for discussion of the problems surrounding mutation environments within nominal phrases. The head-complement configuration does not appear to generalize to *all* instances of mutation. In turn, this implies that one major advantage which Roberts claims for his *v*-trigger analysis – that it brings the environment for syntactic SM into conformity with other mutation contexts – is also lost.

The present section has also presented a number of environments for syntactic SM which cannot be treated as head government by the finite *v* (Roberts' trigger for the mutation). This applies to the mutation on the predicate of *i*-clauses, shown in (41) to (43). It also applies to the mutation of objects of non-finite verbs and impersonal verbs following a parenthetical XP – see (36) and (37) – and to the mutation of displaced subjects, (39). In none of these contexts does an overt functional or lexical head appear to be available as a mutation trigger (see also Tallerman 1999, 2006). The mutation found on the final complement of three-argument predicates – see (38) – is also a problem for the *v*-trigger analysis. Given a typical P&P analysis of such predicates, involving VP shells, each complement will indeed be c-commanded by a head. However, only one can be c-commanded by *v*, and the other must be the complement of a different head.

Of course, it would be entirely possible to maintain the case-linked *v*-trigger account for relatively straightforward data, such as (1) to (3), but to propose different empty heads as the trigger for SM in the various other cases. The problem is that such an account fails to generalize over all instances of syntactic SM. There is no specific head, nor a natural class of heads, which could be regarded as the mutation trigger in all the cases that are problematic for the *v*-trigger account: no generalization covers all the data we have discussed.

7.6   Recent work from a phrase-based perspective

In this section we look at more formal considerations concerning the XPTH, and examine a proposal by Borsley (1999) for a refinement of the hypothesis. Borsley & Tallerman (1996) assume a version of the hypothesis along the lines of (45):

(45)   A constituent bears SM if it is immediately preceded by a phrase which
         c-commands it.   (Borsley 1999: 270)

Although this is relatively successful in accounting for much of the data discussed so far in this chapter, it is also problematic in various ways. First, we examine a theory-internal problem. Classical P&P theory posits two empty categories which are Caseless, PRO and the trace of NP-movement, and two which are Case-marked, *pro* and *wh*-trace. As we saw in section 7.2, the Caseless empty categories do not trigger SM, whilst the Case-marked ones do. Borsley (1999: 276) points out that in order to account for this, (45) would have to be revised, thus:

(46)   A phrase bears SM if it is immediately preceded by another phrase with
         lexical content or Case which c-commands it.

The problem is the following: 'This statement contains a disjunction and there is no obvious way to eliminate it. We cannot say that only phrases with lexical content trigger mutation, given that *pro* and *wh*-trace do so, and we cannot say that only phrases with Case trigger mutation, given that non-NPs do not have Case' (Borsley 1999: 276). There is no simple way to resolve this problem within P&P theory (as Tallerman 1990 observes), but Borsley proposes a straightforward solution within an HPSG framework. HPSG does not accept the existence of the two Caseless empty categories, and complements to control and raising verbs are analysed as VPs rather than clausal complements. If PRO and NP-trace are eliminated, *all* XPs (overt or covert) trigger SM, and the section of (46) which reads 'with lexical content or Case' is now unnecessary.

Looking again at some crucial data from section 7.2 (examples (14) and (15)), we would find the following contrast, given the HPSG analysis:

(47)   Mae   Elen yn   disgwyl   [_VP prynu beic].
         be.PRES.3s Elen PROG expect.INF   buy.INF bike
         'Elen is expecting to buy a bike.'

(48)   Disgwyliodd Elen [_VP brynu   beic].   (*prynu*)
         expect.PAST.3s Elen   buy.INF bike
         'Elen expected to buy a bike.'

In (47), there is no SM on the VP complement, whereas in (48) the VP bears SM, triggered by the immediately preceding subject, *Elen*.

There are further advantages to this analysis. First, it obviates a problem noted in section 7.2, namely that the Caseless empty categories not only fail to trigger SM, they also fail to block it. That fact is problematic for an analysis which assumes the presence of PRO and NP-trace because it means that in just these two contexts, the Trigger Constraint seen in (9) – a highly desirable locality condition – is violated. In an example such as (48), for instance, the triggering XP *Elen* does not immediately precede the target (*brynu beic*) if a PRO subject is assumed: . . . *Elen* [$_{CP}$ PRO *brynu beic*]. However, if we assume a VP complement, as shown in (48), then these contexts also conform to the Trigger Constraint.

Second, the HPSG analysis of control and raising complements avoids the need for a special statement concerning the mutation of CPs (see section 7.2). As shown in (21), full clauses sometimes appear resistant to SM triggered from an external position. But if control and raising complements are also full clauses, then it is problematic that such constituents bear SM when they are immediately preceded by an XP: see (17) and (18). If these complements are only VPs, and not full clauses, then the contrast between (19)/(21) and (17)/(18) is handled straightforwardly.[13]

Given the HPSG account, the disjunction in (46) is removed, and one might assume that the statement of the XPTH in (45) is now adequate. However, two types of evidence suggest that this still requires a crucial amendment. The first involves coordination. Consider (49), where syntactic SM occurs following the subject XP *y ddynes*:

(49)   Prynodd   [y   ddynes] [grys, crys-t a   siaced].   (*crys*)
        buy.PAST.3s the woman   shirt, t-shirt and jacket
        'The woman bought a shirt, a t-shirt and a jacket.'

In this example, the direct object comprises a series of conjuncts. Note that crucially, only the initial conjunct of the whole direct object is marked for SM: *crys > grys*. The second conjunct and any subsequent conjuncts cannot bear SM: we therefore get *crys-t* here and not **grys-t*.[14] Given the version of the XPTH in (45), the mutation pattern in (49) is surprising, because it is reasonable to assume that the first conjunct both immediately precedes and c-commands the second conjunct (and so on, given a string of conjuncts). Since each conjunct is a phrasal category too, under (45) each ought to be a trigger for SM. But this prediction is incorrect: **Prynodd y ddynes grys, grys-t* (etc.) – i.e. the

---

[13] The issue of whether CP blocks mutation is far from settled. Although it has often been noted that CPs (or certain types of CP) cannot bear SM (see for instance Harlow 1989, Tallerman 1990, Borsley & Tallerman 1996), evidence to the contrary is presented in Tallerman (2006). More research is required on this matter.

[14] Note that the final conjunct in (49) is immediately preceded by *a*, 'and', a trigger for aspirate mutation, which – as the closest trigger – would take precedence in any case. In this instance, the target *siaced* 'jacket' does not have a mutable initial consonant, so there is no aspirate mutation.

coordination is ungrammatical with mutation on all conjuncts which are immediately preceded by an XP.

The second type of evidence suggesting a revision to the XPTH involves
adjuncts. Although optional material often does bear SM, this is crucially not
obligatory, even when the adjunct immediately follows an XP:

(50)   A'   i yno   ddydd Llun   / dydd Llun.
        go.FUT.1s I there Monday(+SM) / Monday
        'I'll go there on Monday.'

In (50), either *ddydd Llun* with SM or *dydd Llun* with no SM would be
grammatical. Furthermore, adjuncts may also bear SM even when they do not
follow an XP; for instance, they may mutate in clause-initial position. In fact,
the presence or absence of mutation on adjuncts is generally dialectally or
idiolectally determined, irrespective of syntactic context. This is in stark
contrast to the mutation (say) of a direct object of a finite verb in a VSO
clause, which is never optional. It appears, then, that the mutation of adjuncts
is not triggered at all, and therefore should not fall under the XPTH. What is
now needed is some way of preventing the statement of the XPTH from
triggering the mutation on adjuncts in all instances.

Various solutions (for instance, involving empty category prepositions
which block the mutation) have been proposed to handle both these problematic types of data, i.e. coordination and adjuncts; see for instance Harlow
(1989), Tallerman (1990), Borsley & Tallerman (1996). What seems to us most
satisfactory, though, is the following revision of the trigger hypothesis, from
Borsley (1999: 286):

(51)   A complement bears SM if it is immediately preceded by a phrasal sister.

Restricting the target for SM to complements has the effect that, in (49), the
entire direct object is predicted to bear the mutation – which shows up, as
usual, on its initial segment – but each individual conjunct is *not* a target.
Secondly, this more restrictive formulation entails that any mutation occurring
on adjuncts does not fall under the XPTH at all, and must be treated
separately. This is a good result, because the SM triggered under the XPTH is
one of the most robust kinds of mutation in the entire Welsh language, and is
not subject to dialectal or idiolectal variation. Since, as noted above, the
mutation of adjuncts is much less regulated, it is clearly preferable if it falls
outside the XPTH.

Borsley's HPSG analysis crucially assumes a 'flat' phrase structure, which
means that subjects and objects of VSO clauses are sisters, and the DOM
mutation in examples like (1) is handled straightforwardly under the version

of the XPTH in (51): the subject triggers the mutation on the object. The VP complement which is assumed in examples like (48) is also a sister to the subject, the XP trigger for mutation. In (52) we show the kind of structure that Borsley proposes for examples like (5), which have a displaced subject that bears SM, and (53) gives the structure for examples like (4), with SM on the VP within an infinitival *i*-clause. The mutated elements are shown in italics:

(52)

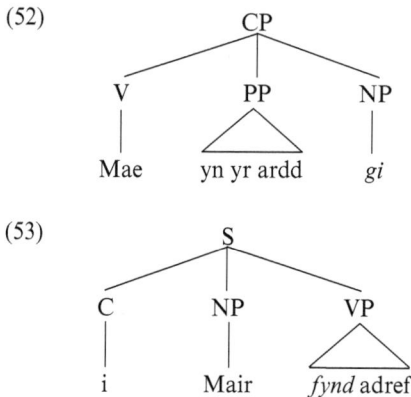

(53)

In both these structures, we have a head followed by its two complements. In (52), the copula *mae* takes a predicate PP and a subject NP complement, and in (53), what Borsley analyses as a complementizer, *i*, takes a subject NP and the predicate VP as its complements.[15] The mutation in both examples is triggered by the immediately preceding phrasal sister.

Note, though, that adopting (51) requires a rather specific definition of 'complement'. In particular, this must include the grammatical function 'subject', in order to account for the SM on postposed subjects in examples such as (5)/(52); see Borsley (1999: 285) for some discussion. The predicate in (53) must also be considered a complement of the head *i*.

Of course, it is essentially an empirical matter whether the XPTH, formulated as in (51), is preferable to other analyses of syntactic SM. However, from the evidence considered in this chapter, we conclude that the phrase-based approach makes the correct predictions over a broad set of data, whilst the case-linked approach does not.

Finally, there are a number of theoretical issues involving the syntax of SM that we have not yet considered, and it is to these we now turn.

---

[15] However, there is good evidence that inflectional *i* is not a complementizer; see section 3.6.3 above. This does not affect the point made in the text concerning the analysis of the mutation in *i*-clauses.

7.7   Theoretical matters and structural considerations

7.7.1   Case and mutation

The first issue concerns the idea within case-based or case-linked approaches that syntactic SM is a reflex of accusative case (or abstract Case; see, for instance, Roberts 2005: ch. 2.3). We have already seen data that cast doubt on this claim: see (30) above, which shows that a post-subject PP predicate in a copular clause bears syntactic SM. Now consider (54):

(54)   Dw   i [$_{AP}$ <u>lawn</u> mor grac â chi].   (*llawn*)
        be PRES.1s I   full   as   angry as you
        'I'm just as angry as you.'

This example shows that AP predicates in a copular clause also bear syntactic SM: under the XPTH, this would be triggered by the subject XP, *i*, 'I'. However, APs and PPs are not case-bearing elements, so an analysis such as Roberts (2005), which views 'DOM' as corresponding to ACC Case-marking, is highly problematic.

A second reason to doubt that syntactic SM equates to Case-marking concerns the very superficial nature of the mutation compared to what is generally known about case. Consider, for instance, (55) versus (56):

(55)   Mae   ci   yn yr ardd
        be.PRES.3s dog in the garden
        'There's a dog in the garden.'

(56)   Mae   [$_{PP}$ yn yr ardd] <u>gi.</u>   (*ci*)
        be.PRES.3s   in the garden dog
        'There's a dog in the garden.'

For Roberts, the subject *ci* in (55) is licensed as NOM in its unmarked position, whilst the subject in (56), in a somewhat more marked position, is licensed as ACC. Yet there is no substantive difference between these examples apart from the word order. In such cases as these, the NOM versus ACC distinction appears to have no independent justification – it is purely diacritic, and in fact could well be replaced with the labels 'bears no SM' (NOM) and 'bears SM' (ACC). Compare this to the situation in German or the Slavonic languages, where (for instance) a fronted *wh*-phrase bears the same case as the XP has when in situ in the clause, and a sentence fragment object must be accusative; see section 7.3. Recall also from section 7.3 that although the objects of VSO clauses bear SM when in situ, fronted objects and sentence fragment objects in Welsh do not bear SM (see (25) and (26) above), and therefore, in Roberts' terms, they are not licensed as ACC.[16] Again, this seems very unlike typical case-marking behaviour. Under the case-linked approach, however, the exact same constituents may be licensed either as ACC or NOM, even where there are no corresponding semantic distinctions.

Consider also the type of data seen in section 7.5. Much of this involved contexts not normally associated with syntactic SM, such as the object of a non-finite verb or the object of an impersonal verb: we saw, though, that if an XP immediately precedes these objects, they do bear SM, contrary to Roberts' predictions; see (36) and (37). The same applies to the subject in (55) versus (56): a subject in the unmarked 'high' clausal position bears no SM, but a subject in a lower position (following an XP) does mutate. Under the 'DOM' analysis, where SM is seen as a reflex of accusative Case, the implication is as follows: there are a number of contexts in which ACC is not normally licensed at all, such as in an impersonal construction, but where ACC somehow *is* licensed if and only if the object is preceded by an XP. Such an account seems to us highly unsatisfactory. It also seems unnecessary – if 'preceded by an XP' is a crucial part of the account, then we essentially have the XPTH, and the 'DOM' account is superfluous. In conjunction with the empirical problems for Roberts' analysis, we see this as further evidence against the idea that syntactic SM equates to ACC Case-marking.

In sum, all the indications are that syntactic SM is a superficial phenomenon. Displacement of constituents often gives rise to the mutation (e.g. in the case of a low subject), yet, on the other hand, fronting an object results in the suppression of a mutation which *would* appear in the unmarked word order: see (25). Mutation appears following an optional parenthetical XP, so that a phrase may bear SM or fail to bear SM under trivially different conditions.

We conclude, then, that syntactic SM displays quite distinct properties from Case-marking. In the next section, we turn to more issues concerning structure.

---

[16] As noted earlier, Roberts (2005: 78) discusses fronted *wh*-objects as in (i):

(i)   Pwy/*bwy   a   welodd   Megan [$_{DP}$ t]?
        who/who(+SM) PRT see.PAST.3s Megan
        'Who did Megan see?'

In his account, the *wh*-trace cannot bear SM as it has no phonological properties; and '*L* cannot attach to the *wh*-word *pwy*, as *L* attaches at PF while *pwy* moves in the syntax'. However, the fact remains that if syntactic SM were case-marking, then one would expect the fronted object to bear the same case as an in situ object.

7.7.2   *Structure and empty categories*

All approaches to syntactic SM must assume the existence of empty categories. Within the P&P framework, a fair amount of empty structure unrelated to the mutation itself will also be assumed. It was noted as far back as Tallerman (1990) that some of these structural assumptions are problematic for a straightforward account of mutation. Non-overt structure prevents elements which are plausibly regarded as triggers for various mutations from being structurally adjacent to their targets.

We turn first to verb movement. In all recent P&P accounts of Welsh verb-initial word order, the finite element originates within a verb phrase, and raises to some initial position. Tallerman (1990) notes that the trace of V-movement is problematic for a phrase-based account of syntactic SM, since it necessarily intervenes between the presumed XP trigger and the target. Consider, for instance, a fairly typical P&P analysis of a VSO clause such as (1); a structure along the lines of the following is representative of many recent accounts (e.g. Tallerman 1998, Willis 1998, 2000):

(57) $[_{AgrSP} [_{AgrS}$ Verb] $[_{TP} [_{DP}$ Subject] $t_v [_{VP} t_{Su} [t_v'$ Object]]]]

Here, both the verb and the subject have raised out of a VP. In terms of the mutation, the result we are looking for is syntactic SM on the direct object in VSO clauses. If the trigger for the SM is the subject, then a number of empty nominal and verbal categories are bound to intervene between trigger and target on such an account. This is inherently problematic for the XPTH within a P&P approach, though not within an HPSG approach as outlined in section 7.6.

Within a case-linked approach, Roberts (2005) in fact makes use of this empty structure: as we have seen, the trigger under his account is *v*, the site through which finite verbs transit as they raise. However, as noted earlier, there is no verb movement within an embedded *i*-clause such as those in (41) to (43) above – and hence, there is no triggering *v*; see also Tallerman (1990: 409). Yet these infinitival clauses nonetheless exhibit syntactic SM on the VP predicate. Again, a case-linked account could presumably give some entirely different explanation for the mutation within *i*-clauses, but Occam's razor suggests that this is not a desirable move.

We turn next to empty nominal categories. Sections 7.2 and 7.6 have already discussed the problems that surround the Caseless empty nominals, PRO and NP-trace, and in section 7.6 we saw that it is desirable to eliminate these two categories, at least within a phrase-based account. Given the importance of maintaining an analysis in which all triggers are adjacent to their targets, any account which assumes that the Caseless empty categories are present at the level at which mutation applies would have serious problems. This is apparently not a problem for the case-linked account: if PRO and trace are regarded as invisible at PF, where mutation applies, they will not prevent the trigger, *v*, from being adjacent to the target. However, what seems to us more problematic for any account within the Minimalist framework is the idea that traces are seen as copies. It is unclear how a copy (as opposed to a trace) could be distinguished from the overt noun phrase itself, but this is an undesirable property for any account of mutation. Within a phrase-based account, a noun phrase copy would itself be a trigger for SM, and under any kind of account, a noun phrase copy ought to block mutation from some preceding trigger. Yet, as we have seen in section 7.2, this is not what happens: a nominal trace/copy is actually inert for mutation purposes; see for instance (15) and (18), repeated here as (58) and (59):

(58)   Mae   Elen wedi dechrau   [~~Elen~~ gyrru   / *yrru   bws].
        be.PRES.3S Elen PERF begin.INF   drive.INF / (+SM) bus
        'Elen has started to drive a bus.'

(59)   Dechreuodd Elen [~~Elen~~ yrru   bws].   (*gyrru*)
        begin.PAST.3S   Elen drive.INF bus
        'Elen started to drive a bus.'

In (59), under the case-linked account, the copy of *Elen* in the embedded clause would be the first element in the complement to *v*, so ought to bear the mutation triggered by *v* (invisibly, of course, since *Elen* does not have a mutable initial consonant). But in fact, the mutation is actually on the *following* constituent, *gyrru bws* (*gyrru* > *yrru*). Roberts (2005: 171–2, n. 21) suggests that a copy could be mutated and then delete, but this gets exactly the wrong result for (59), where what is needed is for the copy to be simply invisible, so that the following constituent is mutated by *v*.[17]

Presumably, either within a phrase-based account or within a case-linked account, one could propose that the mutation applies at some syntactic level at which the unwanted traces/copies, empty nominal elements and excess structure have all been deleted and pruned. The difficulty is that both analyses need to retain *some* non-overt elements in order to account for mutation, because both assume non-overt triggers – for Roberts, *v* is crucial, and for the phrase-based approach, *pro* and *wh*-trace are essential. It is not clear to us what level of structure could be postulated within the P&P framework which retains only the desired empty elements and yet none of the inconvenient ones,

---

[17] An alternative, suggested to us by Ian Roberts (p.c.), is that copies delete and therefore do not affect mutation. Clearly, though, this requires a special statement of what is visible at PF and what is not.

without making ad hoc assumptions. However, the kind of HPSG account proposed by Borsley (1999), outlined in section 7.6 above, would recognize *pro* and *wh*-trace, but excludes the Caseless nominals, so yielding the desired result for the phrase-based approach.

Note finally that a solution based on the XPTH is intrinsically better suited to a syntactic model which assumes a very 'surface' kind of structure, such as HPSG or LFG. It remains to be seen whether any account of syntactic SM which obtains the same level of empirical accuracy can be formulated within the P&P model.

7.8   Conclusion: common ground?

We have outlined in this chapter a number of critical differences between a recent case-linked approach to syntactic SM (Roberts 2005) and recent phrase-based approaches (Borsley & Tallerman 1996, Borsley 1999, Tallerman 2006). It is worth asking, in this brief final section, whether the two approaches have any common ground. The answer is that in fact they do. First, they have in common their adherence to (or a stated aim to adhere to) some version of the Trigger Constraint (see (9) above). In other words, both types of analysis regard it as crucial that triggers for mutation be adjacent to the targets (see, for instance, Roberts 2005: 73). It is worth noting that not all accounts make this assumption. For instance, Zwicky (1984: 387) suggests that in a VSO clause, the trigger for SM on the object is the finite verb, which is of course *not* adjacent to the target. Roberts (2005) essentially retains this view but reformulates it in terms of adjacency, since the trigger is the trace of the moved verb.

Second, all accounts stress that the mutation process 'is sensitive to post-movement configurations only' (Roberts 2005: 71). As we have seen, movement of constituents often makes a difference in terms of availability to undergo mutation. For instance, the fronted object of a finite verb bears no SM (see (25)), while a displaced subject does bear SM in various contexts: see (5), (6) and (39). (See Hannahs & Tallerman 2006 for some discussion of problems concerning the interaction between mutation and other morphophonological processes.) Clearly, whether or not an account literally assumes displacement of constituents depends on the theoretical assumptions made. But all accounts must assume that mutation is triggered at a rather transparent level of structure.

Third, the case-linked approach and recent phrase-based approaches seem to have converged on the importance of the COMPLEMENT relation. Borsley

(1999) explicitly proposes that only complements are targets for syntactic SM, as we saw in section 7.6, and Roberts attempts to build the head-complement relation into his account of *all* mutation processes: see Roberts (2005: 71–4, 88–93), and for some discussion, see Tallerman (2006). As noted in section 7.6, however, not all accounts necessarily agree on what actually constitutes a complement; for Borsley (1999), for instance, complements must include subjects and VP predicates.

There are, then, some areas in which a reasonable amount of agreement occurs across the various approaches. Perhaps the most important remaining challenge for future research on syntactic SM is to formulate an analysis within a P&P framework which not only accounts for all the data discussed in this chapter, but also employs as succinct a generalization as the XPTH.

Note finally that we have concluded in this chapter that syntactic SM is essentially a superficial phenomenon, despite the fact that various empty categories do play a role both in triggering and in blocking the mutation. This observation is noteworthy because chapter 6 suggested that the same is true of agreement in Welsh: it appears to operate on a rather superficial level in the grammar.

8

More on verbal syntax

In this chapter, we discuss some further aspects of verbal syntax. In section 8.1, we look at a number of aspects of the verb *bod* 'be'. Then, in section 8.2, we look at the complex properties of negation. Finally, in section 8.3, we consider valency-changing processes, especially the passive construction and also the impersonal construction.

8.1   The syntax of *bod*

The preceding chapters have highlighted a number of properties of *bod* 'be'. In chapter 2 we looked at aspectual clauses like (1), in which *bod* has a complement containing an aspectual particle and a non-finite verb phrase, and copular clauses like (2), in which *bod* has a non-verbal complement.

(1)   Mae   Rhiannon [yn   cysgu].
       be.PRES.3S Rhiannon PROG sleep.INF
       'Rhiannon is sleeping.'

(2)   Mae   Gwyn [yn   ddiog].
       be.PRES.3S Gwyn PRED lazy
       'Gwyn is lazy.'

We also saw that there is evidence from coordination that there is a single verb *bod* used in both types of sentence. In section 3.3.1, we noted that *bod* has two more tenses than ordinary verbs: the present tense in (1) and (2) and the imperfect tense in (3) and (4).

(3)   Roedd   Rhiannon [yn   cysgu].
       be.IMPF.3S Rhiannon PROG sleep.INF
       'Rhiannon was sleeping.'

(4)   Roedd   Gwyn [yn   ddiog].
       be.IMPF.3S Gwyn PRED lazy
       'Gwyn was lazy.'

We also pointed out that the present and for many speakers the imperfect as well are replaced by the non-finite form *bod* in affirmative declarative complement clauses. Thus, (5) and for many speakers (6) too are replaced by (7).

(5)   *Mae   Aled yn   credu   [**mae**   Elen yn   darllen
        be.PRES.3S Aled PROG believe.INF be.PRES.3S Elen PROG read.INF
        y   llyfr].
        the book
        ('Aled believes that Elen is reading the book.')

(6)   %Mae   Aled yn   credu   [**roedd**   Elen yn   darllen
        be.PRES.3S Aled PROG believe.INF be.IMPF.3S Elen PROG read.INF
        y   llyfr].
        the book
        'Aled believes that Elen was reading the book.'

(7)   Mae   Aled yn   credu   [**bod** Elen yn   darllen y   llyfr].
        be.PRES.3S Aled PROG believe.INF be.INF Elen PROG read.INF the book
        'Aled believes that Elen is/was reading the book.'

We noted, however, that the present and the imperfect do occur in negative declarative and interrogative complement clauses, but that the present tense takes a distinctive form in the third person, *ydy* or *yw* in the singular and *ydyn* in the plural. We also noted in section 4.1.4 that the present tense of *bod* takes the form *sy(dd)* when its subject is extracted, as in (8).

(8)   Beth **sy**   'n   digwydd?
        what be.PRES.REL PROG happen.INF
        'What's happening?'

We also saw in section 4.3.3 that *yw/ydy* appears in examples like the following with a fronted complement.

(9)   a. Diog **ydy**   Gwyn.
           lazy be.PRES.3S Gwyn
           'Gwyn is lazy.'
        b. Athro **ydy**   Gwyn.
           teacher be.PRES.3S Gwyn
           'Gwyn is a teacher.'

There is more to be said about the syntax of *bod*. In particular, we need to discuss variation in third-person forms and the possibility of omitting finite forms of *bod*.

8.1.1   Third-person forms

The present tense of *bod* has distinctive third person forms in negative and interrogative contexts and also in 'if'-clauses. In the singular *yw/ydy* and *oes* appear instead of *mae*, while *ydyn* appears instead of *maen* in the plural. *Yw* and *ydy* appear with a definite subject and *oes* with an indefinite subject. *Yw* occurs in literary Welsh and southern dialects, and *ydy* occurs in northern dialects. With a definite subject, there is a contrast between (10) and (11a)–(11c). The negative and interrogative examples are literary forms.

(10)   **Mae**   Sioned yn   aros.
       be.PRES.3S Sioned PROG stay.INF
       'Sioned is staying.'

(11)   a. Nid **yw**   Sioned yn   aros.
         NEG be.PRES.3S Sioned PROG stay.INF
         'Sioned is not staying.'
       b. A **yw**   Sioned yn   aros?
         Q be.PRES.3S Sioned PROG stay.INF
         'Is Sioned staying?'
       c. os **yw**   Sioned yn   aros
         if be.PRES.3S Sioned PROG stay.INF
         'if Sioned is staying'

As discussed in section 8.2.2, a colloquial counterpart of (11a) would have *dyw* or *dydy* instead of *nid yw* and the negative adverb *ddim* after the subject. A colloquial counterpart of (11b) would lack *a*. Similarly, with an indefinite subject, there is a contrast between (12) and (13a)–(13c). Again, the negative and interrogative examples are literary forms.

(12)   **Mae**   ceffyl yn yr ardd.
       be.PRES.3S horse in the garden
       'There is a horse in the garden.'

(13)   a. Nid **oes**   ceffyl yn yr ardd.
         NEG be.PRES.3S horse in the garden
         'There isn't a horse in the garden.'
       b. A **oes**   ceffyl yn yr ardd?
         Q be.PRES.3S horse in the garden
         'Is there a horse in the garden?'
       c. os **oes**   ceffyl yn yr ardd
         if be.PRES.3S horse in the garden
         'if there is a horse in the garden'

As discussed in section 8.2.3, a colloquial counterpart of (13a) would have *does* instead of *nid oes* and the negative quantifier *dim* before *ceffyl*, i.e. *Does dim ceffyl yn yr ardd*. A colloquial counterpart of (13b) would lack *a*.

The forms *yw, ydy* and *ydyn* also appear in sentences with what appears to be a preverbal adjective phrase or noun phrase complement such as those in (9). As noted in section 4.4, evidence that this constituent is a complement comes from an example like the following, where reconstruction of anaphoric relations is possible and *ei hun* 'himself' may be interpreted as referring to *Ifan*.

(14)   Ei   elyn   gwaethaf ei   hun   yw   Ifan.
         3MS enemy worst   3MS REFL be.PRES.3S Ifan
         'Ifan is his own worst enemy.'

Neither an adjective phrase nor a noun phrase complement may appear in situ. Instead, we have a predicative phrase containing the predicative particle *yn* and an adjective phrase or a noun phrase. Thus, related to the examples in (9), we have not those in (15) but those in (16).

(15)   a. *Mae   Gwyn ddiog.
            be.PRES.3S Gwyn lazy
            ('Gwyn is lazy.')
         b. *Mae   Gwyn athro.
            be.PRES.3S Gwyn teacher
            ('Gwyn is a teacher.')

(16)   a. Mae   Gwyn **yn**   ddiog.
            be.PRES.3S Gwyn PRED lazy
            'Gwyn is lazy.'
         b. Mae   Gwyn **yn**   athro.
            be.PRES.3S Gwyn PRED teacher
            'Gwyn is a teacher.'

One might propose that the initial adjective phrase or a noun phrase is really a predicate phrase with a phonologically empty predicative particle. An overt predicative particle is impossible in pre-verbal position. Hence, it would have to be obligatorily null; compare (9).

(17)   a. *Yn   ddiog yw/ydy   Gwyn.
            PRED lazy   be.PRES.3S Gwyn
            'Gwyn is lazy.'
         b. *Yn   athro yw/ydy   Gwyn.
            PRED teacher be.PRES.3S Gwyn
            'Gwyn is a teacher.'

As noted in section 4.4, there is one situation in which the complement of *bod* must appear pre-verbally. This is in sentences with an identificational interpretation such as the following:

(18)   a. Yr athro   yw/ydy   Megan.
            the teacher be.PRES.3S Megan
            'Megan is the teacher.'
         b. Megan yw/ydy   'r athro.
            Megan be.PRES.3S the teacher
            'The teacher is Megan.'

These examples have no verb-initial counterparts. The following are ungrammatical:

(19)   a. *Mae   Megan yn   yr athro.
           be.PRES.3S Megan PRED the teacher
           ('Megan is the teacher.')

        b. *Mae   'r athro   yn   Megan.
           be.PRES.3S the teacher PRED Megan
           ('The teacher is Megan.')

Identificational sentences normally contain two definite noun phrases but there are examples where the pre-verbal complement is indefinite:

(20)   Rhaff ydy   'r   ateb.
        rope be.PRES.3S the answer
        'The answer is a rope.'   (Jones & Thomas 1977: 49)

When other complements of *bod* occur preverbally, *mae* and *maen* appear. Thus, corresponding to the examples in (21) are those in (22) and not those in (23).

(21)   a. Mae   Gwyn yn   cysgu.
           be.PRES.3S Gwyn PROG sleep.INF
           'Gwyn is sleeping.'
        b. Mae   Gwyn wedi cysgu.
           be.PRES.3S Gwyn PERF sleep.INF
           'Gwyn has slept.'
        c. Mae   Gwyn yn y   dre.
           be.PRES.3S Gwyn in the town
           'Gwyn is in town.'

(22)   a. Cysgu   mae   Gwyn.
           sing.INF be.PRES.3S Gwyn
           'Gwyn is sleeping.'
        b. Wedi cysgu   mae   Gwyn.
           PERF sleep.INF be.PRES.3S Gwyn
           'Gwyn has slept.'
        c. Yn y   dre mae   Gwyn.
           in the town be.PRES.3S Gwyn
           'Gwyn is in town.'

(23)   a. *Cysgu   yw/ydy   Gwyn.
           sing.INF be.PRES.3S Gwyn
           ('Gwyn is sleeping.')
        b. *Wedi cysgu   yw/ydy   Gwyn.
           PERF sleep.INF be.PRES.3S Gwyn
           ('Gwyn has slept.')

    c. *Yn y   dre   yw/ydy   Gwyn.
       in the town be.PRES.3s Gwyn
       ('Gwyn is in town.')

Notice that whereas (21a) contains a Progressive Phrase, the pre-verbal constituent in (22a) looks like a verb phrase. One might, of course, propose that it is really a Progressive Phrase with a null progressive particle, and the fact that it has a progressive interpretation might support such an analysis. However, it would have to be obligatorily null because an ordinary Progressive Phrase is not possible here:

(24)   *Yn   cysgu   mae   Gwyn.
        PROG sing.INF be.PRES.3s Gwyn
        ('Gwyn is sleeping.')

Moreover, a constituent without *yn* is not possible in situ:

(25)   *Mae   Gwyn cysgu.
        be.PRES.3s Gwyn sleep.INF
        ('Gwyn is sleeping.')

The alternation between an in-situ Progressive Phrase in (21a) and what looks like a verb phrase in pre-verbal position in (22a) is rather like the alternation between an in-situ Predicate Phrase in (16a) and (16b) and what looks like an adjective phrase or noun phrase in pre-verbal position in (9a) and (9b). However, as we saw in section 2.2, progressive *yn* and predicative *yn* are two different lexical items. Hence, it is hard to see how there could be a single explanation for the two facts.

8.1.2   Omission of finite forms of bod

A further notable feature of *bod* is that finite forms are sometimes omitted in clause-initial position in colloquial Welsh with certain pronominal subjects. Thus, instead of (26a), we might have (26b).

(26)   a. Wyt   ti   'n   mynd?
          be.PRES.2s you.s PROG go.INF
          'Are you going?'
      b. Ti   'n   mynd?
          you.s PROG go.INF
          'You going?'

It is natural to assume that examples like (26b) involve a phonologically empty form of *bod*. Some evidence for this position comes from the fact that *bod* appears in an associated tag question, whether or not it is overtly present in the main clause. The following illustrate:

(27)   a. Rwyt   ti   'n   mynd, ynd   wyt?
        be.PRES.2S you.S PROG go.INF Q.NEG be.PRES.2S
        'You are going, aren't you?'
     b. Ti   'n   mynd, ynd   wyt?
        you.S PROG go.INF Q.NEG be.PRES.3S
        'You are going, aren't you?'

Bod omission is particularly common with *ti* 'you.s', but it also occurs with *ni* 'we' and *chi* 'you.PL'. Borsley & Jones (2001) note that it also occurs with *fi* 'I' and *nhw* 'they' in the speech of some speakers of southern dialects.

8.1.3   Analyses of bod

Important analytic questions arise about *bod*, notably how many lexical items there are and what determines what form appears in specific situations. These have been addressed in two papers: Rouveret (1996) and Zaring (1996).

Rouveret (1996) proposes that there is a single *bod* in all the examples we have considered. His main aim is to provide an account of the *mae/yw* distinction. He proposes that the complement of *bod* is a stage level predicate, i.e. one which denotes a temporary state, even if it contains an individual level predicate, i.e. one which denotes a permanent state. Thus, he assumes that *yn las* in (28) is a stage level predicate even though the adjective *glas* (which is mutated after *yn*) is an individual level predicate.

(28)   Mae   'r   môr yn   las.
        be.PRES.3S the sea   PRED blue
        'The sea is blue.'   (=Rouveret's (23b))

Similarly, he assumes that *yn (ad)nabod Siôn* in (29) is a stage level predicate even though *adnabod Siôn* is an individual level predicate.

(29)   Mae   Mair yn   (ad)nabod Siôn.
        be.PRES.3S Mair PROG know.INF   Siôn
        'Mair knows Siôn.'   (=Rouveret's (24b))

He proposes that a stage level predicate has a null spatio-temporal external argument, which must be bound by an operator of some kind. The question, then, is how is this argument bound? Rouveret proposes that *mae* and *maen* incorporate an abstract locative clitic, which binds this argument. He also suggests that negatives and interrogatives involve a quantifier which is able to bind this argument and that it is bound by a focus feature in the examples in (9) and (18). He argues that *mae* and *maen* cannot appear in negatives and interrogatives because the locative clitic leaves nothing for the negative and interrogative quantifiers to bind.

This account has a number of questionable features. First, the idea that the complement of *bod* is always a stage level predicate seems quite dubious. Second, it is not obvious that negatives and interrogatives involve quantifiers which bind a variable. Finally, it is not clear why *yw, ydy* and *ydyn* do not appear in examples with a fronted aspect phrase or prepositional phrase: why, that is, we have the examples in (9) and (18) but not those in (22). Hence, we are sceptical about this analysis.

In contrast to Rouveret, Zaring (1996) argues that there are two lexical items: on the one hand, predicational *bod*, which appears in a full set of contexts, and on the other, identity *bod*, which just appears in fronted complement structures. He suggests that this accounts for the fact, highlighted by the contrast between (18) and (19), that identificational interpretations are only available with fronted complement structures. One might suppose that identity interpretations are only available in such structures because they are the only structures which allow *bod* to have a pair of noun phrases as its dependents. As (15b) shows, a noun phrase is not possible as an in-situ complement. However, as Zaring notes, there are examples with an identity interpretation which do not involve a pair of noun phrases, e.g. the following:

(30)   Beth ydy   Siôn ydy   anarferol.
       what be.PRES.3S Siôn be.PRES.3S unusual
       'What John is is unusual.' (=John is unusual)   (=Zaring's (35a))

(31)   Beth mae   Siôn yn ei wneud ydy   gweithio.
       what be.PRES.3S Siôn PROG 3MS do.INF be.PRES.3S work.INF
       'What John is doing is working.' (=John is working)   (=Zaring's (35c))

Here, the fronted complements are probably noun phrases, but this is not true of the subjects *anarferol* and *gweithio*. It looks, then, as if the best explanation for the restriction of identity interpretation to fronted complement structures may be that there is a separate lexical item which only allows such structures.

It seems to us that Zaring's position is quite plausible. However, it raises questions about the relation between a lexical item and its forms since it entails that there are two lexical items, one of which has a subset of the forms of the other. Also it provides no account of why *mae* only allows AspP or PP as a pre-verbal complement, as in (22), and why *yw* only allows adjectival or noun phrases as a pre-verbal complement, as in (9) and (18). It seems to us, then, that *bod* remains an important topic for research.

8.2   Negation

We turn now to negation, which is a particularly complex area of Welsh, discussed in detail in Borsley & Jones (2005). We will look briefly at literary Welsh and then look in more detail at colloquial Welsh.

8.2.1   Negation in literary Welsh

In literary Welsh, as we saw in sections 2.1.2 and 8.1.1, negative main clauses are marked by the pre-verbal particle *ni* (*nid* before a vowel) and negative subordinate clauses have the pre-verbal particle *na* (*nad* before a vowel). Both are optionally accompanied by the negative post-subject adverb *ddim*.[1] Thus, we have examples like the following:

(32)   Nid yw   Gwyn (ddim) yn   darllen.
        NEG be.FUT.3s Gwyn NEG   PROG read.INF
        'Gwyn isn't reading.'

(33)   Gwn   i [nad yw   Gwyn (ddim) yn   darllen].
        know.FUT.1s I   NEG be.PRES.3s Gwyn NEG   PROG read.INF
        'I know Gwyn isn't reading.'

The particles can also be accompanied by a negative subject or object such as *neb* 'no one' or *dim* 'nothing' or by the negative adverbs *byth* and *erioed*. The latter both mean 'never', but differ in that *byth* appears in imperfective contexts and *erioed* in perfective contexts. The following illustrate for *ni(d)*:

(34)   Nid oes   neb   yn yr ystafell.
        NEG be.PRES.3s no one in the room
        'There is no one in the room.'

(35)   Ni   welais   i ddim.
        NEG see.PAST.1s I nothing
        'I saw nothing.'

(36)   Ni   fydd   Gwyn byth yna.
        NEG be.FUT.3s Gwyn never there
        'Gwyn will never be there.'

---

[1] One might suppose that *ddim* is a mutated form, the mutation being triggered by the preceding subject in accordance with the XP trigger hypothesis of chapter 7. However, this element appears as *ddim* in all positions. For example, the following might occur as a notice on a faulty machine:

(i)   ddim yn   gweithio
       NEG PROG work.INF
       'not working'

Thus, it seems that *ddim* is the basic form.

(37)   Ni   fu   Gwyn erioed yna.
        NEG be.PRET.3S Gwyn never   there
        'Gwyn was never there.'

Ddim in (35) is not the adverb that appears in (32) and (33) but the mutated form of *dim*, which is a pronoun. The following show that *neb, dim, byth* and *erioed* can be used in elliptical negative answers, which suggests that they are semantically negative:[2]

(38)   A: Pwy welaist   ti?
           who see.PAST.2S you.S
           'Who did you see?'
        B: Neb
           'No one.'

(39)   A: Beth welaist   ti
           what see.PAST.2S you.S
           'What did you see?'
        B: Dim
           'Nothing.'

(40)   A: Pa   mor aml wyt   ti   'n   gweld Sioned?
           which so often be.PRES.2S you.S PROG see.INF Sioned
           'How often do you see Sioned?'
        B: Byth
           'Never.'

(41)   A: Pa   mor aml wyt   ti   wedi bod   ym Mangor?
           which so often be.PRES.2S you.S PERF be.INF in Bangor
           'How often have you been in Bangor?'
        B: Erioed
           'Never.'

Thus, (34)–(37) show that literary Welsh is a language in which sentences with a number of negative elements have a single negation interpretation.

The verb in a negative sentence sometimes differs in form from the verb in a related affirmative sentence. We saw in the last section that *yw* and *oes* appear in negative sentences where the corresponding affirmative sentences have *mae*. Thus, the affirmative counterparts of (32) and (34), repeated here as (42) and (43), are (44) and (45), respectively.

(42)   Nid yw   Gwyn (ddim) yn   darllen.
        NEG be.PRES.3S Gwyn NEG   PROG read.INF
        'Gwyn isn't reading.'

---

[2] *Byth* and *erioed* also have some important non-negative uses. See Borsley & Jones (2005: section 5.2.4.)

(43)   Nid oes   neb   yn y   stafell.
        NEG be.PRES.3S no one in the room
        'There is no one in the room.'

(44)   Mae   Gwyn yn   darllen.
        be.PRES.3S Gwyn PROG read.INF
        'Gwyn is reading.'

(45)   Mae   rhywun yn y   stafell.
        be.PRES.3S someone in the room
        'There is someone in the room.'

(As was noted in the last section, *yw* appears with a definite subject and *oes* with an indefinite subject.)

The verb in a negative sentence may also differ in form as a result of the mutation effects of *ni(d)*. This triggers soft mutation with *b, d, g, m, ll, rh*, and aspirate mutation with the voiceless stops *p, t, c*. Thus, we have contrasts like the following in literary Welsh:

(46)   a. Caiff   Sioned groeso   cynnes.
           get.FUT.3S Sioned welcome warm
           'Sioned will get a warm welcome.'
        b. Ni   chaiff   Sioned groeso   cynnes.
           NEG get.FUT.3S Sioned welcome warm
           'Sioned will not get a warm welcome.'

8.2.2   Weak negative verbs and negative dependents

We turn now to colloquial Welsh. Here, preverbal *ni(d)* does not occur, but the verb sometimes has a distinctive form. Corresponding to the literary sentences in (32), (34) and (35) are the following:

(47)   Dydy   Gwyn ddim yn   darllen.
        NEG.be.PRES.3S Gwyn NEG PROG read.INF
        'Gwyn isn't reading.'

(48)   Does   neb   yn y   stafell.
        NEG.be.PRES.3S no one in the room
        'There is no one in the room.'

(49)   Welais   i ddim byd.
        see.PAST.1S I nothing
        'I saw nothing.'

Colloquial Welsh normally has *dim byd* as an n-word where literary Welsh has *dim*. (47) and (48) have distinctive verb forms. The initial *d-* is obviously a historical remnant of *nid*. A few other verbs with an initial vowel allow an initial *d-* in the future tense in a negative sentence in certain dialects, for instance, *mynd* and *gwybod* 'know'. (50b) contains a standard northern form, while (51b) contains a more restricted northern form:

(50)   a. Wn   i am hynny.
             know.FUT.1s I for that
             'I know about that.'
         b. Dwn   i ddim am hynny.
             NEG.know.FUT.1s I NEG   for that
             'I don't know about that.'

(51)   a. A'   i yn ôl.
             go.FUT.1s I back
             'I will go back.'
         b. Da'   i ddim yn ôl.
             NEG.go.FUT.1s I NEG   back
             'I will not go back.'

However this is not possible with most verbs. Similarly, some verbs with an initial voiceless stop, *p, t, c*, allow aspirate mutation.

(52)   a. Caiff   Sioned fynd   rwan.
             get.FUT.3s Sioned go.INF now
             'Sioned can/may not go now.'
         b. Chaiff   Sioned ddim mynd   rwan.
             NEG.get.FUT.3s Sioned NEG go.INF now
             'Sioned can/may not go now.'

However, most verbs with an initial *p, t, c* show soft mutation, which is also possible in an affirmative sentence. The following, in which the basic forms of the verbs appear in brackets, are typical examples:

(53)   a. Ganodd   Sioned ddim yn   dda   iawn.   (*canodd*)
             sing.PAST.3s Sioned NEG   PRED good very
             'Sioned did not sing very well.'
         b. Brynodd   Sioned ddim byd.   (*prynodd*)
             buy.PAST.3s Sioned nothing
             'Sioned did not buy anything.'
         c. Dorrodd   Sioned ddim byd.   (*torrodd*)
             cut.PAST.3s Sioned nothing
             'Sioned did not cut anything.'

Hence, it does not seem plausible to attribute the mutation to a phonologically null counterpart of *ni(d)*.

Borsley & Jones (2005: chapter 3) propose that colloquial Welsh negative sentences normally contain a weak negative verb. The examples in (47), (48), (50b), (51b), (52b) contain weak negative verbs which differ in form from their positive counterparts, but such verbs are normally identical in form to positive verbs, which, as noted in section 2.1.2, often show soft mutation. Even when they have a distinctive form they must be accompanied by a negative dependent. Hence the following are not possible alternatives to (47), (48), (52b).

(54)   a. *Dydy   Gwyn yn   darllen.
          NEG.be.PRES.3S Gwyn PROG read.INF
          ('Gwyn isn't reading.')
       b. *Does   dyn yn y   stafell.
          NEG.be.PRES.3S man in the room
          ('There isn't a man in the room.')
       c. *Chaiff   Sioned fynd   rwan.
          NEG.get.FUT.3S Sioned go.INF now
          ('Sioned can/may not go now.')

The negative dependent may be (a) a post-subject adverb, (b) the subject of the verb, or (c) a complement of the verb. (47)–(49) illustrate the three possibilities. Borsley & Jones call this requirement the Negative Dependent Constraint. The following violate the constraint:

(55)   *Wnes   i [weld   dim byd].
        do.PAST.1S I see.INF nothing
        ('I saw nothing.')

(56)   *Dw   i [wedi gweld dim byd].
        be.PRES.1S I PERF see INF nothing
        ('I have seen nothing.')

Here, the bracketed complements contain a negative element. However, the negative element is not the head. Normally a negative constituent has a negative head.[3] These examples can be made grammatical by the addition of post-subject *ddim*, as in the following:

(57)   Nes   i **ddim** [gweld dim byd].
        do.PAST.1S I NEG   see.INF nothing
        'I saw nothing.'

(58)   Dw   i **ddim** [wedi gweld dim byd].
        be.PAST.1S I NEG   PERF see.INF nothing
        'I have seen nothing.'

We see here that colloquial Welsh like literary Welsh allows multiple realizations of negation.

---

[3] For some speakers a prepositional phrase is negative if it contains a negative noun phrase. Thus, some speakers accept examples like the following:

(i)   %Soniodd   Sioned [am   neb].
        mention.PAST.3S Sioned about no one
        'Sioned talked about no one.'

8.2.3   *Negative quantifiers and pseudo-quantifiers*

The preceding examples show that negative pronouns and adverbs play an important role in Welsh negation. Such elements are often known as n-words. Another important Welsh n-word is a quantifier homophonous with the pronoun *dim*, which takes either a bare indefinite noun phrase or a prepositional phrase containing the preposition *o* 'of' and a definite noun phrase as a complement, as in the following:

(59) a. Does   **dim** gwely yn y   stafell.
         NEG.be.PRES.3S NEG bed   in the room
         'There is no bed is in the room.'
      b. Does   **dim** o 'r   dynion yn y   stafell.
         NEG.be.PRES.3S NEG of the men   in the room
         'None of the men is in the room.'

(60) a. Welais   i **ddim** dyn.
         see.PAST.1S I NEG   man
         'I saw no man.'
      b. Welais   i **ddim** o 'r   dynion.
         see.PAST.1S I NEG   of the men
         'I saw none of the men.'

(61) a. Wnes   i ddim gweld **dim** dyn.
         do.PAST.1S I NEG   see.INF NEG man
         'I saw no man.'
      b. Wnes   i ddim gweld **dim** o 'r   dynion.
         do.PAST.1S I NEG   see.INF NEG of the men
         'I saw none of the men.'

The examples in (61) would be ungrammatical without the adverb *ddim* because of the Negative Dependent Constraint. Like the pronoun *dim*, the quantifier *dim* looks like the adverb *ddim* when it is mutated. However, it is clearly a different item. An important difference between the quantifier *dim* and the adverb *ddim* is that the former but not the latter can immediately follow a negative subject. The following illustrate:

(62) Welodd   neb   ddim o 'r   dynion.
      see.PAST.3S no one NEG of the men
      'No one saw any of the men.'

(63) *Does   neb   ddim yn y   stafell.
       NEG.be.PRES.3S no one NEG in the room
       'There's no one in the room.'

Unlike the adverb *ddim*, the adverbs *byth* and *erioed* can follow a negative subject, as the following show:

(64)   Does   neb   byth yn y   stafell.
        NEG.be.PRES.3S no one never in the room
        'No one is ever in the room.'

(65)   Fu   neb   erioed yn y   stafell.
        be.PRET.3S no one never in the room
        'No one has ever been in the room.'

A surprising fact about Welsh negation is that adverb *ddim* may not be immediately followed by an object. Thus, (66) is ungrammatical although (67) is acceptable for many speakers:

(66)   *Fytodd   hi ddim y   siocled.
        eat.PAST.3S she NEG the chocolate
        ('She didn't eat the chocolate.')

(67)   Fytodd   hi ddim hyd yn oed y   siocled.
        eat.PAST.3S she NEG even   the chocolate
        'She didn't even eat the chocolate.'

Instead of (66), colloquial Welsh has the following, in which *mo* is essentially a combination of *dim* and *o*:

(68)   Fytodd   hi mo 'r   siocled.
        eat.PAST.3S she NEG the chocolate
        'She didn't eat the chocolate.'

Mo is also used in literary Welsh. It is inflected like the preposition *o*, as the following show:

(69)   a. Welais   i mono   fo.
           see.PAST.1S I NEG.3MS him
           'I didn't see him.'
        b. Welais   i moni   hi.
           see.PAST.1S I NEG.3FS her
           'I didn't see her.'

Borsley & Jones (2005: section 5.3.2) call *mo* a pseudo-quantifier on the grounds that it doesn't have the kind of partitive interpretation that one expects with a real quantifier. Unlike the quantifier *dim* in (59)–(61), *mo* can only appear within the object of a finite verb for many speakers. Thus, the following are ungrammatical for such speakers:

(70)   *Fydd   Sioned ddim yn yfed   mo 'r gwin.
        be.FUT.3S Sioned NEG PROG drink.INF NEG the wine
        ('Sioned won't be drinking any of the wine.')

(71)   *Fydd   mo 'r   gwin yn   cael   ei   yfed.
    be.FUT.3S NEG the wine PROG get.INF 3MS drink
    ('None of the wine will be drunk.')

As discussed in section 9.5, *mo* had a wider distribution in earlier forms of the language.

8.2.4   Strong negative verbs

Although colloquial Welsh does not have pre-verbal *ni(d)* in main clauses, it does have pre-verbal *na(d)* in subordinate clauses. Thus, (33) is possible in colloquial as well as literary Welsh. A negative dependent is not required here. For Borsley & Jones (2005: sections 3.4 and 3.5), *na(d)*+verb is one of a number of types of strong negative verb, which are not subject to the Negative Dependent Constraint. Colloquial Welsh also has negative subordinate clauses which look just like main clauses, as in (72).

(72)   Wn   i dydy   Gwyn ddim yn   darllen.
    know.FUT.1S I be.PRES.3S Gwyn NEG   PROG read.INF
    'I know Gwyn isn't reading.'

It also has negative subordinate clauses introduced by *bod*, as in (73).

(73)   Wn   i bod   Gwyn ddim yn   darllen.
    know.FUT.1S I be.INF Gwyn NEG   PROG read.INF
    'I know Gwyn isn't reading.'

Another strong negative verb is seen in negative imperatives such as the following:

(74)   Paid/   Peidiwch   â   symud   y   car.
    NEG.IMPER.S/ NEG.IMPER.P with move.INF the car
    'Do not move the car!'

This contains the defective verb *peidio*, which has only imperatives and a non-finite form, whose only content is negation.[4] It is optionally followed by the preposition *â* 'with' (*ag* before a vowel). The non-finite form *peidio* is used to negate non-finite clauses, giving pairs of examples like the following:

(75)   a. Ceisiodd   Gwyn [ateb   y   cwestiwn]
      try.PAST.3S Gwyn answer.INF the question
      'Gwyn tried to answer the question.'
    b. Ceisiodd   Gwyn [beidio (ag) ateb   y   cwestiwn]
      try.PAST.3S Gwyn NEG.INF with answer.INF the question
      'Gwyn tried not to answer the question.'

---

[4] There is also a non-defective verb *peidio* meaning 'stop'.

Notice that *peidio* appears as *beidio* in (75b). This is a standard case of mutation following a subject, discussed in chapter 7.

Further strong negative verbs occur in certain southern dialects. In
particular, these have distinctive negative present tense forms of the copula,
illustrated by (76). The forms *sa, so* and *smo* are dialect variants.

(76)   a. **Sa**   i 'n   gwbod.
            NEG.be.PRES I PROG know.INF
            'I don't know.'
        b. **So**   ni isie hwnna.
            NEG.be.PRES we want that
            'We don't want that.'
        c. **Smo**   fi 'n   mynd â   hwnna.
            NEG.be.PRES I PROG go.INF with that
            'I'm not taking that.'

8.2.5   The licensing of n-words

The Negative Dependent Constraint rules out sentences where a
weak negative verb appears without a negative dependent. It is also necessary
to rule out sentences where a negative dependent appears with an unambiguously positive verb. This means in particular examples with *mae* or *maen*,
discussed in section 8.1.1, and examples with a finite verb preceded by the
affirmative particles *mi* and *fe*, discussed in section 2.1.2.[5]

(77)   *Mae   Gwyn ddim yn   darllen.
         be.PRES.3S Gwyn NEG PROG read.INF
         ('Gwyn isn't reading.')

(78)   *Mi/fe fydd   neb   yn yr ystafell.
         AFF   be.FUT.3S no one in the room
         ('There will be no one in the room.')

For many speakers, an n-word such as *neb* or *dim byd* cannot appear in the
infinitival complement of a finite verb unless it contains *peidio*. Thus, we have
the following contrast:

(79)   a. *Ceisiodd   Gwyn [ddweud dim byd].
             try.PAST.3S Gwyn say.INF   nothing
             'Gwyn tried to say nothing.'
        b. Ceisiodd   Gwyn [beidio (â)   dweud dim byd].
             try.PAST.3S Gwyn NEG.INF with say.INF nothing
             'Gwyn tried to say nothing.'

---

[5] For some further examples of unambiguously positive verbs see Borsley & Jones
(2005: section 3.6).

N-words are also impossible in imperatives unless they contain *paid* or *peidi-wch*, as the following illustrate:

(80)   a. *Ffonia /   Ffoniwch   neb.
           phone.IMPER.S / phone.IMPER.P no one
           ('Phone no one.')
        b. Paid/   Peidiwch   (â)   ffonio   neb.
           NEG.IMPER.S /   NEG.IMPER.P with phone.INF no one
           'Don't phone anyone.'

Borsley & Jones (2005: section 4.4) argue that the n-words are subject to what they call the Negative Context Requirement, which requires them to appear in one of a limited number of 'negative contexts', the most important of which is a constituent headed by a weak or strong negative verb. The ungrammatical examples which we have just considered violate this constraint.

8.2.6   Analyses

The most detailed formal analyses of Welsh negation are the HPSG analyses developed in chapters 8 and 9 of Borsley & Jones (2005). They pay particular attention to the Negative Dependent Constraint and Negative Context Requirement.

Following Borsley (1989a), which was discussed in chapter 2, Borsley & Jones assume that subjects of finite clauses are extra complements. They also argue in chapter 5 that the same is true of post-subject adverbs. This allows them to formalize the Negative Dependent Constraint in chapter 9 as a constraint requiring a weak negative verb to have a negative complement.

Borsley & Jones adopt the standard HPSG assumption that quantifiers, including negative quantifiers, are stored and retrieved from storage at certain clausal nodes which constitute their scope. Within this approach, the contexts in which an n-word can appear can be analysed as contexts which allow a negative quantifier to be retrieved from storage, and the Negative Context Requirement can be formalized as a constraint on the retrieval of negative quantifiers from storage.

Although the most detailed analyses of Welsh negation are within the HPSG framework, there are also P&P analyses of some of the main facts. Rouveret (1994: section 2.4.3) develops an analysis in which negative sentences involve a NegP high in the clause. Within this approach, (47), repeated here as (81), has the structure in (82).

(81)   Dydy   Gwyn ddim yn   darllen.
        NEG.be.PRES.3S Gwyn NEG PROG read.INF
        'Gwyn isn't reading.'

(82) $[_{NegP}$ Neg $[_{AgrSP}$ dydy$_i$ $[_{TP}$ Gwyn t$_i$ $[_{VP}$ ddim $[_{VP}$ t$_i$ yn darllen]]]]]

Rouveret proposes that negative nominals and adverbials including *ddim* move to Spec NegP at LF to satisfy the Neg-criterion of Haegeman (1995) and Zanuttini (1997), which requires a negative operator to be in a Spec-head configuration with a negative head and vice versa. One point to note about this analysis is that it seems to require the postulation of an empty negative operator in cases where there is no overt negative dependent. Willis (2004) develops an analysis in which negative sentences have a NegP low in the clause and *ddim* occupies its specifier position. (Essentially the same analysis was proposed in Rouveret 1991.) Within this analysis, (47)/(81) has the structure in (83). (Willis assumes that finite verbs are in C.)

(83) $[_{CP}$ Neg$_i$-dydy$_j$ $[_{TP}$ Gwyn t$_j$ $[_{NegP}$ ddim t$_i$ $[_{VP}$ t$_j$ yn darllen]]]]

Willis proposes that weak negative verbs have an uninterpretable negative feature, which is eliminated by the minimalist mechanism Agree. Within this approach there is no need to assume an empty negative operator in cases where there is no overt negative dependent. Essentially what Rouveret and Willis provide is an approach to the Negative Dependent Constraint but neither provides a detailed analysis. In particular, they do not consider how examples like (55) and (56) are to be ruled out. Within Minimalism, it would be natural to propose that the negative head and the negative dependent are separated by a phase boundary in such examples, but Borsley & Jones (2005: chapter 10) argue that this approach either allows ungrammatical sentences or excludes grammatical ones depending on the location of Neg. Neither Rouveret nor Willis offer any account of the Negative Context Requirement. Thus, we are some way from a full P&P analysis of Welsh negation.

8.2.7   *Some other negative elements*

Two further negative elements which deserve a mention here are the preposition *heb* 'without' in (84) and the homophonous aspect marker in (85).

(84)   Mae   Sioned wedi croesi   'r   ffordd heb   edrych.
        be.PRES.3s Sioned PERF cross.INF the road   without look.INF
        'Sioned has crossed the road without looking.'

(85)   Mae   Sioned heb   fynd   i   Loegr.
        be.PRES.3s Sioned without go.INF to England
        'Sioned has not gone to England.'

(85) means the same as (86), which is the negative form of an ordinary aspectual clause.

(86)   Dydy   Sioned ddim wedi mynd i   Loegr.
         NEG.be.PRES.3S Sioned NEG PERF go.INF to England
         'Sioned has not gone to England.'

Whereas (86) contains the weak negative form *dydy*, (85) contains the unambiguously positive form *mae*. This suggests that *heb* is a negative head and not
an n-word which must be in a negative context. However, some speakers have
examples like (87).

(87)   Dydy   Sioned heb   fynd i   Loegr.
         NEG.be.PRES.3S Sioned without go.INF to England
         'Sioned has not gone to England.'

It looks, then, as if *heb* may be an n-word for some speakers.
    Two final negative elements are seen in focus sentences, which we discussed
in chapter 4. Consider the following:

(88)   a. Nid/Dim y   dyn welais   i.
            NEG   the man see.PAST.1S I
            'It wasn't the man that I saw.'
         b. Nid/Dim yn yr ardd   mae   Gwyn.
            NEG   in the garden be.PRES.3S Gwyn
            'Gwyn isn't in the garden.'
         c. Nid/Dim darllen llyfr wnaeth   Gwyn.
            NEG   read.INF book do.PAST.3S Gwyn
            'Gwyn didn't read a book.'

Nid is more literary and *dim* more colloquial.[6] Borsley & Jones (2005: section
6.5) suggest that these elements have a focus-negating function. They can also
be used in sentences like the following:

(89)   Welais   i Gwyn, nid/dim Emrys.
         see.PAST.1S I Gwyn NEG   Emrys
         'I saw Gwyn, not Emrys.'

(90)   Pwy welaist   ti?
         who see.PAST.2S you.S
         'Who did you see?'
         Nid/Dim Emrys.
         NEG   Emrys
         'Not Emrys.'

(91)   Dw   i wedi cael   llythyr nid/dim oddi wrth Mair ond
         be.PRES.1S I PERF get.INF letter NEG   from   Mair but
         oddi wrth Sioned.
         from   Sioned
         'I have received a letter not from Mair but from Sioned.'

---

[6] Some speakers use *ddim* here.

Notice that this is the third element *dim* that we have encountered, the others being the pronoun mentioned in section 8.2.1 and the quantifier discussed in section 8.2.3.

8.3   Valency-changing processes

Like most languages, Welsh has a number of valency-changing processes. As in many languages, the most important is the passive. We first discuss this. Then we go on to consider some others.

8.3.1   *The passive*

As is well known, passives involve the demotion or deletion of a subject and the promotion of an object. They were the focus of the earliest work on Welsh syntax within modern syntactic theory, Awbery (1976). In Welsh, the examples in (92) have the passive counterparts in (93).

(92)   a. Tarodd   Rhodri Emrys.
         hit.PAST.3S Rhodri Emrys
         'Rhodri hit Emrys.'
       b. Mae   Rhodri wedi taro   Emrys.
         be.PRES.3S Rhodri PERF hit.INF Emrys
         'Rhodri has hit Emrys.'

(93)   a. Cafodd   Emrys ei   daro   (gan Rhodri).
         get.PAST.3S Emrys 3MS hit.INF by   Rhodri
         'Emrys was hit (by Rhodri).'
       b. Mae   Emrys wedi cael   ei   daro   (gan Rhodri).
         be.PRES.3S Emrys PERF get.INF 3MS hit.INF by   Rhodri
         'Emrys has been hit (by Rhodri).'

As these examples show, Welsh passives standardly contain the auxiliary *cael* 'get', a subject, a non-finite verb preceded by a clitic agreeing with the subject, and an optional PP headed by *gan* 'by'. The non-finite verb in a passive construction cannot be followed by a pronoun, as is normally possible when a verb is preceded by a clitic.

(94)   a. Cafodd   Emrys ei   daro   (*o)   (gan Rhodri).
         get.PAST.3S Emrys 3MS hit.INF him by Rhodri
       b. Mae   Emrys wedi cael   ei   daro (*o)   (gan Rhodri).
         be.PRES.3S Emrys PERF get.INF 3MS hit.INF him by   Rhodri

This is reminiscent of *wh*-questions in which the object of a non-finite verb is questioned. Here too the non-finite verb is commonly preceded by a clitic and cannot be followed by a pronoun.

(95)   Pwy mae   Emrys wedi ei   daro   (*o)?
         who be.PRES.3S Emrys PERF 3MS hit.INF   him
         'Who has Emrys hit?'

We will return to this comparison shortly.

As one might expect, passives allow various kinds of subject. Most commonly the subject bears the patient relation to the non-finite verb, but this is not always the case. Consider first the following:

(96)   a. Mae   Gwyn wedi cael   ei   benodi   'n   gadeirydd.
            be.PRES.3S Gwyn PERF get.INF 3MS appoint.INF PRED chairman
            'Gwyn has been appointed chairman.'
         b. Mae   Gwyn yn   cael   ei   alw   yn   ffŵl.
            be.PRES.3S Gwyn PROG get.INF 3MS call.INF PRED fool
            'Gwyn is called a fool.'

Here it is arguable that the subjects only bear a semantic relation to the predicates *cadeirydd* and *ffŵl*. The active counterparts of these examples in (97) would be analysed in some frameworks as involving a small clause complement.

(97)   a. Maen   nhw wedi penodi   Gwyn yn   gadeirydd.
            be.PRES.3P they PERF appoint.INF Gwyn PRED chairman
            'They have appointed Gwyn chairman.'
         b. Maen   nhw' n   galw   Gwyn yn   ffŵl.
            be.PRES.3P they   PROG call.INF Gwyn PRED fool
            'They call Gwyn a fool.'

There are also examples which seem to involve an expletive subject, for example the following:

(98)   Mae   wedi cael   ei   gadarnhau fod   Nigel Barry wedi
         be.PRES.3S PERF get.INF 3MS confirm.INF be.INF Nigel Barry PERF
         symud   i   'r   clwb o   Ynys Môn.
         move.INF to   the   club from   Anglesey
         'It has been confirmed that Nigel Barry has moved to the club from
         Anglesey.'

Here, it is natural to assume that there is an empty expletive subject.

An interesting fact about passives is that *cael* 'get' is optional after *wedi*. Thus, instead of (93b) the following is possible:

(99)   Mae   Emrys wedi ei   daro   (gan Rhodri).
         be.PRES.3S Emrys PERF 3MS hit.INF by   Rhodri
         'Emrys has been hit (by Rhodri).'

It seems that *wedi* may combine with either an active verb phrase or a passive verb phrase. A consequence of this is that an example like (100) is ambiguous.

(100)   Mae   Gwyn wedi ei   daro.
          be.PRES.3S Gwyn PERF 3MS hit.INF
          'Gwyn has hit him.'
          'Gwyn has been hit.'

The addition of the pronoun after the non-finite verb disambiguates such examples, as (101) shows:

(101)   Mae   Gwyn wedi ei   daro   o.
          be.PRES.3S Gwyn PERF 3MS hit.INF him
          'Gwyn has hit him.'

This is because, as noted above, a non-finite verb in a passive construction cannot be followed by a pronoun.

As noted earlier, passives seem rather like certain *wh*-questions in having a clitic before a non-finite verb and not allowing a following pronoun. If the clitic in *wh*-questions like (95) is associated with a post-verbal trace, one might suppose that the same is true of the clitic in a passive. Things are not so simple, however. First, as noted in section 4.1.5, the clitic is optional in *wh*-questions in which the object of a non-finite verb is questioned. Thus, (102) is also possible:

(102)   Pwy mae   Emrys wedi daro/taro?
          who be.PRES.3S Emrys PERF hit.INF
          'Who has Emrys hit?'

In passives, however, the clitic is obligatory. Thus, (103) is not possible as an alternative to (93a).

(103)   *Cafodd   Emrys daro/taro (gan Rhodri).
          get.PAST.3S Emrys hit.INF   by Rhodri
          'Emrys was hit (by Rhodri).'

Second, there is no clitic in certain other cases where there would be a postverbal trace on standard transformational assumptions. Consider first raising sentences. Here, as noted in section 6.2.2, there is no clitic although on transformational assumptions the raising verb would be followed by a trace. Thus, we have (104) and not (105).

(104)   Mae   Gwyn wedi dechrau [*t* darllen y   llyfr].
          be.PRES.3S Gwyn PERF begin.INF   read.INF the book
          'Gwyn has begun to read the book.'

(105)   *Mae   Gwyn wedi ei   ddechrau [*t* darllen y   llyfr].
          be.PRES.3S Gwyn PERF 3MS begin.INF   read.INF the book
          ('Gwyn has begun to read the book.')

Consider also unaccusative sentences. Here, on transformational assumptions, an example like (106) would have a trace following the non-finite verb *diflannu*, as indicated.

(106)   Mae   o wedi diflannu   *t.*
         be.PRES.3S he PERF disappear.INF
         'He has disappeared.'

However, there is no clitic here, and a clitic is impossible, as (107) shows.

(107)   *Mae   o wedi ei   ddiflannu.
         be.PRES.3S he PERF 3MS disappear.INF

It looks, then, as if the appearance of clitics in passives is probably not a consequence of some general principle.

8.3.2   Other valency-changing processes

8.3.2.1   Other valency-reducing processes

The best known valency-reducing operation is the passive, discussed in section 8.3.1, which primarily has the syntactic effect of promoting direct objects to become subjects, as well as demoting or deleting the former subject, the agent argument. Welsh also exhibits two lexical transitivity alternations which are valency-reducing in the sense of suppressing the agent, though (as with the passive) there are no concomitant morphological effects – such as verbal inflections – to mark this. The first of these is the inchoative (change of state) or anticausative alternation, illustrated in (108) and (109). The (a) sentences show the transitive verbs, which are lexical causatives (section 8.3.2.2), and the (b) sentences the corresponding intransitive verbs, the inchoatives, where the patient argument is the syntactic subject:

(108)   a. Dw   i wedi **toddi**   'r rhew.
            be.PRES.1S I PERF melt.INF the ice
            'I've melted the ice.'
         b. Mae   'r eira wedi **toddi**   dros nos.
            be.PRES.3S the snow PERF melt.INF over night
            'The snow has melted overnight.'

(109)   a. Mae   'r dynion wedi **duo**   eu gwynebau.
            be.PRES.3S the men   PERF blacken.INF 3P faces
            'The men blackened their faces.'
         b. Rhostiwch   pedwar pupur nes bydd   y   croen wedi
            roast.IMPER.2P four   pepper until be.FUT.3S the skin PERF
            duo.
            blacken.INF
            'Roast four peppers till the skin has blackened.'

Other verbs of this kind are numerous, and include *berwi* 'boil', *sychu* 'dry', *drysu* 'confuse/be confused', *deffro* 'wake/wake up' and *siomi* 'disappoint/be disappointed'. Note from the last three cases that not all the alternating verbs in Welsh have an English lexical counterpart which displays the transitive/intransitive alternation.

The second type is the so-called middle alternation, illustrated in (110) and (111). Again, the (a) sentences show the transitive verbs, and the (b) sentences the corresponding intransitive verbs – the middles – where the patient argument is the syntactic subject. The middle is typically characterized as requiring an adverbial element to modify the verb, as in these examples.

(110) a. Rhaid   i   ni **rewi**   'r   ffa.
          necessity to us freeze.INF the beans
          'We have to freeze the beans.'
       b. Dydy   mefus   ddim yn **rhewi**   'n   dda.
          NEG.be.PRES.3S strawberries NEG PROG freeze. INF PRED good
          'Strawberries don't freeze well.'

(111) a. Mae   'r   plant   wedi **gwerthu** 'r ci.
          be.PRES.3S the children PERF sell.INF   the dog
          'The children have sold the dog.'
       b. Mae   llyfrau Cymraeg yn **gwerthu** 'n well nag erioed.
          be.PRES.3S books Welsh   PROG sell.INF   PRED better than ever
          'Welsh books are selling better than ever.'

8.3.2.2 Increases in valency

We note first that Welsh has no equivalent to the familiar dative movement (applicative) process found in English and in many other languages, which takes an indirect object (or other oblique argument) and promotes it to direct object position, with the former direct object becoming some kind of secondary object:

(112) Mae   Aled wedi **rhoi**   'r llyfr i Elin.
       be.PRES.3S Aled PERF give.INF the book to Elin
       'Aled has given the book to Elin.'

(113) *Mae   Aled wedi **rhoi**   Elin y llyfr.
       be.PRES.3S Aled PERF give.INF Elin the book
       ('Aled has given Elin the book.')

In turn, this means that only the direct object (the theme argument in these examples, *y llyfr* 'the book') is eligible for promotion to subject in a passive sentence: unlike in English, there is no possibility of creating a new direct object, which can then undergo passivization:

(114)   *Mae   Elin wedi cael   ei   rhoi   (o) 'r   llyfr   gan Aled.
         be.PRES.3S Elin PERF get.INF 3FS give.INF of the book by Aled
         ('Elin has been given the book by Aled.')

This is grammatical when the direct object is passivized:

(115)   Mae   'r   llyfr wedi cael   ei   roi   i   Elin gan Aled.
         be.PRES.3S the book PERF get.INF 3MS give.INF to Elin by Aled
         'The book has been given to Elin by Aled.'

Welsh does, however, have a valency-increasing causative construction, consisting synchronically of two distinct syntactic patterns. The first occurs with a small set of verbs, including *gorfodi* 'make, force' and *hala* 'make':

(116)   Fydd   o ddim yn   ein **gorfodi**   ni i   adael.
         NEG.be.FUT.3S he NEG PROG 1P force.INF us to leave.INF
         'He won't make us leave.'

(117)   Mae   jyst gweld y   plant   yn   fy **hala**   fi i   lefain.
         be.PRES.3S just see.INF the children PROG 1S make.INF me to cry.INF
         'Just seeing the children makes me cry.'

These occur in the following pattern:

(118)   Mae   X yn   gorfodi/ hala   rhywun   **i wneud** rhywbeth.
         be.PRES.3S   PROG force.INF/ make.INF someone to do.INF something
         'X makes/forces someone to do something.'

This pattern has an unambiguous structure, with a postverbal direct object noun phrase in the matrix clause, and an embedded (control) clause introduced by complementizer *i* (see section 3.5). For instance, within a Principles and Parameters framework, we could suggest a structure of the following kind:

(119)   *gorfodi/hala* **Direct Object** $[_{CP} [_C$ **i**$] [_{TP}$ PRO **verb** Y $]]$

The pattern shown in (119) also occurs in most, though not all, object control contexts, such as the following; see also section 3.5:

(120)   Mae   Alys yn   dysgu   Gwyn i   siarad   Llydaweg.
         be.PRES.3S Alys PROG teach.INF Gwyn to speak.INF Breton
         'Alys is teaching Gwyn to speak Breton.'

The second pattern is as follows; compare (118):

(121)   Mae   X yn   *gwneud* **i rywun**   wneud rhywbeth.
         be.PRES.3S   PROG make.INF to someone do.INF something
         'X makes someone do something.'

This pattern occurs with a larger set of verbs, including *gwneud* 'make', *achosi* 'cause', *peri* 'cause' and *gadael* 'let':

(122)   Mae   hwn yn   **gwneud**   iddyn nhw deimlo 'n   well.
         be.PRES.3S this PROG make.INF to.3P them feel.INF PRED better
         'This makes them feel better.'

(123)   Mae   'r   goeden fawr yn yr ardd   yn **achosi**   i 'r
         be.PRES.3S the tree   big   in the garden PROG cause.INF to the
         tai   gwympo.
         houses   fall.INF
         'The big tree in the garden is making the houses fall down.'

(124)   Bydd   ffôn   yn   eich ystafell wely yn **peri**   i chi
         be.FUT.3S phone   in   2P   room   bed   PROG cause.INF to you
         deimlo   'n   ddiogel.
         feel.INF PRED safe
         'A phone in your bedroom will make you feel safe.'

With this pattern, there is a potential syntactic ambiguity. One possible structure is (125).

(125)   *gwneud/peri/achosi* [$_{CP}$ [$_C$ **i**] [$_{TP}$ [noun phrase] verb Y]]

Here, the *i* is a complementizer marking the start of an embedded clause, and the following noun phrase is the subject of the lower clause. The *i* + noun phrase sequence in infinitival *i*-clauses in general is argued not to be a constituent (Borsley 1986, Sadler 1988, Rouveret 1994, Tallerman 1998); see section 3.6.2. Alternatively, this pattern can have the structure in (126):

(126)   *gwneud/peri/achosi* [$_{PP}$ **i** [noun phrase]] [$_{TP}$ PRO verb Y]

Here, *i* is not a complementizer, but part of a postverbal PP complement in the matrix clause, and the embedded clause is a control clause with no complementizer, at least in the standard case. This is generally accepted as the historically older pattern: see section 9.9.2.2, which reviews proposals for the historical development of the innovative *i*-clause construction.

The likelihood is that the structures in both (125) and (126) are available synchronically for many of the causatives formed with these verbs, so that they are often syntactically ambiguous – as indeed is often the case in English. Furthermore, speakers are often unsure whether or not the embedded clause should take complementizer *i*, so that it is not uncommon to find examples with both an *i*-PP in the matrix clause *and* a complementizer *i* introducing the embedded clause:

(127) Mae   llif   gostyngol y   gwaed   yn   **achosi**   i
       be.PRES.3S flow   reduced   the   blood   PROG cause.INF to
       gelloedd   yr   ymennydd   yn   y   man   hwnnw   [i
       cells   the   brain   in   the   place that.MASC to
       farw   o   ddiffyg   ocsigen].
       die.INF   from   lack   oxygen
       'The reduced flow of blood causes the brain cells in that region to die from
       a lack of oxygen.'

Welsh has no morphological causative, i.e. no specifically causative verbal inflections; this is also the case with the passive (section 8.3.1). Both the constructions in (118) and (121) are known as syntactic or periphrastic causative constructions, because they involve the addition of an extra causative verb into the syntax; as in English, French and German, a causative 'make' or 'let' type verb is added. Both constructions are valency-increasing in the sense that a new causative agent is added to the structure; in (123), for example, *y goeden fawr* 'the big tree' is the causative agent. Note that the addition of the causative verb and its agent argument also results in the formation of a complex (biclausal) structure.

Welsh (like English) also has a large number of lexical causatives, as noted in section 8.3.2.1, such as *toddi* 'melt', *sychu* 'dry', *plygu* 'bend', *troi* 'turn', *codi* 'rise/raise' and many more. As seen in the previous section, these are zero-marked morphologically (i.e. there is no morphology marking them as lexically causative), instead consisting of valency-alternating transitive and intransitive pairs. Lexically related forms (like English *rise* vs. *raise*) also exist, such as *bwyta* 'eat' and *bwydo* 'feed'. There is also a highly productive causative N > V derivational suffix *-eiddio*, parallel to English *-ify/-ize*, as in *modwlareiddio* 'modularize' and *semestereiddio* 'semesterize', *Cymreigeiddio* 'Cymricize (i.e. to make Welsh)', and a far less productive A > V causative derivational suffix *-(h)au*, as in *tristáu* 'sadden' (< *trist* 'sad'), *pruddhau* 'sadden' (< *prudd* 'sad'), *symlhau* 'simplify' (< *syml* 'simple'), *rhyddhau* 'free, liberate' (< *rhydd* 'free').

8.3.3   Impersonals

Awbery (1976) discussed not just passives but also impersonals. Unlike passives, which occur in both literary and colloquial Welsh, impersonals are largely confined to the literary language. The following is a typical example:

(128)   Torrwyd   y   cwpan (gan Megan).
        break.PAST.IMPERS the cup   by   Megan
        'The cup was broken by Megan.'

Like passives, impersonals allow the notional subject to be expressed by a PP
headed by *gan*. Otherwise, however, they are rather different. Blevins (2003)
argues that passives have a different argument structure from the corresponding actives but that impersonals have the same argument structure as the
related active sentences and just do not allow the normal realization of the
subject argument. On this view, impersonals are not the result of a valency-
changing process.

One difference between passives and impersonals in Welsh is that whereas
the auxiliary in a passive agrees with the following subject, impersonal forms
show no agreement and are only marked for tense. A second difference is that
the impersonal construction is not confined to transitive verbs. In fact all
verbs, even *bod*, have an impersonal form. The following illustrate:

(129)   a. Rhedwyd   yno.
           run.PAST.IMPERS there
           'People ran there.'
        b. Eisteddwyd   ar y   gadair gan Mair.
           sit.PAST.IMPERS on the chair by Mair
           'The chair was sat on by Mair.'
        c. Soniwyd   am y   mater gan y   pwyllgor.
           talk.PAST.IMPERS about the matter by the committee
           'The matter was talked about by the committee.'
        d. Yr oeddid   yn   canu.
           PRT be.IMPF.IMPERS PROG sing.INF
           'People were singing.'

A further difference is that there is good evidence that a postverbal noun
phrase in the impersonal construction is not a subject but an object. As noted
in section 6.1, literary Welsh allows an object to be realized by a clitic attached
to a pre-verbal particle. As Comrie (1977) points out, these clitics can appear
instead of or in addition to a postverbal pronoun in impersonal sentences.
This is illustrated by (130).

(130)   Fe 'm gwelwyd   (i).
        AFF 1S see.PAST.IMPERS I
        'I was seen.'

A further point to note is that the object of an impersonal verb is not mutated.
Thus, (131) has the basic form *draig* and not the mutated form *ddraig*.

(131)   Gwelwyd   draig.
        see.PAST.IMPERS dragon
        'A dragon was seen.'

We noted in section 2.6.1 that the object of a finite verb is mutated and that this is true whether or not there is an overt subject. The following illustrate:

(132)   Gwelais   i geffyl.   (*ceffyl*)
         see.PAST.1S I horse
         'I saw a horse.'

(133)   Gwelais   geffyl.   (*ceffyl*)
         see.PAST.1S horse
         'I saw a horse.'

In chapter 7 we proposed that the mutation of objects is one instance of mutation triggered by a preceding phrase. On this approach, the mutation in (133) is triggered by a phonologically empty subject. One might suppose that impersonals have an empty expletive subject. The fact that the object is not mutated suggests, however, that there may be no subject in the syntactic structure of impersonals. The understood subject can act as a controller, as in (134).

(134)   Aethpwyd   ati   i ysgrifennu 'r   ddogfen.
         go.PAST.IMPERS to.3FS to write.INF   the document
         'They went to her to write the document.'

However, this may just mean that control refers to argument structures. Recall that impersonals have the same argument structure as the related active sentences for Blevins (2003).

As noted earlier, there seems to be just one similarity between passives and impersonals, that both allow a *gan*-phrase. However, Awbery (1976: chapter 5) notes that some impersonals do not in fact allow a *gan*-phrase. They are not possible with impersonals with an intransitive or stative verb. Thus, (135) contrasts with (128).

(135)   *Rhedwyd   yno gan Ifor.
         run.PAST.IMPERS there by Ifor
         ('Ifor ran there.')

Similarly, a *gan*-phrase is not possible in (136).

(136)   Gwyddys   yr ateb   (*gan bawb).
         know.PAST.IMPERS the answer   by   everyone
         'The answer is known by everyone.'

8.4   Conclusions

This chapter has explored some further aspects of verbal syntax. We began by looking at some aspects of the verb *bod* 'be', especially variation in third person forms and the possibility of *bod*-omission. Then, we considered the complex properties of negation, highlighting among other things the contrast between weak and strong negative verbs, and the role of negative dependents, including dependents containing negative quantifiers or pseudo-quantifiers, and the licensing of n-words. Finally, we discussed valency-changing processes, especially the passive construction and also the impersonal construction.

9

Historical syntax

In this chapter, we turn to the historical development of Welsh syntax, concentrating mostly on the Middle Welsh period (1150–1500) to the present day. Welsh has undergone major changes in a number of areas, particularly in word order, negation and the syntax of embedded non-finite verbs. This chapter will give an overview of the main changes, as well as looking at some areas of syntax where the language has remained fairly conservative (agreement, *wh*-constructions, noun phrases). The major issues that will be considered are:

(i)	the status of non-VSO word orders in Middle Welsh
(ii)	the grammaticalization of aspect markers
(iii)	the shift of negation from pre-verbal to postverbal position (Jespersen's Cycle)
(iv)	the integration of mutation from phonology into syntax
(v)	the spread of predicate marker *yn* and word-order changes in the syntax of the copula
(vi)	the emergence of main-clause affirmative particles from earlier pronouns
(vii)	the loss of an 'ergative' system of case-marking in embedded non-finite clauses
(viii)	the emergence of clauses introduced by the preposition *i* 'to'

For reasons of space, it has not been possible to discuss every syntactic change. In particular, the emergence of dialectally specific grammatical items, such as the northern past-tense marker *ddaru* and the southern negative marker *smo*, will not be covered. The same applies to syntactic developments before the Middle Welsh period, and to some more minor developments in the Middle Welsh and modern periods (decline of subjunctive; reanalysis of *os* 'if' from a cleft marker to a complementizer) and so on. Examples in this chapter are Middle Welsh (MW) unless marked otherwise as Old Welsh (OW), Early Modern Welsh (1500–1700) (EMW), Modern Welsh (1700–present day) (ModW) or Middle Breton (MB).

9.1   Word order in main clauses

9.1.1   Verb-second structures

Pre-modern stages of all the Brythonic Celtic languages are characterized by a verb-second (V2) constraint in main clauses. While this constraint
has survived in Breton and Cornish, the major development in Welsh finite
main clauses has been the emergence of a dominant VSO word-order pattern.

The most characteristic syntactic pattern of Middle Welsh is the main-
clause construction known traditionally as the abnormal sentence. The term
is rather inappropriate, since the pattern is overwhelmingly the most frequent
one for main clauses. It derives from the perception of a speaker of Modern
Welsh, for whom the norm is VSO order. The abnormal sentence is not verb-
initial; rather some other phrasal constituent precedes the finite verb, which is
itself preceded by a verbal particle in the following basic schema:

(1)   phrase (topic) – pre-verbal particle *a* / *y*(*d*) – finite verb

The pre-verbal constituent is typically one familiar from the preceding
discourse, and it is generally accepted that the abnormal sentence is a
fronting device that allows topic – comment order to be realized (Fife 1988).
The topic – comment nature of the word-order rule has been demonstrated for
a number of Middle Welsh texts. The main studies are Poppe (1989, 1990,
1991a, 1991b, 1993); Watkins (1977c, 1983–4, 1988, 1990, 1993). Examples are
given in (2)–(4). The form of the particle, which is common to the abnormal
sentence and to relative clauses and *wh*-questions, is determined by the nature
of the pre-verbal constituent. It appears as *a* after a nominal element fronted
from subject position, as in (2); or from object position, as in (3); or from the
object of a preposition, as in (4). For further examples of the last type, see
Willis (1998: 89–90).

(2)   **Riuedi   mawr o sswydwyr** a   gyuodassant y uynyd . . .
       numbers large of officials   PRT rise.PAST.3P   up
       'Large numbers of officials got up . . .'   (*PKM* 16.18–19)

(3)   Ac **ystryw** a   wnaeth   y   Gwydyl.
       And trick   PRT make.PAST.3S the Irish
       'And the Irish played a trick.'   (*PKM* 44.11)

(4)   **Y   prenneu ereill** a   deuei   ffrwyth arnunt . . .
       the trees   other PRT come.IMPF.3S fruit   on.3P
       'Fruit grew on the other trees . . .'   (*YSG* 4387–8)

In another form of the abnormal sentence, a non-finite verb (verb-noun) may
be fronted over the auxiliary *gwnuethur* 'do'. In most cases, the direct object,

if there is one, is fronted together with the verb, as in (5), although there are some examples where the object does not move, as in (6). Other complements (for instance, prepositional-phrase complements) and adjuncts may freely move or remain (Lewis 1928: 181–2). In all cases, the particle is *a*. For further examples, see Mac Cana (1997: 188–96).

(5)   [$_{VP}$ Kyrchu   tref arall] **a**   wnawn.
          head.for.INF town other PRT do.PRES.1P
          'We shall head for another town.'   (*PKM* 54.3)

(6)   [$_V$ Gwyssyaw] **a**   oruc   Arthur milwyr yr ynys honn.
          summon.INF PRT do.PAST.3s Arthur soldiers the island DEM.FS
          'Arthur summoned the soldiers of this island.'   (*CO* 922–3)

There is an analogue of this construction in Modern Welsh, where, however, the entire non-finite verb phrase must be fronted, including the object (for examples, see section 4.3.3).

The initial phrase of the abnormal sentence may be adverbial, as in (7), or a fronted prepositional-phrase complement, as in (8), both being followed by the verbal particle *y(d)*:

(7)   Yn Hardlech **y**   bydwch   seith mlyned ar ginyaw . . .
          in Harlech PRT be.FUT.2P seven years   at dinner
          'In Harlech you will be at dinner for seven years . . .'   (*PKM* 45.2–3)

(8)   Ac ar y kynghor hwnnw **y**   trigwyt.
          and on the advice   DEM.MS PRT settle.PAST.IMPERS
          'And on that decision they agreed.'   (*PKM* 20.21–2)

When a predicate adjective phrase or noun phrase is fronted, it is followed by soft mutation of the verb (*bu* becomes *uu* in (9)), but no particle (Richards 1938: 108, Willis 1998: 52):

(9)   Llawen uu   pob un wrth   y gilid   o honunt.
          happy be.PRET.3s every one towards each-other of.3P
          'Everyone one of them was (became) happy towards each other.'
                                                                  (*PKM* 6.17–18)

As recent studies have shown, the abnormal sentence is statistically far and away the commonest word-order pattern in Middle Welsh. Verb-initial main clauses in fact account for an insignificantly small proportion of main clauses, being largely confined to coordination contexts (see section 9.1.3.2 below). The distribution of word-order patterns found in affirmative main clauses in studies of a number of Middle Welsh texts is given in Table 9.1. From there it can be seen that abnormal sentences with fronting account for upwards of 90% of main clauses in all texts, with adverbial phrases, followed by subjects and non-finite verbs and verb phrases, being the most commonly fronted elements.

Table 9.1. *Distribution of word-order patterns in affirmative main declarative clauses in Middle Welsh.*

	word-order pattern						
	verb-second main clauses clause-initial constituent (%)					V1 (%)	sample size
	Adv	S^{NOM}	S^{PRO}	O^{NOM}	V/VP		
Branwen	41	17	16	8	14	4	181
Breuddwyd Maxen	43	5	16	20	8	9	154
Breudwyt Ronabwy	45	12	6	9	26	2	139
Culhwch ac Olwen	25	16	12	12	26	9	253
Ked. Amlyn ac Amic	47	5	7	6	32	3	293
Cyfranc Lludd a Llefelys	39	24	22	4	10	0	67
Manawydan	24	6	31	12	27	0	154
Pwyll	38	11	22	10	17	3	376

Note:
Adv   adverbial phrase/clause (incl. adverbial complement)
S^{NOM} nominal subject   V/VP verb-noun/non-finite verb phrase
S^{PRO} pronominal subject   V1   finite verb in initial position
O^{NOM} nominal object
Sources: Poppe (1989, 1990, 1991a, b, 1993), Watkins (1977c, 1983–4, 1988, 1993).

The status of the abnormal order in Middle Welsh has been controversial. According to a prominent account of the development of Welsh word order, developed originally by Proinsias Mac Cana, topicalization in the abnormal order was a literary fashion in Middle Welsh, unrepresentative of the spoken language of the period. It is claimed that the order was introduced from southeastern dialects, which once formed a dialect continuum with the dialects of Brythonic that subsequently gave rise to Breton and Cornish, and which supposedly formed the basis of the literary language (Mac Cana 1973, 1979, 1991, 1992: 62–6; Fife 1988: 126–9; Fife & King 1991; see also McCone 2006: 16–17). This hypothesis is intended to account for a paradox in the history of the language. In Old Welsh both the verb-initial order as in (10) and the abnormal order as in (11) are attested. Although the evidence is sparse and difficult to interpret, it has generally been assumed that the verb-initial pattern was the usual one (Mac Cana 1973: 113; Watkins 1987).

(10)   . . . imguodant   ir   degion   guragun   tagc . . .   OW
        . . . declare.PAST.3P the noblemen make.IMPER.1P peace
        'The noblemen declared "Let us make peace."'   (Surexit)

(11)   Gur dicones   remedaut elbid anguorit...   OW
        man create.PAST.3S wonder   world PRT+1P.ACC+redeem.PRES.3S
        'The man who created the wonder of the world redeems us . . .'

                                                                (Juv. 5a–b)

Similarly, in contemporary Welsh, verb-initial orders predominate. It is
therefore tempting to believe that the intermediate period must also have seen
dominant verb-initial main-clause order.

   However, there is considerable evidence against this. First the 'abnormal'
pattern is the dominant main-clause order in all medieval Brythonic languages, and its properties are virtually identical in all three. Examples from
Middle Breton are given in (12)–(15). Note in particular that the use of particles is identical in the two languages: *a* after a subject in (12) or object in (13);
e(z) (Middle Welsh *y(d)*) after an adverbial phrase in (14); and no particle but
a soft mutation (*bizy* becomes *vizy*) after a predicate noun phrase in (15).
Moreover, since similar topicalization structures are productive in modern
Breton, there is no reason to doubt their true productivity in earlier stages of
that language.[1]

(12)   Cesar **a** respontas   deze...   MB
        Caesar PRT reply.PAST.3S to.3P
        'Caesar replied to them . . .'   (Ca. 12)

(13)   ...hac an holl doueouse... **a** meux   an oll   MB
        and the all gods-those PRT have.PRES.1S the all
        dispriset . . .
        renounce.PASTPART
        '. . . and I have renounced all those gods . . .'   (Ca. 8)

(14)   ...hac en continant **ez** aparissas   an eal   dezy   MB
        and immediately PRT appear.PAST.3S the angel to.3FS
        '. . . and immediately the angel appeared to her . . .'   (Ca. 13)

(15)   Ma guir cares **vizy**...   MB
        my true love be.FUT.2S
        'You shall be my true love . . .'   (*B* 506)

Middle Breton also has fronting of non-finite verbs, just like Middle Welsh.
As in Middle Welsh, either a non-finite verb alone, or a non-finite verb
phrase may be fronted over auxiliary 'do' (*ober*). The former option is
illustrated in (16), paralleling (6); the latter option is illustrated in (17),
paralleling (5).

---

[1] For statistical studies of the distribution of the various word-order patterns in a
   Middle Breton text, see George (1987–8, 1990).

(16)   ... [ᵥ fezaff]   agra   en holl tut   sauant: MB
                    beat.INF PRT+do.PRES.3S the all   people wise
        '... she beats all the wise people ...'   (Ca. 12)

(17)   [ᵥₚ Gouuernn en splann   un queffrann didann haff an bet ...
             govern.INF in splendour a   part   under.1S   the world
        euel penn] a   mennaff...   MB
        as head PRT want.PRES.1S
        'I want to govern in splendour a part of the whole world under me as its
        head ...'   (B 34)

A similar variety of orders is attested in Cornish (George 1990, 1991). Further
syntactic similarities in points of detail discussed below also lead to the conclusion that the abnormal order in Middle Welsh is sufficiently close to the
other medieval Brythonic Celtic languages that speakers of Middle Welsh
must have had productive control over the complexities of the construction,
and that it therefore reflects spoken usage.

These word-order patterns have been interpreted as a verb-second (V2)
constraint in Middle Welsh (Willis 1998) and Modern Breton (Borsley &
Kathol 2000; Schafer 1994, 1995), and such a constraint appears to have held
for all three medieval Brythonic languages. This V2-constraint is broadly
comparable to that in modern continental Germanic languages, such as
German, Dutch and Swedish. Extending standard analyses of verb-second,
we can suppose that the particle is a complementizer (in C). It agrees in form
with the topic constituent, which moves to precede it, thereby forming the
specifier of the complementizer phrase. If phrases are limited to having only
a single specifier position, then there is therefore a unique clause-initial topic
position. The movement is analysed as A'-movement, of the same type as
the movement of the *wh*-word in *wh*-questions. Whether the verb also raises
to C in medieval Brythonic languages as in Germanic is difficult to determine. In the following discussion it will be assumed that the verb raises
to adjoin to particles in C. Thus the left edge of a main clause will have
the general form given in (18), a formal instantiation of the basic template
given in (19).

(18)

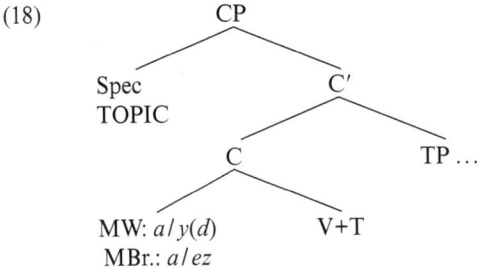

(19)   phrase (topic) – preverbal particle *a* / *y(d)* / ø – finite verb

There are a number of other properties of verb-second topicalization in the medieval Brythonic languages that make it parallel to A′-movement in *wh*-constructions. Long-distance topicalization is possible from an embedded non-finite clause. This pattern, which is illustrated in (20), is exactly the same pattern as that found in Middle Welsh relative clauses (see section 9.10 below) (for further examples, see Willis 1998: 87–8). Here *toat y neuad* 'the ceiling of the hall' is the subject of the verb *bot* 'be' in the embedded clause, but is topicalized to initial position in the main clause, across a clause boundary. The freedom to topicalize from an embedded clause into a main clause is not a self-evident property, and it is difficult to see how someone applying a literary rule would know that the literary rule allowed this quite complex construction. Even more striking is the fact that Middle Breton permits exactly the same construction, illustrated in (21), where *houz seruicheres espressaff* 'your most obedient servant' has been topicalized from its position in the embedded clause. The only sensible conclusion is that this construction is inherited from late Brythonic, which inevitably entails that it was a living part of the language.

(20)   **Toat y neuad** a   tebygei   y   vot   yn   eur oll.
ceiling the hall   PRT suppose.IMPF.3S 3MS.GEN be.INF PRED gold all
'The ceiling of the hall he supposed to be all gold.'   (*BM* 3.3)

(21)   **Houz seruicheres espressaff**   ez   vennaff   bezout . . .   MB
your servant   most.obedient PRT want.PRES.1S be.INF
'Your most obedient servant I wish to be . . .'   (*B* 517)

Furthermore, reconstruction of binding relations is found in Middle Welsh V2-structures. Thus, in (22), *y* 'his' is understood as having *neb* 'anyone' as its antecedent. It is normally assumed that a quantifier such as *neb* must c-command an element in order to serve as its antecedent (quantifier binding). In *wh*-structures in many languages, however, reconstruction effects obtain, and binding operates as though the moved element was in its original position. This is what we have here. For binding to take place, *y geuyn* 'his back' needs to be c-commanded by *neb* 'anyone', and hence for binding it must be interpreted in its base position as the object of *dangos* 'show'. For this to happen *y geuyn* must have topicalized (undergone A′-movement) from a lower clausal position, one after and below *neb*. This is the sort of behaviour that general properties of *wh*-constructions in other languages lead us to expect, but it is a property that someone applying an artificial literary rule would be unlikely to devise for themselves. Adherence to complex rules of this type should therefore also be taken as evidence that the 'abnormal sentence' was a productive and living feature of Middle Welsh.

(22)   Nyt y   geuyn a   dyly   neb   y   dangos
        NEG 3MS.GEN back   PRT should.PRES.3S anyone 3SM.GEN show.INF
        y   elynnyon . . .
        to+3MS.GEN enemies
        'It is not his back that anyone should show to his enemies . . .'
        (i.e. 'No one should show his back to his enemies.')

(YCM 140.26–7)

The verb-second system is complicated somewhat by rules of adverb placement. There has been considerable discussion in the literature on 'multiple
frontings' in the Middle Welsh abnormal sentence. These are instances where
a number of constituents precede the verb, leaving it apparently in third or
even fourth position or later. An extreme example is given in (23).

(23)   Ac [o 'r dywed] [gan wuyhaf grym a   llafvr] [gwedy kaffael
        and of the end   with greatest power and toil   after   get.INF
        o 'r Brytanyeyt penn e   mynyd], [en e   lle] [wynt] a
        of the Britons   top the mountain in the place they   PRT
        dangossassant . . .
        show.PAST.3P
        'And in the end with the greatest power and toil once the Britons had
        gained the top of the mountain in that place they showed . . .'

(BB 795–7, Poppe 1991b:178)

It has been suggested that the multiple frontings are an indication that the
abnormal sentence in Middle Welsh is a literary device pursued to extremes
(Fife & King 1991:89–90). Tallerman (1996) suggests that these cases motivate
an analysis of the Middle Welsh abnormal sentence as multiple adjunction of
both arguments and non-arguments to CP.

The most important objection to these analyses is that, in cases of multiple
fronting, apart from clear instances of left dislocation, all the pre-verbal elements except one must be non-argument adverbials. A maximum of one of the
pre-verbal constituents may be an argument, and this argument must 'count'
for the purposes of determining the form of the pre-verbal particle. So, in (23),
the particle is *a*, the form required by the single fronted argument of the verb,
namely the subject *wynt* 'they'. All the other fronted elements are adverbial.
This is the typical pattern. Crucially, we never find two arguments, say a
subject and an object, or a subject and prepositional-phrase complement, in
fronted position.

Adverbs may be placed before a topicalized argument as in (23) and (24), or
between the topicalized argument and the pre-verbal particle, as in (25).
Again, the facts are the same in Middle Welsh, in the (a)-examples, and in
Middle Breton, in the (b)-examples. The Cornish data are generally parallel

(see George 1991: 212). As before, the strict parallelism across the medieval Brythonic languages suggests a productive, inherited system.

(24) a. **[Hir bylgeint]** Guydyon a   gyuodes.
          early.morning Gwydion PRT get.up.PAST.3S
          'Early next morning, Gwydion got up.'   (*PKM* 82.5–6)
      b. ...ha **[goudese]** ny a   rento   dict respond.   MB
          and after.this we PRT give.FUT.3s to.2s response
          '... and after this we shall give you a response.'   (Ca. 6)

(25) a. Gwalchmei **[yn ieuenctit y   dyd]** a   deuth   y dyffryn ...
          Gwalchmai in youth   the day PRT come.PAST.3S to valley
          'Early in the day Gwalchmai came to a valley ...'   (*P* 59.9–10)
      b. ...ha neuse an rouanes **[dre   an carantez he deffoye**
          and now the queen   through the love   have.PAST.3FS
          cõmeret   ouz   an guerhes sanctes Cathell,] a
          take.PASTPART towards the virgin saint   Catherine PRT
          yez   en   nos ...   MB
          go.PAST.3S in.the night
          '... and now the queen through the love that she had taken towards the
          virgin saint Catherine went in the night ...'   (Ca. 19)

Adverbs preceding the topic can be analysed as adjoined to the top of the clause (CP). Since left-dislocated elements are generally considered to adjoin to CP, such an analysis predicts that left-dislocated elements and adverbs will be ordered freely relative to one another. This prediction is indeed borne out. In (26), for instance, an adverbial clause (*rac guelet ...* 'lest I should see ...') precedes a left-dislocated phrase (*punt ...* 'a pound ...'), which is doubled by an object clitic (*'e*) later in the clause.

(26) Arglwyd ... [rac guelet gwr kyuurd   a thidi   yn y   gueith
      lord   lest see.INF man of.such.rank as you.REDUP in the act
      hwnnw], [punt a   geueis   i o   gardotta], mi a 'e
      DEM.MS pound PRT receive.PAST.1S I from beg.INF I PRT 3S.ACC
      rodaf   it ...
      give.PRES.1S to.you
      'Lord ... lest I should see a man of such rank as you in that act, a pound
      that I received from begging, I shall give (it) to you ...'   (*PKM* 62.9–11)

Adverbs appearing between the topic may be analysed as adjoining to C′, or to some phrase within a split CP, or to TP if the verb does not raise to C. The result is that a unique topic position is maintained. Consequently there is only one landing site for movement to a pre-verbal position, and only one argument may be moved there. Adverbials on the other hand may be freely adjoined around this topic. The basic tree-structure for the verb-second construction is given in (27), representing the template in (28) (Willis 1998: 58–78; cf. Poppe 1989: 51).

(27)

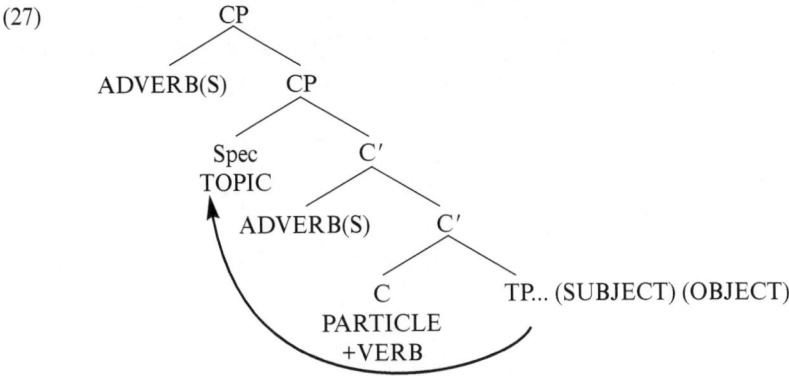

(28)   (adv$_1$ – adv$_2$ – adv$_3$ . . .) – topic – (adv$_4$ – adv$_5$ – adv$_6$ . . .) particle verb (subject) (object)

Breton has essentially maintained this system to the present day (see Schafer 1995; Stephens, 1982), although perhaps with less tolerance of adjoined adverbs. In Welsh, however, topicalization of constituents other than subjects and adverbs became less frequent. The evidence of informal texts suggests that by the seventeenth century the spoken language alternated only between VSO and SVO order in main clauses. The verb-second constraint, which required a pre-verbal topic in most main clauses, was lost. A crucial role seems to have been played by the phonological erosion of the preverbal particles, omitted (or used interchangeably) in informal texts from the sixteenth century. Omission of *a* after a subject topic is shown in (29); and omission of *y(d)* after an adverbial topic in (30) (see also Evans 1968a: 335; Willis 1998: 188–9). In both cases, the position where the particle would have appeared in earlier Welsh is marked as ø.

(29)   . . . Jessu ø gwnnwys   y   olwc y vynydd . . .   EMW
        Jesus   raise.PAST.3S 3MS.GEN look up
        'And Jesus looked up.'   (*RhG* i.85.16–17, 1550–75)

(30)   Yn vffern ø peraist   gyffro . . .   EMW
        in hell   cause.PAST.2S commotion
        'In hell you caused a commotion . . .'   (*TWRP*, 'Y Dioddefaint' 825, 1552)

It seems that the loss of the particles in speech obscured the nature of the verb-second constraint, and triggered a reanalysis in the structural position of pre-verbal adverbs (Evans 1968a: 336–7, Willis 1998: 190–200). Recall that, in Middle Welsh, a pre-verbal adverb could fill the topic position, but could also simply be disregarded for calculating the verb-second rule. When it filled the topic position, for instance when it was the only pre-verbal constituent (as in (7) above), this fact was shown by the appearance of the pre-verbal particle *y(d)*. On the other hand, adverbs in multiple fronting constructions such as (23)–(26) would have been in adjoined positions, and did not trigger topic-particle agreement. Thus, in (26), the particle is *a* despite all the adverbials, because the topic position is filled by the subject. The particle system thus helped distinguish between two types of adverbial: those that determined the choice of particle and counted for determining verb-second, and those that did not determine the particle and did not count for verb-second.

With the loss of the particles, the distinction between adverbials in the topic position and those in adjoined positions was lost. For instance, in (30), there is no particular reason to suppose that *yn vffern* 'in hell' is in topic position, because it is no longer necessary to assume this in order to explain the choice of the pre-verbal particle. Consequently, an analysis would be possible with *yn vffern* in adjoined position with the clause having no syntactic topic at all.

Since adjoined adverbs are typically optional, it would be expected that a clause like (30) would have a grammatical counterpart without the adverb, that is, an absolute verb-initial main clause. Such clauses begin to be attested freely from the sixteenth century, outside of the limited environments (typically coordination) where they were allowed previously (for further examples, see Willis 1998: 196):

(31)   Gorvüost   ar dy   elynion ...   EMW
        overcome.PAST.2S on 2S.GEN enemies
        'You overcame your enemies . . .'   (*RhG* i.22.28–9, *c.* 1514)

Affirmative SVO orders remained alongside the new VSO patterns. Since the sixteenth century, however, the use of SVO order in Welsh has declined to the extent that it has disappeared entirely from most dialects in neutral main clauses. Extensive variation between SVO and VSO, showing complex stylistic conditioning, appears in prose texts from the sixteenth century on (Currie 2000; Willis 1998: 251–6). The shift is partly due to the emergence of affirmative markers from preverbal pronominal subjects (see section 9.1.2 below), and to the continued spread of periphrastic verb-initial constructions (see section 9.2.1 below), as well as competition from VSO orders of the type in (31). On agreement patterns in verb-second structures, see section 9.3.2 below.

9.1.2 Expletive subjects and the emergence of the pre-verbal particle fe

Alone among the medieval Brythonic languages, Middle Welsh had a fully productive expletive-pronoun construction.[2] The expletive subject *ef* (the masculine third-person singular pronoun) appears in the pre-verbal topic position when the clause contains no other topic constituent:

(32) **Ef** a   doeth   makwyueit a   gueisson ieueinc y
      it PRT come.PAST.3S squires   and lads   young to+3MS.GEN
      diarchenu . . .
      disrobe.INF
      'There came squires and young lads to disrobe him . . .'   (*PKM* 4.8–9)

Effectively, then, *ef* acts as a dummy topic when the clause lacks a real topic.

Expletive subjects are restricted in their distribution in Middle Welsh. They are found with unaccusative intransitive verbs in presentational contexts as in (32). In this case the only restriction on the subject is that it should refer to an entity new to the discourse, whether it is definite or indefinite. They also occur as the subject of impersonal forms of the verb:

(33) . . . ac eissoes **ef** a   anet   meibon idaw   ef . . .
      and yet   it PRT be.born.PAST.IMPERS sons   to.3MS him
      '. . . and yet sons were born to him . . .'   (*YCM* 30.6–7)

A third environment for the expletive subject is in main clauses with an extraposed clausal argument. In (34), the clausal subject of *damweinaw* 'to happen' is (obligatorily) extraposed rightwards. An expletive subject must appear in the pre-verbal topic position.

(34) A   gwedy gwascaru y   llu   dan y   coedyd **ef** a
      and after scatter.INF the force among the woods it PRT
      damweinawd y Ywein . . . [kyrchu y   coet . . .]
      happen.PAST.3S to Owain   attack.INF the forest
      'And after scattering the force among the woods, Owain . . . happened to
      attack the forest . . .'   (*BT* 96.28–9)

The expletive subject *ef* is only ever found in pre-verbal topic position. Where there is some other topic in a main clause, or in a subordinate clause, it is never found. Note that *ef* is comparable in the contexts in which it appears to the English expletive subjects *there* and *it*.

---

[2] The Breton interrogative marker *hag-eñ* derives historically from the conjunction *hag* 'and' and an expletive pronoun *eñ* 'it'. This suggests that an expletive construction was once available throughout Brythonic. Modern Breton also has an 'expletive verb' *bez'* (< *bezañ* 'be'), used rather like Middle Welsh *ef*.

Although this represents the distribution of the expletive subject in canonical Middle Welsh texts, by late Middle Welsh (from the end of the fourteenth century at the latest) the range of contexts in which the expletive subject is found expands to include clauses with transitive verbs:

(35)   **Ef** a   danuon   Duw ... taryan itt...
        it PRT send.PRES.3S God   shield to.you
        'God will send a shield to you ...'   (*YSG* 247–8)

There was a sharp increase in the use of this construction in the late sixteenth and seventeenth centuries, evidenced in less literary texts. At this period the expletive subject appears in various reduced forms such as *fo, fe* and *e. Fo* is a phonologically reduced form of the reduplicated (strong) pronoun *efo* plus pre-verbal particle *a*; *fe* is a reduced form of a variant of this, *efe. E* is the direct descendant of the Middle Welsh expletive *ef a*. The pronoun was reanalysed as a verbal particle (affirmative main-clause complementizer). Compare *vo* in (36), which seems essentially to function as an affirmative marker.

(36)   ...**vo** drôdd   dy   atteb   y lleuad y 'w   gwrthwyneb.
        PRT turn.PAST.3S 2S.GEN answer the moon to 3SF.GEN reverse
        '... your answer turned the moon around.'   (*TCh* 10.117–18)

The three forms competed as pre-verbal particles for a while, with *fe* coming to dominate in late Modern Welsh.

The spread of this construction in Welsh naturally led to a significant increase in the frequency of VSO word orders, and has been a significant factor in the spread of dominant VSO word order in Modern Welsh.

9.1.3   Verb-initial order

9.1.3.1   Absolute and conjunct verbal morphology

Old Welsh shows some survivals of an earlier division between what are traditionally referred to as absolute and conjunct verbal endings, found productively in Old Irish (Cowgill 1975, Isaac 1993, 2000, McCone 1979, 1987, 2006, Meid 1968, Sims-Williams 1984, Watkins 1963). Absolute forms were used when the verb stood at the beginning of the sentence, with conjunct forms elsewhere. Although the distinction had largely been lost before Old Welsh, some evidence of it remains. In the third-person singular some absolute forms in -*(h)it* and -*yt* are found in Old Welsh. In (37), the absolute form of the third-person singular past tense of the verb 'give' is found, *rodesit*, rather than the conjunct form *rodes* that is generalized later. For further examples of absolute forms in Old and Middle Welsh, see Rodway (2002).

(37)   Rodesit   Elcu guetig   *equs* . . .
        gave.PAST.3S.ABS Elgu afterwards horse
        'Elgu gave afterwards a horse . . .'   (Surexit)

The existence of absolute verbal morphology points to an earlier stage of the Brythonic languages where VSO was the unmarked order in main clauses, or at least a major word-order pattern. The most likely scenario for the earlier development of Brythonic word order is that VSO word order gave way to a verb-second system as a clefting (focus) construction was generalized to all main clauses (Willis 1998: 97–101) (on the clefting construction, see also section 9.7.2 below). This is a variant of the earliest view (Richards 1938: 104–6, Evans 1968a) that the 'abnormal' verb-second order was the result of the influence of clefts on the SVO order. For other views, see Lewis (1942) and Mac Cana (1973). Lewis argues that pre-verbal particles were inserted into SVO structures to host object clitics. Mac Cana (and following him Isaac 1996) suggests that the abnormal sentence developed from left-dislocation structures.

Even in the later medieval Brythonic languages verb-initial orders do appear, but they are restricted to well-defined environments, most notably in coordination contexts and with the verb 'be'. It is to these special cases that we now turn.

9.1.3.2 VSO in coordination contexts

In all the medieval Brythonic languages verb-initial orders appear productively in the second of a pair of conjoined clauses (and any subsequent clauses). The pre-verbal particles provide clear evidence for the syntactic structure involved. Middle Welsh and Middle Breton data are presented here, following the analysis in Willis (1997). For Cornish, see George (1990: 231).

In two clauses sharing a subject in pre-verbal topic position in both clauses, the second subject may be omitted. This is illustrated for Middle Welsh in (38a) and for Middle Breton in (38b). In (38a), *mi* 'I' acts as the subject of both conjoined clauses. Despite this, syntactic effects remain: the particle *a* in the second clause indicates agreement with a subject topic. This indicates that the coordination is at a level below the subject but above the verb: subject [[particle – verb] AND [particle – verb]].

(38)   a. . . . **mi** [a rodaf   Pryderi a Riannon it]   ac   [a
            I   PRT give.PRES.1S Pryderi and Rhiannon to.you and PRT
            waredaf   yr hut a   'r lletrith y   ar Dyuet].
            remove.PRES.1S the spell and the magic   from on Dyfed.
        '. . . I shall give Pryderi and Rhiannon to you and remove the spell and
        magic from Dyfed.'   (*PKM* 64.18–20)

b. goudese **hon saluer Iesus-Christ** [a   aparissas   dezy gant
after.this our saviour Jesus Christ PRT appear.PAST.3S to.3FS with
vn nompr bras a aelez ha guerheset] hac [alauaras
a number big of angels and virgins   and PRT+say.PAST.3S
dezy . . .]   MB
to.3FS

'After this our saviour Jesus Christ appeared to her with a great number of
angels and virgins and said to her . . .'   (Ca. 21)

In both of the examples in (38), the second clause is apparently verb-initial,
but the particle *a* preceding the verb in this clause indicates that there is a
nominal (subject or object) topic. In (38), the presence of *a* could be because
the second clause shares a nominal topic with the first.

Consider now (39), where the topic in the first clause is an adverbial (*yna*
'then' in (39a)), triggering the particle *y(d)/ez*. The presence of the particle
a in the second clause cannot be due to this adverb, since *a* requires a
nominal topic. The two clauses do not therefore share a single topic, and
we cannot suggest that the coordination is at a level below the adverb as we
did before. The only solution seems to be to suggest an understood topic in
the second clause, syntactically, a non-overt (null) topic in the topic position of the second clause (marked as __). This topic is understood as referring to *Sabot*, and acts as the topic of the second clause; it is also the
understood subject; hence we find particle *a*. Essentially, then, the syntax
and semantics of this example makes sense only if we understand *Sabot* in
place of the gap __. The Breton example in (39b) is essentially identical but
with a clausal adverbial *euel maz testify an scriptur sacr* 'as the holy scripture testifies'. Once again, the near identity in structure in a complex construction between Middle Welsh and Middle Breton suggests that speakers
of Middle Welsh had a productive, non-learnèd grasp of the syntax of this
construction.

(39)   a. . . . ac [**yna** y kyuodes   sabot] ac [__ a elvis
and then PRT arise.PAST.3S Sabot and __ PRT call.PAST.3S
ar bovn . . .]
on Bown
'And then Sabot arose and called on Bown . . .'   (*YBH* 2825–6)
        b. . . . **euel maz testify**   **an scriptur sacr**, ez cryont
like as   testify.PRES.3S the scripture holy PRT cry.PRES.3P
vengeancz, hac à so alyes dré   punition   diuin
vengeance and PRT is often through punishment divine
castiet   en   betman . . .   MB
punish.PASTPART in.the world.this
'. . . as the holy scripture testifies, they cry vengeance and are often
punished in this world . . .'   (GK 2.96.4–6)

An analysis containing understood (non-overt) topics is further supported by the fact that in some cases a particle in the second of a pair of conjoined clauses does not seem to be conditioned by a single element in the first clause. In (40), the particle in the final clause is *a* and the verb in that clause is plural, evidently to be understood as having 'Peredur, Bwrt and Galâth' as its subject. The particle *a* is triggered by a nominal element, hence we must understand the topic of the final clause to be a subject noun phrase referring to 'Peredur, Bwrt and Galâth'. However, the preceding context never actually contains such a noun phrase, only *Paredur a Bwrt* in the first clause and *Galaath* in the second.

(40)   Ac yna [**Paredur a   Bwrt**$_i$ a   gymerassant y   tal blaenaf y 'r
        and then Peredur and Bwrt PRT take.PAST.3P the end front   to the
        tabyl], a [**Galaath**$_j$ ehun a   gymerth   y   tal   arall], ac
        table   and Galâth 3MS.self PRT take.PAST.3S the end   other and
        [___$_{i+j}$ a   aethant   ac ef tua   'r   dref].
        ___$_{i+j}$ PRT go.PAST.3P with it towards the town
        'And then Peredur and Bwrt took the front end of the table, and Galâth himself took the other end and (they) carried it towards the town.'
                                                               (*YSG* 5599–5601)

Clauses introduced by Middle Welsh *y(d)* or Middle Breton *ez* + a verb are often analysed as VSO. Almost all of the cases of verb-initial order in Table 9.1 are of this type. Examples of the sort of clauses involved are given in (41). In the light of the foregoing discussion, it would be desirable to account for the appearance of *y(d)* or *ez* rather than *a* in the second conjunct in terms of agreement with a relevant topic. This can be achieved by positing an adverbial non-overt topic in the second conjunct in (41), marked by a gap ___. Its contribution to the meaning is to provide narrative continuity in the absence of any topic, roughly equivalent to 'and then' (see analyses of verb-initial clauses in V2 languages, for instance Diesing 1990 on Yiddish, and Sigurðsson 1990 on Old Icelandic). If this analysis is accepted, then cases such as (41) are actually part of the verb-second system, and not an exception to it.

(41)   a. . . . ac [ef a   deuth   y 'r   weirglawd]. Ac [__ **y**
        and he PRT come.PAST.3S to the meadow   and   PRT
        deuth   [y] wreic ohen   a 'r   vorwyn at
        come.PAST.3S the woman very.old and the maiden to
        y   gwr llwyt].
        the man grey
        '. . . and he came to the meadow, and the very old woman and the maiden came to the grey man.'   (*P* 38.9–10)

b. Neuse [ann drouc berger   so   conuertisset en un men
now   the bad   shepherd be.PRES.REL turn.PASTPART in a   stone
mabr] ... Hac [__ **ez** lauar   Sante Barba ...]   MB
marble and   PRT say.PRES.3S Saint Barbara
'Now the bad shepherd is turned into a marble stone ... and Saint
Barbara says ...'   (*B* 383)

These coordination rules have not survived the loss of verb-second in
Welsh. Since acquisition of the null topic depended on the presence of the
particle *y(d)*, the phonological erosion of the particle introduced verb-initial
clauses into the language that did not need to be analysed as part of the verb-
second system. This in itself probably contributed to its abandonment. For
instance in the sixteenth century sentences like (42) are found, where only the
appearance of *ac*, the form required before a vowel, rather than *a*, indicates
the loss of the particle *y(d)*. Soon afterwards, even this is lost in most cases,
indicating that the last clause of a sequence of conjoined clauses was already
being analysed as verb-initial.

(42)   ... ef aeth   anyssbrydoedd ac   ef ... ac yr agores   y
        it go.PAST.3S evil.spirits   with him   and PRT open.PAST.3S the
        ddayar, **ac llyngkawdd**   y   wyr ef oll.   EMW
        earth   and swallow.PAST.3S 3MS.GEN men him all
        '... evil spirits took him to eternal torment, and the earth opened and it
        swallowed all his men.'   (*DFfEL* 162.3–5, 1595)

9.1.3.3   Verb-initial order with 'be'

In Middle Welsh, verb-initial order is required with the present tense
of *bot* 'be', as illustrated in (43), and occurs optionally (alongside verb-
second) with the past tense, as shown by the pair in (44) versus (45).

(43)   Ie, ... y **mae**   yno ryw   ystyr   hut.
        yes   PRT be.PRES.3S there some meaning magic
        'Yes, ... there is some magic meaning there.'
                                           (*PKM* 10.10, see Watkins 1993:122)

(44)   Arglwyd, ... yd **oed**   yn   ediuar gennym ni gwneuthur hynny.
        lord   PRT be.IMPF.3S PRED sorry with.1P us do.INF   DEM.NS
        'Lord, ... we were sorry to have done that.'   (*YSG* 4679–80)

(45)   A   drws y pebyll a **oed**   yn agoret ...
        and door the tent   a PRT be.IMPF.3S PRED open
        'And the doorway of the tent was open ...'   (*P* 10.11)

Since *bot* 'be' was also used as the auxiliary in the periphrastic progressive and
perfect constructions, the rise of these constructions also helped to generalize

verb-initial order (see also section 9.2.1 below). Again, the patterns and developments are rather similar to those found in Middle and Modern Breton.

9.2   Periphrastic verbal forms

Although the earliest stages of the Brythonic languages expressed virtually all tenses, moods and voices synthetically, the modern languages are characterized by extensive use of periphrastic verbal forms. Particularly noticeable are the emergence of periphrastic forms for the passive and progressive.

9.2.1   Periphrastic aspectual constructions

All Brythonic languages have innovated periphrastic progressive constructions of the form 'be' + subject + aspect marker + verb-noun. In all cases the aspect marker has arisen historically from a preposition. In Welsh, the marker developed out of *yn* (+ nasal mutation) 'in' with loss of nasal mutation; and in Breton and Cornish it developed from Middle Breton *ouz*, Cornish *orth* 'by' (Hewitt 1990).

In Middle Welsh, the most frequent use of *yn* + verb-noun is as an adjunct, often to a noun phrase (cf. modern French *en*):

(46)   . . . ef   a   welei   varchawc **yn   dyfot   yn y erbyn** . . .
          he PRT see.IMPF.3s knight   PROG come.INF towards.3MS
          '. . . he saw a knight coming towards him . . .'   (*P* 61.17–18)

However, *yn* + verb-noun is also used as a true periphrastic verbal form, albeit not as frequently as in Modern Welsh:

(47)   Ac   y   mae   Matholwch yn   rodi   brenhinaeth Iwerdon y
          and PRT be.PRES.3s Matholwch PROG give.INF kingdom   Ireland   to
          Wern   uab Matholwch . . .
          Gwern   son Matholwch
          'And Matholwch gives the kingdom of Ireland to Gwern son of
          Matholwch . . .'   (*PKM* 41.9–10)

The periphrastic construction in (47) has greatly increased in frequency in Modern Welsh, replacing the synthetic forms almost entirely in expressing present time reference. The development of the new periphrastic present tense in this way led to a realignment of the tense – aspect system, such that the former synthetic present-tense paradigm has largely been shifted into a function as a modal future (see Poppe 1996, Haspelmath 1998: 36–7). Scots Gaelic has undergone a similar development (Poppe 1996: 151) (see also section 1.4.2.1).

The construction in (47) probably arose from a reanalysis of cases where *yn* appeared after *bot* 'be'. So, in cases like (48), there would once have been potential ambiguity as to whether the prepositional phrase headed by *yn* was an adjunct or an aspectual complement of 'be'. At some point the second option was chosen over the first and the construction was reinterpreted as referring to a single event.

(48)   ... wythnos y   bu   yn   bwrw   marchawc beunyd ...
         week   PRT be.PRET.3S PROG throw.INF knight   every.day
         '... for a week (there) he was, unseating a knight every day ...'
         or 'for a week he unseated a knight every day ...'   (*P* 41.12)

Judging from the existence of examples such as (47), the introduction of a true present tense with *yn* had already taken place by the Middle Welsh period. The construction is already used with stative verbs in Middle Welsh:

(49)   Ac nyt **yttoed**   Selyf   **yn** **gwybot** pa   ffuryf y
         and NEG be.IMPF.3S Solomon PROG know.INF which way   PRT
         gallei   wneuthur peth a   barhaei   yn   gyhyt   a hynny ...
         can.IMPF.3S make.INF thing PRT last.IMPF.3S PRED long.EQ as DEM.NS
         'And Solomon didn't know how he could make something that would last
         as long as that ...'   (*YSG* 4435–7)

Modern Welsh has at least one other aspect marker used in this way, namely the perfect marker *wedi* which has emerged from the preposition *wedi* (Middle Welsh *(g)wedy*) 'after' (see section 2.2.1). As shown in (50), this already existed in Middle Welsh, where, however, it is extremely rare. Again, it seems likely that a reanalysis of *wedi* from preposition to aspect marker has contributed to its status as the unmarked perfect construction in Modern Welsh.

(50)   ... yny doeth   rybudyeu idaw, a   menegi   uot   y
         until come.PAST.3S warnings to.3SM and indicate.INF be.INF the
         crydyon   wedy duunaw   ar y   lad.
         shoemakers PERF conspire.INF on 3SM.GEN kill.INF
         '... until warnings came to him, indicating that the shoemakers had
         conspired to kill him.'   (*PKM* 58.17–19)

9.2.2   The periphrastic passive

The Brythonic languages have no inherited passive forms, although impersonal (subjectless) verbal forms fulfil much the same function (see section 8.3.3). Breton and Cornish developed a new periphrastic passive using a past participle on the model of French and English. Middle Welsh also developed a periphrastic passive, this time using the verb *caffael* (Modern

Welsh *cael*) 'get, receive' as an auxiliary. A Middle Welsh example is given in (51) (from D. S. Evans 1964:164). The internal argument (patient) of the verb *goganu* 'disgrace' is *ni* 'we / us'. It is promoted to subject position of the passive auxiliary (here in the mutated form *gawn*). At the same time, a first-person plural object clitic *yn* (but no overt object) accompanies the verb. Although rare in Middle Welsh, the construction has become extremely productive in Modern Welsh (see section 8.3.1).

(51)   . . . **ni** a   **gawn**   **yn**   goganu   gan yr unben . . .
        we PRT get.PRES.1P 1P.GEN disgrace.INF by the chieftain
        onys   guahodwn.
        if + NEG + 3S.ACC invite.PRES.1P
        '. . . we'll be disgraced by the chieftain . . . if we do not invite him.'
                                                                    (*PKM* 84.26–7)

9.3   Agreement patterns and null arguments

9.3.1   *General principles of agreement*

Medieval Brythonic languages all have verbal paradigms manifesting rich subject – verb agreement licensing null subjects. There are also object clitics which may co-occur with overt pronominal objects or with a null object (see section 9.8 below). Many prepositions show agreement with their objects and similarly allow either overt or null objects. In most respects the properties of the agreement system are identical to those of the modern literary languages (see section 6.1 for relevant paradigms in Modern Welsh).

With the exception of subject – verb agreement in V2-structures (see section 9.3.2 below), a (null or overt) pronominal subject triggers rich agreement, and nominal subjects trigger default third-person singular agreement, just as in Modern Welsh (see section 6.1).

One difference between Middle Welsh and the modern language concerns postverbal non-pronominal subjects, which sometimes co-occur with full agreement in Middle Welsh, as in (52), where a plural postverbal nominal subject *Pryderi a Manawydan* triggers a plural verb *orugant* 'did', contrary to Modern Welsh usage (D. S. Evans 1971). These have generally been attributed to foreign literary influence (Morris-Jones 1931: 191 and D. S. Evans 1971, but contra this Lewis 1942: 16–17), and were probably not possible in spoken Middle Welsh.

(52)   ... kymryt eu   gwledeu ... a **orugant**   Pryderi a
         take.INF 3P.GEN feats   PRT do.PAST.3P Pryderi and
         Manawydan.
         Manawydan
         '... Pryderi and Manawydan had their feast ...'   (*PKM* 37.7–8)

9.3.2   Subject–verb agreement in V2-structures and the 'mixed' sentence

It is generally said that, in Middle Welsh affirmative verb-second ('abnormal') structures, the verb usually agrees in person and number with a subject in pre-verbal topic position (Fife 1988: 116–18, Fife & King 1991: 139 although D. S. Evans 1964: 180 is more cautious). This is illustrated in (53), where the subject *y deu urenhin* 'the two kings' is in the pre-verbal topic position and triggers a plural verb *nessayssant* 'drew near' (compare also (2) above).

(53)   Ac ar hynny y   deu urenhin a **nessayssant**   y gyt
         and on DEM.NS the two king   PRT draw.near.PAST.3P together
         am perued y   ryt e ymgyuaruot.
         at middle the ford to meet.INF
         'And then the two kings approached one another in the middle of the ford
         to meet.'   (*PKM* 5.19–20)

On the other hand, in Middle and Modern Breton and Middle Cornish, the verb remains in the 'default' third-person singular form in this environment. Even in Middle Welsh, however, agreement is not always observed, as seen from example (54) (see D. S. Evans 1971). In this example, the plural subject *y gwyr* 'the men' in preverbal position is nevertheless accompanied by a singular verb *wiscawd* 'dressed'. This fact may suggest an early period where both patterns were productive (cf. Koch 1991: 38).

(54)   Y gwyr a **wiscawd**   amdanunt ...
         the men PRT dress.PAST.3S around.3P
         'The men got dressed ...'   (*PKM* 29.22)

The agreement in Welsh in (53) is problematic, given the fact that in other A'-constructions (*wh*-questions, relative clauses) there is no subject – verb agreement when subjects are extracted.

In negative clauses, the verb agrees with a pre-verbal subject in all the medieval Brythonic languages.

A related construction in Welsh shows absence of agreement parallel to Breton and Cornish. This is what is traditionally referred to as the mixed sentence, similar in appearance to the abnormal sentence, but having a focus interpretation. As in the abnormal sentence, the order is fronted constituent – particle – verb, but agreement between a fronted subject and the verb is absent. Hence, in (55), the subject is first person *mi* 'I', yet the verb is third person.

(55)   Mi a   'e   heirch . . .
        I   PRT 3FS.ACC seek.PRES.3S
        'It is I who seek her.'   (*CO* 562)

Unlike the abnormal sentence, the mixed sentence may be embedded, using one of the embedded-focus markers *panyw* or *pan yw, (y) may* or *(y) taw*. The first two are illustrated in (56). In the first subordinate clause, *pan yw* allows *o'm anuod inheu* 'against my will' to be focused in a mixed sentence; in the second, *y may* allows *brawt un uam a mi* 'my half-brother' to be focused in the same way.

(56)   . . . menegwch   ydaw . . . **[p]an yw**   o 'm   anuod
        indicate.IMPER.2P to.3MS   COMP.FOCUS of 1S.GEN unwillingness
        inheu y   gwnaethpwyt   hynny; ac **y may**   brawt
        I.CONJ PRT made.PAST.IMPERS DEM.NS and COMP.FOCUS brother
        un   uam   a mi a   wnaeth   hynny . . .
        same mother as me PRT do.PAST.3S DEM.NS
        'Tell him that it was against my will that this was done; and that it was my
        half-brother who did it . . .'   (*PKM* 33.21–3)

Use of *panyw* died out in the sixteenth century, but the other two markers have survived as *mai* and *taw* to this day (see section 4.3.4). There are further syntactic differences between the mixed and abnormal sentences; see Evans (1964: 179–81); Fife (1988); Fife & King (1991: 83ff.); and Tallerman (1996).

These cleft markers are reasonably transparent as sequences of complementizer *pan* 'that, when, whence' or *y(d)* + part of the verb 'be' (*yw* or *may*). It seems that a reanalysis took place reducing the construction from two clauses, an existential copular clause plus a relative clause, into a single clause, with *panyw* etc. being reanalysed as clefting particles taking a clausal complement in the process (Tallerman 1996: 117–18). The fact that in Middle Welsh the particle *y* may be omitted, resulting in *may*, suggests that the reanalysis may already have taken place by this time, since otherwise this particle is not optional in the language.

9.3.3   The decline of null arguments

Null arguments have been declining for some time in Welsh, primarily through reanalysis of the word division between inflectional endings and

Table 9.2. *Possible interpretation of agreement paradigms in modern colloquial Welsh.*

	gan 'with' coll. northern	*gweld* 'see' coll. southern
1s	*gynna i*	*weles i*
2s	*gynna ti*	*weles ti*
3MS	*gynno fo*	*welodd e*
3FS	*gynni hi*	*welodd hi*
1P	*gynno ni*	*welso ni*
2P	*gynno chi*	*welso chi*
3P	*gynnyn nhw*	*welso nhw*

pronouns. In much colloquial Welsh the endings of prepositions and verbs have effectively been reanalysed as part of the following pronoun and consequently a morphologically poorer inflected form has been generalized; see Jones (1988: 143–5). Consider a possible interpretation of the colloquial paradigms for the preposition *gan* 'with' and the past tense of the verb *gweld* 'see' in Modern Welsh in Table 9.2. Although conventional spellings such as *gynnon ni, gynnoch chi* and *gynnon nhw* are normally used to represent even the spoken variants in these cases, there is every reason (for instance, from syllabification and the absence of a geminate consonant phonetically) to suspect that the apparently distinct ending in these cases actually forms part of the following pronoun today.

Null arguments are not permitted with the ambiguous forms in such dialects. Evidence of a move away from null arguments is found at least as early as the sixteenth century (cf. their relative rarity in the slander cases in Suggett 1983).

9.4   Morphological case

The continental Celtic languages exhibited a full system of six cases. A similar system of morphological case marking had already been lost by the time of the earliest records in all Brythonic languages (Koch 1983). Pronominal object clitics are the only exception (see section 9.8). A rare attested productive instance of morphological case is the following Old Welsh example, where the genitive form *nyf* (spelled *nym*) of *nef* 'heaven' appears (cf. Old Irish *nem* 'heaven', genitive *nime*):

(57)   Ath   uodi   gwas nym   gwerth na   thechut . . .
                                                                            OW
PRT+2S.ACC be.SUBJ.3S+you abode heaven.GEN because NEG flee.IMPF.2S
'May you have the abode of heaven because you did not flee . . .'
                                                                    (*CA* 233)

Traces of an earlier case system remain, however, in certain fossilized forms, such as Welsh *erbyn*, Cornish *erbyn* < *ar* 'on' + dative of *pen* 'head'; Welsh *heddiw*, Breton *hiziv* < dative of demonstrative + dative of *dydd/deiz* 'day'; Middle Welsh *dywieu* etc. 'Thursday' < dative of *dyd* 'day' + *Ieu* 'Jupiter'; and Welsh *eleni*, Breton *hevlene* 'this year' and Middle Welsh *yrllyned*, Breton *warlene* 'last year' from an oblique case form of the word for 'year' (Morris-Jones 1913: 414, 436; Lewis and Pedersen 1937: 162, 164, 171; Fleuriot 1964: 238–41). In Middle Breton *pemdez*, Middle Welsh *beunyd* 'every day', the nasal consonant shows the effect of an earlier accusative inflection.

9.5   Negation

In Middle Welsh, negation is marked by the negative marker *ny(t)* preceding the verb, most frequently in initial position, as in (58).

(58)   **Ny** welei   ef y   twrwf   rac tywyllet y   nos.
        NEG saw.IMPF.3S he the commotion for dark.EQ the night
        'He could not see the commotion because the night was so dark.'
                                                                    (*PKM* 22.23)

Negative main clauses are optionally verb-second. A constituent may be moved (topicalized) to precede the negative marker and the verb, although, in contrast to affirmative clauses, this is not compulsory. The optional nature of verb-second in negative clauses makes Welsh (and the other Brythonic languages) rather different from the Germanic languages in this area. The order with fronting, shown in (59), contrasts with the non-fronted order in (58). In the majority of cases, there is no topicalization in negative main clauses in Middle Welsh (Watkins 1990).

(59)   A hynny **ny** thygywys   idaw.
        and DEM.NS NEG avail.PAST.3S to.3MS
        'And that didn't work for him.'   (*PKM* 11.2)

Fronted objects (and fronted non-finite verbs) in negative main clauses optionally induce the appearance of an object agreement clitic *-s* on the negative marker, giving *nys*. This possibility is shown in (60). The optionality of the clitic is shown in (61), where the marker appears as *ny*.

(60)   . . . a   hynny   **nys**   gallei.
         and   DEM.NS   NEG+3S.ACC can.IMPF.3S
         '. . . and that he could not do.'   (*YSG* 1780–1)

(61)   . . . ac   attep   **ny**   chauas   ef genthi   hi   yn hynny.
         and   answer   NEG   receive.PAST.3S   he with.3FS   her   in   DEM.NS
         '. . . and no answer did he receive from her in that (respect).'

                                                                    (*PKM* 7.12–13)

The availability of optional topicalization across negation is also a feature
of Middle Breton and Cornish (George 1990: 231, 234).

Main clauses like the one in (61) have also been analysed as left-dislocation
structures (Isaac 1996: 58–9), with the fronted object in an extraclausal
position and the -*s* object clitic either fulfilling the direct-object function or
licensing a null element in object position. On this analysis, (60) would be
interpreted as meaning '. . . and that, he couldn't do it.'

However, there are good reasons for treating the fronted element in (60) and
(61) as internal to the clause. Non-referential quantified noun phrases, such as
dim o Seint Greal 'any of the Holy Greal' in (62), may precede the verb in this
construction. These are cross-linguistically resistant to left dislocation,
because it is not normally possible to use a pronoun to refer back to a noun
phrase that has no reference (compare the ungrammatical English *Any of the
films, I haven't seen them* versus grammatical *That film, I've seen it*). This suggests that sentences like (62) involve topicalization rather than left dislocation.
Fronting of such phrases is not possible in Modern Welsh.

(62)   . . . eissyoes **dim**   o **Seint Greal** nys   gweles   ef.
         however anything of Holy Grail   NEG+3S.ACC   see.PAST.3S   he
         '. . . however, he did not see the Holy Grail at all.'   (*YSG* 1335)

Negative object relative clauses show the same pattern with -*s* (see section 9.10
below).

9.5.1   *The shift of negative-polarity indefinite pronouns to negative quantifiers*

Middle Welsh has negative polarity items such as *dim* 'anything', *neb*
'anyone, any' (cognate with Breton *neb* 'any'), *e(i)ryoet* 'ever' and *byth* 'ever'.
These occur in negative (63), interrogative (64), and conditional / subjunctive
contexts only.

(63)   Ny   wnn   i **dim**   y wrth honno . . .
         NEG   know.PRES.1S   I anything   about   DEM.FS
         'I know nothing about her . . .'   (*PKM* 54.9)

(64)   . . . a   dywedy   di   ymi   **dim**   o 'th   negesseu?
         INT tell.PRES.2S you to.me anything of 2S.GEN errands
'. . . will you tell me anything of your errands?'   (*PKM* 12.18–19)

Dim and *neb* have become negative quantifiers 'nothing' and 'no one' (see Rouveret 1994: 128–9), used in a negative sense in the absence of the negative marker *ni(d)* or other mark of negation (see section 8.2). Evans cites the following example from as early as the fourteenth century, although such examples are sporadic until the modern period:

(65)   . . . y neb   a   wybu   wneuthur pob   peth o   dim . . .
         anyone PRT know.PAST.3S make.INF every thing from nothing
'. . . he who knew how to make everything from nothing . . .'
                              (*LlALl* 60.13–14, Evans 1964:107)

Other negative quantifiers have also emerged from phrases once used as the equivalent of indefinite pronouns: for instance, *dim byd* 'nothing' < *dim yn y byd* 'nothing in the world' or *nunlle* 'nowhere' < *yn un lle* 'in any place'.

9.5.2   The Welsh Jespersen's Cycle

The mutated form of *dim*, namely *ddim*, has become a marker of pure negation in own right, initially as a marker of emphatic negation, where it generally appears in sentence-final position. This position is typically that of adverbials, and suggests that at this stage *ddim* functioned as a negative adverbial right-adjoined to the verb phrase. This use is attested from the mid-thirteenth century (Willis 2006b). A Middle Welsh example is given in (66). Note that, in (66), *dim* follows the indirect object *idaw* 'to him'.

(66)   . . . ac   **nyt** argwedwys   idaw   **dim.**
         and NEG harm.PAST.3S to.3MS at.all
'. . . and it didn't harm him at all.'   (*YCM* 27.18)

In Early Modern Welsh, *ddim* acquired the status of an unemphatic marker of negation, positioned between the subject and the aspect markers. The result of these changes was the creation of bipartite negation marking, *ni(d)* . . . *ddim* in main clauses, and *na(d)* . . . *ddim* in embedded clauses as in (67).

(67)   Ac velly pawb   a   wybu   **nad**   oedd   hi **ddim**
         and so   everyone PRT know.PAST.3S NEG.COMP be.IMPF.3S she NEG
         yn   pechu . . .   EMW
         PROG sin.INF
'And so everyone knew that she wasn't sinning . . .'
                   (Peniarth 218, 'Teithie Syr Sion Mandefyl', 127–8, 1605–10)

Ddim appears to have undergone reanalysis from an adverbial to a simple marker of negation, analogous to the development of French *pas* from noun 'step' > minimiser 'at all' > marker of negation. Ultimately, postverbal *ddim* became obligatory in negative main clauses in spoken Welsh and informal written Welsh. The pre-verbal marker *ni(d)* has itself been eroded, surviving only as a soft or aspirate mutation on verbs in negative sentences and in special negative forms of the verb 'be' (*nid ydwyf* 'I am' > *dydw*) and, in some dialects, of other verbs (see section 8.2.2). As a result *ddim* has become the primary marker of negation in spoken Welsh.

Breton has experienced a broadly similar, but independent, series of developments, innovating a new postverbal negative marker *ket* (Middle Breton *quet*), the source of which is unknown. Cornish has been the most conservative of the Brythonic languages with respect to negation, preserving the pre-verbal negative marker *ny* alone (Lewis 1946: 48–9, Poppe 1995: 103). On negation throughout Brythonic, see also Poppe (1995).

9.5.3   Definite direct objects in negative sentences

In Middle Welsh, definite direct objects are preceded by the preposition *o* 'of, from' after the negative marker *dim*. Originally this seems to have been a partitive construction (cf. English *none of the food*), but already in Middle Welsh it is found both in partitive senses (68) and in more neutral contexts (69).

(68)   ...heb   anuon   dim o   'r   bwyt udunt...
          without send.INF NEG of the food to.3P
          '...without sending any of the food to them...'   (*YSG* 1823)

(69)   Vy   enw   i, ...ny   elly   di   wybot   dim ohonaw...
          1S.GEN name me   NEG can.PRES.2S you know.INF NEG of.3MS
          'My name, you cannot know it...'   (*YSG* 590)

By the seventeenth century, a reduced form of *ddim o* had evolved into a negative marker *mo*, used before definite objects, subjects of unaccusative verbs and before non-finite verbs in the periphrastic tenses. These cases are exemplified in (70)–(72). In (70), *mo* marks a negative definite object *moth neges* 'your message'; in (71), it marks the subject of an unaccusative verb *bod* 'be', namely *moi chystled* 'its like'; and in (72), it marks the verb *mo'i wnevthyd* 'do it' in a non-finite clause dependent on a negative clause *ni allai* 'he couldn't'.

(70)   ...ni   chei   di   yn wir **moth**   neges.   EMW
          NEG get.FUT.2S you indeed NEG+2S.GEN request
          '...you'll never get your request.'   (*HGC* 14.15.4, *c.* 1640)

(71) Ni   bu   ar fôr **moi**   chystled . . .   ModW
      NEG be.PRET.2S on sea NEG+3FS like
      'There was never its like on the sea . . .'   (*ERRG* 1.2.8, 1782)

(72) . . . am ryw negess ni   allai   **mo** 'i   wnevthyd . . . EMW
      for some errand NEG can.IMPF.3S NEG 3MS.GEN do.INF
      '. . . for some errand that he couldn't do . . .'   (*RhG* ii.50.28, 1582)

9.6   Mutations

The phonology of the mutations has, in so far as can be determined
from the textual record, remained constant in the attested historical period.
The soft mutation of /g/, formerly /ɣ/, became zero in the ninth century
(Jackson 1953: 469–70), as a result of the loss of /ɣ/ in most environments by
regular sound change. For details of the phonology of mutation in modern
Welsh, see section 1.4.4.

Mutations were once predictable from the phonological environment,
specifically the final segment of the preceding word. By the time of Middle
Welsh, however, mutations can be predicted only by reference to a list of arbitrary triggering environments, as in Modern Welsh. However, there are
differences in these environments as compared with the modern language.

The overwhelming majority of mutations are triggered by individual lexical
items onto the initial consonant of the word immediately following them.
These have remained largely constant. Discussion will be limited here to those
mutations triggered by a particular syntactic structure. For details of mutations within the noun phrase, see section 9.11 below.

Mutations are indicated sporadically in Middle Welsh texts. In general, if
mutation is indicated orthographically, then this can be taken as evidence that
a particular context was a mutation trigger, but absence of orthographic mutation is inconclusive. Investigation of mutation rules therefore has to be done
by generalizing from cases where mutation is indicated. Absence of mutation
can be inferred only from larger numbers of cases where it is not indicated in
the orthography or from cases of alliteration in poetry.

9.6.1   *Direct-object mutation in Welsh*

In Middle Welsh, soft mutations on subjects and objects occur if the
immediately preceding word is a mutation trigger. If a noun phrase immediately follows a verb and that verb is a mutation trigger, it mutates irrespective

of whether it is a subject or an object. Verb forms triggering mutation include imperfect and pluperfect verbs in *-ei*, the preterite of the verb *bot* 'be' and its compounds (*bu* and *-fu*) and other forms of the verb *bot* 'be'. Other verbs (including present-tense verbs, the present subjunctive in *-(h)o* and past tense verbs in *-awd, -s* and *-th/-t*) leave the following noun phrase unmutated (Morgan 1952: 182–233). For instance, an imperfect or pluperfect verb form triggers soft mutation on the subject (from *Bendigeituran* with initial /b/ to *Uendigeituran* with initial /v/) in (73)), and on the object (from *llannerch* with initial /ɬ/ to *lannerch* with initial /l/) in (74)).

(73)   Ny   angassei   **Uendigeituran** eiryoet y mywn ty.
                                                    (*Bendigeituran*)
        NEG contain.PLUPERF.3S Bendigeidfran ever   in   house
        'Bendigeidfran had never fitted inside a house.'   (*PKM* 31.12)

(74)   Ac ef a   welei   **lannerch** yn y   coet . . .   (*llannerch*)
        and he PRT see.IMPF.3s glade   in the forest
        'And he saw a glade in the forest . . .'   (*PKM* 1.13–14)

If a verb is a mutation trigger, it will trigger mutation on the first overt element following, irrespective of whether that element is a subject or an object. Hence, if a verb is a mutation trigger and the subject is null or has been topicalized, then the object bears the mutation that would otherwise have been triggered on the subject. Where the subject is immediately postverbal and overt, whether it mutates depends on the ending of the verb before it.

Where there is a postverbal subject, the mutation on a following object depends on the nature of the subject. If the subject is a personal pronoun, mutation is the norm from the start. If the subject is a lexical, then both options seem to be available (Morgan 1952: 195–200, 224–7).

Mutation of subjects triggered by a preceding verb was lost in Early Modern Welsh. Evans (1968b) finds that the mutation of the subject of the verb *bod* 'be' was declining by the late sixteenth century, although mutation of the subject of imperfect and pluperfect tense verbs remained the norm. On the other hand, mutation spread to the objects of all verb forms, rather than just those which had originally triggered mutation. There is some evidence of this spread already in Middle Welsh. The result is the modern situation in which the direct object of a tensed verb mutates (except for objects of impersonal verbs), whereas the subject does not normally mutate unless it is separated from the verb (see chapter 7).

Morgan (1952) suggests that the crucial factor in these developments was the fact that objects mutated after subject pronouns, whereas there was no parallel context in which subjects mutated frequently and regularly. Consequently a high proportion of objects mutated, but a much lower proportion of subjects. This set the scene for the generalization of direct-object mutation in Modern Welsh.

9.6.2 *Mutation of comparative adjectives in negative and interrogative clauses*

In Middle Welsh, as in Modern Welsh, adjectives modifying masculine or plural nouns do not normally undergo mutation. However, if a comparative adjective modifies a noun in a negative or interrogative clause, it must undergo mutation, whatever the gender and number of the noun it modifies. Thus, in (75), the object, *ansyberwyt* 'arrogance', is masculine, but the adjective that modifies it must mutate because the clause is negative (*mwy* > *uwy*). Again, in (76), a comparative adjective modifying a subject mutates (*gwell* > *well*) because the clause is negative.

(75)   Ny weleis   ansyberwyt **uwy**   ar wr . . .   (*mwy*)
        NEG see.PAST.1S arrogance   greater on man
        'I have never seen greater arrogance in a man . . .'   (*PKM* 2.14–15)

(76)   . . . nyt oes   seith cantref **well** noc wy.   (*gwell*)
              NEG be.PRES.3S seven cantref better than them
        '. . . there are no seven cantrefs (administrative division) better than them.'
                                                                   (*PKM* 49.21)

This is another case where a mutation is triggered syntactically. In this case the relevant trigger environment is that a comparative adjective must be c-commanded by a negative or interrogative operator to undergo mutation. This mutation survived into Early Modern Welsh but no further in literary texts (Morgan 1952: 66–7).

This mutation is normally explained historically as the result of elision of a relative clause (Williams 1938: 127–8; Evans 1964: 43–4). It appears that, in the early Celtic languages, comparative adjectives could not be used attributively and had to be introduced using a relative clause instead (Lewis & Pedersen 1937: 186–7; Thurneysen 1946: 232–3). If so, then a sentence like (75) would at one time have contained a relative clause, as in the hypothetical (77).

(77)   **Ny weleis   ansyberwyt a   uei   uwy . . .
          NEG see.PAST.1S arrogance   PRT be.IMPF.SUBJ.3S greater
        'I have never seen arrogance that might be greater . . .'

Here, the mutation of *mwy* 'greater' to *uwy* is the regular mutation of an adjective in predicative position. When comparative adjectives began to appear in predicative position, it was via a reduction of this pattern, with the mutation being retained, but only in negative and interrogative contexts (but see Morgan 1952: 342–3 for an alternative view).

9.7   Copular constructions and inversion structures

9.7.1   Delayed subjects and objects in Middle Welsh

Delayed subjects, that is, subjects that appear after complements or adjuncts of the verb, are relatively common in Middle Welsh compared to Modern Welsh, where they are quite rare. There are two types of inversion in Middle Welsh. In the first, exemplified in (78), either a heavy noun phrase is postposed or the clause presents some new element in the discourse. The noun phrase must not be a pronoun, and there are no restrictions on the verb. This type remains in Modern Welsh.

(78)   . . . kanys ny   wisgawd   arueu eiryoet **uarchawc urdawl   well**
              since NEG wear.PAST.3S arms ever   knight   honourable better
              noc   ef.
              than   he
              '. . . since a better knight than he never bore arms.'   (*YSG* 3972–3)

The second type is restricted to the unaccusative group of intransitive verbs, but allows pronominal subjects. It also seems to be pragmatically neutral. Thus, in (79a), the subject *ef* 'he' follows the complement of *aeth* 'went', and in (79b), the subject *chwi* 'you' follows the complement of the verb, namely *yma* 'here'.

(79)   a. . . . yn y   deudecuet dyd wedy Calan Mei yd   aeth   [PP o
                 in the twelfth   day after May.Day PRT go.PAST.3S   from
                 'r   byt   hvn]   **ef** y tragywyd[avl] teyrnas wlat nef . . .
                 the world DEM.MS he to eternal   kingdom land heaven
                 '. . . on the twelfth day after May Day he went from this world to the
                 eternal kingdom of the land of heaven . . .'   (*BD* 207.22–3)
              b. Pa   neges   y   dodyvch   [AP yma] **chwi**?
                 which mission PRT come.PERF.2P   here you
                 'On what mission have you come here?'   (*CO* 476–7)

Delayed objects, that is, direct objects that appear after other complements or adjuncts of the verb, are also found in Middle Welsh. Again this construction seems to be pragmatically neutral and may apply to any noun phrase including a pronoun. In (80), the object *wy* 'them' follows the complement of the verb, namely *y mywn* 'in'.

(80)   Gellwng   [AP y mywn] **wy** . . .
              let.IMPER.2S   in   them
              'Let them in . . .'
                                                                                    (*PKM* 81.27)

Very similar phenomena occur to this day in the form of pronoun postposing in Irish (see Chung & McCloskey 1987; Ó Siadhail 1989: 207–10).

Delayed subjects and objects (except of the presentational/heavy NP-shift type) have both been lost in the transition to Modern Welsh. The loss of delayed subjects with unaccusative verbs in (79) may be linked to the loss of the expletive *ef* construction discussed in section 9.1.2 above. For further discussion, see Evans (1965).

9.7.2   Copular constructions

The verb *bot* 'be' had five present indicative forms in the third person in Old and Middle Welsh: *mae, yw, oes, ys* and *ysydd*. As in Modern Welsh (section 8.1.1), *yw* functions (together with a negative or interrogative particle) as the regular negative and interrogative of *mae* if the subject is definite; *oes* fulfils the same function if the subject is indefinite; *ys* is used only as a copula with a predicative adjective or noun phrase; and *ysydd* is found in A'-constructions (*wh*-questions, relative clauses). Historically, *mae, yw* and *ys* have all been used in affirmative copular constructions, but *mae* has spread at the expense of *ys*.

Typical of Old and early Middle Welsh are copular constructions of the form copula – predicate – subject. The form of the copula is *ys* (imperfect *oed*, preterite *bu*, future *byd*):

(81)   Ys   <u>gohilion</u>   **hwnn** . . .
        be.PRES.3S remainder DEM.MS
        'He is what remains . . .'   (*CO* 472)

Throughout this section, predicates are underlined, and subjects are marked in bold.

The *ys*-copula is found in Old Breton as *is* (Fleuriot 1964: 321) but was lost early on, being replaced by a construction involving the equivalent of *yw* (Breton *eo*). The Middle Welsh copula system is very similar to that found in the modern Goidelic Celtic languages. The cognate of *ys* (*is*) has survived productively in Scottish Gaelic, and, in particular, in Irish.

The negative of *ys* is *nyt* (imperfect *nyt oed*, past *ny bu*), identical in form in the present with the negative marker itself, but presumably still a verb in this context, since sentences containing it do not need another verb:

(82)   Dioer . . . nyt   <u>da</u>   **dy**   **gynghor uynet** y 'r gaer . . .
        certainly NEG.be.PRES.3S good 2S.GEN advice   go.INF to the castle
        'Certainly . . . your advice to go to the castle is not good . . .'
                                                                    (*PKM* 56.1–2)

This construction is found also with right dislocation of the predicate noun phrase when the predicate is definite:

(83)   Ys   <u>hwy</u> **yr rei hynny**, <u>Nynhyaw a   Pheibyaw</u> . . .
        be.PRES.3S they the ones DEM.P Nynniaw and Peibiaw
        'Those are Nynniaw and Peibiaw . . .'   (*CO* 598)

The type in (83) represents an archaic pattern, even in Middle Welsh, in that the pronoun and the right-dislocated element agree, both being third person plural. More usually, the masculine singular pronoun *ef* is found with predicates of all person/number combinations. By the time of most Middle Welsh texts *ys ef* 'it is he' has been reduced to *sef* and reanalysed as an expletive element permitting right dislocation of a focused (new) element (Evans 1958):

(84)   Sef   a   doeth   dy   nyeint   ueibion dy   chwaer.
        FOCUS PRT come.PAST.3S 2S.GEN nephews sons   2S.GEN sister
        'Your nephews, your sister's sons, were the ones who came.'
                                                                (*PKM* 74.10)

In Modern Welsh *sef* has grammaticalized as an adverb meaning 'namely'.

The Middle Welsh copular construction described above and illustrated in (81) has been replaced by a construction of the form (particle +) copula – subject – predicate marker *yn* – predicate.[3] In Middle Welsh, a similar construction with the order copula – predicate marker *y(n)* – predicate – subject is, broadly speaking, required in clauses with a non-finite verb (Watkins & Piette 1962: 300). This order is found in the bracketed embedded non-finite clauses in (85).

---

[3] The predicative marker *yn* may derive historically either from an earlier oblique (probably instrumental) form of the definite article, or from a construction involving the preposition *yn* 'in' (Richards 1934: 107–12). The parallel development in Old Irish of a copular construction involving the preposition *i n-* 'in' (e.g. *Atá sé i n-a rígh* 'He is a king,' lit. 'He is in his king') has been used to support the second view. However, in Welsh the preposition *yn* requires a nasal mutation, the predicative marker a soft mutation, a fact which argues against their common origin and is consistent only with the first hypothesis (Watkins & Piette 1962: 295–9). Most plausible is the suggestion that *yn* spread from functioning as an adverb marker to become also a predicate marker: it is used as the adverb marker regularly in Welsh, commonly in Cornish (*yn*), and sporadically also in Middle Breton (*en/ez*). The distribution suggests that *yn* was used solely as an adverb marker in the parent language. In Welsh it was generalized into the predicate marker function, in Breton it was (eventually) lost completely, and Cornish retained the conservative pattern (Watkins & Piette 1962: 299–301). Presumably this spread could have been the result of reanalysis of verb phrases of the type 'stand *yn* steadfast', where '*yn* steadfast' might reasonably interpreted either as an adverb 'steadfastly' or as a secondary predicate. See also Gensler (2002).

(85)   a. Duw . . . a   wyr   [bot   yn   <u>eu</u>   **hynny**   arnaf i].
            God   . . . PRT know.PRES.3S be.INF PRED false DEM.NS on.1S me
            'God . . . knows that that is a wrong against me.'   (*PKM* 21.2–3)
        b. . . . a   thebygu [y   uot   yn   <u>wannach</u> o   hynny   **ef**].
            and think.INF 3MS.GEN be.INF PRED weaker   from DEM.NS he
            '. . . and thinking that he was weaker as a result of that.'   (*BD* 47.27–8)

In finite clauses, the older order copula *ys* – predicate – subject is still commonly found, but, already in Middle Welsh, the predicative marker begins to appear in tensed clauses. Note that, when it is used in tensed clauses, the subject generally precedes the predicate. In this construction the copula has the forms present *mae* (negative *nyt yw*) and imperfect *oed* (negative *nyt oed*):

(86)   Kyn   kyuyl y 'r ulwydyn, yd oed   **ef** yn   <u>holl iach</u>.
        before end   to the year   PRT be.IMPF.3S he PRED recovered
        'Before the end of the year he was recovered.'   (*PKM* 90.19–20)

Finally, in late Middle Welsh and early Modern Welsh, this subject – predicate order spreads back to clauses with non-finite *bod*:

(87)   . . . a   dywedut [vot   **kanmwyaf y tir   hynny** y[n] <u>gyuanned</u>].
            and say.INF be.INF most   the land DEM.NS PRED inhabited
            '. . . and they say that most of that land is inhabited.'   (*FfBO* 46.13–14)

For further details, see Richards (1934) and Watkins & Piette (1962).

9.8   Pronouns

Pronouns in Middle Welsh vary in the main according to a strong (independent) vs. weak (dependent) distinction rather than grammatical function. The four simple series are given, according to the traditional classification (Evans 1964: 49–58), in Table 9.3. Large-scale homophony means that the contrast between independent and affixed pronouns and between accusative and genitive infixed forms operates only in a minority of person – number combinations.

With some exceptions discussed below (notably with the accusative dependent series), the distribution of these is broadly the same as in Modern Welsh. Independent pronouns are used for the subject in pre-verbal topic position, for the direct object when used without a corresponding accusative agreement clitic and for the object of an uninflected preposition. Examples are given in (88)–(90). In (88), the subject pronoun is topicalized to pre-verbal position and appears in the independent form *mi*. In (89), the verb is imperative, a form that cannot host clitics, hence the object pronoun must appear in the

Table 9.3. *Traditional classification of personal pronouns in Middle Welsh.*

		dependent		
	independent	accusative (object)	genitive (possessive)	affixed
first-person singular	*mi*	*'m*	*vy*^{N} (*'m*)	*i* (*ui* after /v/)
second-person singular	*ti*	*'th*^{S}	*dy*^{S}(*'th*^{S})	*di* (*ti* after /t/)
third-person singular masculine	*ef*	*'e* (*h-*), *-s*	*y*^{S} (*'e*^{S})	*ef*
third-person singular feminine	*hi*	*'e* (*h-*), *-s*	*y*^{A} (*'e*^{A})	*hi*
first-person plural	*ni*	*'n*	*yn* (*'n*)	*ni*
second-person plural	*chwi*	*'ch*	*ych* (*'ch*)	*chwi*
third-person plural	*wy(nt)*	*'e, -s*	*eu* (*'e*)	*wy(nt)*

Note: soft mutation triggers marked as ^{S}; aspirate mutation triggers as ^{A} and nasal mutation triggers as ^{N}.

independent form. Since it is in a mutation environment, it appears as mutated *ui* rather than unmutated *mi*. In (90), the pronoun *mi* appears as the object of the uninflectable preposition *a* 'with' and is in the independent form for this reason.

(88) **Mi**   a   'th   rodaf   di   y   'm   lle   i   yn
      1S.IND PRT 2S.ACC PUT.PRES.1S 2S.AFF in   1S.GEN place 1S.AFF in
      Annwuyn . . .
      Annwfn
      'I shall put you in my place in Annwfn . . .'   (*PKM* 3.8)

(89) "Dyro   di   **ui**   idaw   ef," heb   hi . . .
      give.IMPER.2S 2S.AFF 1S.IND to.3MS him QUOT 3FS.IND
      ' "Give me to him," she said . . .'   (*PKM* 14.21)

(90) A   reuedawt rygyueryw   a   **mi.**
      and wonder PERF.meet.PRES.3S with me
      'And a wonder has befallen (met with) me.'   (*PKM* 32.25)

Independent pronouns are also found in a number of miscellaneous other 'strong' contexts, for instance, standing alone, as predicates and in apposition. They cannot follow a verb showing agreement, and therefore have essentially the same distribution as non-pronominal noun phrases.

The accusative and genitive series are essentially agreement clitics. The accusative clitics attach to the end of the particle preceding a finite verb; the genitive clitics precede a non-finite verb. A minimal pair showing the two is provided in (91) and (92). In (91), the verb is finite and is preceded by an accusative clitic (*'e* plus no mutation); in (92), the verb is non-finite, there being a finite auxiliary *wnaf* 'do', and the object clitic is therefore genitive (*y* plus soft mutation, *kymryt > gymryt*).

(91) "Ie," heb ef,   "mi   a   'e   kymeraf."
      yes   QUOT 3MS.IND 1S.IND PRT 3S.ACC take.PRES.1S
      "'Yes," he said, "I shall take it."'   (*PKM* 92.7)

(92) "**Y**   gymryt a   wnaf,"   heb y Pwyll.   (*kymryt*)
      3MS.GEN take.INF PRT do.PRES.1S QUOT Pwyll
      "'I shall take it," said Pwyll.'   (*PKM* 17.27)

Genitive clitics also attach to nouns, indicating the possessor noun phrase (see section 9.11). Both series license a null pronoun in the postverbal (or postnominal) argument position itself. This argument position may also be filled by an overt pronoun, in which case pronouns of the affixed series are used (as with *di* in (88) in conjunction with a genitive clitic). Null subjects are permitted in postverbal position, although they are not obligatory, and once again affixed pronouns may be used in their place. After inflected prepositions, either an overt affixed pronoun or a null pronoun is possible.

In the third person the accusative form *-s* is used after negative markers *ny* and *na*, and after various particles and complementizers (for instance, affirmative particle *neu*, complementizers *o* 'if' and *ony* 'unless').

The possibilities for null arguments are shown in (93). Here, the subject is null, identified as second-person singular by the form of the verb *dechreueist*. A genitive agreement clitic precedes the non-finite verb *llad* 'kill', allowing the postverbal object to be null.

(93) Canys dechreueist   uy   llad,   gorffen.
      since   start.PAST.2S 1S.GEN kill.INF finish.IMPER.2S
      'Since you have begun to kill me, finish (it).'   (*PKM* 5.28)

Middle Welsh also had pragmatic distinction manifested on the independent and affixed series of pronouns. In addition to the simple forms given above, there is also a conjunctive paradigm of both independent and affixed pronouns, and a reduplicated paradigm of independent pronouns. These are given in Table 9.4.

These have the same syntactic distribution as their simple counterparts but differ pragmatically. The conjunctive pronouns are used in contrastive contexts (for instance, topic shift, see Mac Cana 1990), and the reduplicated series

Table 9.4. *Paradigms of conjunctive and reduplicated pronouns in Middle Welsh.*

	Independent Conjunctive	Affixed Conjunctive	Independent Reduplicated
'I'	*minheu*	*inheu*	*miui*
'you (singular)'	*titheu*	*ditheu*	*tidi*
'he'	*ynteu*	*ynteu*	*efo*
'she'	*hitheu*	*hitheu*	*hihi*
'we'	*ninheu*	*ninheu*	*nini*
'you (plural)'	*chwitheu*	*chwitheu*	*chwichwi*
'they'	*wynteu*	*wynteu*	*wyntwy*

is emphatic. Examples of conjunctive pronouns are given in (94). The subject in topic position is a first-person independent conjunctive pronoun. Another conjunctive pronoun *inheu* occupies the object position of the preposition *ymdanaf*, this time in the affixed form because it doubles the agreement morphology on the preposition *ymdanaf*.

(94)   Arglwydes, . . . gwisc   ymdan y gwryanc   hwnn.   A
        lady   dress.IMPER.2S around the young.man DEM.MS and
        minheu . . . a   wiscaf   ymdanaf **inheu**.
        1S.IND.CONJ PRT dress.PRES.2S around.1s 1S.AFF.CONJ
        'Lady, . . . arm this young man. And I (meanwhile / on the other hand) will
        arm myself.'   (*PKM* 82.24–6)

Reduplicated pronouns are shown in (95) in subject and object position. Note that when they occupy object position, reduplicated pronouns may not co-occur with object clitics in canonical Middle Welsh.

(95)   **Miui**   a   rodaf   vyg   cret . . . na   charaf   i
        1S.REDUP PRT give.PRES.1S 1S.GEN oath   NEG love.PRES.1S 1S.AFF
        tidi . . .
        2S.REDUP
        'I give you my word . . . that I do not love you . . .'   (*P* 36.1–2)

9.8.1   Loss of accusative clitics

In Middle Welsh independent pronouns are required as the objects of imperatives (as in (89) above), where there is no pre-verbal particle for an object clitic to cliticize onto. With other finite forms of the verb, an accusative object clitic (optionally doubled with an affixed pronoun) is more usual, as in (91). The bare independent pronoun is, however, also possible, as with *di* 'you' in (96).

(96) kanys heb dy genyat ti y gwnaeth duw **di**
for without 2S.GEN permission 2S.AFF PRT make.PAST.3S God 2S.IND
'. . . for God made you without your permission . . .'
(*CC* 23.21, Evans 1964: 50)

The pattern with an independent pronoun in direct object position has spread at the expense of the pattern with agreeing clitic and affixed pronoun. In spoken Welsh, the accusative clitics have become largely obsolete. In some northern varieties they remain at least at an underlying level, since their mutation effects remain. For instance in (97), the verb *lladdodd* 'killed' does not mutate, even though it is preceded by the particle *mi*, a soft mutation trigger. Absence of mutation here can only be explained as the result of deletion of an accusative object clitic *'i*, which blocks mutation.

(97) . . . mi lladdodd Rofar ni o.   ModW
AFF kill.PAST.3S Rover us him
'. . . our Rover killed him.'   (*GPB* 203)

Also in some northern dialects, the accusative clitics were replaced by genitive ones with finite verbs. For instance, in (98), we find the genitive object clitic *dy* proclitic to the verb, where more traditionally we would expect an accusative clitic *'th*.

(98) '. . . os na nei di, mi dy ladda di'   ModW
if NEG do.PRES.2S you AFF 2S.GEN kill.FUT.1S you
'. . . if you don't, I'll kill you.'   (*GT* 29)

9.8.2 *Effects of phonological reduction of pronouns*

The history of both simple and reduplicated independent pronouns in Welsh has been one of phonological reduction. In Middle Welsh, simple independent pronouns are clearly full pronouns, failing standard tests for clitic status. For instance, in (99), the simple independent pronouns *ef* 'he' and *hi* 'she' are conjoined to form a complex subject.

(99) A phan vu barawt bwyt, **ef** **a** **hi** a aethant
and when be.PRET.3S ready food 3MS.IND and 3FS.IND PRT went.3P
y eisted y gyt . . .
to sit.INF together
'And when food was ready, he and she went to sit together . . .'
(*YSG* 3279–80)

By Early Modern Welsh, such coordination was no longer possible. Similarly, in Middle Welsh, a pre-verbal subject pronoun could be modified by an emphatic reflexive such as *ehun* 'himself', but this too died out in Early Modern Welsh. It seems that, by this time, pre-verbal independent subject pronouns cliticized to the front of the verb.

Similar weakening of the reduplicated series was underway too. Reduplicated subject pronouns begin to be found as expletive subjects in the sixteenth century, as with *y vo* in (100). This suggests that they were no longer understood as emphatic.

(100)   ... **y vo**   a   uu   y   kyuriw dymesdyl ynGymhrv y
         3MS.REDUP PRT be.PRET.3S the such   storm   in.Wales   the
         dethwn yma ...   EMW
         day   DEM
         '... there was such a storm in Wales that day ...' (*RhG* i.32.16–17, *c.* 1530)

Furthermore, phonologically reduced forms appear. For instance, in (101), *vo* is a reduced form of the Middle Welsh masculine third person singular reduplicated pronoun *efo*.

(101)   **Vo**   aeth   oddiwrth yr holl gythrelied ...   EMW
         3MS.REDUP go.PAST.3S away.from the all   devils
         'He went away from all the devils ...' (*TWRP*, 'Y Dioddefaint' 777, 1552)

The full paradigm of the reduced reduplicated forms is given in Table 9.5.

The reduced forms of the reduplicated pronouns were very similar in form to the simple independent pronouns and merged with them, with variant forms coming to be distinguished by new conditioning factors. For instance, whereas in late Middle Welsh both reduplicated *efo* (later also *efe*) for emphasis and unemphatic simple *ef* were possible in postverbal subject position, in spoken Modern Welsh the reduced reduplicated forms *fe* / *fo* came to be used after a vowel (for instance, *deuai fe* 'he'd come'), with the simple form appearing after a consonant (for instance, *daeth e* 'he came'). Stylistic variation also arose, with descendants of Middle Welsh reduplicated forms (*fi, di, fo/fe* and *nhw*) being more colloquial, and variants descended from Middle Welsh simple forms (*mi, ti, ef* and *hwy*) being more formal.

Another effect of the phonological reduction of pronouns is that pre-verbal subject pronouns were reanalysed as affirmative verbal particles (see section 2.1.2). In the eighteenth century, doubling with both pre-verbal and postverbal subject pronouns appears in colloquial Welsh for the first time. For instance, in (102), pre-verbal independent pronouns, *mi* and *ti*, are doubled by postverbal affixed pronouns *i* and *di*.

(102)   a. mi   dewes   i   fy spectol gartre   ModW
         1S.IND leave.PAST.1S 1S.AFF 1S glasses at.home
         'I left my glasses at home.'   (BL1. 8.22)

Table 9.5. *Reduction of pronominal forms in Early Modern Welsh.*

	full forms	semi-reduced forms	reduced forms
'I'	*myfi*	*y fi*	*fi*
'you (singular)'	*tydi*	*y di*	*di* *thdi** (*> chdi*)
'he'	*efo / efe*	*y fo / y fe*	*fo / fe*
'she'	*hyhi*	*y hi*	*hi*
'we'	*nyni*	*y ni*	*ni*
'you (plural)'	*chwychwi*	*y ch(w)i*	*chi*
'they'	*hwyntwy*	*ynhwy*	*nhw*

Note: * After *a*^A 'and', *â*^A 'with', *â*^A 'as', *gyda*^A 'with' and *efo*^A 'with'.

b. Ti   elli   di   fyn'd lle   gwelech   di
2S.IND can.PRES.2S 2S.AFF go.INF where see.PRES.SUBJ.2S 2S.AFF
'n   dda.   ModW
PRED good
'You can go wherever you please.'   (*PN* 13.19)

The appearance of this type of clause provides good evidence that, by this time, pre-verbal subject pronouns, such as *mi* and *ti* in (102), had become main-clause affirmative complementizers, agreeing with the subject and the verb. This is confirmed by the fact that, at the same time, conjunctive subject pronouns disappear from pre-verbal position in low-style texts and must be placed in a postverbal position. That is, sentences of the type in (103), where a conjunctive subject pronoun *nineu* 'we' appears pre-verbally, are replaced with sentences of the type in (104), where the conjunctive subject pronoun *inne* 'I' appears postverbally and the pre-verbal position is filled by a simple pronoun *mi*, presumably now treated as an affirmative main-clause complementizer.

(103)   Felly **nineu**   aethom   i   weled   y   *'Lecsiwn.*   ModW
        SO   1P.IND.CONJ go.PAST.1P to see.INF the election
        'So we went to see the election.'   (*GBC* 20.7–8, 1703)

(104)   Os lleddis   i fy mab fy hun
        if kill.PAST.1S I 1S son 1S self
        Mi af   **inne**
        PRT go.FUT.1S I.AFF.CONJ
        i   run   ddihenudd.
        to the-same death
        'If I killed my own son, I shall go to the same death.'
                                                    (*HGC* 35.19–20, *c.* 1716)

Finally, in the mid eighteenth century, agreement between complementizer and verb ceases to be enforced consistently. In particular, the former first-person marker *mi* and the former masculine third-person marker *fe* appear before all person – number combinations and acquire the status of general affirmative main-clause complementizers, a status that they have maintained today. Innovative examples are given in (105) and (106). In (105), *mi* appears before a third-person plural verb; in (105), *fe* appears before a first-person singular verb.

(105)   Mi welen   yno ffenest . . .   ModW
         AFF see.COND.3P there window
         'They saw there a window . . .'   (*ER*, Lloyd 1937: 98)

(106)   Fe fydda   fi   bôb Boreu   yn   gorfod   gweiddi . . .
                                                                    ModW
         AFF be.FUT.1S 1S.AFF every morning PROG have-to.INF shout.INF
         'Every morning I'll have to shout . . .'   (*BDaf.* 16.25–6, ?*c.* 1765)

The doubling construction in (102b) has died out, although it is widely attested in the nineteenth century and was maintained until the twentieth century in parts of the southeast (see C. Thomas 1993).

9.9   Subordinate clauses

9.9.1   *Embedded finite clauses*

Embedded tensed clauses in Middle Welsh are verb-initial clauses of the form complementizer – verb – subject – object, essentially as in Modern Welsh:

(107)   O gwnaeth   hitheu   gam,   kymeret   y   phenyt   amdanaw.
         if do.PAST.3S she.CONJ wrong take.IMPER.3S 3FS punishment for.3MS
         'If she has done wrong, let her take her punishment for it.'
                                                                (*PKM* 21.17–18)

As in Modern Welsh, embedded finite clauses may act as complement to a preposition, as in (108), although the set of prepositions that allow this has changed slightly.

(108)   Ac yn y lle,   **y gyt** **ac**   y   doeth   y 'r   mor,
         and in the place together with PRT come.PAST.3S to the sea
         annyan y   mor a   gauas . . .
         nature the sea PRT get.PAST.3S
         'And there and then, as he came into the sea, he acquired the nature of the
         sea . . .'   (*PKM* 77.24–5)

Embedded verb-second order is confined to embedded clefts (section 9.7.2) and to positions after a few complementizers, such as *canys* 'since' (historically also a cleft < *can* 'since' + copula *ys*).

9.9.2   *Embedded infinitival clauses*

9.9.2.1   Complement clauses to declarative and epistemic verbs

In Middle Welsh, as in Modern Welsh, clausal complements of verbs that take propositions as their complements (declarative and epistemic verbs) must contain a non-finite verb under certain circumstances, even though they fill a finite gap in the paradigm of clause types (see section 3.3). The set of verbs involved includes *clybot* 'hear', *credu* 'believe', *dywedut* 'say', *gwelet* 'see', *gwybot* 'know', *medylyaw* 'think', *mynegi* 'indicate', *ryuedu* 'marvel' and *tebygu* 'suppose'. If the complement clause is affirmative and refers to an event preceding that of the main clause, then it is syntactically non-finite, as in (109).

(109)   . . . mi a   gigleu   [dyuot   y 'r Deheu y   ryw bryuet   ni
         I   PRT hear.IMPF.1S come.INF to the south   the sort creatures NEG
         doeth   y 'r ynys honn   eiroet].
         come.PAST.3S to the island DEM.FS ever
'. . . I have heard that creatures the like of which have never come to this island have come to the south.'   (*PKM* 68.16–17)

On the other hand, embedded questions and clefts, embedded negative clauses and conditional and future clauses after these verbs are finite, as in (110).

(110)   . . . mi a   tebygaf   [y byd   gwr idi   yn y   lle . . .]
         I   PRT suppose.PRES.1S PRT be.FUT.3S man to.3FS in the place
'. . . I suppose that he will be her husband now . . .'   (*P* 63.20–1)

The non-finite type in (109) manifests a pattern of argument marking not found in Modern Welsh. With the unaccusative group of intransitive verbs, such as *cleuychu* 'fall ill', *cyuodi* 'rise, get up', *dyuot* 'come', *hanuot* 'come from, originate', *mynet* 'go', *marw* 'die', *troi* 'turn (intrans.)' or *tyfu* 'grow', the sole, internal argument behaves as a direct object, following the verb if it is lexical, as with *y ryw bryuet* 'the sort of creatures' in (109). If it is pronominal, it appears as a genitive object clitic, as with third-person plural marker *eu* in (111).

(111)   Ac wynteu   a   dywedassant **eu**   hanuot   o   lys   Arthur.
         and they.CONJ PRT say.PAST.3P   3P.GEN originate.INF from court Arthur
'And they said that they were from Arthur's court.'   (*YSG* 4614–17)

This pattern of marking, whereby the sole argument of an intransitive / unaccusative verb is treated as a direct object, is the same as that found more generally in languages that have ergative-absolutive case systems, for instance, Basque, Hindi and Australian languages such as Dyirbal and Warlpiri.

Conversely, if the embedded clause contains an unergative intransitive verb, such as *kerdet* 'walk' or *marchogaeth* 'ride', or a transitive verb, such as *gwneuthur* 'do', *llad* 'kill' or *rhoi* 'give', a completely different pattern is found, and the external argument (subject / agent) is marked using the preposition *o* 'from, of':

(112)   a. A   gredy   di ... [gwneuthur **o   Duw** Adaf]?
           INT believe.PRES.2S you   make.INF   of God Adam
           'Do you believe that God made Adam?'   (*YCM* 30.4–5)
        b. Yr ymdidan yssyd   yn   dywedut ... [uarchogaeth **ohonaw** ...
           the story   be.PRES.REL PROG say.INF   ride.INF   of.3MS
           yny   doeth   hyt   y vanachlawc ...]
           until come.PAST.3S as.far.as to monastery
           'The story says that he rode ... until he came to a monastery ...'
                                                                  (*YSG* 1112–15)

Under some circumstances, the internal argument (subject, theme) of an unaccusative verb may be marked using this pattern. Manning (1995) suggests that [+human] is the conditioning factor, with [+human] noun phrases allowing *o*. It is certainly clear that if the subject is conceived of as being agentive, marking with *o* is more likely. An example where this seems to be the case is given in (113).

(113)   ... dan   amot   [mynet **o 'th   tad** ... y wrha
             under condition go.INF of 2S.GEN father to pay.homage.INF
             y 'r amherawdyr Arthur ...]
             to the emperor   Arthur
          '... on condition that your father ... go to pay homage to Emperor
          Arthur ...'   (*P* 39.8–9)

Here, it looks as though *o* is used in order to highlight the conscious and deliberate nature of going to pay homage; zero-marking (*mynet dy dad* ...) would merely state the change of location. Most of these exceptional examples are with a pronominal subject, hence another possibility in keeping with the typology of ergative systems is that it is pronouns that may be marked with *o*. In some languages with ergative systems (for instance, Dyirbal), there is 'split' ergativity with pronouns exhibiting nominative-accusative patterns of marking, with ergativity being manifested only with non-pronominal noun phrases.

Tenseless clauses of the type in (109), (111) and (112)–(113) are also found in various other syntactic environments, such as the clausal complement of various prepositions (*cyn* 'before', *gan* 'for, since', *rac* 'in front of, lest', (*g*)*wedy* 'after'), adjectives (*ryued* 'strange', *drwc* 'bad, sorry') and nouns (*amot* 'condition', *cred* 'belief'). Examples with a non-finite complement clause to a preposition are illustrated in (114) (unaccusative pattern) and (115) (transitive pattern).

(114)   A   gwedy eu   diflannu . . .
         and after   3P.GEN disappear.INF
         'And after they had disappeared . . .'   (*P* 47.9)

(115)   . . . gwedy y   adnabot   o 'r   rei   guarchaedic ef . . .
         after   3MS.GEN recognize.INF of the ones besieged   him
         '. . . after the besieged ones had recognized him . . .'   (*BD* 146.4)

They are also found in main clause contexts, either in a series of conjoined main clauses where only the first is specified for tense and person, or independently (the so-called 'historic infinitive', Fowkes 1991):

(116)   Ac yna y   gyrchu   o   'r   marchawc ef   yn   llityawc . . .
         and then 3MS.GEN attack.INF from the knight   him PRED angry
         'And then the knight attacked him angrily . . .'   (*P* 14.18)

For fuller discussion, see Lewis (1928: 182–4), Manning (1995), Morgan (1938) and Richards (1949–51).

In some Middle Welsh texts, the preposition *y* 'to' is found instead of *o* 'of' marking the subject in this type of construction. For instance, in (117), we have *y'r llew* 'to the lion' rather than the more frequent *o'r llew* 'of the lion'.

(117)   Yna agori   y   safyn y 'r   llew . . .
         then open.INF 3MS.GEN mouth to the lion
         'Then the lion opened its mouth . . .'   (*YBH* 31.1296–7, Evans 1964: 162)

In the transitive construction, both subject – object order, as in (115) and (116), and object – subject order, as in (118), are attested. However, the former outnumbers the latter by a substantial margin (Morgan 1938: 204), which seems to suggest that the subject – object order is basic, with object – subject order being derived by extraposition of the subject.

(118)   A   gwedy adnabot   hynny o Ywein . . .
         and after   recognize.INF DEM.NS of Owain
         'And after Owain had recognized that . . .'   (*BT* 78.16)

Note also that although the order non-pronominal subject – pronominal object is attested (as in (115) and (116) above), the order non-pronominal object – pronominal subject is rare. Assuming that extraposition of pronouns is dispreferred, this confirms that subject – object order is basic.

Complement clauses of this type have become severely restricted. By the seventeenth century the number of verbs involved in the construction had shrunk to just one, namely the verb *bod* 'to be', and even before this the considerable uncertainty of usage including hypercorrection suggests a disintegrating system. The pattern with *bod* 'be' remains in contemporary Welsh (see section 3.3). In other environments, the older construction has been replaced by the *i*-clause, see section 9.2.2.2 below.

A parallel construction existed in Middle Breton, but was already far more restricted in distribution, occurring with a very narrow set of embedded verbs, consisting perhaps only of three unaccusative verbs *bout/bezaff* 'be', *donet* 'come' and *monet* 'go'. Similar data are found in Cornish, but only with the verb *bos* 'be' (George 1993: 460).

9.9.2.2 The innovation of *i*-clauses

In chapter 3, two types of Modern Welsh infinitival clauses with overt subjects introduced by *i* 'to' were distinguished. Finite *i*-clauses, found as complements to declarative and epistemic verbs and nouns and as complements to prepositions, are illustrated in (119).

(119)   a. Dywedodd Steffan [i Nia baentio 'r   llun].   ModW
say.PAST.3S Steffan to Nia paint.INF the picture
'Steffan said that Nia had painted the picture.'
b. Er   [i lemyriaid ddiflannu   o   fannau eraill], maen
although to lemurs   disappear.INF from places other be.PRES.3P
nhw wedi ffynnu   ar Madagascar.
they PERF flourish.INF on Madagascar.
'Although lemurs have disappeared from other places, they have flourished on Madagascar.'

Non-finite *i*-clauses, found as complements to verbs of expectation, volition and various other control verbs, nouns and adjectives, and as complements to prepositions, are illustrated in (120).

(120)   a. Byddai   'n   syniad da   [i Nia baentio 'r   llun].   ModW
be.COND.3S PRED idea   good to Nia paint.INF the picture
'It would be a good idea for Nia to paint the picture.'
b. Roedd   y   maniffesto yn   galw   am [i 'r gweithwyr gael
be.IMPF.3S the manifesto PROG call.INF for to the workers   get.INF
rheoli   'r pyllau glo].
manage.INF the mines coal
'The manifesto called for the workers to be allowed to manage the coal mines.'

As we saw in section 3.4, in the former case, the event of the *i*-clause is real and anterior to that of the main clause: in (119a), Nia did paint the picture, and she did so before Steffan reported it. In the latter case, the event of the *i*-clause is potential, with generic or future time reference: in (120a), Nia may (or may not) paint the picture in the future.

There are broadly two types of account of the origin of these patterns. Lewis (1928: 182–4) relates them to the syntax of control verbs and adjectives and other similar verbs. A number of control verbs, such as *erchi* 'ask', *peri* 'cause' and *adolwyn* 'ask', required a prepositional-phrase complement headed by *i* 'to' in Middle Welsh. This indirect object had to act as controller for the unexpressed subject (PRO) of the embedded clause (object control):

(121)   A   chyt   archo   yti   [PRO$_i$ rodi   yr eil . . .]
        and though ask.PRES.SUBJ.3S to.you   give.INF the second
        'And though he may ask you to give him the second . . .'   (*PKM* 3.19–20)

Lewis suggests that it was 'by analogy' with this group that the construction with *i* marking the subject in all non-finite clauses spread. Miller (2004) adopts a related approach, but, focusing in particular on the nonfinite type in (120), suggests specifically that there was an early reanalysis of the verb *peri* 'cause', with the diffusion supported by the existence of superficially similar constructions with control adjectives such as *iawn* 'right' (see also section 8.3.2.2 on causative verbs and the syntax of *peri*).

A second type of account links the construction to verbs of happening or finishing. Morgan (1938: 209–13) distinguishes the two types of *i*-clause, and concentrates on the historical origin of the finite type. He argues that this has its origins in impersonal uses of the verb *daruot* 'finish, happen'. *Daruot* takes two arguments: a prepositional-phrase experiencer headed by *i* 'to', and either a noun phrase (122) or a verb phrase (123) for the event (theme).

(122)   A   gwedy daruot   idaw   y   ginyaw . . .
        and after   finish.INF to.3MS 3MS.GEN dine.INF
        'And after he had finished his dinner . . .'   (*O* 379–80)

(123)   A   gwedy daruot   im   goruot   ar bob   camhwri . . .
        and after   finish.INF to.me overcome.INF on every feat
        'And after I had mastered (finished mastering) every feat of arms . . .'
                                                                    (*O* 33–4)

He suggests that loss of *daruot* in (123) gave rise to the modern Welsh finite *i*-clause.

Richards (1949–51: 78–81) notes that a number of predicates, notably *damwein(y)aw* 'happen', allowed either a non-finite complement clause of the 'ergative' type discussed above, or an indirect object followed by a control clause. These two cases are illustrated in (124) and in (125) respectively.

(124)   Ynghyfrug hynny y   damweinawd [dyuot   llu   o 'r
in.means DEM.NS PRT happen.PAST.3S come.INF force of the
Flemisseit o   Ros y Gaer Uyrdin] . . .
Flemings from Rhos to Carmarthen
'In this way it happened that a force of the Flemings came from
Rhos to Carmarthen.'   (*BT* 98.6–7)

(125)   . . . ef a   damweinyawd [y wynt] [dwyn   yr ysgraff ymeith
it PRT happen.PAST.3S to wind take.INF the boat   away
odyno   hyt   yn ynys arall bell].
from.there as.far.as in island other distant
'It happened that a wind took the boat away from there to another distant
island.'   (*YSG* 4175–6)

He suggests that this alternation spread to verbs such as *dywedut* 'say' which
had originally had only the type in (124), thereby innovating sentences like
(119a) and so on.

   All accounts are compatible with the suggestion that a reanalysis took place,
with one generation of speakers interpreting the *i* – noun phrase sequence as
indirect object of a main-clause verb, and the next interpreting it (in some
cases) as subject of the embedded clause, illustrated for a control structure
source (like *erchi* 'ask' or *peri* 'cause') in (126).

(126) $[_{PP}$ i NP $]\,[_{TP}$ PRO verb $\ldots\,] \Rightarrow [_{TP}\,[_{T}$ i$]\,[_{vP}$ NP $[_{VP}$ verb $\ldots\,]\,]\,]$

For instance, according to the Lewis–Miller account, we could say that a verb
like *erchi* 'ask' acquired a second possible complement pattern. The sentence
in (121) might easily have been (mis)interpreted as also having the meaning
'although he may ask [someone] that you give him the second', with object of
'ask' and subject of 'give' distinct. The subcategorization frame of the verb
would be extended to allow for this second possibility and a new type of
embedded clause would be created.

(127)   Stage I
         erchi 'ask'   — $[_{PP}$ i NP] TP

         Stage II
         erchi 'ask'   — $[_{PP}$ i NP] TP
                          — $[_{TP}\,[_{T}$ i$]\,[_{vP}$ NP $\ldots\,]\,]$

Once embedded clauses headed by *i* became possible with this verb, their
appearance generally in contexts where embedded non-finite clauses were possible was a natural consequence.

   The earliest examples of the spread of *i*-clauses come from canonical
Middle Welsh texts. However, these are extremely rare – Miller (2004: 243)

cites the two examples, both non-finite *i*-clauses, that have been noted to date
– and are open to dispute (Morgan 1938: 209–10). Note that, in (128) and in
the Middle Welsh examples below, the preposition is spelled *y* according to
usual Middle Welsh practice.

(128)   . . . ny thebygaf   i [y un o hyn   uynet ar dy   geuyn di].
         NEG suppose.PRES.1S I to one of DEM.NS go.INF on 2S.GEN back   you
         'I do not think that any of these people will (want to) go on your back.'

(*PKM* 25.16)

More general use comes only from late Middle Welsh onwards. At this time,
we find finite *i*-clauses as objects of prepositions (129) and complements of
declarative and epistemic verbs (130).

(129)   A   [gwedy **idaw**   disgyn],   wynt a   barassant   ystabyl
         and after   to.3MS dismount.INF they PRT cause.PAST.3P stable
         y 'w   varch . . .
         to 3MS.GEN horse
         'And after he had dismounted, they had a stable prepared for his horse . . .'

(*YSG* 525–6)

(130)   Pan wybu   bobyl y wlat   [**ymi** dyuot   odyno yn
         when know.PAST.3S people the country to.me come.INF away PRED
         vyw] . . .
         alive
         'When the people of the country realized that I had come away alive . . .'

(*FfBO* 57.1)

Although superficially contradictory, the various accounts may be compatible
with each other. Lewis (1928) does not distinguish between finite and non-finite
i-clauses, but he seems to envisage that the pattern spread from control verbs
to both types. Miller's (2004) account is similar, but restricts itself essentially
to the non-finite type. Reanalysis of the syntax of control verbs is reasonable
as a source for this type, but this proposal makes less sense for the origin of
finite *i*-clauses, since they exhibit a past-tense/anterior restriction on their interpretation. The proposals of Morgan (1938) and Richards (1949–51), on the
other hand, account straightforwardly for this restriction, but it is hard to see
how they could account for the generic or future meaning of non-finite *i*-
clauses. A reasonable conclusion is that Modern Welsh *i*-clauses have two
sources: finite *i*-clauses derive from reanalysis of raising verbs such as *daruot*
'finish, happen' and *damwein(y)aw* 'happen'; and non-finite *i*-clauses derive
from reanalysis of control verbs such as *erchi* 'ask' and *peri* 'cause'.

9.10   *Wh*-constructions

In most cases, *wh*-constructions in Middle Welsh have properties identical to those of topicalization in the V2-construction discussed above (section 9.1.1). Examples here are given from relative clauses, but the same properties are found in *wh*-questions and other *wh*-constructions.

As in modern literary Welsh (see chapter 4, especially section 4.7), the basic distinction is between relative clauses formed using the particle (complementizer) *a* and those formed using the particle Middle Welsh *y(d)* (Modern Welsh *y(r)*, Middle Breton *ez*). The former is obligatory in extractions from subject position (131) and the direct-object position of a synthetic verb (132). In relative clauses formed on subject position, the verb does not agree with the extracted subject, but appears in a default third-person singular form. Hence the verb in (131) is singular (*oed* 'was') even though the antecedent of the clause is plural (*megineu* 'bellows'). Note that, although in Middle Breton and Cornish there is no agreement either in a *wh*-construction or in a V2-structure, in Welsh there is a contrast between relative clauses, where there is no agreement, and V2-structures, where there is full agreement (see section 9.3.2 above).

(131)   y   megineu **a**   oed   wedy eu   gossot yg kylch y   ty
         the bellows PRT be.IMPF.3S PERF 3P.GEN set.INF around the house
         'the bellows that had been set up around the house'   (*PKM* 36.15)

(132)   a   'r   arglwydiaeth **a**   gaussam   ninheu
         and the government   PRT receive.PAST.1P we.CONJ
         '... and the government that we had ...'   (*PKM* 8.15–16)

With relative clauses formed on other positions, usage is variable in the medieval languages, with both particles generally possible. For instance, (133) shows both particles used in the formation of relative clauses on the object of a preposition in Middle Welsh. In these cases, full agreement is generally required at the extraction site. For instance, in (133) the preposition *yndi* agrees with the feminine singular antecedent in both cases.

(133)   a. ffiol eur   **a**   anho   llawn diawt y   brenhin yndi
         vial gold PRT fit.PRES.SUBJ.3S full   drink the king   in.3FS
         'a golden vial that the king's fill of drink would fit into'   (*LIB* 3.22)
         b. Nyt oed   long **y**   kynghanei   ef yndi.
         NEG be.IMPF.3S ship PRT fit.IMPF.SUBJ.3S he in.3FS
         'There was no ship that he could fit into.'   (*PKM* 40.10–11)

This variability has been removed in the development of literary Welsh, which has generalized the particle *y(r)* in all cases except the first two above, namely clauses formed on subject position and the object position of a synthetic verb. Colloquial Welsh has continued the Middle Welsh pattern in a slightly different way, deleting the particles, but leaving the mutation effect of *a* (on loss of *a*, see section 9.1.1 above), and generalizing it (see chapter 4).

Overt relative pronouns are a feature of literary varieties of all the medieval Brythonic languages, for instance, *yr hynn* 'the one' and *y rei* 'the ones' in (136) below (compare also Middle Breton *pere* 'which ones' in this function). Their use seems to reflect imitation of the syntax of Latin or of the dominant neighbouring languages, rather than natural developments in speech.

In the negative, relative clauses formed on subject position show full subject – verb agreement, as in (134). The contrast between affirmative and negative clauses here again demonstrates the parallelism between relative clauses and V2-structures.

(134)   gwraged a   meibon a   dynyon didraha diwala,   ny   ellynt ...
        women and boys   and men   meek   contented NEG can.IMPF.3P
        nac   ymladeu na   ryueloed
        neither battles nor wars
        'women and boys and meek, contented men, who could undertake neither
        battles nor wars'   (*P* 7.13–16)

In negative object relatives, an object agreement marker -*s* optionally attaches to the negative marker in Middle Welsh, as in (135), which contrasts with (136), where this option is not taken and we find *ny* alone.

(135)   Llawer o betheu enryued ... y   rei ... **nys**   credei
        many of things strange   the ones NEG+3S believe.IMPF.3S
        neb
        anyone
        'Many strange things that no one would believe.'   (*FfBO* 46.8–9)

(136)   Medylyaw yd wyf ...   yr hynn   **ny** medylyut   ti
        think.INF PRT be.PRES.1S the DEM.NS NEG think.IMPF.SUBJ.2S you
        amdanaf i.
        about.1s me
        'I'm thinking what you wouldn't think about me.'   (*PKM* 86.10–11)

Again this parallels verb-second main-clause structures (section 9.5, especially examples (60) and (61)). The negative relative marker, Middle Welsh *ny(t)*, homophonous with the main-clause negative marker, has given way to modern Welsh *na(d)*, homophonous with the negative marker used in subordinate clauses. The optional object agreement has been lost.

9.11   Noun phrases

All Insular Celtic languages have had a definite article from their earliest attested stages (Welsh *y(r)*, Breton and Cornish *an*, Old Irish *ind*). The gender mutations and other aspects of the use of the article have remained essentially the same since Middle Welsh.

In Middle Welsh, agreement within the noun phrases is indicated, as in Modern Welsh, by mutation patterns, with feminine singular nouns triggering mutation on adjectives (see section 5.4.1). At earlier periods, morphological marking of gender and number (see section 5.4.2) was more widespread than today.

Within the noun phrase it is the syntax of numerals that has undergone the most significant and interesting change. In Modern Welsh, singular forms of nouns are used with numerals, although the phrases themselves are syntactically plural (see section 5.3). In Middle Welsh, however, a few nouns have special numerative forms for use after numerals (*brawd* 'brother', numerative *broder*, plural *brodyr*; *blwydyn* 'year', numerative *blwyd/blyned*, plural *blynyded*; *llwdn* 'young animal', numerative *llydn*, plural *llydnot*). Some other nouns appear in forms identical to the plural after numerals (*chwaer* 'sister' ~ *chwiored*; *gwraig* 'woman' ~ *gwraged*; *merch* 'girl' ~ *merchet*; *iarll* 'earl' ~ *ieirll*; *march* 'horse' ~ *meirch*; *tarw* 'bull' ~ *teirw*). Four nouns appear in the singular after *deu* 'two' (*mab* 'son', *gwas* 'servant', *gwr* 'man' and *dyd* 'day') but in numerative forms after other numerals (namely, *meib, gweis, gwyr* and *dieu* respectively). Most of these gave way to the singular in later Middle Welsh.

Phrases headed by a numeral present particular difficulties of agreement in Middle Welsh. Adjectives are plural if the adjective has a separate plural form, despite the fact that the head noun may be singular:

(137)   a. deu was   ieueinc
            two servant.S young.P
            'two young servants'   (*PKM* 81.23)
         b. dwy   genedyl vvdron
            two.F nation.S dirty.P
            'two foul nations'   (*BY* 36)

Remnants of an earlier dual number survive in the mutation patterns in phrases headed by *deu* (masculine) or *dwy* (feminine) 'two'. Here adjectives in Middle Welsh undergo soft mutation regardless of gender. Hence, in (138), the head noun is *milgi* 'greyhound', which is masculine, and would not normally trigger a mutation on a following adjective (cf. section 5.4.1). However, the adjectives *bronwynyon* 'white-breasted' and *brychyon* 'speckled' mutate to *vronwynyon* and *vrychyon* respectively because of the numeral *deu* 'two', making the whole phrase 'dual'.

(138)   deu vilgi   vronwynyon   vrychyon
         two greyhound.s   white-breasted.P speckled.P
         'two white-breasted speckled greyhounds'   (*P* 48.9–10)

In all cases, Modern Welsh has generalized singular adjectives and regularized mutation according to gender (see section 5.3.2).

9.12   Conclusion

This chapter has presented a selection of the main features of Middle Welsh and the most important developments that gave rise to the syntactic patterns of Modern Welsh. We have seen that, in some areas, the language has been syntactically very innovative. Particularly notable are major changes in main clause word order, in negation, in aspects of the system of pronouns and pre-verbal particles, and in embedded non-finite clauses. Inevitably a chapter on historical syntax has to focus more on change than on stability, but it is worth noting that, in other areas, there is remarkable continuity between Middle and Modern Welsh: basic patterns of agreement, underlying VSO word order (as revealed in embedded clauses), and core aspects of the syntax of *wh*-constructions and noun phrases have changed little.

10

Welsh as a VSO language

Subject-initial constituent order predominates in the languages of the world. Perhaps 10–12% of the world's languages have verb-initial finite clauses (Ruhlen 1987), so from a typological perspective, Welsh – with VSO surface word order – is in a relatively rare class. In this chapter we examine, both from a traditional typological and from a generative perspective, the question of whether or not there exists a distinct VSO – or more generally, verb-initial – syntactic 'type'.

Proposed universals from work in traditional syntactic typology are discussed in section 10.1. Welsh has a strongly head-initial phrase structure, but how exactly should this be characterized, and what specific word order correlations are predicted to occur? What kinds of explanation have been proposed for the observed patterns?

Proposals from the generative literature are discussed in section 10.2. Various properties have been claimed to characterize verb-initial languages, including verb agreement only with the first conjunct in coordinate structures; inflecting prepositions; lack of a lexical verb 'have'; agreement inflections closer to the verb stem than tense inflections; existence of pre-verbal particles marking tense/mood/aspect, interrogatives and polarity. We evaluate these, and other, claims in light of data from Welsh and other verb-initial languages, and conclude that no syntactic features uniquely characterize verb-initial languages.

Section 10.3 briefly considers various analyses of verb-initial languages within generative frameworks, and concludes that there are a number of distinct analytical pathways to VSO (and VOS) word order. It therefore seems clear that neither in terms of superficial distinguishing features, nor in terms of appropriate analysis, is there a single verb-initial language type.

10.1 Traditional typology: universal ordering principles and VSO languages

One of the earliest systematic investigations into typological universals of grammar was undertaken by Greenberg (1963). Working on the basis of a thirty-language sample, of which Welsh was in fact a member, Greenberg proposed a total of forty-five universals of syntax and morphology. Given the inclusion of Welsh in the original work, it is unsurprising that most of the universals which are relevant to Welsh are in fact supported by the data. However, in a wider context, not all of the proposed correlations are corroborated by more recent research. In section 10.1.1 we set out just those universals which have some relevance to verb-initial languages, together with commentary and illustration where necessary.

10.1.1   Welsh and the Greenbergian universals

Here we discuss proposed language universals from Greenberg (1963). Greenberg's work makes some strong predictions, but relies on what would now be considered a small and rather unrepresentative sample of the world's languages. Later work, for instance by Matthew Dryer (1988a, 1991, 1992), uses a much larger database: this contains a genetically and areally representative sample of 625 languages (Dryer 1992), and, as we will see, the results often reveal exceptions to the Greenbergian universals.

Universal 1. In declarative sentences with nominal subject and object, the dominant order is almost always one in which the subject precedes the object.

Universal 1 in part coincides with the word-order generalization noted at the start of the introduction. The vast majority of the world's languages have subject-initial order in unmarked clauses, but even those that do not, including Welsh, typically have a word order in which the subject precedes the object. Welsh, like all the Celtic languages, adheres to subject – object order in all unmarked clause types, whether finite, non-finite or verbless.

Universal 2. In languages with prepositions, the genitive almost always follows the governing noun, while in languages with postpositions it almost always precedes.

Universal 3. Languages with dominant VSO order are always prepositional.

Welsh adheres strictly to Universals 2 and 3: it is prepositional, as seen in (1), and has noun – genitive (NGEN) word order, as in (2):

(1)   i Fangor; am   y   ddynes; wrth y   drws
        to Bangor; about the woman; by   the door
        'to Bangor; about the woman; at the door'

(2)   a. llyfr Sioned   b. pen yr Wyddfa   c. brawd fy mam
          book Sioned   head the Snowdon   brother 1s mother
          'Sioned's book'   'the summit of Snowdon'   'my mother's brother'

Universal 3 forms part of a broader pattern of general head-initial word order: the head verb precedes its dependants, and the head preposition does likewise. Universal 2 also appears to instantiate the generalization that heads are either initial in their phrase or final, which in the generative grammatical tradition is often known as the head order parameter.

In fact, though, the head order parameter is taken to predict the order of a head and its *complement* (see Chomsky & Lasnik 1993: 518), in which case it applies to preposition – noun phrase sequences, as in (1), but is not so obviously relevant for NGᴇɴ sequences as in (2). In much generative work, the possessor NP is not regarded as a complement to the head noun, but rather, as a specifier of some kind: see the discussion of various possible accounts in section 5.6.3.4. However, Borsley (1989a), working within an HPSG framework, and Sadler (2000), in an LFG framework, both propose that possessors are in fact complements, in which case data such as (2) do indeed instantiate head-initial order in the general sense.

Note that Universals 2 and 3 are not exceptionless: see Dryer (1991, 1992). Universal 2 is in any case presented by Greenberg as a statistical, not an absolute, universal, and there are certainly exceptions to it in Dryer's sample: Garawa (Australian non-Pama-Nyungan) and Wembawemba (Pama-Nyungan) are both prepositional, but have GᴇɴN order. Universal 3 is presented as an absolute universal, but in fact there are four VSO languages in Dryer's sample (1991: 448) which are postpositional.

> *Universal 6.* **All languages with dominant VSO order have SVO as an alternative or the only alternative basic order.**

Specifically, Greenberg (1963: 79) notes that 'all VSO languages apparently have alternative basic orders among which SVO always figures'. The VSO/SVO alternation in basic word order noted by Greenberg does indeed occur frequently, for instance in varieties of Arabic, and in Berber, illustrated in (3):

(3)   a. ad-y-segh   Moha ijn teddart
          FUT-3MS-buy Moha one house
          'Moha will buy a house.'

       b. Moha ad-y-segh   ijn teddart
          Moha FUT-3MS-buy one house
          'Moha will buy a house.'   (Ouhalla 1991: 106–7)

Universal 6 seems to imply that VSO order alternates with SVO order, which is interesting from the generative perspective, since VSO order is typically seen as deriving from SVO order within the Principles Parameters framework: see section 2.3. It has also been shown by Dryer (1991) that SVO languages overwhelmingly pattern with VSO languages in terms of word order correlations, rather than being intermediate between VSO and SOV. However, assuming Greenberg's generalization to apply solely to finite clauses, as is clearly intended, Modern Welsh does not generally instantiate Universal 6.[1] Nor do the other Celtic languages, since the SVO alternative is not a possible unmarked order in finite clauses. Example (4) illustrates for Welsh:

(4)   a. Gwelodd   y   ddynes ddraig.
          see.PAST.3S the woman dragon
          'The woman saw a dragon.'
       b. *Y ddynes gwelodd   draig.
          the woman see.PAST.3S dragon
          ('The woman saw a dragon.')

As noted in sections 2.1 and 4.3, the subject may precede the verb if it is focused, but the same is true of any constituent in Welsh, including the object. Moreover, a clause with focus has a distinctive intonation pattern, with stress on the focused XP, and also displays a specific mutation on the verb:

(5)   *Y ddynes* welodd   ddraig.   (*gwelodd*)
        the woman see.PAST.3S dragon
        'It was the woman who saw a dragon.'

As discussed in section 4.3, focus constructions are *wh*-constructions. In colloquial Welsh the verb undergoes soft mutation in *wh*-constructions when a gap is formed on the subject (or object) position; see section 4.1.1. So in (5), *gwelodd > welodd*; the literary construction would have a pre-verbal particle, *a*, which also triggers soft mutation on the verb. No such mutation occurs on the verb in (4b).

Note secondly that in all varieties of Welsh, the object in (5) also undergoes soft mutation, *draig > ddraig*. In section 7.2 we propose that such mutation in a focus clause is triggered by the *wh*-trace in subject position. Such an analysis of examples like (5) depends on the assumption that SVO order is *not* basic, but involves movement from the subject position: the *wh*-movement provides a *wh*-trace which triggers the mutation. In (4), if the ungrammatical (b) were

---

[1] Welsh does, however, have non-finite SVO clauses, as outlined in chapter 3.

a possible basic order, there would be no *wh*-movement and hence no trace to trigger the mutation. The object in (4) is then incorrectly predicted not to bear soft mutation: **draig*; cf. the mutated form *ddraig* in (5).

In sum, subject-initial order in the modern language is generally a marked rather than a basic order. However, as noted in section 9.1, the emergence of predominant verb-initial word order is a relatively recent phenomenon, with unmarked SVO order remaining widespread in speech until the eighteenth century. Remnants of SVO as an unmarked word order also survive in some modern south-eastern Welsh dialects, though not in any northern dialects; cf. Thomas (1993).

> *Universal 9.* **With well more than chance frequency, when question particles or affixes are specified in position by reference to the sentence as a whole, if initial, such elements are found in prepositional languages, and, if final, in postpositional [languages].**

Universal 9 offers a further correlation concerning head – complement order: when prepositional languages have what we might call an interrogative complementizer, it is predicted to be in initial position, selecting a clausal complement. Complementizers in general are often etymologically preposi-tions (cf. English *for*), or may synchronically be classed as prepositional complementizers (see chapter 3 on *i* and *o* in Welsh infinitival clauses). Assuming that the complementizer is a head, it is then entirely expected to find ordering correlations between adposition and noun phrase complement, and complementizer and clausal complement.

Literary Welsh has overt question particles, and as predicted, these are clause-initial:

(6)   **A**   oedd   Piwritaniaid yr ail   ganrif   ar bymtheg yn
      INT be.IMPF.3S Puritans   the second century on fifteen   PRED
      chwyldrowyr?
      revolutionaries
      'Were the Puritans of the seventeenth century revolutionaries?'

(7)   **Onid**   twyll   yw   hynny?
      NEG.INT deception be.PRES.3S that
      'Isn't this cheating?'

However, in colloquial Welsh, most question particles are normally absent, though one exception is the interrogative particle *ai*, used in affirmative clauses with a focused XP:

(8)   **Ai**   [ein adran   ni] sy   'n   gyfrifol?
      FOC.INT 1P department us be.PRES.REL PRED responsible
      'Is it our department which is responsible?'

More generally, it is clear that Universal 9 is not exceptionless. For instance, Macaulay (2005) reports sentence-final question particles in two dialects of the VSO language Chalcatongo Mixtec (Diuxi-Tilantongo and Yosondúa), spoken in the Mexican state of Oaxaca; and Lee (2005) also reports sentence-final question particles in another VSO language from the same Otomanguean family, San Lucas Quiaviní Zapotec.[2] Dryer (1991) reports sentence-final question particles both in this family, and also in Nilotic and Chadic, families unrelated to Otomanguean.

> **Universal 12.** **If a language has dominant order VSO in declarative sentences, it always puts interrogative words or phrases first in interrogative word questions; if it has dominant order SOV in declarative sentences, there is never such an invariant rule.**

Welsh exemplifies Universal 12 straightforwardly, since, as seen in chapter 4, a *wh*-phrase always occurs in initial position in *wh*-questions:

(9)   **Pwy** gafodd   y   wobr?
        who get.PAST.3s the prize
        'Who got the prize?'

Again, though, Dryer's work indicates that Universal 12 is not an exceptionless generalization: there are thirteen verb-initial languages in his sample (1991: 449) which have *wh*-in-situ, rather than a fronted *wh*-element.

> **Universal 16.** **In languages with dominant order VSO, an inflected auxiliary always precedes the main verb. In languages with dominant order SOV, an inflected auxiliary always follows the main verb.**

As we have seen throughout, Welsh does have inflected auxiliaries before the main verb, though not immediately before it, since the subject normally intervenes:

(10)   **Gwnaeth** Sioned agor   yr anrheg.
        do.PAST.3s Sioned open.INF the present
        'Sioned opened the present.'

If we assume that the auxiliary is a head that takes the VP as its complement, then Universal 16 is again predictable in terms of the generalization that in VSO languages, heads precede complements throughout their syntax. In the Principles & Parameters model, the analysis would rely on this idea: a finite auxiliary is generated lower down in the clause, taking a VP complement, and

---

[2] However, Lee argues that the particles are actually base-generated in the CP domain, and that the remnant of the clause is fronted to the specifier of ForceP, giving the appearance of sentence-final particles.

raises to a position above the subject; see section 2.3.3. So in a possible analysis such as (11), the auxiliary *gwnaeth* 'do.PAST.3s' is generated in (a) as the head of *v*P, and raises to T, as shown in (b):

(11)   a. [$_{TP}$ [$_{T'}$ [$_{vP}$ Sioned [$_{v}$gwnaeth] [$_{VP}$ agor yr anrheg]]]] ⇒
         b. [$_{TP}$ [$_{T}$ gwnaeth$_j$] [$_{vP}$ Sioned [$_{v}$ t_j]   [$_{VP}$ agor yr anrheg]]]]

Universal 16 is clearly a robust generalization, but nonetheless, Dryer's sample contains one verb-initial language (a Maipuran language, Island Carib) which displays the opposite order of verb and auxiliary (1991: 448).

> ***Universal 17.* With overwhelmingly more than chance frequency, languages with dominant order VSO have the adjective after the noun.**

> ***Universal 19.* When the general rule is that the descriptive adjective follows, there may be a minority of adjectives which usually precede, but when the general rule is that descriptive adjectives precede, there are no exceptions.**

Chapter 5 showed that the unmarked word order is indeed N – Adj in Welsh:

(12)   y   gath ddu
         the cat   black
         'the black cat'

As noted by Greenberg (1963: 87), Welsh illustrates the first part of the generalization in Universal 19: most attributive adjectives follow the head noun, but a subset typically precede it (see section 5.4.3). Both orders are seen in (13):

(13)   a. fy llyfr   newydd   b. fy hoff   lyfr
            1s book   new   1s favourite book
            'my new book'   'my favourite book'

However, Greenberg's Universal 17 is decisively *not* borne out by the languages in Dryer's large and representative database. Dryer (1988a, 1992) demonstrates that in fact, VO languages (i.e. the set of languages in which the verb precedes the object) display no greater propensity for N – Adj ordering than do OV languages. So although Welsh conforms to Universal 17, nothing in particular could be said to follow from this. On the basis of his data, Dryer (1992) shows that the order of noun and adjective is not what he terms a *correlation pair*; there is no universal correlation between the order of the verb and its object (OV vs. VO) and the order of the noun and adjective.[3]

---

[3] Dryer assumes a basic OV vs. VO division. Elements whose position correlates with the position of the object (either pre- or post-head) are termed *object patterners*, and elements whose position correlates with that of the verb are *verb patterners* (Dryer 1996: 1052). For instance, an adposition is a verb patterner and its complement is an object patterner, since statistically, a strong correlation is found between the order of these two elements and the order of the <verb, object> pair. The pair <adposition, noun phrase> is then termed a correlation pair.

Universal 20. **When any or all of the items (demonstrative, numeral and descriptive adjective) precede the noun, they are always found in that order.**

The relevant portion of this universal – involving the relative order of numeral and pre-nominal adjective – is certainly observed in Welsh:

(14) y tair hen gath
      the three old cat
      'the three old cats'

As section 5.4 showed, the demonstrative is a postnominal element in Welsh.

Universal 21. **If some or all adverbs follow the adjective they modify, then the language is one in which the qualifying adjective follows the noun and the verb precedes its nominal object as the dominant order.**

Adjectival intensifiers (Greenberg's adverbs) are generally predicted by Greenberg to follow the head adjective, but he himself notes (1963: 106, fn. 17) that in Welsh, some intensifiers precede and others follow the adjective they modify. Examples of both orders are shown in (15):

(15) a. Intensifier + adjective:
      tra chymhleth 'quite complex'
      eitha(f) pwysig 'quite important'
      rhy gyflym 'too fast'
      gweddol dda 'fairly good'
    b. Adjective + intensifier
      hapus iawn 'very happy'
      oer uffernol 'awfully cold'
      cas dychrynllyd 'terribly nasty'
      tal [dros ben] 'exceedingly tall'

Despite this variation, Universal 21 clearly applies to Welsh, given that *some* intensifiers follow the adjective, attributive adjectives generally follow the noun and the verb precedes its nominal object.

It might appear at first glance that Universal 21 again indicates a correlation between head-initial order in head/complement relations (such as a verb and its object) and head-initial order in phrases generally. However, this is not the case. We have already observed that Universal 17, which predicts a prevalence of noun – adjective order in VSO languages, is not supported by Dryer's more representative database. Dryer (1991: 448–9) also notes that a number of verb-initial languages (fifteen in his sample) do not conform to the predicted adjective – intensifier order. Moreover, Dryer (1992: 97) shows that cross-linguistically, the items 'adjective + intensifier' – like the items 'noun + adjective' – do not form a correlation pair. In simple terms, the order of the elements within these pairs fails to correlate in any way with the VO or OV status of a language (see footnote 3).

It seems, then, that absolute head-initial word order across all categories is not an inevitable characteristic of verb-initial languages; we return to the characterization of 'head-initial' in section 10.1.2.

Note also that in Welsh, the pattern in (15a) is undoubtedly the unmarked order; furthermore, only a few intensifiers obligatorily follow the adjective (*iawn*, 'very', probably the most frequent intensifier, is one of these). The most likely explanation for the post-head status of *dros ben*, 'exceedingly', is that as a phrasal intensifier (etymologically a PP meaning 'over the head' or 'over the top'), it is a heavy constituent, and must therefore be postposed, like all PP adjuncts in Welsh.[4]

> ***Universal 23.*** **If in apposition the proper noun usually precedes the common noun, then the language is one in which the governing noun precedes its dependent genitive.**

Welsh conforms to Universal 23: (16) illustrates the fact that proper nouns may precede a common noun in apposition, and we have already seen in (2) that head nouns precede their dependent genitive.[5]

---

[4] A very few intensifiers have the option of appearing in either pre-head or post-head position:

(i)   eithriadol   oer / oer   eithriadol
        exceptional cold / cold exceptional
        'exceptionally cold'

(ii)   digon   parod / parod ddigon
        enough   ready / ready enough
        'willing enough'

The fact that *digon* undergoes soft mutation (> *ddigon*) in the post-head position in (ii) suggests that this is a marked word order; see Tallerman (1999). Some adjectival intensifiers appear in yet a third construction, illustrated in (iii); see P. W. Thomas (1996: 217–22):

(iii)   eithriadol   o oer
        exceptional of cold
        'exceptionally cold'

And one intensifier, *braidd* 'rather', appears either in post-adjectival position or alternatively in a fourth construction, using predicative *yn*, as in (iv):

(iv)   braidd yn   wan
        rather PRED weak
        'rather weak'

[5] Dryer concludes that noun and genitive do form a correlation pair, though noting that 'while there is an overwhelming preference for GenN order among OV languages, the preference for NGen order among VO languages is much weaker' (1992: 91).

(16)   a. Ioan Fedyddiwr   b. Dafydd Frenin   c. Duw Dad
           John baptist   David king   God father
           'John the Baptist'   'King David'   'God the father'

Note, however, that the ordering in (16) is by no means exceptionless. For instance, river names and the place name by which a lord is known are proper nouns which always follow the common noun, as shown in (17). And if a determiner is used in the noun phrase, then the order is determiner – common noun – proper noun, as shown in (18):

(17)   a. afon Menai   b. Arglwydd Tonypandy
           river Menai   lord   Tonypandy
           'Menai strait'   'Lord Tonypandy'

(18)   a. y Brenin Siarl   b. y Fam   Teresa
           the king   Charles   the mother Teresa
           'King Charles'   'mother Teresa'

Furthermore, the common nouns in (16) all bear soft mutation (*fedyddiwr* < *bedyddiwr*; *frenin* < *brenin*; *dad* < *tad*), despite the absence of any specific lexical trigger, which suggests that the order proper noun – common noun is in fact the *marked* order: see footnote 4.

This completes our discussion of the major Greenbergian universals as they apply to Welsh. What, though, should we conclude from the generalizations noted? Probably the most straightforward observation is that Welsh behaves like a canonical head-initial language in the sense that lexical heads precede complements across all phrase types: verbs precede objects; prepositions precede objects; nouns precede genitives; complementizers precede the clause; and auxiliaries precede the verb phrase. However, various predictions made by Greenberg concerning the relative ordering of other elements were shown to be unreliable: note particularly the discussion of Universals 17 and 21 above, where it was shown that adjectives do not invariably follow the head noun in head-initial languages, nor do intensifiers invariably follow the head adjective. What, then, *is* a consistently head-initial language? In section 10.1.2 we briefly consider this question.

10.1.2   *Some extensions and proposed explanations*

In early work building on the Greenbergian tradition, it was generally assumed that word-order correlations reflect a general cross-linguistic tendency for heads to either consistently precede, or consistently follow, their syntactic dependants; see, for instance, Lehmann (1973, 1978) and Vennemann (1975, 1976). Hawkins (1983) builds on these intuitions with his principle of

Cross-Category Harmony, which essentially claims that languages have a strong tendency to 'harmonize' the order of heads and dependents across all categories.

Dryer (1992) shows that simply referring to the order of 'head' and 'dependent' in word-order correlations is problematic, whether the correlation is taken to refer to a head and *any* of its dependents (which Dryer terms the Head-Dependent Theory) or only to a head and its complements (the Head-Complement Theory). If the proposal is intended to cover any head + dependent pair, then it makes a number of incorrect predictions, as we saw with respect to noun + adjective pairs and adjective + intensifier pairs in section 10.1.1: the theory is too strong, since it predicts correlation pairs which do not in fact occur; further examples are provided by Dryer (1992: 95–9). If relevant pairs are restricted just to a head and its complements, then the theory is too weak, since certain pairs which are indeed correlation pairs will be excluded. These include <verb + adjunct> (i.e. an adverb or PP modifying the verb) and <noun + relative clause>: the dependents in these cases are not complements. (In Welsh, as expected, the verb precedes any adjuncts in the unmarked case, and head nouns always precede relative clauses; see section 4.2.) How, then, can the intuition that a language is 'head-initial' or 'head-final' be captured successfully?

Dryer (1992) proposes the Branching Direction Theory (BDT) as a replacement for both the Head-Dependent Theory and the Head-Complement Theory. The basic intuition behind the BDT is as follows: 'languages tend towards one of two ideals: right-branching languages, in which phrasal categories *follow* non-phrasal categories, and left-branching languages, in which phrasal categories *precede* non-phrasal categories' (Dryer 1992: 109).[6] Specifically, heads will tend either to consistently precede their phrasal dependents, as in Welsh, or consistently follow them, as in Japanese or Turkish. Of course, in many cases all three hypotheses make identical predictions: for instance, the order of an adposition and its noun-phrase complement is successfully determined either with reference to a head and its dependent/complement or with reference to a head and its phrasal dependent.

---

[6] Dryer's formal version of the BDT (1992: 89) is as follows:

> Verb patterners are non-phrasal (non-branching, lexical) categories and object patterners are phrasal (branching) categories. That is, a pair of elements X and Y will employ the order XY significantly more often among VO languages than among OV languages if and only if X is a non-phrasal category and Y is a phrasal category.

This formulation is subsequently revised by Dryer (1992) but the later formulations do not materially affect the discussion in this chapter.

But the crucial test cases are ones where the BDT makes distinct predictions from the other two hypotheses (Dryer 1992: 107–8).

As a first instance, only the BDT distinguishes correctly between two types of adjuncts to noun heads, namely adjectives and relative clauses. As we have seen, noun + adjective is not a correlation pair; on the other hand, noun + relative clause *is* (Dryer 1992: 86–7). On the assumption that unmodified adjectives are non-phrasal dependents, the BDT correctly makes *no* predictions about their order relative to the head noun. Relative clauses, however, are always phrasal categories, and so in VO languages they are predicted by the BDT to follow the head noun. Differing behaviours amongst these two types of nominal adjuncts are successfully predicted by the BDT.

Secondly, consider two types of dependents of adjectives: intensifiers and standards of comparison. As noted in section 10.1.1 in connection with Greenberg's Universal 21, <adjective + intensifier> is not a correlation pair; again, this is correctly predicted by the BDT on the assumption that intensifiers are (canonically) non-phrasal dependents. However, <adjective + standard of comparison> *is* a correlation pair (Dryer 1992: 91–2), displaying an overwhelming preference for the order Adj–Standard in VO languages, as (19) illustrates for Welsh:

(19)   Dw   i 'n   [$_{AP}$ henach na   ti].
        be.PRES.1S I PRED   older than you
        'I'm older than you.'

Since the standard of comparison (*na ti* 'than you' in (19)) is a phrasal dependent of the adjective, the observed ordering is predicted under the BDT.

On the basis of a number of contrasts of this nature, Dryer concludes that the critical generalizations in word-order correlations must be based neither on the head-dependent nor the head-complement relation, but 'on the distinction between phrasal and non-phrasal elements' (Dryer 1992: 108).

Dryer's principle is based on a structural contrast between branching and non-branching elements, but it seems likely to have a more fundamental explanation in terms of efficiency of parsing, as Dryer himself notes (1992: 128). A very similar proposal for a parsing principle termed Early Immediate Constituents (EIC) is first advanced by Hawkins (1990, 1994); see now Hawkins (2004). The basic intuition here is that the human parser prefers word orders which allow it to recognize quickly all the immediate constituents of a phrase or clause. The idea is to minimize the number of words which must be processed in order to identify each constituent. As Dryer notes (1992: 131), consistently left- or right-branching structures are highly preferred under this proposal, which means that the EIC and the BDT predict very similar structures.

Two remaining correlations are worth mentioning here. Both articles and numerals tend to precede nouns in VO languages (Dryer 1991, 1996: 1053), i.e. articles and numerals are verb patterners (see footnote 3), with the noun as object patterner. Welsh exemplifies both of these correlation pairs; see section 5.2.1 above. For numerals, the correlation is weaker, universally, and as Dryer (1992) points out, it is likely that numerals are heads in some languages, taking the noun as complement, but in other languages are not. Whether the BDT makes any predictions in these cases depends on what structural assumptions are made: for instance, if the article (D) is a head selecting a branching NP as complement, as discussed with reference to Welsh in section 5.6, then the BDT would indeed predict article – noun phrase order in VO languages. As Dryer (1996: 1054) notes, Hawkins' earlier principle of Cross-Category Harmony (Hawkins 1983) predicts that verb-initial languages in which *all* modifiers are postnominal should be the preferred type. But this is incorrect, given a definite preference for pre-nominal articles and numerals in verb-initial languages.

Note finally that <noun, demonstrative> is not a correlation pair (Dryer 1992: 96–7), i.e. there is no universal correlation between the order of verb and object and the order of noun and demonstrative. Welsh neatly illustrates the difference between articles and numerals on the one hand and demonstratives on the other, since demonstratives are in postnominal position (section 5.4 above).

In conclusion, we can say that Welsh is a typologically highly consistent verb-initial language in terms of the generalization that heads precede branching dependents across all phrasal categories.

10.2   Approaches to word-order typology in generative grammar

Various typological correlations with VSO word order have been suggested not only in the Greenbergian tradition, but also within the generative literature. However, it seems highly unlikely that any of these will prove to be robust in the longer term, since counterexamples are plentiful.

10.2.1   Proposals by Ouhalla (1991): are the Celtic languages typologically VSO?

In this section we discuss work by Ouhalla (1991) concerning the typology of the Celtic family. His central claim is that Celtic languages are not VSO languages at all, but rather, typologically SVO – despite the fact that none of them allows unmarked SVO word order in finite clauses.[7] Ouhalla predicts the following universal word order correlations (1991: 110):

(20)   VSO languages:
        (i)   have Agr inside Tense
        (ii) have SVO as an alternative order
        (iii) lack non-inflected infinitives

(21)   SVO languages:
        (i)   have Agr outside Tense
        (ii) tend not to have VSO as an alternative order
        (iii) have non-inflected infinitives

His claim is that the Celtic languages display the pattern in (21). Note that property (21ii) does not *prevent* an SVO language from displaying a VSO alternative, which is how Ouhalla accounts for the existence of Celtic VSO word order.

10.2.1.1 Inflected infinitival clauses

We start the discussion with the third property proposed by Ouhalla, (20)/(21iii), concerning infinitival clauses. The idea is that SVO languages typically have uninflected infinitivals, 'that is, infinitival clauses which do not display an Agr element' (Ouhalla 1991: 108). On the other hand, VSO languages are predicted always to have inflected infinitival clauses, as illustrated for Berber in (22):

(22)   a. y-arzu   uxwwan [ad-y-awer]
           3MS-try.PAST thief   to-3MS-escape
           'The thief tried to escape.'
        b. t-uggur   a madrasa hama   [ad-t-rmed]
           3FS-go.PAST to school   in.order to-3FS-learn
           'She went to school to learn.'   (Ouhalla 1991: 108–9)

Ouhalla proposes the following as an implicational universal:

(23)   All languages with dominant VSO order lack non-inflected infinitives, while all languages with dominant SVO order have them.
                                                            (Ouhalla 1991: 109)

---

[7] Breton, as a verb-second language, is exceptional amongst the modern Celtic languages. In Breton affirmative main clauses, one of the more unmarked word orders involves a fronted subject, but this does not alternate with VSO, since that word order is generally ungrammatical in matrix clauses. Embedded finite clauses *are* VSO in Breton, and no alternation with SVO is possible. See also the discussion of Greenberg's Universal 6 in 10.1.1 above.

Ouhalla's view is that the Celtic languages lack inflected infinitivals; he illustrates using Welsh examples parallel to those in (24):

(24)   a. Disgwyliodd   Aled [i   Mair fynd].
           expect.PAST.3S Aled   to   Mair go.INF
           'Aled expected Mair to go.'
        b. Disgwyliodd   Aled [i   'r   genod ddarllen y   llyfr].
           expect.PAST.3S Aled   to the girls   read.INF the book
           'Aled expected the girls to read the book.'

Clearly, though, citing examples of non-inflected infinitives does not establish that inflected infinitives do not exist in the language, and in fact, Welsh does have inflected infinitival clauses, as discussed extensively in chapter 3. Like all head-dependent relations in Celtic, the relationship between the clause-initial *i* element and the subject of the infinitival clause conforms to the general principle of agreement with following pronominal arguments only (see section 6.1): *i* agrees with a pronominal subject, but not with a full noun phrase subject, as seen in (24). Changing the subjects to pronominals, as in (25), we see that Welsh indeed has infinitivals which display an obligatory agreement element, realized here as an inflection on the clause-initial *i*:

(25)   a. Disgwyliodd   Aled [**iddi**   hi   fynd].
           expect.PAST.3S Aled   to.3FS her go.INF
           'Aled expected her to go.'
        b. Disgwyliodd   Aled [**iddyn** nhw ddarllen y   llyfr].
           expect.PAST.3S Aled   to.3P   them read.INF the book
           'Aled expected them to read the book.'

Furthermore, *bod*-clauses (section 3.3) also exhibit obligatory agreement (in the form of an agreement proclitic) when the subject is pronominal:

(26)   Dywedodd   y   genod [**ei**   fod   o   'n   hwyr].
        say.PAST.3S the girls   3MS be.INF he PRED late
        'The girls said that he was late.'

And the other Celtic languages also display infinitival clauses with obligatory subject agreement, with the difference that only Welsh generally allows the pronominal subject to be overt, rather than null (see section 6.1):

(27)   Le linn **dom** bheith go mo shearradh . . .   (Connacht Irish)
        while to.1S be.INF to 1S   stretch.INF
        'While I was stretching myself . . .'   (Ó Siadhail 1989: 282)

(28)   Koulz eo   [**din**   mont].   (Breton)
        time be.PRES.3S for.1S go.INF
        'It's time for me to go.'

However, Ouhalla's use of the term 'inflected infinitive' might be taken to refer solely to a non-finite verb with agreement marking, whereas the examples in (25), (27) and (28) all involve an inflected functional element (etymologically a preposition in each case), and (26) has an inflected copula. Nonetheless, Welsh does have inflected infinitives in the first sense too, though with the agreement marking taking the form of a proclitic which agrees with the following object, rather than the preceding subject:[8]

(29) Disgwyliodd Aled [i 'r genod **ei** **ddarllen** o].
      expect.PAST.3S Aled to the girls 3MS read.INF it(3MS)
      'Aled expected the girls to read it.'

Of course, Ouhalla's generalization in (23) does not exclude SVO languages which do have inflected infinitivals, such as European Portuguese; it merely states that such infinitivals are not obligatory. Nonetheless – contrary to Ouhalla's claim – the Celtic languages appear to be typologically VSO by this generalization, since the inflections are in fact obligatory, given a pronominal (and, apart from Welsh, null) subject in the infinitival clause.

10.2.1.2 The order of tense and agreement inflections

Property (20)/(21i) refers to the order of tense and agreement inflections in relation to the verb stem.

Ouhalla accounts for the differences that he proposes between VSO and SVO languages by assuming a distinct underlying structure for each language type. True VSO languages are claimed to have a Tense projection above a (subject) Agreement projection, as in (30), while SVO languages (including of course Celtic, in his view) are said to have the Agreement projection outside the Tense projection, as in (31) (Ouhalla 1991: 113):

(30) $[_{\text{TENSEP}} [_{\text{AGRP}} [_{\text{VP}}$ [Subject] $[_{v'}]]]]$ VSO languages

(31) $[_{\text{AGRP}}$ [Subject] $[_{\text{TENSEP}} [_{\text{VP}}$ $[_{v'}]]]]$ SVO languages

Assuming the correctness of the Mirror Principle (Baker 1985), structures reflect the order in which inflections are attached to a stem. A language with the Tense projection over Agreement, as in (30), will have the agreement affix attached closer to the stem than the tense affix; this order follows from the order of the verb movement operations. Such is indeed the case in Berber and Arabic, as illustrated in (3) and (32) respectively. The concatenative morphology in these examples clearly shows that the tense marker is outside the agreement marker; that is, the agreement marker is closer to the stem than the tense marker.

---

[8] We regard it as largely a matter of realization that the agreement in (29) takes the form of a clitic rather than an affix; see sections 6.3 and 6.4 for discussion.

(32)   **sa-ya**-shtarii Zayd-un   dar-an.
         FUT-3MS-buy Zayd-NOM house-ACC
         'Zayd will buy a house.'   (Ouhalla 1991: 106)

This ordering is argued by Ouhalla to be indicative of a true VSO language.

The relevance of Ouhalla's proposal concerning the relative order of the tense and agreement inflections – and thus, the tense and agreement projections – lies in the selectional requirements of each element. If the Tense head selects an AgrP, as in (30), then Agr cannot fail to project. One result of this is that the set of Tense-initial languages – the set that Ouhalla regards as the true VSO group – will always display an Agreement projection, including in infinitival clauses. This accounts for property (20iii). Conversely, in the Agr-initial languages, Agr itself is not selected by Tense, (31), and thus, Ouhalla claims, Agr may sometimes fail to project at all. Where Agr does nonetheless project in infinitival clauses, then we get SVO languages with inflected infinitivals, such as European Portuguese.

Using Welsh as illustration, Ouhalla goes on to suggest that the Celtic languages display the opposite ordering of tense and agreement inflections from Berber and Arabic; in other words, he suggests that the tense inflection is closer to the verb stem than the agreement inflection, as in (31). Rouveret (1991) also proposes that this is the case in Welsh, claiming that 'the agreement affix is clearly external to the tense affix' (1991: 374), and illustrating with forms such as (33):

(33)   can – a   – f
         sing – T   – Agr
         sing – FUT – 1s
         'I sing/will sing.'

However, this conclusion is not supported by the evidence. As seen in chapter 1, Welsh verbal morphology is actually highly fusional, rather than concatenative, with no distinct identifiable tense and agreement morphemes in most cases. Consider, for instance, the full paradigm of the literary present tense of the verb *canu* 'sing', from which (33) is taken.[9] As Table 10.1 clearly shows, there are no recurring tense or agreement morphemes throughout the paradigm, and thus no justification for treating *a* and *f* as discrete morphemes, as Rouveret proposes. The consensus in the literature is that functional structure can only be said to reflect morpheme order if the morphology is concatenative; see Baker (1985: fn. 5; and 401–2) and also Rouveret (1991). Given the overwhelmingly fusional morphology of Welsh,

---

[9] As noted in section 1.4.2.1, literary Welsh has a true present tense which corresponds to the future tense in colloquial Welsh.

Table 10.1 *Literary Welsh present tense of* canu *'sing'.*

1s	can-af	1P	can-wn
2s	cen-i	2P	cen-wch
3s	cân	3P	can-ant

Ouhalla's proposal in (20)/(21i) is effectively irrelevant to the question of whether or not Welsh is a 'true' VSO language.[10]

Finally, it is worth noting that Ouhalla's prediction that verb-initial languages generally have tense outside subject agreement, even as a surface generalization, does not appear to be very robust. Siewierska (1993) reports that verb-initial languages are split fairly evenly between Tense outside Agr ordering – in Siewierska's notation T(A) – and Agr outside Tense ordering – in Siewierska's notation A(T). Only 54% of verb-initial languages were found to display T(A), although this is claimed by Ouhalla to be the order which is typologically associated with verb-initial word order. Obviously, reliable statistics are only available for languages that have concatenative morphology, which, as noted, is not the case for Welsh. Moreover, of the total set of T(A) languages in her sample, Siewierska reports that only 57% are verb-initial. As she notes (1993: 111): 'These figures suggest that a T(A) language has about a 50% chance of displaying V1 order, and conversely that the occurrence of T(A) order in a V1 language is virtually just as probable as that of A(T) order.'[11]

10.2.1.3 Subject positions and agreement

A further prediction by Ouhalla is that the subject occupies a different position in SVO and VSO languages. SVO languages typically have the subject in what he regards as the canonical subject position, Spec, AgrP, as shown in (31). VSO languages may use this subject position too, or alternatively, Ouhalla suggests, may have a subject which remains within the Spec, VP position, as shown in (30). Either way, if the verb moves to the highest functional

---

[10] An alternative view of Welsh agreement is presented in chapter 6. If Welsh verbal morphology is not built up from functional heads in the way that Ouhalla assumes, then the point he attempts to make concerning the ordering of tense and agreement projections would in any case be irrelevant.

[11] Whilst Ouhalla suggests that the basic constituent order of a language (verb-initial or subject-initial) can be discovered from the ordering of the tense and subject agreement affixes, Siewierska (1993: 112) also notes that this is not the case: 'basic order seems to have a stronger conditioning effect on affix order than vice versa'. In other words, the direction of the relationship is the converse of the one posited by Ouhalla.

head position, Tense, it will precede the subject in the unmarked word order. Within Ouhalla's analysis, the alternative SVO word order found in Tense-initial languages such as Standard Arabic and Berber, and illustrated in (3b) above, arises when a topic (not a canonical subject) is base-generated in the highest specifier position in the clause in (30), namely Spec, TenseP.[12]

Despite the fact that Ouhalla places the Celtic languages in a different typological class to Arabic, there is one significant respect in which the Celtic languages pattern like Arabic. This concerns the lack of number agreement between a plural full noun phrase subject and the finite verb, as illustrated for Arabic in (34) and for Welsh in (35):

(34)   a. jaaʔ-at /*jiʔ-na   l-banaat-u
            came-3FS/came-3FP the-girls-NOM
            'The girls came.'
         b. jaaʔ-a /*jaaʔ-uu   l-ʔawalaad-u
            came-3MS/came-3MP the-boys-NOM
            'The boys came.'   (Ouhalla 1991: 124–5)

(35)   Diflannodd/   *diflannon   y   dreigiau.
         disappear.PAST.3S/ disappear.PAST.3P the dragons
         'The dragons disappeared.'

Ouhalla's account of the absence of agreement observed in both language families relies on the claim that the non-pronominal subject fails to occupy the canonical Spec, AgrP position, the position in which subject agreement occurs in his framework. For Arabic, Ouhalla proposes that non-pronominal subjects in VSO clauses remain in the low Spec, VP position, where they are assigned the nominative case seen in (34). On the other hand, the topic subject of an Arabic SVO clause, in Spec, TenseP, is assigned accusative case, as seen in the embedded clause in (36), where the complementizer ʔinna is the case-assigner:

(36)   qaal-uu [ʔinna **Zayd-an**   wasal-a   mutaʔaxxir-an]
         said-3P that   Zayd-ACC arrived-3MS late-ACC
         'They said that Zayd arrived late.'   (Ouhalla 1991: 119)

In Ouhalla's account, non-pronominal subjects cannot raise to Spec, AgrP. However, he proposes that *pro* must raise to that position, which accounts for the presence of full agreement on the verb in (37), where the subject is null:

(37)   ʔishtar-u   daar-an
         bought-3MP house-ACC
         'They bought a house.'   (Ouhalla 1991: 124)

[12] Borsley (1995) presents an alternative account of the word order distinctions between Welsh and Syrian Arabic within an HPSG framework. See also Borer (1995) on VSO and SVO word orders in Modern Hebrew.

The proposal is extended to Celtic under the assumption that non-pronominal subjects also remain within VP in that family, so accounting both for the word order – V raises to the higher functional head, Agr, in the structure in (31), while the subject remains in Spec, VP – and also for the observed lack of subject/verb agreement. Ouhalla's idea is that Celtic subjects are also assigned case in this lower position, just as he proposes for Arabic.

However, the proposal that Celtic subjects remain in their underlying position is not supported by the evidence. For both Welsh and Irish, the subject must in fact raise from VP; see also chapter 2 above. For instance, in both languages, subjects (in bold type) are higher than adverbials (in italics) which modify material within VP:

(38)   a. Mae   **hogia** *bob* *amser* yn   brolio.
          be.PRES.3s lads   every time PROG boast.INF
          'Lads are always boasting.'   *(AN* 28)
    b. Doeddwn   **i** *prin*   yn   fy nal fy hun yn   ôl.
          NEG.be.IMPF.1s I scarcely PROG 1s hold 1s REFL PRED back
          'I could scarcely hold myself back.'   *(AN* 135)

(39)   a. Chuala **Róise** *go minic* roimhe   an t-amhrán sin.   (Irish)
          heard   Róise often   before.3MS the song   DEM
          'Róise had often heard that song before.'
    b. Deireann **siad** *i gcónai* paidir roimh am luí.
          say   they always   prayer before time lie.INF
          'They always say a prayer before bedtime.'   (McCloskey 1996: 269)

The fact that the subject is sited in a higher position than medial adverbials is typically considered to be evidence that it has raised from VP. Such adverbials are generally assumed to be adjoined to VP, or some higher position: in (38b), *prin* is above the progressive aspect marker *yn*, and might therefore be adjoined to an AspP. And for Irish, McCloskey (2001) demonstrates that these adverbials are in fact outside VP, since they are retained rather than deleted under VP-ellipsis. Further evidence that case-driven movement of the subject occurs in Irish is provided by McCloskey (1996, 1997, 2001).

Finally, it is worth asking whether verb-initial (or VSO) languages invariably lack full subject/verb agreement. In fact, they do not: for instance, the VSO language Chalcatongo Mixtec has subject/verb agreement (Macaulay 1996, 2005), and so does the VSO language Chamorro (Chung 1998, 2004: 201):

(40)   a. **Ha**-ottu i   petta i   patas-su.
          3s-bang the door the foot-1s
          'The door banged my foot.'

b. **Ma**-fa'gasi   i   lalahi i   kannai-ñiha.
3DUAL/P-wash the men   the hand-3DUAL/P
'The men washed their hands.'   (Chung 1998: 36)

In sum, Ouhalla's suggestion that the Celtic languages are not genuinely VSO in terms of their typology is not well supported. But two questions remain: are there any genuinely universal syntactic correlates of verb-initial order, and is there really a syntactically distinct VSO (or more generally, verb-initial) language *type*? In the next section we examine a number of other proposals for language universals, and conclude that both these questions must be answered in the negative.

10.2.2 Further proposals for correlates of verb-initial order

In their introduction to Carnie & Guilfoyle (2000), the editors suggest the following as typical (though not exceptionless) correlates of VSO word order:

(41)   Carnie & Guilfoyle's proposed syntactic correlates of VSO order
    i.   Head initiality
    ii.   Prepositional
    iii. Postnominal adjectives
    iv.   Pre-verbal tense, mood/aspect, question and negation particles
    v.   Inflected prepositions
    vi.   Left-conjunct agreement
    vii. Lack of a verb 'have'
    viii. Copular constructions without verbs
    ix.   Verbal noun infinitives   (Carnie & Guilfoyle 2000: 10)

The first three are Greenbergian, and we have already examined their status in section 10.1.1.

10.2.2.1 Pre-verbal particles

Moving on to correlate (iv), it is certainly true that pre-verbal particles of various kinds are common in all the Celtic languages, and in many other verb-initial languages. We have already commented on the status of initial question particles in Welsh in section 10.1.1, in connection with Greenberg's Universal 9. It is not the case that Welsh always has some pre-verbal particle in a finite clause. As discussed in section 8.2, literary Welsh does have pre-verbal negation particles, but these do not appear in most contexts in colloquial Welsh. Instead, the postverbal negative adverb *ddim*, which is optionally present in the literary variety, has become the sole marker of negation in colloquial Welsh in contexts such as (42):

(42)   Dw   i **ddim** wedi gweld y   ffilm.
        be.PRES.1S I NEG PERF see.INF the film
        'I haven't seen the film.'

Colloquial Welsh is therefore a counterexample to what Dryer (1988b) proposed as an exceptionless generalization concerning verb-initial languages, namely that the negative element always comes before the verb in unmarked word order, not after it.[13]

Within a transformational framework, Bury (2005) in fact proposes that verb-initial languages which are derived by verb-movement (like Welsh) actually *require* pre-verbal particles. He suggests (2005: 148) that the verb moves to the complementizer position, but that such head-movement could only be learnable if the target position for movement contains an overt lexical item at least some of the time. If the pre-verbal particles are complementizers, then their prevalence in verb-initial languages is predicted. We have seen that literary Welsh has overt question and negation particles, though these are normally absent in colloquial Welsh. The pre-verbal particles most likely to occur in the colloquial variety are the affirmative markers *mi* or *fe* (see section 2.1), illustrated in (43):

(43)   **Mi/fe** es   i allan.
        AFF   go.PAST.1S I out
        'I went out.'

Note, though, that an affirmative marker is by no means obligatory in (43). *Mi/fe* both trigger soft mutation on the following verb, and since the verb may appear in its soft mutated form even when the particle is absent, it is often suggested that the mutation is triggered by a phonologically empty particle; Bury (2005) also proposes this. However, it is rather hard to sustain the view that the particle is in some sense always 'there', since both it and its mutation effects

---

[13] Dryer (1991: 446, fn.5) notes a further exception, the Chadic language Lamang. Note, though, that in some verb forms colloquial Welsh does display an initial *d-*, a remnant of the literary negative complementizer *ni(d)* (see section 8.2.2); for instance, *dydy* (*d* + *ydy*), NEG.be.PRES.3S 's/he is not', and *dwn* (*d* + *wn*), NEG.know.FUT.1S 'I do not know'. However, as discussed in section 8.2.2, it does not seem plausible to propose a phonologically null counterpart of *ni(d)* in all negative contexts. When overtly present, the morpheme *ni* triggers aspirate mutation on verbs beginning with the voiceless stops (*p*, *t*, *c*), whereas in spoken Welsh, which has no *ni*, the majority of verbs with initial *p*, *t* or *c* display soft mutation, not aspirate. This strongly implies that a null complementizer is in fact not present in these contexts, nor indeed (contra Roberts 2005: 73) is *ni* 'subject to a late deletion rule at PF'.

may be absent. Moreover, as noted in section 2.1.2, pre-verbal particles are obligatorily absent with some forms of *bod* 'be'.[14]

Roberts (2005: chapter 4) makes a very similar proposal concerning the obligatoriness of pre-verbal particles to that of Bury. He suggests that Welsh pre-verbal particles such as *mi, fe* and *y* are members of the C-system; specifically, they occupy the Fin head within a split-C system (Rizzi 1997). The proposal is that initial verbs also merge in Fin, but that verb-movement alone is not licit; therefore, either the particles are required, or else there must be some other mechanism preventing verbs from being in absolute initial position, such as the filled specifier found in V2 syntax (as in Germanic).

10.2.2.2 Inflected prepositions

Correlate (v), the idea that inflected prepositions only occur in verb-initial languages (see section 6.1), was proposed by Kayne:

(44)   Agreement between a preposition and its lexical complement is possible
        only in a V . . . S . . . language.   (1994: 50).

Specifically, Kayne's theory predicts that agreement between an adposition and its complement is always a reflex of head/specifier agreement, so in order to derive a preposition that agrees with its complement, the latter would have to raise to the specifier position in the PP, to trigger agreement, after which the head P would raise to a higher head position. Kayne also notes that (44) is a conjecture which requires an explanation. However, (44) does not predict that *all* verb-initial languages display inflected prepositions, so although the Celtic languages do all have them, we cannot conclude that this is an inevitable concomitant of verb-initial status. In fact, the majority of verb-initial languages certainly do appear to have person marking on prepositions. However, this is not the case for Konjo, Tinrin or Nandi, which all have prepositions without inflections.[15]

---

[14] Roberts (2005: 33–4, 123) proposes that the complementarity between various forms of *bod* 'be' and pre-verbal particles is accounted for by the fact that all are in the same position (the Fin head in the C-system). However, as discussed in section 2.1.2, the situation is in fact more complex than Roberts' account allows for. For instance, in some varieties of colloquial Welsh the affirmative particle *mi* can co-occur with forms of *bod* in the first and second person singular present tense: *mi (r)ydw, mi (r)wyt*. Clearly, strict complementarity between finite forms of *bod* and the pre-verbal particles does not occur.

[15] We thank Anna Siewierska for providing information on prepositions and inflections, gathered from her extensive database.

10.2.2.3 Left-conjunct agreement

Correlate (vi), left-conjunct agreement, was illustrated in section 6.2. Consider (45), where the verb is in the first-person singular form *gwelais*, agreeing with the first conjunct *i* 'I', while the subject itself is plural, a coordination of the two noun phrases *i a Megan*:

(45)   Gwelais   [i a   Megan] ddraig yn yr ardd.
        see.PAST.1S I and Megan dragon in the garden
        'Megan and I saw a dragon in the garden.'

Left-conjunct agreement, or first conjunct agreement as the phenomenon is also known, is attested in a number of languages and language families. It occurs in languages with basic VSO word order, such as the Celtic family, and Semitic (e.g. Biblical Hebrew, Standard Arabic), but it also occurs in languages with other basic word orders, such as Slavonic (e.g. Polish, Russian), Frisian and Swahili. Examples (46) and (47) illustrate further:

(46)   way-yiqqaḥ   šem   ɛwa:-yɛpɛt̪ ʔɛt̪-haṣṣimla: (Biblical Hebrew)
        and-took.3MS Shem and-Japheth ACC.the-garment
        'And Shem and Japheth took a garment.' (Genesis 9:23)

                                                                (Doron 2000: 75)

(47)   Do pokoju weszła   młoda kobieta i   chłopiec.   (Polish)
        to room entered.F.S young woman and boy
        'Into the room walked a young woman and a boy.'   (Citko 2004)

It is often noted that first conjunct agreement is sensitive to word order. Doron (2000: 77), for instance, points out that it occurs in Hebrew (and in other languages with variable constituent order) in VS clauses, but not in SV clauses. Citko (2004) also observes that first conjunct agreement is possible with postverbal subjects in Slavonic, as shown in (47), but is not generally found with pre-verbal subjects (with some rare exceptions).[16] She also notes that 'the agreeing conjunct simply has to follow the element it agrees with' (fn. 2). The latter generalization is in fact crucial to an analysis of first conjunct agreement in the Celtic languages, since all heads (not just verbs) display agreement with an immediately following pronominal first conjunct: see section 6.3 above.

10.2.2.4 The lack of lexical 'have'

Correlate (vii) suggests that VSO languages lack a lexical verb 'have'; see, for instance, Freeze & Georgopoulos (2000: 167), who, citing the Mayan VOS language Yucatec as illustration, state that 'there are no "have" lexicalizations in the possessive sentences of verb initial languages'. It is certainly

---

[16] However, there are important differences between Celtic and Slavonic: whereas first-conjunct agreement is compulsory in Celtic, it is merely possible in Slavonic.

true of most of the Celtic family – apart from Breton and Cornish – that a
lexical 'have' does not occur. Three alternative constructions, all involving a
PP, are common in Welsh, as illustrated in (48) to (50):

(48)   Mae   **gen**   **i**   feic/ annwyd/ dri   o blant.
        be.PRES.3s with.1s me bike/ cold/   three of children
        'I've got a bike/a cold/three children.'

(49)   Mae   pen tost/ dwy chwaer **'da** **fi**.
        be.PRES.3s head sore/ two sister   with me
        'I've got a headache/two sisters.'

(50)   Mae   annwyd / peswch   / haint   / hiraeth   **arni** **hi**.
        be.PRES.3s cold(n.) / cough(n.) / bug(n.) / homesickness on.3FS her
        'She's got a cold / a cough / a bug / homesickness.'

The difference between (48) and (49) is mainly dialectal, with the former used
in northern dialects and the latter in southern ones; both can be used for either
alienable or inalienable possession, and both are also used to indicate temporary states, such as having an illness or pain. The construction in (50), with a
PP headed by *ar* 'on', is restricted to temporary states of mind and body, and
cannot be used for possession.

    In Breton, possession can also be indicated in a similar way to Welsh, using
a PP construction: *gant* 'with' in (51) is cognate with Welsh *gan* 'with' in (48):

(51)   **Ganti**   e   oa   teir   yar.
        with.3FS PRT be.IMPF.3s three hen
        'She had three hens.'   (Press 1986: 140)

However, Breton does have a lexical verb 'have', *endevout* or *kaout* in the
infinitival form; this construction is illustrated in (52):

(52)   Bremañ Azenor ha Iona **o** **deus**   un ti.
        now   Azenor and Iona 3P have.PRES a house
        'Azenor and Iona have a house now.'   (Jouitteau 2005: 373)

This is also the only verb in Breton which fails to obey the complementarity
principle (see section 1.4.3), a constraint by which fully inflected forms can
only co-occur with a null pronominal argument. (As we have often seen, agreement in Welsh is allowed with either an overt or null pronominal, but in most
varieties of Breton, agreement only co-occurs with a null pronominal.) This
constraint does not hold in (52), where an overt non-pronominal subject co-
occurs with a fully agreeing verb form *o deus* ('have.3P').[17]

---

[17] Historically, the finite forms of Breton *kaout/endevout* 'have' derive from the verb
bezañ 'be' plus a prefixed personal pronoun. However, the 'have' verb has now developed an entirely independent existence in Breton, as is clear from its morphology
and the fact that it has an infinitival form and is used as a perfect auxiliary.

Other environments where a 'have' verb typically occurs cross-linguistically include existentials, psych constructions (as in French *avoir peur/faim*, have.INF fear/hunger 'to be afraid/hungry'), modals and the perfect. Examples of these contexts in Welsh – all without a 'have' verb – are illustrated in (53) to (56):

(53)   Mae   gan y   ganolfan theatr â   lle   i   365 o bobl.
       be.PRES.3s with the centre   theatre with room for 365 of people
       'The centre has a theatre with room for 365 people.'

(54)   a. Mae   gen/   arna i   ofn.
          be.PRES.3s with.1s/ on.1s me fear
          'I'm afraid.'
       b. Dw   i 'n   ofni   nadroedd.
          be.PRES.1s I PROG fear.INF snakes
          'I'm afraid of snakes.'
       c. Dw   i ofn   nadroedd.
          be.PRES.1s I fear(n.) snakes
          'I'm afraid of snakes.'

(55)   a. Maen   nhw 'n   gorfod   mynd.
          be.PRES.3P they PROG must.INF go.INF
          'They have to go.'
       b. Rhaid   iddyn nhw fynd.
          necessity to.3P them go.INF
          'They have to go.'

(56)   Maen   nhw wedi mynd.
       be.PRES.3P they PERF go.INF
       'They have gone.'

The different possibilities shown in the examples in (54) and (55) are, in each case, widely used alternative constructions conveying the same meanings. The construction in (54c) is more colloquial than that in (54b).

The lack of a verb 'have' is certainly not an inevitable concomitant of verb-initial word order. Apart from Breton and Cornish, Chalcatongo Mixtec is cited by Macaulay (2005) as an example of a verb-initial language with a robust possessive 'have'. Conversely, many other languages which are not verb-initial also lack a lexical verb 'have', such as Finnish, Hungarian, Japanese, Russian and Turkish. Clearly, the lack of 'have' does not correlate with the head-initial property, though as a one-way implication (if verb-initial then no 'have'), it is a strong, though not exceptionless, generalization.

10.2.2.5 Verbless copular constructions

Correlate (viii) proposes that VSO languages display copular constructions without verbs. In the Irish construction in (57), the initial element *is* (glossed as COPULA) is often argued to be a functional element synchronically rather than a verb of any kind; see Ahlqvist (1972), Carnie (1995, 2000), Doherty (1996):

(57)   Is dochtúir capall   (é) Cathal.
        COP doctor   horses.GEN AGR Cathal
        'Cathal is a doctor of horses.'   (Carnie 2000: 67)

Carnie regards *is* as a complementizer, while Doherty sees it as an inflectional head I. Regarding correlate (viii), Doherty (1996: 7) reports that *is* can indeed be omitted in casual speech.

Welsh does have a collection of proverbs which generally appear without a copula, as illustrated in (58):

(58)   a. Nid aur popeth   melyn.
           NEG gold everything yellow
           'All that glitters is not gold.'
        b. Hir pob   aros.
           long every wait
           'A watched pot never boils.'

There is, though, always the possibility of adding the copula, to give *Nid aur yw popeth melyn*, *Hir yw pob aros*. Furthermore, these constructions are lexicalized, whereas in Irish, the construction shown in (57) is productive. In Modern Welsh, the omission of the copula is a hallmark of formal rather than casual style, although this construction was formerly far more productive in the spoken language. Nonetheless, Modern Welsh does not in a meaningful sense display copular constructions without verbs: these are obsolescent even in literary Welsh. Conversely, as is well known, many non-VSO languages display verbless copular constructions, for instance, Modern Hebrew and Russian. See also section 8.1.2.

10.2.2.6 The use of nominalized verb forms in place of finite verbs

Correlate (ix) proposes that verb-initial languages have a tendency to use nominalized forms such as 'verbal noun' infinitives in contexts where SVO languages would have finite verbs (Myhill 1985: 188). However, we have argued in section 3.1.1 that syntactically, the infinitive in Welsh is not a nominalized form at all, but a genuine verb, non-finite except in the case of *bod* 'be' (section 3.3.2). Myhill specifically proposes relative clauses and other subordinate clauses, and cleft or focus constructions as examples of environments which demand nominalized rather than verbal forms, or alternatively require special dependent forms of the verb. He cites Welsh *bod*-clauses as an example of a subordinate context with a nominalized verb form, but in fact *bod*-clauses behave like fully finite clauses, as seen in section 3.3.2 above, and *bod* itself is not a nominalized form. Furthermore, section 3.2 shows that – contrary to Myhill's predictions – ordinary finite verbs can occur perfectly well in Welsh subordinate clauses.

Welsh *wh*-constructions also fail to support Myhill's proposals. In general, the same finite verb forms occur both in ordinary VSO clauses and in relative clauses and focus constructions; there is no paradigm of special dependent verb forms used in the latter contexts, with the exception of a special present tense form of *bod*, namely *sy(dd)* (section 4.1.4), which is used in subject extraction *wh*-constructions. There are certainly distinct agreement effects in focus constructions (section 4.3.2), and Myhill takes these effects to be indicative of a special verbal status; but in fact a general account of the lack of person agreement in focus (and other) contexts is available on the premise that a head agrees with a *following*, but not a preceding, pronominal element (section 6.3).

In sum, we can conclude first that no other syntactic properties correlate uniquely with verb-initial word order, and second, that none of the proposed characteristics discussed in this section uniquely defines a set of verb-initial languages. On the other hand, verb-initial languages from unrelated families often share remarkably similar properties, for instance the lack of agreement between full NP subjects (as opposed to pronominal subjects) and finite verbs, which occurs both in the Celtic languages and in the Semitic languages: see (34) and (35) above, and section 6.1 for further illustration from Welsh.

10.3   Conclusion: the derivation of verb-initial word order

The transformational generative tradition has largely assumed that verb-initial languages are derived from an underlying SVO word order. For Welsh, for instance, the 'underlying SVO' proposal dates back to an early generative work, Jones & Thomas (1977). A natural question then arises, as noted by Carnie, Harley & Dooley (2005) in their editors' introduction: is there a single way of deriving verb-initial word order universally, or at least, is there one derivation for VSO order and another for VOS order? The answer in both cases is again negative.

Even assuming a uniform underlying structure, a number of different ways of deriving verb-initial word order are proposed in the literature. Three main analyses involving movement can be distinguished. The Celtic languages and also the verb-initial Semitic languages are generally analysed as involving head-movement of the finite verb/auxiliary, typically to I or to one of the functional heads replacing I, such as T.

Conversely, for the alternating VSO/VOS language Chamorro, Chung (1990, 1998) has argued that the most appropriate analysis involves the lowering of the subject; more generally, she confirms the view that there is no universal verb-initial language 'type'.

Yet a third broad possibility, the raising of an entire VP (or other XP) predicate, or else VP remnant raising, has become well established in the recent transformational literature; see, for instance, a number of papers in Carnie & Guilfoyle (2000) and Carnie, Harley & Dooley (2005). The raising of a remnant VP would entail that everything but the verb has previously been moved out of the VP, so that raising the remnant – overtly, just the verb – derives VSO order. VOS order can also be derived if the object cannot move independently of the verb (for reasons relating to Case assignment, for instance), but must raise along with the verb, resulting in an entire fronted VP. Analyses along these lines are proposed by Lee (2000) for Quiaviní Zapotec, Massam (2000, 2005) for Niuean, Rackowski & Travis (2000) for Malagasy and Niuean, and Travis (2005) for Malagasy. The empirical motivation behind the predicate-raising analysis for such languages comes from the fact that their syntax is not merely verb-initial, but more generally predicate-initial. Two examples illustrate:

(59)   sidâi   ɛnâ.   (Maasai)
        nice.ACC this.NOM
        'This is nice.'   (Koopman 2005: 286)

(60)   hā   he fale   gagao a   ia.   (Niuean)
        PRED in house sick   ABS she
        'She's in hospital.'   (Otsuka 2005: 67)

We can conclude that the verb-initial languages so far investigated form a highly disparate set, in terms of both syntactic properties and appropriate analysis.

In fact, it seems clear that even closely-related languages (such as the Celtic languages) do not necessarily follow the same route to derive their observed word orders. As McCloskey (1996) remarks, there is no 'VSO parameter', and even within the Celtic language family, there are major distinctions in terms of appropriate analyses. He continues: 'recent work on VSO languages . . . has shed great doubt on the idea that they might form a unitary class' (McCloskey 1996: 273–4).

References

Modern Welsh texts

AN   Doherty, Berlie (1991 [1993]). *Annwyl neb*. Translated by Emily Huws. Llandysul: Gwasg Gomer.

COG   Elis, Islwyn Ffowc (1952). *Cyn oeri'r gwaed*. Llandysul: Gwasg Gomer.

DE   Martell, Owen (2003). *Dyn yr eiliad*. Llandysul: Gwasg Gomer.

DHMH Meredith, Owain (1997). *Diwrnod hollol mindblowing heddiw*. Talybont: Y Lolfa.

GPB   Davies, E. Tegla (1923). *Gŵr Pen y Bryn*. Cardiff: Hughes a'i Fab.

GT   Owen, Daniel (1992 [1894]). *Gwen Tomos*. Cardiff: Hughes a'i Fab.

TMC   Roberts, Kate (1988 [1936]). *Traed mewn cyffion*. Llandysul: Gwasg Gomer.

WJ   Hughes, T. Rowland (1944). *William Jones*. Llandysul: Gwasg Gomer.

Historical Welsh texts

BB   Roberts, Brynley F. (ed.) (1971). *Brut y Brenhinedd. Llanstephan MS. 1 version*. Dublin: Dublin Institute for Advanced Studies.

BD   Lewis, Henry (ed.) (1942). *Brut Dingestow*. Llandysul: J. D. Lewis a'i Feibion.

BDaf.   Jones, Hugh & Cadwaladr, John (?*c.* 1765). *Enterlut, neu ddanghosiad o'r modd y darfu i'r Brenhin Dafydd odinebu efo gwraig Urias*. Caerlleon [Chester]: W. Read a T. Huxley.

BLl.   Y Brenin Llyr. (*c.* 1700–50). National Library of Wales, Cwrtmawr MS 212A.

BM   Williams, Ifor (ed.) (1908). *Breuddwyd Maxen*. Bangor: Jarvis a Foster.

BT   Jones, Thomas (ed.) (1955). *Brut y tywysogyon or the chronicle of the princes. Red Book of Hergest version*. Cardiff: University of Wales Press.

BY   Jones, Thomas (ed.) (1940). *Y Bibyl Ynghymraec*. Cardiff: Gwasg Prifysgol Cymru.

CA   Williams, Ifor (ed.) (1938). *Canu Aneirin*. Cardiff: Gwasg Prifysgol Cymru.

CC   Lewis, Henry (ed.) (1925). Cynghorau Catwn. *Bulletin of the Board of Celtic Studies* 2. 16–25.

CO   Bromwich, Rachel & Evans, D. Simon (eds.) (1992). *Culhwch ac Olwen. An edition and study of the oldest Arthurian tale*. Cardiff: University of Wales Press.

DFfEL   Kyffin, Maurice (Morys) (1595). *Deffyniad Ffydd Eglwys Loegr*. Williams, W. P. (ed.) (1908). Bangor: Jarvis & Foster.

ER   Roberts, Ellis (1759). *Dwy o gerddi newyddion*. Y Mwythig [Shrewsbury]. Stafford Prys.

ERRG   Roberts, Ellis & Gruffudd, Robert (1782). *Dwy o gerddi newyddion . . .* Trefriw: Dafydd Jones.

FfBO   Williams, Stephen J. (ed.) (1929). *Ffordd y Brawd Odrig*. Cardiff: Gwasg Prifysgol Cymru.

GBC   Ellis Wynne (1703). *Gweledigaetheu y bardd cwsc*. Morris-Jones, John (ed.) (1948). Cardiff: Gwasg Prifysgol Cymru.

HGC   Anon. (ed.) (17th–18th c.) *Hanes-gerddi Cymraeg. Casgliad o hanes-gerddi Cymraeg* 1903. Cardiff: William Lewis.

HLlTN   Edwards, Thomas (Twm o'r Nant) (1789, 1799–1806). *Hunangofiant a llythyrau Twm o'r Nant*. Ashton, Glyn M. (ed.) (1948). Cardiff: Gwasg Prifysgol Cymru.

Juv.   Juvencus englynion. In Haycock, Marged (ed.) (1994). *Blodeugerdd Barddas o ganu crefyddol cynnar*. Llandybïe: Cyhoeddiadau Barddas. 3–16.

LlALl   Morris-Jones, John & Rhŷs John (eds.) (1894). *The Elucidarium and other tracts in Welsh from Llyvyr Agkyr Llandewivrevi, A. D. 1346 (Jesus College MS. 119)*. Oxford: Clarendon Press.

LlB   Williams, Stephen J. & Powell, J. Enoch (eds.) (1961). *Cyfreithiau Hywel Dda yn ôl Llyfr Blegywryd*. Cardiff: Gwasg Prifysgol Cymru.

O   Thomson, Robert L. (ed.) (1968). *Owein or Chwedyl Iarlles y Ffynnawn*. Dublin: Dublin Institute for Advanced Studies.

P   Goetinck, Glenys W. (ed.) (1976). *Historia Peredur vab Efrawc*. Cardiff: Gwasg Prifysgol Cymru.

Peniarth   Teithie Syr Sion Mandefyl. National Library of Wales, ms. Peniarth 218
218   (1605–10). References are to line numbers in *Corpws Hanesyddol yr Iaith Gymraeg 1500–1850* (http://people.pwf.cam.ac.uk/dwew2/hcwl/pen218/ pen218_frames.htm).

PKM   Williams, Ifor (ed.) (1930). *Pedeir Keinc y Mabinogi*. Cardiff: Gwasg Prifysgol Cymru.

PN   Jones, Hugh (1783). *Enterlute newydd; ar ddull ymddiddan rhwng Protestant a Neilltuwr . . .* Mwythig [Shrewsbury]: T. Wood.

RhG   Parry-Williams, T. H. (ed.) (1954). *Rhyddiaith Gymraeg*. Vol. i: 1488–1609. Vol. ii: 1547–1618. Jones, Thomas (ed.) (1956). Cardiff: Gwasg Prifysgol Cymru.

Surexit   Dafydd Jenkins, & Owen, Morfydd E. (eds.) (1983–4). The Surexit Memorandum. The Welsh marginalia in the Lichfield Gospels. *Cambridge Medieval Celtic Studies* 5. 37–66, 7. 91–120.

TCh   Davies, W. Beynon (ed.) (1976). *Troelus a Chresyd (o lawysgrif Peniarth 106)*. Cardiff: Gwasg Prifysgol Cymru.

TWRP   [16th c.] Jones, G. (ed.) (1939). *A study of three Welsh religious plays*. Bala: R. Evans & Son.

YBH   Watkins, Morgan (ed.) (1958). *Ystorya Bown de Hamtwn*. Cardiff: Gwasg Prifysgol Cymru.

| YCM | Williams, Stephen J. (ed.) (1930). *Ystorya de Carolo Magno.* Cardiff: Gwasg Prifysgol Cymru. |
| YSG | Jones, Thomas (ed.) (1992). *Ystoryaeu Seint Greal.* Cardiff: Gwasg Prifysgol Cymru. |

Middle Breton texts

B	Ernault, Émile (ed.) (1888). *Le mystère de sainte Barbe.* Paris: Libraire du Collège de France.
Ca.	Ernault, Émile (ed.) (1887). La vie de sainte Catherine. *Revue Celtique* 8. 76–95.
GK	Ernault, Émile (ed.) (1928–30). Le breton de Gilles de Keranpuil. *Revue Celtique* 45. 202–71, 47. 72–159.

Secondary Literature

Abney, Steven Paul (1987). The English noun phrase in its sentential aspect. Doctoral dissertation, Cambridge, MA: MIT.

Ackema, Peter & Neeleman, Ad (2004). *Beyond morphology: interface conditions on word formation.* Oxford: Oxford University Press.

Ahlqvist, Anders (1972). Some aspects of the copula in Irish. *Éigse* 14. 269–74.

Aldridge, Michelle, Borsley, Robert D., Clack, Susan, Creunant, Gwenan & Jones, Bob Morris (1997). The acquisition of noun phrases in Welsh. In Sorace, Antonella, Heycock, Caroline & Shillcock, Richard (eds.), *Proceedings of the GALA '97 Conference on Language Acquisition.* Edinburgh: Human Communication Research Centre, University of Edinburgh. 6–9.

Alexopoulou, Theodora (2006). Resumption in relative clauses. *Natural Language and Linguistic Theory* 24. 57–111.

Anderson, Stephen R. (1982). Where's morphology? *Linguistic Inquiry* 13. 571–612.

(1992). *A-morphous morphology.* Cambridge: Cambridge University Press.

Anwyl, E. (1899). *A Welsh grammar for schools, part II – syntax.* London: Swan Sonnenschein & Co. Ltd.; New York: Macmillan.

Awbery, Gwenllïan Mair (1976). *The syntax of Welsh: a transformational study of the passive.* Cambridge: Cambridge University Press.

(1977). A transformational view of Welsh relative clauses. *Bulletin of the Board of Celtic Studies* 27. 155–206.

Baker, Mark (1985). The Mirror Principle and morphosyntactic explanation. *Linguistic Inquiry* 16. 373–417.

Ball, Martin J. (1987–8). The erosion of the Welsh pre-sentential particle system. *Studia Celtica* 22/23. 134–45.

Ball, Martin J. (ed.) (1988a). *The use of Welsh.* Clevedon: Multilingual Matters.

Ball, Martin J. (1988b). Variation in grammar. In Ball (ed.). 58–69.

Ball, Martin J. (ed.) (1993). *The Celtic languages.* London: Routledge.

Ball, Martin J., Fife, James, Poppe, Erich & Rowland, Jenny (eds.) (1990). *Celtic linguistics, Ieithyddiaeth Geltaidd: readings in the Brythonic languages, a festschrift for T. Arwyn Watkins.* Amsterdam: John Benjamins.

Ball, Martin J. & Müller, Nicole (1992). *Mutation in Welsh*. London: Routledge.

Beavers, John & Sag, Ivan A. (2004). Ellipsis and apparent non-constituent coordination. In Müller, Stefan (ed.), *Proceedings of the 11th International Conference on Head-Driven Phrase Structure Grammar*. Stanford, CA: CSLI Publications. 70–92.

Blevins, James (2003). Passives and impersonals. *Journal of Linguistics* 39. 473–520.

Bondaruk, Anna (1995). Resumptive pronouns in English and Polish. In Gussman, Edmund (ed.), *Licensing in syntax and phonology*. Lublin: Folium. 27–55.

Borer, Hagit (1995). The ups and downs of Hebrew verb movement. *Natural Language and Linguistic Theory* 13. 527–606.

Borsley, Robert D. (1984). VP complements: evidence from Welsh. *Journal of Linguistics* 20. 277–302.

(1986). Prepositional complementizers in Welsh. *Journal of Linguistics* 22. 67–84.

(1989a). An HPSG approach to Welsh. *Journal of Linguistics* 25. 333–54.

(1989b). Phrase structure grammar and the Barriers conception of clause structure. *Linguistics* 27. 843–63.

(1993). On so-called 'verb-nouns' in Welsh. *Journal of Celtic Linguistics* 2. 35–64.

(1995). On some similarities and differences between Welsh and Syrian Arabic. *Linguistics* 33. 99–122.

(1997). Mutation and case in Welsh. *Canadian Journal of Linguistics* 42. 31–56.

(1999). Mutation and constituent structure in Welsh. *Lingua* 109. 263–300.

(2005). On the superficiality of Welsh agreement and related matters. Unpublished manuscript, University of Essex.

(2006). On the nature of Welsh VSO clauses. *Lingua* 116. 462–90.

Borsley, Robert D. & Jones, Bob Morris. (2001). The development of finiteness in early Welsh. *Journal of Celtic Language Learning* 6. 9–20.

(2005). *Welsh negation and grammatical theory*. Cardiff: University of Wales Press.

Borsley, Robert D. & Kathol, Andreas (2000). Breton as a V2 language. *Linguistics* 38. 665–710.

Borsley, Robert D., Rivero, María-Luisa & Stephens, Janig (1996). Long head movement in Breton. In Borsley & Roberts (eds.), 53–74.

Borsley, Robert D. & Roberts, Ian (eds.) (1996a). *The syntax of the Celtic languages*. Cambridge: Cambridge University Press.

Borsley, Robert D. & Roberts, Ian (1996b). Introduction. In Borsley & Roberts (eds.) 1–52.

Borsley, Robert D. & Stephens, Janig (1989). Agreement and the position of subjects in Breton. *Natural Language and Linguistic Theory* 7. 407–427.

Borsley, Robert D. & Tallerman, Maggie (1996). Phrases and soft mutation in Welsh. *Journal of Celtic Linguistics* 5. 1–49.

Bresnan, Joan (2001). *Lexical-functional syntax*. Blackwell: Oxford.

Bury, Dirk (2005). Pre-verbal particles in verb-initial languages. In Carnie, Harley & Dooley (eds.). 135–54.

Cardinaletti, Anna & Starke, Michal (1999). The typology of structural deficiency: a case study of the three classes of pronouns. In Van Riemsdijk, Henk (ed.), *Clitics in the languages of Europe*. Berlin: Mouton de Gruyter. 145–233.

Carnie, Andrew (1995). Nonverbal predication and head movement. Doctoral dissertation, Cambridge, MA: MIT.

(2000). On the definition of X^0 and XP. *Syntax* 3. 59–106.

Carnie, Andrew & Guilfoyle, Eithne (2000). *The syntax of verb initial languages.* Oxford & New York: Oxford University Press.

Carnie, Andrew, Harley, Heidi & Dooley, Sheila Ann (eds.) (2005). *Verb first: on the syntax of verb-initial languages.* Amsterdam/Philadelphia: John Benjamins.

Chomsky, Noam (1982). *Some concepts and consequences of the theory of government and binding* (Linguistic Inquiry Monographs 6). Cambridge, MA: MIT Press.

(1999). Derivation by phase. *MIT Occasional Papers in Linguistics* 18. Cambridge, MA: MIT Press.

Chomsky, Noam & Lasnik, Howard (1993). The theory of principles and parameters. In Jacobs, Joachim, von Stechow, Arnim, Sternefeld, Wolfgang & Vennemann, Theo (eds.), *Syntax: an international handbook of contemporary research.* Berlin: Walter de Gruyter. 506–69.

Chung, Sandra (1990). VPs and verb movement in Chamorro. *Natural Language and Linguistic Theory* 8. 559–19.

(1998). *The design of agreement: evidence from Chamorro.* Chicago, IL & London: University of Chicago Press.

(2004). Restructuring and verb-initial order in Chamorro. *Syntax* 7. 199–233.

Chung, Sandra & McCloskey, James (1987). Government, barriers, and small clauses in modern Irish. *Linguistic Inquiry* 18. 173–237.

Cinque, Guglielmo (1994). On the evidence for partial N-movement in the Romance DP. In Cinque, Guglielmo, Koster, Jan, Pollock, Jean-Yves, Rizzi, Luigi & Zanuttini, Raffaella (eds.), *Paths towards universal grammar: Studies in honor of Richard S. Kayne.* Washington, DC: Georgetown University Press. 85–110.

(1999). *Adverbs and functional heads.* Oxford: Oxford University Press.

Citko, Barbara (2004). Agreement asymmetries in coordinate structures. In Arnaudova, Olga, Browne, Wayles, Rivero, María Luisa & Stojanović, Danijela (eds.), *Formal approaches to Slavic linguistics 12: The Ottawa meeting 2003.* Ann Arbor, MI: Michigan Slavic Publications. 91–109.

Comrie, Bernard (1977). In defense of spontaneous demotion: the impersonal passive. In Cole, Peter & Sadock, Jerrold (eds.), *Grammatical relations.* Syntax and Semantics 8. New York: Academic Press. 47–58.

Corbett, Greville G. (1993). The head in Russian numeral expressions. In Corbett, Greville G., Fraser, Norman M. & McGlashan, Scott (eds.), *Heads in grammatical theory.* Cambridge: Cambridge University Press. 11–35.

Cowgill, Warren (1975). Two further notes on the origin of the insular Celtic absolute and conjunct verb endings. *Ériu* 26. 27–32.

Culicover, Peter W. & Jackendoff, Ray (2005). *Simpler syntax.* Oxford: Oxford University Press.

Currie, Oliver (2000). Word order stability and change from a sociolinguistic perspective: the case of early modern Welsh. In Sornicola, Rosanna, Poppe, Erich & Shisha-Halevy, Ariel (eds.), *Stability, variation and change of word-order patterns over time.* Amsterdam: John Benjamins. 203–30.

Diesing, Molly (1990). Verb movement and the subject position in Yiddish. *Natural Language and Linguistic Theory* 8. 41–79.

Doherty, Cathal (1996). Clausal structure and the modern Irish copula. *Natural Language and Linguistic Theory* 14: 1–46.

Doron, Edit (1988). On the complementarity of subject and subject-verb agreement. In Barlow, Michael & Ferguson, Charles A. (eds.), *Agreement in natural languages*. Stanford, CA: CSLI Publications. 201–18.

(2000). VSO and left-conjunct agreement: Biblical Hebrew vs. Modern Hebrew. In Carnie & Guilfoyle (eds.), 75–95.

Dryer, Matthew (1988a). Object-verb order and adjective-noun order: dispelling a myth. *Lingua* 74. 77–109.

(1988b). Universals of negative position. In Hammond, Michael, Moravcsik, Edith A. & Wirth, Jessica (eds.), *Studies in syntactic typology*. Amsterdam/ Philadelphia: John Benjamins. 93–124.

(1991). SVO languages and the OV:VO typology. *Journal of Linguistics* 27. 443–82.

(1992). The Greenbergian word order correlations. *Language* 68. 81–138.

(1996). Word order typology. In Jacobs, Joachim (ed.), *Handbook on syntax*, Vol. ii. Berlin/New York: Walter de Gruyter. 1050–65.

Duffield, Nigel (1996). On structural invariance and lexical diversity in VSO languages: arguments from Irish noun phrases. In Borsley & Roberts (eds.). 314–40.

Emonds, Joseph E. (1985). *A unified theory of syntactic categories*. Dordrecht: Foris.

Evans, D. Simon (1964). *Grammar of Middle Welsh*. Dublin: Dublin Institute for Advanced Studies.

(1968a). The sentence in Early Modern Welsh. *Bulletin of the Board of Celtic Studies* 22. 311–37.

(1968b). The verbal predicate in Early Modern Welsh. *Études Celtiques* 12. 236–60.

(1971). Concord in Middle Welsh. *Studia Celtica* 6. 42–56.

Evans, Emrys (1958). Cystrawennau 'sef' mewn Cymraeg Canol. *Bulletin of the Board of Celtic Studies* 18. 38–54.

(1965). Gohirio'r rhagenw mewn Cymraeg Canol. *Bulletin of the Board of Celtic Studies* 21. 141–5.

Fassi Fehri, Abdelkader (1999). Arabic modifying adjectives and DP structures. *Studia Linguistica* 53. 105–154.

Fife, James (1988). *Functional syntax: a case study in Middle Welsh*. Lublin: Redakcja Wydawnictw Katolickiego Uniwersytetu Lubelskiego.

(1990). *The semantics of the Welsh verb*. Cardiff: University of Wales Press.

Fife, James & King, Gareth (1991). Focus and the Welsh 'abnormal sentence': a cross-linguistic perspective. In Fife & Poppe (eds.). 81–154.

Fife, James & Poppe, Erich (eds.) (1991). *Studies in Brythonic word order*. Amsterdam: John Benjamins.

Fleuriot, Léon (1964). *Le vieux breton: éléments d'une grammaire*. Paris: Librairie C. Klincksieck.

Fowkes, Robert A. (1991). Verbal noun as 'equivalent' of finite verb in Welsh. *Word* 42. 19–29.

Freeze, Ray & Georgopoulos, Carol (2000). Locus operandi. In Carnie & Guilfoyle (eds.). 163–83.

Fynes-Clinton, O. H. (1913). *The Welsh vocabulary of the Bangor district*. Oxford: Oxford University Press. [Facsimile reprint, Felinfach: Llanerch Publishers, 1995.]

Gensler, Orin D. (2002). Why should a demonstrative turn into a preposition? The evolution of Welsh predicative *yn*. *Language* 78. 710–64.

George, Kenneth J. (1987–8). Quelques réflexions sur l'ordre des mots dans la pièce en moyen breton: Buhez Santez Nonn. *Bretagne Linguistique* 4. 175–87.

(1990). A comparison of word-order in Middle Breton and Middle Cornish. In Ball, Fife, Poppe & Rowland (eds.). 225–40.

(1991). Notes on word order in *Beunans Meriasek*. In Fife & Poppe (eds.). 205–50.

(1993). Cornish. In Ball (ed.). 410–68.

Green, Anthony D. (2006). The independence of phonology and morphology: the Celtic mutations. *Lingua* 116. 1946–85.

Greenberg, Joseph H. (1963). Some universals of grammar with particular reference to the order of meaningful elements. In Greenberg, Joseph H. (ed.), *Universals of language*. Cambridge, MA: MIT Press. 73–113.

Guilfoyle, Eithne (1988). Parameters and functional projections. In Blevins, James & Carter, Judi (eds.), *Proceedings of the North Eastern Linguistic Society 18*. Amherst, MA: Dept. of Linguistics, University of Massachusetts. 193–207.

Haegeman. Liliane (1995). *The syntax of negation*. Cambridge: Cambridge University Press.

Hannahs, S. J. & Tallerman, Maggie (2006). At the interface: selection of the Welsh definite article. *Linguistics* 44. 781–816.

Harlow, Stephen (1981). Government and relativization in Celtic. In Heny, Frank (ed.), *Binding and filtering*. London: Croom Helm. 213–54.

(1983). Celtic relatives. *York Papers in Linguistics* 10. 77–121.

(1989). Syntax of Welsh soft mutation. *Natural Language and Linguistic Theory* 7. 289–316.

(1992). Finiteness and Welsh sentence structure. In Obenauer, Hans-Georg & Zribi-Hertz, Anne (eds.), *Structure de la phrase et théorie du liage*. Paris: Presses Universitaires de Vincennes. 93–119.

Haspelmath, Martin (1998). The semantic development of old presents: new futures and subjunctives without grammaticalization. *Diachronica* 15. 29–62.

Hawkins, John A. (1983). *Word order universals*. New York: Academic Press.

(1990). A parsing theory of word order universals. *Linguistic Inquiry* 21. 223–62.

(1994). *A performance theory of order and constituency*. Cambridge: Cambridge University Press.

(2004). *Efficiency and complexity in grammars*. Oxford: Oxford University Press.

Heinecke, Johannes (1999). *Temporal deixis in Welsh and Breton*. Heidelberg: Universitätsverlag C. Winter.

Hendrick, Randall (1988). *Anaphora in Celtic and universal grammar*. Dordrecht: Kluwer.

Hendrick, Randall (ed.) (1990). *The syntax of the modern Celtic languages*. San Diego, CA: Academic Press.

Hendrick, Randall (1991). The morphosyntax of aspect. *Lingua* 85. 171–210.

(1994). The Brythonic copula and head-raising. In Lightfoot, David & Hornstein, Norbert (eds.), *Verb movement*. Cambridge: Cambridge University Press. 163–88.

(1996). Some syntactic effects of suppletion in the Celtic copulas. In Borsley & Roberts (eds.). 75–96.

Hewitt, Steve (1990). The progressive in Breton in the light of the English progressive. In Ball, Fife, Poppe & Rowland (eds.). 167–88.

Hurford, James R. (1975). *The linguistic theory of numerals*. Cambridge: Cambridge University Press.

(2003). The interaction between numerals, and nouns. In Plank, Frans (ed.). *Noun phrase structure in the languages of Europe*. Berlin: Mouton. 561–620.

Isaac, Graham R. (1993). Issues in the reconstruction and analyses of Insular Celtic syntax and phonology. *Ériu* 44. 1–32.

(1996). *The verb in the Book of Aneirin*. Tübingen: Max Niemeyer Verlag.

(2000). The most recent model of the development of absolute and conjunct flexion. *Ériu* 51. 63–8.

Jackson, Kenneth (1953). *Language and history in early Britain*. Edinburgh: Edinburgh University Press.

Jones, Bob Morris (1990a). Linguistic causes of change in pronominalization in children's Welsh. *Bulletin of the Board of Celtic Studies* 37. 43–70.

(1990b). Variation in the use of pronouns in verbnoun phrases and genitive noun phrases in child language. In Ball, Fife, Poppe & Rowland (eds.). 53–76.

(1993). Ascriptive and equative sentences in children's Welsh. *Studies in child language: Aberystwyth education papers*. University of Wales, Aberystwyth.

(1999). *The Welsh answering system*. Berlin, New York: Mouton de Gruyter.

Jones, Bob Morris & Thomas, Alan R. (1977). *The Welsh language: studies in its syntax and semantics*. Cardiff: University of Wales Press.

Jones, Dafydd Glyn (1988). Literary Welsh. In Ball (ed.). 125–71.

Jones, Mari C. (1998). *Language obsolescence and revitalization: linguistic change in two sociolinguistically contrasting Welsh communities*. Oxford: Clarendon Press.

Jones, Robert Owen (1993). The sociolinguistics of Welsh. In Ball (ed.). 536–605.

Jones, T. J. Rhys (1977). *Living Welsh*. Sevenoaks: Hodder & Stoughton.

Jouitteau, Mélanie (2005). La syntaxe comparée du breton. Doctoral dissertation, Université de Nantes.

Kathol, Andreas (2000). *Linear syntax*. Oxford: Oxford University Press.

Kayne, Richard S. (1994). *The antisymmetry of syntax*. Cambridge, MA & London: MIT Press.

King, Gareth (1993). *Modern Welsh: a comprehensive grammar*. London: Routledge.

(2003). *Modern Welsh: a comprehensive grammar*. Second edition, London: Routledge.

Koch, John T. (1983). The loss of final syllables and loss of declension in Brittonic. *Bulletin of the Board of Celtic Studies* 30. 201–33.

(1991). On the prehistory of Brittonic syntax. In Fife & Poppe (eds.). 1–44.

Koopman, Hilda (2005). On the parallelism of DPs and clauses: evidence from Kisongo Maasai. In Carnie, Harley & Dooley (eds.). 281–301.

Larson, Richard (1988). On the double object construction. *Linguistic Inquiry* 19. 595–621.

Lee, Felicia (2000). VP remnant movement and VSO in Quiaviní Zapotec. In Carnie & Guilfoyle (eds.). 143–62.

(2005). Force first: clause-fronting and clause typing in San Lucas Quiaviní Zapotec. In Carnie, Harley & Dooley (eds.). 91–106.

Lehmann, Winfred P. (1973). A structural principle of language and its implications. *Language* 49. 47–66.

(1978). The great underlying ground-plans. In Lehmann, Winfred P. (ed.), *Syntactic typology: studies in the phenomenology of language*. Austin, TX: University of Texas Press. 3–55.

Lewis, Henry (1928). Y berfenw. *Bulletin of the Board of Celtic Studies* 4. 179–89.

(1931). *Datblygiad yr iaith Gymraeg*. Cardiff: Gwasg Prifysgol Cymru.

(1942). *The sentence in Welsh*. London: Humphrey Milford Amen House.

(1946). *Llawlyfr Cernyweg Canol*. Cardiff: Gwasg Prifysgol Cymru.

Lewis, Henry & Pedersen, Holger (1937). *A concise comparative Celtic grammar*. Göttingen: Vandenhoeck & Ruprecht.

Lieber, Rochelle (1983). New developments in autosegmental morphology: consonant mutation. In Barlow, Michael, Ferguson, Charles A., Flickinger, Daniel & Wescoat, M. (eds.), *Proceedings of the West Coast Conference on Formal Linguistics*. Stanford, CA: Stanford University Press. 165–75.

Lloyd, D. Myrddin (1937). Casgliad o hen faledi. *Journal of the Welsh Bibliographical Society* 5. 93–9.

Longobardi, Giuseppe (2001). The structure of DPs: some principles, parameters, and problems. In Baltin, Mark & Collins, Chris (eds.), *Handbook of contemporary syntactic theory*. Oxford: Blackwell. 562–603.

Macaulay, Monica (1996). *A grammar of Chalcatongo Mixtec*. Berkeley, CA: University of California Press.

(2005). The syntax of Chalcatongo Mixtec: preverbal and postverbal. In Carnie, Harley & Dooley (eds.). 341–66.

Mac Cana, Proinsias (1973). Celtic word-order and the Welsh abnormal sentence. *Ériu* 24. 90–120.

(1979). Notes on the 'abnormal sentence'. *Studia Celtica* 14–15. 174–93.

(1990). On the uses of the conjunctive pronouns in Middle Welsh. In Ball, Fife, Poppe & Rowland (eds.). 411–33.

(1991). Further notes on constituent order in Welsh. In Fife & Poppe (eds.). 45–80.

(1992). On the early development of written narrative prose in Irish and Welsh. *Études Celtiques* 29. 51–67.

(1997). Notes on periphrasis with verbal noun and verb 'to do' in Middle Welsh. In Mac Mathúna, Séamus & Ó Corráin, Ailbhe (eds.), *Miscellanea Celtica in memoriam Heinrich Wagner*. Uppsala: Acta Universitatis Upsaliensis, 183–96.

McCloskey, James (1990). Resumptive pronouns, A'-binding, and levels of representation in Irish. In Hendrick (ed.). 199–248.

(1991). Clause structure, ellipsis and proper government in Irish. *Lingua* 85. 259–302.

(1996). Subjects and subject positions in Irish. In Borsley & Roberts (eds.). 241–83.

(1997). Subjecthood and subject positions. In Haegeman, Liliane (ed.), *Elements of grammar: handbook of generative syntax*. Dordrecht: Kluwer Academic Publishers. 197–235.

(2001). The distribution of subject properties in Irish. In Davies, William & Dubinsky, Stanley (eds.), *Objects and other subjects: grammatical functions, functional categories and configurationality* (Studies in Natural Language and Linguistic Theory, Vol. 52). Dordrecht: Kluwer Academic Publishers. 157–92.

McCloskey, James & Hale, Kenneth (1984). On the syntax of person-number inflection in Modern Irish. *Natural Language and Linguistic Theory* 1. 487–533.

McCone, Kim R. (1979). Pretonic preverbs and the absolute verbal endings in Old Irish. *Ériu* 30. 1–34.

(1987). *The early Irish verb*. Maynooth Monographs 1. Maynooth: An Sagart.

(2006). *The origins and development of the Insular Celtic verbal complex*. Maynooth Studies in Celtic Linguistics 6. Maynooth: Department of Old Irish, National University of Ireland, Maynooth.

Manning, H. Paul (1995). Fluid intransitivity in Middle Welsh: gradience, typology and 'unaccusativity'. *Lingua* 74. 171–94.

(1996). What Welsh relatives are really like. In Dobrin, Lise M., Singer, Kora & McNair, Lisa (eds.), *Proceedings from the main session of the Chicago Linguistic Society's thirty-second meeting*. Chicago, IL: Chicago Linguistic Society. 251–65.

Martin, Roger (2001). Null Case and the distribution of PRO. *Linguistic Inquiry* 32. 41–166.

Massam, Diane (2000). VSO and VOS: Aspects of Niuean word order. In Carnie & Guilfoyle (eds.). 97–116.

(2005). Lexical categories, lack of inflection and predicate fronting in Niuean. In Carnie, Harley & Dooley (eds.). 227–42.

Maxwell, John T. & Manning, Christopher D. (1996). A theory of non-constituent coordination based on finite-state rules. In Butt, Miriam & King, Tracy Holloway (eds.), *Proceedings of the First LFG Conference, Grenoble, France*, online publication, http://cslipublications.stanford.edu/LFG/1/lfg1.html.

Meid, Wolfgang (1968). Remarks on the origin of the Old Irish absolute and conjunct inflexion. *Studia Celtica* 2. 1–8.

Miller, D. Gary (2004). The origin of the Welsh conjugated infinitive. *Diachronica* 21. 329–50.

Mittendorf, Ingo & Sadler, Louisa (2005). Numerals, nouns and number in Welsh NPs. In Butt, Miriam & King, Tracy Holloway (eds.), *Proceedings of the LFG05 Conference, University of Bergen*. Stanford, CA: CSLI Publications. 294–312.

Morgan, T. J. (1938). Braslun o gystrawen y berfenw. *Bulletin of the Board of Celtic Studies* 9. 195–215.

(1952). *Y treigladau a'u cystrawen*. Cardiff: Gwasg Prifysgol Cymru.

Morris, W. Meredith (1910). *A glossary of the Demetian dialect of north Pembrokeshire with special reference to the Gwaun Valley*. Tonypandy: Evans and Short. [Facsimile edition, Felinfach: Llanerch Publishers, 1991]

Morris-Jones, John (1913). *A Welsh grammar*. Oxford: Oxford University Press.

(1931). *Welsh syntax: an unfinished draft*. Cardiff: University of Wales Press.

Myhill, John (1985). Pragmatic and categorial correlates of VS word order. *Lingua* 66. 177–200.

Ó Siadhail, Mícheál (1989). *Modern Irish: grammatical structure and dialectal variation*. Cambridge: Cambridge University Press.

Otsuka, Yuko (2005). Two derivations of VSO: a comparative study of Niuean and Tongan. In Carnie, Harley & Dooley (eds.). 65–90.

Ouhalla, Jamal (1991). *Functional categories and parametric variation*. London: Routledge.

(1993). Subject-extraction, negation and the Anti-Agreement Effect. *Natural Language and Linguistic Theory* 11. 477–518.

Pedersen, Holger (1909–13). *Vergleichende Grammatik der keltischen Sprachen.* Göttingen: Vandenhoeck and Ruprecht.

Pollard, Carl J., Kasper, Robert & Levine, Robert (1993). *Studies in constituent ordering: towards a theory of linearization in Head-driven Phrase Structure Grammar.* Research Proposal to the National Science Foundation, Ohio State University.

Pollard, Carl J. & Sag, Ivan A. (1994). *Head-driven Phrase Structure Grammar.* Chicago: University of Chicago Press.

Poppe, Erich (1989). Constituent ordering in Breudwyt Maxen Wledic. *Bulletin of the Board of Celtic Studies* 36. 43–63.

(1990). Word-order patterns in Breudwyt Ronabwy. In Ball, Fife, Poppe & Rowland (eds.). 445–460.

(1991a). *Untersuchungen zur Wortstellung im Mittelkymrischen.* Hamburg: Helmut Buske Verlag.

(1991b). Word order in Cyfranc Lludd a Llefelys: notes on the pragmatics of constituent-ordering in MW narrative prose. In Fife & Poppe (eds.). 155–204.

(1993). Word order in Middle Welsh: the case of Kedymdeithyas Amlyn ac Amic. *Bulletin of the Board of Celtic Studies* 40. 95–118.

(1995). Negation in Welsh and 'Jespersen's Cycle'. *Journal of Celtic Linguistics* 4. 99–107.

(1996). Convergence and divergence: the emergence of a 'future' in the British languages. *Transactions of the Philological Society* 94. 119–60.

Press, Ian (1986). *A grammar of modern Breton.* Berlin: Mouton de Gruyter.

Rackowski, Andrea & Travis, Lisa (2000). V-initial languages: X or XP movement and adverbial placement. In Carnie & Guilfoyle (eds.). 117–43.

Reape, Michael (1994). Domain union and word order variation in German. In Nerbonne, John, Netter, Klaus & Pollard, Carl (eds.), *German in Head-driven Phrase Structure Grammar.* Stanford, CA: CSLI Publications. 151–98.

Rhys, Siôn Dafydd (1592). *Cambrobrytannicæ Cymraecæue linguæ institutiones et rudimenta.* Londini: Excudebat Thomas Orwinus.

Richards, Melville (1934). Yr *yn* traethiadol yn y Pedair Cainc. *Bulletin of the Board of Celtic Studies* 7. 96–112.

(1938). *Cystrawen y frawddeg Gymraeg.* Cardiff: Gwasg Prifysgol Cymru.

(1949–51). The subject of the verb noun in Welsh. *Études Celtiques* 5. 51–81, 293–313.

Ritter, Elizabeth (1988). A head-movement approach to construct-state noun phrases. *Linguistics* 26. 909–29.

Rizzi, Luigi (1990). On the anaphor-agreement effect. *Rivista di Linguistica* 2. 27–42.

(1997). The fine structure of the left periphery. In Haegeman, Liliane (ed.), *Elements of grammar.* Dordrecht: Kluwer Academic Publishers. 281–337.

Robert, Gruffydd. (1939 [1567]). *Gramadeg Cymraeg*, ed. G. J. Williams. Cardiff: Gwasg Prifysgol Cymru.

Roberts, Anna E. (1988). Age-related variation in the Welsh dialect of Pwllheli. In Ball (ed.). 104–22.

Roberts, Gareth (2000). Bilingualism and number in Wales. *International Journal of Bilingual Education and Bilingualism* 3. 44–56.

Roberts, Ian G. (1997). The syntax of direct object mutation in Welsh. *Canadian Journal of Linguistics* 42. 141–68.

(2005). *Principles and parameters in a VSO language: a case study in Welsh.* Oxford Studies in Comparative Syntax. New York: Oxford University Press.

Roberts, Ian & Shlonsky, Ur (1996). Pronominal enclisis in VSO languages. In Borsley & Roberts (eds.). 171–99.

Rodway, Simon. 2002 [1998]. Absolute forms in the poetry of the Gogynfeirdd: Functionally obsolete archaisms or working system? *Journal of Celtic Linguistics* 7: 63–84.

Rottet, Kevin J. & Sprouse, Rex A. (2006). Tag questions in Welsh. Unpublished paper, Indiana University.

Rouveret, Alain (1990). X-bar theory, minimality and barrierhood in Welsh. In Hendrick (ed.). 27–79.

(1991). Functional categories and agreement. *Linguistic Review* 8. 353–87.

(1994). *Syntaxe du gallois: principes généraux et typologie.* Paris: CNRS Éditions.

(1996). *Bod* in the present tense and in other tenses. In Borsley & Roberts (eds.). 125–70.

(2002). How are resumptive pronouns linked to the periphery? In Pica, Pierre & Rooryck, Johan (eds.), *Linguistic Variation Yearbook: Volume 2 (2002).* Amsterdam: Benjamins. 123–84.

Ruhlen, Merritt (1987). *A guide to the world's languages.* Vol. i: *Classification.* Stanford, CA: Stanford University Press.

Russell, Paul (1995). *An introduction to the Celtic languages.* London: Longman.

Sadler, Louisa (1988). *Welsh syntax: a Government-Binding approach.* London: Croom Helm.

(1999). Non-distributive features and coordination in Welsh. In *Proceedings of the LF699 Conference,* http://cslipublications.stanford.edu/LFG/4/lfg99-toc.html.

(2000). Noun phrase structure in Welsh. In Butt, Miriam & King, Tracy Holloway (eds.), *Argument realization.* Stanford, CA: CSLI Publications. 73–109.

(2006). Function sharing in coordinate structures. *Lingua* 116. 1777–1806.

Sag, Ivan A., Wasow, Thomas & Bender, Emily (2003). *Syntactic theory.* Second edition, Stanford, CA: CSLI Publications.

Sag, Ivan A., Gazdar, Gerald, Wasow, Thomas, & Weisler, Stephen (1985). Coordination and how to distinguish categories. *Natural Language and Linguistic Theory* 3. 117–71.

Salesbury, William (1969 [1550]). *A brief and plain introduction, 1550.* Menston: Scolar Press.

Schafer, Robin (1994). Nonfinite predicate initial constructions in Breton. Doctoral dissertation, University of California, Santa Cruz.

(1995). Negation and verb second in Breton. *Natural Language and Linguistic Theory* 13. 135–72.

Shlonsky, Ur (1992). Resumptive pronouns as a last resort. *Linguistic Inquiry* 23. 443–68.

Sichel, Ivy (2000). Evidence for DP-internal remant movement. In Hirotani, Masako, Coetzee, Andries, Hall, Nancy & Kim, Ji-yung (eds.), *Proceedings of the North East Linguistic Society 30.* New Brunswick, NJ: Rutgers University. 568–81.

Siewierska, Anna (1993). On the ordering of subject agreement and tense affixes. In Siewierska, Anna (ed.), *EUROTYP Working Papers* II/5, 5. 101–24.

Sigurðsson, Halldór Ármann (1990). V1 declaratives and verb raising in Icelandic. In Maling, Joan & Zaenen, Annie (eds.), *Modern Icelandic syntax*. San Diego, CA: Academic Press. 41–69.

(1991). Icelandic case-marked PRO and the licensing of lexical arguments. *Natural Language and Linguistic Theory* 9. 327–63.

Sims-Williams, Patrick (1984). The double system of verbal inflexion in Old Irish. *Transactions of the Philological Society* 82. 138–201.

(1990). Dating the transition to Neo-Brittonic: phonology and history, 400–600. In Bammesberger, Alfred & Wollmann, Alfred (eds.), *Britain 400–600: language and history*. Heidelberg: Winter. 217–61.

(1991). The emergence of Old Welsh, Cornish and Breton orthography 600–800: the evidence of archaic Old Welsh. *Bulletin of the Board of Celtic Studies* 38. 20–86.

Sommerfelt, Alf (1925). *Studies in Cyfeiliog Welsh: a contribution to Welsh dialectology*. Oslo: I Kommision hos J. Dybwad.

Sproat, Richard (1985). Welsh syntax and VSO structure. *Natural Language and Linguistic Theory* 3. 173–216.

Sproat, Richard & Shih, Chilin (1991). The crosslinguistic distribution of adjective ordering restructions. In Georgopoulos, Carol & Ishihara, R. (eds.), *Interdisciplinary approaches to language: essays in honor of S. Y. Kuroda*. Dordrecht: Kluwer. 565–94.

Stephens, Janig (1982). Word order in Breton. Doctoral dissertation, University of London.

(1990). Non-finite clauses in Breton. In Ball, Fife, Poppe & Rowland (eds.). 151–65.

Stump, Gregory T. (1984). Agreement vs. incorporation in Breton. *Natural Language and Linguistic Theory* 2. 289–348.

(1989). Further remarks on Breton agreement: a reply to Borsley and Stephens. *Natural Language and Linguistic Theory* 7. 429–471.

Suggett, Richard F. (1983). An analysis and calendar of early modern Welsh defamation suits (mss. 16th–19th c.). SSRC Final Report (HR 6979).

Szabolcsi, Anna (1994). The noun phrase. In Kiefer, Ferenc & Kiss, Katalin É, *The syntactic structure of Hungarian*. San Diego, CA: Academic Press. 197–274.

Tallerman, Maggie (1983). Island constraints in Welsh. *York Papers in Linguistics* 10. 197–204.

(1987). Mutation and the syntactic structure of modern colloquial Welsh. Doctoral dissertation, University of Hull.

(1990). VSO word order and consonantal mutation in Welsh. *Linguistics* 28. 389–416.

(1991). The directionality of head subcategorization in Welsh. In Fife & Poppe (eds.). 311–27.

(1996). Fronting constructions in Welsh. In Borsley & Roberts (eds.). 97–124.

(1997). Infinitival clauses in Breton. *Canadian Journal of Linguistics* 42. 205–33.

(1998). The uniform case-licensing of subjects in Welsh. *Linguistic Review* 15. 69–133.

(1999). Welsh soft mutation and marked word order. In Darnell, Michael, Moravcsik, Edith, Newmeyer, Frederick, Noonan, Michael & Wheatley, Kathleen (eds.) *functionalism and formalism in linguistics*. Vol. ii: *Case studies*. Amsterdam: John Benjamins. 277–94.

(2006). The syntax of Welsh 'direct object mutation' revisited. *Lingua* 116. 1750–76.

Ternes, Elmar (1992). The Breton language. In MacAulay, Donald (ed.), *The Celtic languages*. Cambridge: Cambridge University Press. 371–452.

Thomas, Beth & Thomas, Peter Wynn (1989). *Cymraeg, Cymrâg, Cymrêg: cyflwyno'r tafodieithoedd*. Cardiff: Gwasg Taf.

Thomas, Ceinwen H. (1974). Y tafodieithegydd a 'Chymraeg Cyfoes'. *Llên Cymru* 13. 113–52.

(1993). *Tafodiaith Nantgarw. Astudiaeth o Gymraeg llafar Nantgarw yng Nghwm Taf, Morgannwg*. Cardiff: Gwasg Prifysgol Cymru.

Thomas, Peter Wynn (1996). *Gramadeg y Gymraeg*. Cardiff: Gwasg Prifysgol Cymru.

Thorne, David A. (1993). *A comprehensive Welsh grammar*. Oxford: Blackwell.

Thurneysen, Rudolf (1946). *A grammar of Old Irish*. Dublin: Dublin Institute for Advanced Studies.

Toman, Jindřich (1998). A discussion of resumptives in Colloquial Czech. In Bošković, Željko, Franks, Steven & Snyder, William (eds.), *Annual workshop of formal approaches to Slavic linguistics: the Connecticut meeting 1997*. Ann Arbor: Michigan Slavic Publications. 303–18.

Travis, Lisa (2005). VP-internal structure in a VOS language. In Carnie, Harley & Dooley (eds.). 203–24.

Vanden Wyngaerd, Guido (1994). *PRO-legomena: distribution and reference of infinitival subjects*. Berlin: Mouton de Gruyter.

Vennemann, Theo (1975). Analogy in generative grammar: the origin of word order. In Heilmann, Luigi (ed.), *Proceedings of the eleventh International Congress of Linguists*. Bologna: Il Mulino. 79–83.

(1976). Categorial grammar and the order of meaningful elements. In Juilland, Alphonse (ed.), *Linguistic studies offered to Joseph Greenberg on the occasion of his sixtieth birthday*. Saratoga, CA: Anma Libri. 615–34.

Watkins, Calvert (1963). Preliminaries to a historical and comparative analysis of the syntax of the Old Irish verb. *Celtica* 6. 1–49.

Watkins, T. Arwyn (1961). *Ieithyddiaeth*. Cardiff: Gwasg Prifysgol Cymru.

(1977a). The Welsh personal pronoun. *Word* 28. 146–65.

(1977b). Y rhagenw ategol. *Studia Celtica* 12–13. 349–66.

(1977c). Trefn yn y frawddeg Gymraeg. *Studia Celtica* 12–13. 367–95.

(1983-4). Trefn y constitwentau brawddegol yn Branwen. *Studia Celtica* 18–19. 147–57.

(1987). Constituent order in the Old Welsh verbal sentence. *Bulletin of the Board of Celtic Studies* 34. 51–60.

(1988). *Constituent order in the positive declarative sentence in the medieval Welsh tale 'Kulhwch ac Olwen'*. Innsbruck: Institut für Sprachwissenschaft der Universität Innsbruck.

(1990). Constituent order in the negative declarative sentence in the White Book Version of Kulhwch ac Olwen. In Matonis, A. T. E. & Melia, D. F. (eds.), *Celtic language, Celtic culture*. Van Nuys, CA: Ford & Bailie. 247–52.

(1993). Constituent order in main/simple clauses of Pwyll Pendeuic Dyuet. *Language Sciences* 15. 115–39.

Watkins, T. Arwyn & Piette, J. R. F. (1962). Ffurfiant a chystrawen y geirynnau adferfol/traethiadol mewn Cymraeg, Cernyweg a Llydaweg. *Bulletin of the Board of Celtic Studies* 19. 295–315.

Welsh Assembly Government Statistical Directorate (2007). *Schools in Wales: general statistics 2006. Ysgolion yng Nghymru: ystadegau cyffredinol 2006.* Cardiff: Welsh Assembly Government.

Williams, Ifor (1938) (ed.). *Canu Aneirin.* Cardiff: Gwasg Prifysgol Cymru.

Williams, Stephen J. (1959). *Elfennau gramadeg Cymraeg.* Cardiff: Gwasg Prifysgol Cymru.

(1980). *A Welsh grammar.* Cardiff: University of Wales Press.

Willis, David (1997). Clausal coordination and the loss of verb-second in Welsh. *Oxford Working Papers in Linguistics, Philology and Phonetics* 2. 151–72.

(1998). *Syntactic change in Welsh: a study of the loss of verb-second.* Oxford: Oxford University Press.

(2000). On the distribution of resumptive pronouns and *wh*-traces in Welsh. *Journal of Linguistics* 36. 531–73.

(2004). A minimalist approach to Jespersen's Cycle in Welsh. Unpublished manuscript, University of Cambridge.

(2006a). Against N-raising and NP-raising analyses of Welsh noun phrases. *Lingua* 116. 1807–39.

(2006b). Negation in Middle Welsh. *Studia Celtica* 40. 63–88.

Willis, Penny (1988). Is the Welsh verbal noun a verb or a noun? *Word* 39. 201–24.

Woolford, Ellen (1999). More on the anaphor agreement effect. *Linguistic Inquiry* 30. 257–87.

Zanuttini, Rafaella (1997). *Negation and clause structure: a comparative study of Romance languages.* Oxford: Oxford University Press.

Zaring, Laurie (1996). Two 'be' or not two 'be': identity, predication and the Welsh copula. *Linguistics and Philosophy* 19. 103–42.

Zwicky, Arnold M. (1984). Welsh soft mutation and the case of object NPs. In Drogo, Joseph, Mishra, Veena, Testen, David (eds.), *Proceedings of the twentieth Regional Meeting of the Chicago Linguistic Society.* Chicago, IL: Chicago Linguistic Society. 387–402.

Index

a(c) 'and' 43–4, 158, 177, 302 (*see also* coordination)
A′-Disjointness Requirement 109
A′-movement 104–51, 291–2, 334–5
abnormal sentence 287–93, 299, 306–7
absolute clauses 43, 48, 53
absolute verbal inflections 298–9
accusative case 196, 231–2, 309 (*see also* accusative clitics)
accusative clitics 319–23
Ackema, Peter 215
adjectives 8, 22–3, 153–4, 167–70, 171, 174, 175, 177–83, 184, 186, 187–91, 334–9;
    agreement with nouns 165–6, 178–9;
    mutations affecting 22–3, 177–8, 188–94, 195, 196;
    in pre-nominal position 23, 179–80;
    word order pertaining to 22–3, 154, 167–8, 179–83, 184, 186, 187, 223, 344–6
    (*see also* comparative adjectives, equative adjectives, superlative adjectives)
adjunct *wh*-constructions 146–7
adverbs 288, 290, 293–6, 318 n. 3;
    propositional 124
affirmative particles/complementizers (*fe, mi*) 11, 35, 36, 124, 271, 296, 297–8, 324–6, 359, 360
Agree 212, 273
agreement 17–19, 34, 54 n.10, 65, 70–5, 77–9, 95, 96–8, 115, 198–222, 352, 355–8;
    adjective-noun agreement 336; agreement in the noun phrase 160–1, 165–6, 178–9, 360
    (*see also* subject – verb agreement)
agreement morphology 308
Aldridge, Michelle 187
anaphora 51, 55, 71, 80, 83, 86, 95, 131–2
Anderson, Stephen 212
antiagreement 107, 109, 112, 120, 141–2
Anwyl, Edward 43

Arabic 108, 340, 353, 354, 356, 361
aspect markers 8, 12, 39–40, 12, 39–41, 46 n. 7, 57, 58, 98, 127, 260, 273–4, 357, 363
aspectual clauses 12, 39–41, 43, 56–8, 127
aspirate mutation (*see* mutation, aspirate)
aspiration 157, 158, 197
AspP 41, 241 n. 11, 357
attributive noun phrases 191–2
auxiliaries 32, 37, 38, 44–7, 49, 54 n.10, 68, 98, 343–4
auxiliary–initial/AuxSVO clauses 11–12, 32, 38–44, 48, 56–60, 75, 97–9, 224, 231, 236, 343–4
Awbery, Gwenllïan 106, 113, 114, 137, 160, 275, 282, 284

Basque 328
Berber 107, 108, 340, 351, 353, 354, 356
binding 71–2, 83, 84, 87, 109, 292
Blevins, James 283, 284
bod 'be' 33, 35, 37, 39, 43, 57–8, 66, 255–2, 302–3, 314, 317–19, 352, 365;
    forms in copular constructions 130–1;
    omission of 260–1;
    relative forms of 109–10, 131, 136, 141, 150
bod-clauses 76–81, 203, 352, 364–5
Borsley, Robert 35, 37, 38, 53–4, 54 n.10, 55, 56, 90–2, 99, 126, 211, 215, 225–7, 228, 230, 232 n. 4, 234, 238, 239 n. 9, 240, 245, 247–8, 253–4, 261, 263, 264 n.2, 266, 267, 269, 270, 271 n.5, 272, 273, 274, 281, 291, 340, 356 n. 12
Borsley's paradox 90–2, 99, 103
branching direction theory (BDT) 348–50
Bresnan, Joan 52
Breton 18, 37–8, 65–6, 68, 287, 289, 295, 297 n. 2, 303, 304, 306, 309, 312, 336, 351 n. 7, 352, 362, 363
byth '(n)ever' 263–4, 269

Case, abstract 91, 92, 94, 96, 228, 236–7, 245, 249–50, 252–3
case 308–9;
   lack of morphological 15–16, 26–9, 74 n. 3
   (*see also* accusative case, ergative–absolutive case systems; genitive case)
causative construction 280–2
Celtic languages 1, 2, 97, 107, 236, 243, 339, 341, 350–4, 356–8
Chamorro 357–8
child language 159
clausal subjects 61–2, 80, 226, 297
Chomsky, Noam 212
Cinque, Guglielmo 40
cleft constructions 299 (*see also* focus clauses)
clitics 23, 26–7, 70–5, 77–8, 198, 201–4, 207, 208, 209, 210, 217–8, 220–1, 223, 229, 232, 275, 277–8, 283, 352, 353
   (*see also* accusative clitics; object-agreement clitics; possessive clitics; -*s*, third-person object clitic)
colloquial Welsh 5–7, 9–10, 34–6, 41, 64, 78, 79, 110, 111, 139, 144, 163, 167, 176, 204, 257, 260, 265–7, 269, 274, 282, 341, 352, 358, 359, 360 n. 14
comparative adjectives 136, 179, 180, 315–16
   (*see also* adjectives)
complement clauses, finite 75–81, 83;
   tense restrictions in 75–6, 82, 142–3
Complementarity Principle 18–19
complementizers 34, 36–7, 49, 88–90, 92–6, 102–3, 291, 342, 356, 359, 364 (*see also* Focus complementizers)
complex numerals 164–5, 166–8, 184
Comrie, Bernard 283
conditional 310–11, 327
conditional clauses 129
conditional complementizer (*os*) 129
conjunct verbal inflections 298–9
conjunctive pronouns 321–2, 325
construct-state effect 184–5
Continental Celtic 308
control 87–90;
   control verbs 330–2
coordination 51–2, 56, 57, 64–6, 79, 83, 86, 205–6, 212, 218, 246–7, 255, 299–302, 323–4, 361
   (*see also* a(c) 'and'; left-conjunct agreement)
copular clauses 43–4, 56–8, 129–33, 255, 317–19;
   verbless 363–4

Copy Theory of Movement 126, 252
Cornish 287, 289, 291, 293–4, 303, 304, 306, 309, 310, 312, 318 n. 3, 334, 336
correlatives 136
count nouns 172–3
CP-recursion 128–9
Croatian 108
Cross-category Harmony, principle of 348, 350
Culicover, Peter 54–5
cyclic *wh*-movement,
   via, Spec, CP 148–50; via Spec, vP 113, 150–1
Czech 108

ddaru (past tense auxiliary) 12, 42–3, 47, 58–60, 127, 286
ddaru-clauses 12, 42–3, 58–60
ddim (negative adverb) 42, 44–7, 52, 257, 263, 267, 268, 269, 273, 358–9
definite article 155–7, 174, 175, 182, 184–5, 187, 195, 336; form of, 15 n. 6
definiteness 153, 155, 184–5, 317
demonstratives 165, 175–7
determiners 154–63
Determiner Phrase 73–5, 187–194
dialect differences 4–7, 128, 247, 342, 362
dim byd 'nothing' 265–7, 271
direct object mutation (DOM) 60–1, 224, 225, 226 n. 2, 231, 233–43, 246, 247, 249, 250, 251, 271, 284, 313–15
direct *wh*-constructions 137
Dryer, Matthew 348–50
dual 336–7
Duffield, Nigel 186
Dutch 291
Dyirbal 328

Early Immediate Constituents (EIC) 349
ellipsis 51–2, 55–6
empty operator (*see* null operator)
English 181, 187, 297
English influence 116
epistemic verbs 75, 76, 82, 84, 98, 330, 333
equative adjectives 136 (*see also* adjectives)
ergative–absolutive case systems 328
erioed '(n)ever' 263–4, 269
Evans, D. Simon 295, 299, 311, 315
expletive subjects 59, 61–3, 176–7, 224, 297–8, 318, 324
extraposition 152, 215, 297, 329

Fife, James 287, 293
finiteness, nature of in Welsh 97–8
finite subordinate clauses 13–14, 33, 35–8, 49,
    75–81, 82–5 (*see also* subordinate
    clauses)
finite verb 9–13, 33–4, 35, 37, 48–9, 52, 53, 54
    n.10, 56, 63, 198, 199, 204, 211, 214, 217,
    218
floating autosegments 188–91
focus clauses 33, 45, 54, 72, 123–9, 128, 138,
    206–8, 212–5, 219, 228, 306–7, 341, 342,
    365
focus complementizers (*mai, taw*) 124, 128–9,
    132, 143, 307
foreign influence 119, 305
French 187, 312
fronting 287–90; of verb noun/verb phrase
    126–8, 138, 287–8; in copular
    constructions 130–1
future tense 9, 10, 11, 303, 327

gan 'with' (marker of possession) 63, 362–3
gap dependencies 112–14, 120, 123, 135,
    137–8, 140–1, 141–6
gender 22–3, 153, 156, 163, 169, 170, 174,
    175, 176, 177–9, 183, 184, 188–94, 195,
    336
genitive case 308–9, 331–2
German 49, 175, 291
Germanic languages 48–9
grammaticalization 318
Greenberg, Joseph 338–41, 344–5, 347
gwneud (auxiliary) 12, 41–2, 46, 51, 52, 55,
    58–60, 127, 280–1
gwneud-clauses 12, 41–2, 51, 52, 55, 58–60,
    98, 343

Haegeman, Liliane 273
Hale, Kenneth 204, 209 n.3, 214
Hannahs, S. J. 15, 253
Haspelmath, Martin 303
Harlow, Stephen J. 37, 51, 78, 80, 83, 93, 97,
    226, 228, 230, 234, 246
Hawkins, John A. 347, 349–50
'have', lack of in Welsh 12, 232 n. 5, 361–3
Head-driven Phrase Structure Grammar
    (HPSG) 53–4, 55, 59, 209, 211, 215–20,
    234, 239 n. 9, 242, 245–7, 253, 272
head-initial characteristics 7–8, 152, 340,
    345–6, 347–8, 363
heb (see negative aspect marker *heb*)
Hebrew 108, 185, 356 n. 12, 361, 364

Hendrick, Randall 56, 57.
Highest Subject Restriction 108
Hindi 328
historical infinitive 329
Hungarian 159, 160
Hurford, James 175

i, complementizer 87–96
i, inflectional 92–8
i-clauses 81–96, 224, 242, 244, 248, 251,
    330–3;
    finite 82–5, 133, 134, 146;
    non-finite 85–7
Icelandic 301
identificational sentences 130–2, 258–9, 262
imperfect tense 9, 10, 33, 34, 109–10, 141–2,
    144, 314
impersonals 13, 232, 238–9, 244, 250, 282–4,
    297, 314
inchoative/anticausative alternation 278
indefinite article, lack of 155
indefinite pronouns 310–11
indirect *wh*-constructions 137
individual level predicate 261
infinitival clauses, inflected 78, 97–8, 327, 329,
    351–3
infinitival relatives 133–4
infinitives 68–73, 98, 144, 329, 351–3, 358,
    364–5 (*see also* non-finite verbs; verb-
    nouns)
interrogative clauses 36, 44, 45, 49, 310–11,
    315–16, 317 (*see also wh*-questions)
Irish 18, 37, 52 n. 8, 108, 118, 142, 160, 178,
    181, 187, 317, 352, 357, 363–4
Isaac, Graham 310
island constraints 146–9
Italian 187

Jackendoff, Ray 54–5
Jackson, Kenneth 313
Jespersen's Cycle 311–12
Jones, Bob Morris 35, 37, 42, 45 n.6, 48, 51,
    55, 259, 261, 263, 264 n.2, 266, 267, 269,
    270, 271 n.5, 272, 273, 274
Jones, T. J. Rhys 226

Kathol, Andreas 215, 291
King, Gareth 225

Larson, Richard 56
language acquisition 187
language contact 116, 304

left-conjunct agreement 205–6, 218, 361 (*see
     also* coordination)
left dislocation 293–4, 299, 310
Lewis, Henry 299, 331, 333
Lexical Functional Grammar (LFG) 52–3,
     55, 65, 209, 211, 239 n. 9, 253
Lieber, Rochelle 20, 188, 227, 231
linearization-based HPSG 215–20
literary Welsh 4–7, 28, 75, 79, 82, 106, 111,
     112, 115, 117, 119, 120, 121, 122, 132,
     137, 139–40, 144, 157–8, 165, 179, 228,
     232, 341, 342, 354–5, 358, 359, 364
LOCAL 219
long-distance topicalization 292
long-distance *wh*-constructions 141–51

Maasai 366
Mac Cana, Proinsias 289, 299
mai (*see* focus complementizers)
mass nouns 172–3
McCloskey, James 108, 204, 209 n.3, 214, 357,
     366
Manning, H. Paul 113, 114, 137, 328
middle alternation 279
Middle Breton 290–1, 292, 293–4, 299–302,
     303, 306, 310, 312, 318 n. 3, 320, 334, 335
Middle Welsh 286–337;
     period dating for 2–3
Miller, D. Gary 331, 333
mixed sentence 306–7
mo (negative pseudo-quantifier) 140, 269–70,
     312–13
modal verbs 111, 120, 138
Morgan, T. J. 225, 230, 314–16, 331, 333
multiple *wh*-questions 118
mutation 19–26, 35–6, 39, 40, 43, 60–1, 70,
     72, 74, 78, 124, 223–54, 313–6, 341–2,
     346 n. 4, 347, 359, 359 n. 13;
     absence of 184, 186; and case 249–50;
     as head government 243–4;
     exceptions to 24–5, 229–30, 242;
     fossilized 25;
     of subjects 224, 241–2, 249;
     of *wh*-clauses 230, 242;
     phonetic realization of 19–20 (*see also*
        adjectives, mutations affecting; direct
        object mutation; mutation, aspirate;
        mutation, nasal; mutation, soft; nouns,
        mutations affecting)
mutation, aspirate 20–1, 157, 158, 163–4, 168,
     177; 196, 223, 229, 246 n. 14, 265–6, 312,
     320, 359 n. 13

mutation, direct object (*see* direct object
     mutation)
mutation, nasal 20–1, 39, 78, 157, 164, 196–7,
     303, 309, 320
mutation, soft 21, 35–6, 40, 43, 60–1, 74, 78,
     223–54, 265–7, 312, 313–14, 320, 323,
     336–7, 341–2, 346 n. 4, 347, 359;
     in copular constructions 132;
     in focus constructions 127;
     in relative clauses 122;
     in long-distance *wh*-constructions 143. n. 5,
        149–51;
     in the noun phrase 22–3, 152–3, 156–7,
        163–6, 168–9, 177–8, 185–6, 188–94,
        195–6;
     in *wh*-questions 106, 109, 111, 114–15, 117,
        142, 341;
     syntactic 24, 224–54

nasal mutation (*see* mutation, nasal)
N-word 265, 268, 271–2, 274
neb 'no one' 263–5
Neeleman, Ad 215
negation/negative 44, 55, 139–41, 263–75,
     306, 309–13, 315–16, 317, 319, 327,
     358–9
negative aspect marker (*heb*) 39, 40, 273–4
negative auxiliaries (*sa, smo, so*) 271, 286
negative particle/complementizer (*na(d)*) 36,
     139–40, 263
negative particle/complementizer (*ni(d)*) 257,
     263, 265, 274, 359 n. 13
Negative Context Requirement 272, 273
Negative Dependent Constraint 267–8, 270,
     272–3
negative dependents 265–73
negative polarity items 310–11
negative quantifiers 257, 268, 272, 310–11
negative particles 36, 45, 358, 359
'neuter' gender 176
Niuean 366
non-finite clauses 13–14, 62, 66, 68–103,
     200–1, 217, 318, 327–33 (*see also i-
     clauses*)
non-finite verbs 10, 12, 28, 68–103, 198,
     203–4, 205, 207, 208, 209, 210, 220, 255,
     256, 270, 275, 276, 287–8, 319, 321,
     327–33 (*see also* infinitives, verb-nouns)
non-restrictive relatives 122–3
non-standard Welsh 115–16, 156, 159, 161,
     164
noun/appositive word order 346–7

noun/genitive word order 26, 152–3, 340 (*see also* posssessor noun phrases)

nouns 70–3, 152–97, 198, 201–2, 205, 208–10, 211, 217–8

noun phrases 152–97, 336–7

noun-raising 186–7, 189–94

null arguments 15–16, 34, 60–1, 95, 228, 305, 307–8, 321, 352, 356, 362 (*see also pro*)

null operator 119–20, 135, 213

numerals 156–7, 163–71, 174–5, 178, 195–7, 336–7

(*see also* complex numerals, ordinal numerals)

numerative forms of nouns 163, 165–6, 336

objects 15, 51, 54 n.10, 55, 59, 60, 61, 65, 198–200, 202–3, 204, 207, 209, 211, 220, 221, 222, 269, 275, 277, 279–80, 283–4; position of 316–17

object-agreement clitics 23, 28, 109–10, 112–14, 126, 134–5, 138, 159–61, 196–7, 308, 320–2, 323, 327 (*see also* possessive clitics)

obviation effects 71 n. 2, 158

Old Breton 317

Old Irish 298, 308, 318 n. 3, 336

Old Welsh 286, 289, 298–9, 308–9

order domains 215–20

ordinal numerals 156, 169, 195

os 'if' 286

Ouhalla, Jamal 56, 107, 350–6, 358

pam 'why' 106, 117, 119, 129, 133, 148

passives 13, 208, 275–7; passive voice 304–5

past tense 7, 11, 12, 14, 33–4, 42, 45, 47, 59, 82, 85–6, 314

peidio (negative marker) 79, 84, 87, 270, 271

perfect aspect marker *wedi* 12, 39–41, 46 n. 7, 57, 98, 363

perfect tense 302–3, 304

PerfP 41, 57–8

periodization of Welsh 3, 286

periphrastic verb 38, 231, 238

phonology 15 n. 6, 19 n. 9, 25 n. 12, 27, 313

phrasal affixes 210, 217

pied-piping 73, 114–16, 116–17, 120–21, 134

Piette, J. R. F. 318 n. 3

pluperfect tense 5, 10, 314

plural adjectives used as nouns 182–3

Polish 108, 361

Pollard, Carl 205, 209, 211, 215, 219

Poppe, Erich 287, 295, 303

possessive clitics 28, 78, 157–62, 187

possessor noun phrases 26, 73, 74, 153, 158, 161–2, 178, 183, 184–6, 192–4, 198, 201–2, 208, 211, 221, 339–40 (*see also* noun/genitive word order)

predicates 288, 290, 317–19; predicative adjectives 179

predicative *yn* 3, 8, 20–1, 24 n. 11, 58, 235, 258, 260, 318–19, 346 n. 4

preposition stranding 115–16, 120–21

prepositional phrases 288; in noun phrases 185

prepositions 17, 77, 81, 91–3, 198, 199–200, 205, 207, 211, 221–2, 308, 326, 328–9, 330, 333, 339, 340, 353, 360; inflected 17, 115, 360

pre-verbal particle *a* 34–7, 158, 295; in V2-structures 287, 290–1, 293, 299–302; in *wh*-constructions 106–7, 111, 138, 334–5

pre-verbal particle *y(d)* 295–6; in V2-structures 287, 290–1

pre-verbal particle *y(r)* 34–7, 111, 115, 121, 122; in literary Welsh 136–8

Principles and Parameters theory (P&P) 48, 56, 65, 80, 90–91, 95–7, 99, 209, 215, 224, 228, 234, 236, 237, 244, 245, 251, 252–4, 341, 343

pro 71, 72, 80, 94, 95, 113, 228, 245, 252–3 (*see also* null arguments)

PRO 80, 91, 95, 96, 99, 228–9, 239, 245–6, 252

ProgP 41, 57

progressive aspect 12, 302, 303–4

progressive aspect marker *yn* 12, 22, 39, 58, 98, 127, 260, 357

pronouns 34, 61, 78, 198–204, 205, 207–8, 209–10, 212, 213–4, 215, 219–20, 221, 222, 319–26; case on 26–9; in focused position 27, 125–6; pronoun postposing 316–17; strong (independent) pronouns 27, 159, 161, 319–20, 323–5; weak vs. strong distinction 27, 78, 125, 213–4, 219–20

quantifiers 171–3, 174–5, 195; quantifier binding 292 (*see also* negative quantifiers)

raising constructions 59–60, 99–103, 208, 277

reconstruction (in *wh*-constructions) 131, 292

reduplicated pronouns 28, 321–2, 324–5

reflexives 51, 220–2; emphatic reflexives
221–2, 324
relative clauses 118–23, 315, 317;
subject relatives 118–20;
object relatives 118–20;
prepositional relatives 120–1;
possessor relatives 121–2;
adjunct relatives 122–3, 134 (see also
infinitival relatives)
relatives, infinitival (see infinitival relatives)
relative pronouns 106, 108, 119, 335
responsives 45–7
resumptive pronouns 104–5, 108–9, 112–7,
120–3, 126, 134, 135, 138, 139–41, 143–4,
145–6, 147–8, 149, 150, 151, 207
Richards, Melville 43, 137, 299, 318 n. 3, 331,
333
Roberts, Ian 37, 50, 54, 97, 126, 129, 186–7,
188–9, 204, 209, 212, 214, 231, 232 n. 4,
233, 235–44, 249–54, 359 n. 13, 360
Romance languages 48
Rouveret, Alain 35, 41, 42, 49, 50, 54, 58,
64–5, 73–5, 93, 113, 114, 132, 137, 170,
186, 205, 208, 209, 212, 213, 261–2,
272–3, 281, 354

-s (third-person object clitic) 140, 309–10,
321, 335
Sadler, Louisa 34, 65–6, 83, 86–7, 92, 93, 113,
160, 188, 193
Sag, Ivan 205, 209, 211, 215, 219
scope 181–2
Schafer, Robin 291
Scots Gaelic 37, 118, 159, 303, 317
sef 'namely' 318
Semitic languages 185, 361
Serbian 108
serial construction 16, 64–6
Siewierska, Anna 355
SLASH 219
Slovene 108
soft mutation (see mutation, soft)
Sproat, Richard 41, 51
stage level predicate 261–2
storage 272
strong negative verbs 270–1, 272
stylistic variation 111, 120, 136–7, 139, 144,
158, 324
subjacency 146–8
subject 33, 34, 42, 49, 50, 51, 53–4, 54 n.10,
60–6, 71, 78, 80, 81, 87, 91, 198, 199, 203,
205–6, 208, 211, 212–4, 215, 256, 257,

260, 263, 267, 268, 269, 272, 275–6,
278–9, 281, 283–4; position of 316–17
subject-initial word order 33, 338, 339, 342,
355 n. 11 (see also SVO word order)
subject/object alignment 14–16
subject – verb agreement 14–15, 33–4, 107–8,
112, 120, 125–6, 199, 305–7, 357;
in wh-constructions 107–8, 112, 120, 125–6,
206–7, 212–14, 219, 334–5
subjunctive 286, 310–11, 314
subordinate clauses 326–33
superiority effects 118
superlative adjectives 134, 179, 180 (see also
adjectives)
SVO word order 295–6
Swedish 291
SYNSEM 216
synthetic verb 9, 12, 38

tag questions 45–7, 66, 260–1
Tallerman, Maggie 78, 80, 83, 85, 90, 91, 94,
96, 100, 102, 128, 223, 227, 230, 232,
234, 238–42, 244, 245, 246, 247, 251, 253,
293
taw (see focus complementizers)
that-trace effects 143
Thomas, Alan 42 48
Thomas, Peter Wynn 137, 181
topics 287–96, 297, 299–302, 306
tough-constructions 133, 135
transitive verbs 328–9
Trigger Constraint 227–30, 246, 253
Turkish 107, 108, 160
Tzutujil 159

un 'one' 162, 163, 182, 195
unaccusative verbs 278, 297, 312–13, 316,
327–30
unergative verbs 328
universals, Greenbergian 339–47

valency-changing processes 275–83
verbs 9–13, 32–4, 37–8, 39, 42, 44–6, 48–50,
52–4, 65, 66; regular paradigms of 9
verb-nouns 10, 69–75, 159 (see also infinitives,
non-finite verbs)
verb-movement/fronting 48–52, 54–6, 251,
253
verb-second word order 37, 66, 287, 291–2,
295, 301–2, 305, 306–7, 327, 334, 335,
351 n. 7;
in negative clauses 309–10

VoiceP 54
VSO word order 11, 13, 31, 38, 51, 55, 58, 75, 84, 97, 99, 224, 233, 236, 237, 247, 249, 251, 253, 287, 288–9, 295–6, 298, 299–303, 340–6, 350–8, 361, 363, 365, 366

Warlpiri 328
Watkins, T. Arwyn 287, 318 n. 3
weak negative verbs 265–7
wedi (*see* perfect aspect marker *wedi*)
Welsh, history of 2–4
Welsh, number of speakers 4
Welsh syntax, research on 29–30
wh-constructions 104–51;
    adjunct wh-constructions 138;
    object wh-constructions 138
    (*see also* relative clauses, *wh*-questions, focus constructions, copular constructions, *tough*-constructions, infinitival questions, infinitival relatives)
wh-questions 106–18, 317, 334;
    subject *wh*-questions 106–9;
    object *wh*-questions 106–14;
    prepositional *wh*-questions 114–16;
    possessor *wh*-questions 116–17;
    adjunct *wh*-questions 117
wh-trace 112–13, 126, 228, 245, 250 n. 16, 252
Williams, Ifor 315
Williams, Stephen J. 43, 159
Willis, David 113, 114, 137, 188, 193, 273, 291, 295–6, 299, 311
word order 26, 75, 97, 98–9, 236, 240, 241, 249, 251, 287–303, 342;
    in copular constructions 317–19;
    in non-finite clauses 329

XP trigger hypothesis (XPTH) 226–8, 232 n. 4, 233, 235, 239–54, 263 n. 1, 284

Yiddish 301
yn (*see* progressive aspect marker *yn*)
Yup'ik 159
yw/ydy 256–60, 261–2

Zanuttini, Raffaella 273
Zaring, Laurie 131, 262
Zwicky, Arnold 227, 231, 233, 253

Printed in Great Britain
by Amazon.co.uk, Ltd.,
Marston Gate.